From Founding Fathers
To Fire-Eaters

From Founding Fathers To Fire-Eaters

The Constitutional Doctrine of States' Rights in the Old South

James Rutledge Roesch

SHOTWELL PUBLISHING
Columbia, South Carolina

Produced in the Republic of South Carolina by

Shotwell Publishing, LLC
Post Office Box 2592
Columbia, South Carolina 29202

www.ShotwellPublishing.com

Cover Design: Hazel's Dream / Boo Jackson TCB

ISBN-13: 978-1947660083
ISBN-10: 194766008X

10 9 8 7 6 5 4 3 2 1

To my fifth great-grandfather, HUGH RANDOLPH, who fought for the freedom of his people in the War of *American* Independence

To his grandson, JAMES B. RANDOLPH, who died defending the freedom of his people in the War of *Southern* Independence

And to my grandfather, LT. COLONEL JOHN RUTLEDGE, JR., who taught me what that meant.

I declare that if twelve States had adopted it, I would, with manly firmness, and in spite of an erring world, reject it. You are not to enquire how your trade may be increased, nor how you are to become a great and powerful people, but how your liberties can be secured; for liberty ought to be the direct end of your government ... I am fearful I have lived long enough to become an old-fashioned fellow. Perhaps an invincible attachment to the dearest rights of man, may, in these refined, enlightened days, be deemed old-fashioned ... I say, the time has been when every pulse of my heart beat for American liberty, and which, I believe, had a counterpart in the breast of every true American ... The voice of tradition, I trust, will inform posterity of our struggles for freedom. If our descendants be worthy of the name of Americans, they will preserve, and hand down to their latest posterity, the transactions of the present times; and though I confess my exclamations are not worthy the hearing, they will see that I have done my utmost to preserve their liberty...The first thing I have at heart is American liberty; the second thing is American union.
– Patrick Henry at Virginia's Ratification Convention, 1788

If [I] were called upon to establish a criterion, an infallible touchstone of the soundness of political principles, it should be made to consist of nothing so much as a sacred regard for the rights of the States. An enlarged and liberal construction of State rights was, with [me], an indispensable requisite ... [I view] the proposed measure but as the commencement of a series, as an entering wedge. If they begin with declaring one law of one State unconstitutional, where were they to stop? They might, they would go on (it was the natural tendency of power never to be satiated, so long as there was anything left to devour) until the State governments, stripped of all authority ... mere skeletons of governments, the shadows of their former greatness, should be forever abolished, and a great consolidated empire established upon their ruins. [I look forward] to such an event as the death warrant of the existing Constitution, and of the people's liberties. If they wished to preserve the Constitution, they must learn to respect the rights of the States, and not bring the whole artillery of the federal government to bear upon them. In such a contest, the States must fall, and when they did fall, there was an end of all republican government in the country.
 – John Randolph of Roanoke in the Congress, 1807

I wish ... that the President would lift himself up to a higher and loftier pinnacle of statesmanship and at once yield to the propriety of a recognition of the Southern Confederacy. A commercial treaty and a treaty of alliance offensive and defensive with them, would save much of the Union under which we have all lived so long and happily. If all cannot be saved, save as much as can be saved, even of the fragments; for every fragment will be a gem glorious and priceless. But I fear that this policy is not to be their policy. Italy can rise up from the thralldom of centuries and win the bright coronet of free government. The iron crown of Austria may be removed from the brow of its wearer to do honour to Hungary. But Mr. Lincoln recognises no such principle as lying at the base of American institutions, as the right of the people of any of these States to seek their happiness under any government than that inaugurated by himself, of a sectional majority.
– John Tyler, Jr., at Virginia's Secession Convention, 1861

Contents

Introduction

IT IS OFTEN SNIDELY (and stupidly) quipped, 'States' *rights*? More like States' *wrongs!*' In the midst of studying the political, economic, cultural, and social/racial conflict between the North and the South which culminated in the War of Southern Independence, I was dismayed at the dismissive-to-contemptuous manner with which the constitutional doctrine of States' rights in the Old South was regarded. States' rights are either not taken seriously or scorned outright, considered to be nothing more than a code word for the right to own slaves.

In his ambition to get elected in Illinois, Abraham Lincoln impishly mocked the idea that the constitutional doctrine of States' rights meant anything to Southerners other than slavery. 'We began by declaring that all men are created equal, but now from that beginning we have run down to the other declaration, that for some men to enslave others is a "sacred right of self-government,"' he sneered. 'The Democracy [Democratic Party] of today hold the liberty of one man to be absolutely nothing, when in conflict with another man's right of property,' he snapped. 'The perfect liberty they sigh for is the liberty of making slaves of other people,' he scoffed. Of course, the liberty for which the Old South 'sighed' – the right of self-government – was the very same liberty for which Colonial America had 'sighed,' but Lincoln's aim was not to tell the truth and save the Union, but simply to beat the Democrats in the North and obtain office in Washington, D.C. Shortly after his presidential election, Lincoln, replying to a letter from his former colleague, Georgia Congressman and future Confederate Vice President Alexander H. Stephens, claimed that 'the only substantial difference between us' was whether 'slavery is right and should be extended' or 'slavery is wrong and ought to be restricted.' Throughout his war against Southern independence, Lincoln continued to smear the Southern political tradition. 'We all declare for liberty, but in using the same *word* we do not all mean the same *thing*,' remarked Lincoln. 'With some the word liberty may mean for each man to do as he pleases with himself, and the product of his labor, while with others the same word may mean for some men to do as they please with other men, and the product of other men's labor.' Because of these contradictory definitions, concluded Lincoln, the wartime emancipation of the slaves was 'hailed by some as the advance of liberty, and bewailed by others as the destruction of all liberty.' Lincoln made it clear that 'the Confederacy stands for slavery and the Union for freedom.'

Some Southerners saw such deception coming. James H. Thornwell, a prominent Presbyterian preacher and seminary professor in South Carolina, predicted that if the South were defeated, then the North would not only revolutionise 'the whole character of the government' from 'a federal republic, the common agent of sovereign and independent States' to a 'central despotism, with the notion of States forever abolished,' but also would brand the South with the stigma of slavery:

> And what have we to expect if our enemies prevail? Our homes, too, are to be pillaged, our cities our property confiscated, our true men hanged, and those who escape the gibbet, to be driven as vagabonds and wanderers in foreign climes. This beautiful country is to pass out of our hands. The boundaries which mark our States are, in some instances, to be effaced, and the States that remain are to be converted into subject provinces, governed by Northern rulers and by Northern laws. Our property is to be ruthlessly seized and turned over to mercenary strangers, in order

to pay the enormous debt which our subjugation has cost. Our wives and daughters are to become the prey of brutal lust. The slave, too, will slowly pass away, as the red man did before him, under the protection of Northern philanthropy; and the whole country, now like the Garden of Eden in beauty and fertility, will first be a blackened and smoking desert, and then the minister of Northern cupidity and avarice. There is not a single redeeming feature in the picture of ruin which stares us in the face, if we permit ourselves to be conquered. It is a night of thick darkness that will settle upon us. Even sympathy, the last solace of the afflicted, will be denied to us. The civilised world will look coldly upon us, or even jeer us with the taunt that we have deservedly lost our own freedom in seeking to perpetuate the slavery of others. We shall perish under a cloud of reproach and of unjust suspicions, sedulously propagated by our enemies, which will be harder to bear than the loss of home and of goods. Such a fate never overtook any people before.

Thornwell's avowal that the South was fighting for the 'noble cause' of 'constitutional freedom' and against 'a government of force' and 'remorseless despotism' was to no avail. Thornwell's worst fears came true: the South was conquered and her political tradition (America's oldest, with roots in her mother country and even classical antiquity) was smeared as a mere reactionary defence of slavery. As Lincoln decreed, 'The South is to be destroyed and replaced by new propositions and ideas.' Yet States' rights formed a systematic, popular constitutional doctrine which lasted for generations (from the American Revolution to the 'Tenth Amendment' revival), crossed sectional lines (there were Yankee nullifiers and secessionists), and was fundamental to American 'small-f federalism' and 'small-r republicanism' (which in Thornwell's words were 'the great principles which our fathers bequeathed us,' 'the very liberty for which Washington bled,' and 'the true doctrines of the Federal Constitution').

The ruling elite's conspiracy against the constitutional doctrine of States' rights is a terrible crime against the integrity and authenticity of American history. Today, States' rights are merely *written off*, but tomorrow they may be *written out* – and it will not stop there! The hateful and hysteric purging of Confederate history is a symptom of a disease in the body politic which, unless cured, will ultimately be the death of our self-consciousness and self-confidence as a people – that is, of our sense of heritage and identity as well as our love of and loyalty to our country. That disease is an anti-American, anti-white racial consciousness – ascendant since the civil-rights and mass-immigration revolutions of the 1960s – and has nothing to do with 'States' rights' or 'the Civil War' per se, but rather attacks historical figures and events as 'racist' insofar as they are perceived as 'American' and 'white.' Andrew Jackson has already been turned from a hero of the War of 1812 (who fought the Indians as fiercely as they fought the Americans) and a popular President (who overrode the rights of the Indian nations and the State sovereignties alike in the name of the Union) to a genocidal maniac and an evil tyrant. The European conquest of the North-American continent and creation of a new country is seen as nothing more than the genocide of indigenous peoples, even though populations have been migrating and fighting over land and resources for all of human history (and these indigenous 'noble savages' conquered one another more savagely than any conquistador or cowboy). Thomas Jefferson, due to his supposed hypocrisy on the issue of slavery – that hypocrisy being the fact that he was not a radical abolitionist, something he never could have been, even if he had wanted to be – has been mortally wounded and will not live much longer. Slavery, of course, must be remembered forever and ever as America's original sin, yet while slavery has been practiced around the world for all of human history, Europe and her colonies were the only civilisation which voluntarily abolished the institution. 'What we are seeing in this concerted and protracted attack on Southern and even on national and other ethnic symbols,' warns the paleo-conservative renegade Samuel T. Francis, 'is nothing less than a crusade for the overthrow of any symbol that suggests the white – dare I say the real – heritage and history of this country and their replacement by their own symbols and their own racial propaganda and mythology.'

There are three other reasons for this misplaced rejection of States' rights as a legitimate constitutional doctrine. The first is simply cynicism. In today's political culture, when politicians talk out of both sides of their mouths and ghost-write vapid autobiographies, it is difficult to imagine statesmen who stood for principles and wrote brilliant political treatises. Furthermore, 'liberty' is no longer the gold standard of American political ideals, having been replaced by the counterfeit currencies of 'economic prosperity,' 'global hegemony,' and 'human equality.' Thus, by modern standards, Southerners could not have been sincere when they spoke of States' rights; there simply must have been some ulterior motive. By these standards, the practices of present politicians are illogically and unfairly projected onto their predecessors – an insult for which the latter would never have stood. Indeed, imagine what the legendary John Randolph of Roanoke (that indomitable old Virginian who strode about Capitol Hill booted, spurred, and flanked by his hunting hounds, captivated Congressmen with his spellbinding oratory, dueled the greatest men of his time with words as well as pistols, defended Jeffersonian principles against Hamiltonians, Jacksonians, and even errant Jeffersonians, and denounced democracy as 'King Numbers') would have to say about today's boorish, buffoonish political culture!

The second reason, related to the aforementioned anti-American, anti-white racial consciousness, is the grip of Marxist historical theory on American intellectuals, now modernised from *Klassenkampf* (class war) to *Kulturkampf* (culture war). Freudian and Frankfurt-School social scientists, disillusioned by the rise of left-totalitarianism in the East (Stalinism in the Soviet Union, Maoism in the People's Republic of China, etc.) and right-authoritarianism in the West (fascist regimes ruling countries such as

Spain, Italy, and Germany), sought to explain the apparent failure of classical Marxism. They came to the conclusion that Western Civilisation had been the key bulwark against Communism, meaning that 'culture,' rather than 'class,' must be the new target of the revolution. Communists should continue to employ the tried-and-true tactics of subversion and agitation, but rather than organising a revolt against the *bourgeoisie* (the capitalist class), they should organise a revolt against the traditions, institutions, and identities of the *bourgeoisie* as well as the *proletariat*. Indeed, since the Western *proletariat* (the working class) had failed as a revolutionary class, they would be replaced by immigrants from the 'Third World' (countries unaligned with NATO or the Communist Bloc, mostly former European colonies in Africa, Latin America, and Asia) as well as the Western *lumpenproletariat* (counter-cultural groups on the social margins). The Old South, stained with a history of slavery and treason in the minds of many Americans, is not only an easy target under this 'Cultural-Marxist' strategy, but also an entering wedge for the further perversion and degradation of Western Civilisation. The constitutional doctrine of States' rights, which was entangled with slavery in the Old South, is thus caught up in this conspiracy against Western Civilisation. Instead of dying with dignity, then, Marxism (the most deadly, destructive, and discredited ideology in human history) has, like a cockroach, survived the fallout of its own failure and crawled from politics and economics into history and culture, tricking new generations of humanity into hating who they are, where they come from, and what they believe. 'We are witnessing a cultural and political atrocity – an increasingly successful attempt by the media and an academic elite to strip young white Southerners, and arguably black Southerners as well, of their heritage, and therefore, of their identity,' declares the Marxist-turned-Catholic historian of the Old South, Eugene D. Genovese. 'They are being taught to forget their forebears or to remember them with shame.'

The third reason, and the shallowest, is because the Union defeated the Confederacy, which historians decree decided all the outstanding issues between the North and the South (including/especially the constitutional dispute over States' rights). This is illogical and unprincipled, however: force can only decide questions of power, not questions of right. 'The Yankee interpretation of the Constitution prevailed not because it was intellectually superior but because the North won a test of physical strength,' argues Genovese. 'Indeed, it is remarkable with what ease so many liberal historians declare that the meaning of the Constitution was settled by the Union victory, for it would be hard to imagine a clearer example of the doctrine that might makes right – a doctrine supposedly anathema to liberals.'

For these three reasons, the constitutional doctrine of States' rights has never been accorded the respect it deserves. It has never been refuted, however, merely ridiculed. Yet as Thomas Jefferson once observed to James Madison, 'Resort is had to ridicule only when reason is against us.'

With no end in sight to this intellectual reign of terror, I decided to study and share the best constitutional treatises on States' rights by the best statesmen of the Old South. The series begins with James Madison and Thomas Jefferson's seminal *Virginia and Kentucky Resolutions* and ends with Robert B. Rhett's fiery *Address to the People of the Slaveholding States*. Neither of these documents are, strictly speaking, treatises, but rather manifestos of political movements: for the former, nullification/interposition and the Principles of '98; for the latter, secession and 'romantic nationalism.' Since Jefferson and Madison's *Resolutions* formed the cornerstone of States' rights, they are simply the best place to begin. Rhett's *Address*, on the other hand, represents the dramatic culmination of the ideas which the Principles of '98 inspired. By beginning and ending with these manifestos, the continuity in the Southern political tradition from the Founding Fathers to Fire Eaters is apparent.

Each essay begins with a brief biography of the author of each constitutional treatise. These biographies are intended to place the treatises in their historical context as well as provide some understanding of the authors' importance. Most are probably aware of whom Thomas Jefferson and James Madison were and what they did (though perhaps this is too optimistic given today's dumbed-down population and dysfunctional schools), but have probably never even heard of their equally brilliant friends and allies, St. George Tucker and John Taylor of Caroline. These biographies, arranged in chronological order, also amount to a shortened version of the history of the sectional conflict that I had originally intended (and still intend) to write, which was a pleasant coincidence.

Researching and writing these essays has been an enlightening and emotional experience. I have done my best to do justice to the lives and minds of these men whom I so deeply admire. Indeed, I hold them in the highest esteem as the 'best and brightest' of America's true 'greatest generation.' After the conquest of the Confederacy, my third great-grandfather, who was wounded at Shiloh and refused to swear the Oath of Allegiance when captured, named his second son after John C. Calhoun, the Old South's greatest statesman and a world-renowned political theorist. Another third great-grandfather, who went west rather than to war, named his firstborn son (with a Yankee wife, at that!) after Jefferson Davis, Calhoun's protégé and the President of the Confederate States of America. I share my ancestors' sentiments: the American federal republic which the men of these essays defended in words and deeds (and which their sons and grandsons defended to the death) was not just what America was supposed to be, but what she still could and should be. 'Strict construction and state rights have represented a distinct Southern republicanism,' explains Genovese, 'which opposed the Leviathan state and determined to concentrate power as close to home as possible.' In the areas in which our ancestors perhaps fell short, such as the seemingly insoluble problem of slavery, they were well-intentioned and made the best of a bad situation. The cure which was forced upon their descendants was far from the only available option and was in some aspects much worse than the disease, for blacks as well as whites. Although the relationship between States' rights and slavery is grossly overstated, there was indeed a relationship, and thus when thinking and writing about one it is impossible not to think and write about the other. I have done my best to avoid condemning (out of misplaced feelings of guilt) or defending (out of misplaced feelings of pride) slavery, and to tell the truth about this difficult subject. On the subject of slavery, as well as many other historical topics, I have found that left-wing historians (who stress that Antebellum America was essentially a white-nationalist country) are often right for the wrong reasons, while neo-conservative historians (who have disarmed themselves of intellectual defences against the Left's arsenals of 'isms' and 'phobias') embarrass themselves with 'politically correct' revisionism. Regardless of our ancestors' shortcomings by contemporary standards on past social and racial issues, their political and constitutional beliefs are timeless (and, in fact, today more timely than ever), and the politicisation of slavery (which is causing Communist-style purges of American history) must be stopped.

One other pleasure of writing these essays was in learning who the Founding Fathers really were and reclaiming their memory from perversion and abuse. The Founders were not progressives, neo-conservatives, or libertarians: they were 'Country' Whigs (as opposed to 'Court' Tories), classical liberals (as opposed to mercantilists and statists), and aristocratic gentlemen (as opposed to egalitarian radicals) – a truly unique ruling class which changed (and the legacy of which continues to change) the course of world history.

The Founding Fathers were not the forefathers of the neo-conservative icon Abraham Lincoln; they would have considered his politicisation of slavery to be self-serving and self-righteous, as well as his physical preservation of the Union tantamount to its philosophical destruction. Nor were they the forefathers of the progressive icon Franklin D. Roosevelt; they would have found his economic programme to be expensive, his wartime regime oppressive, and the sheer length of his time in office monarchical. Nor were they the forefathers of the libertarian icon Ronald Reagan; they would have found his universalist immigration policies and deficit-finance economics to have mortgaged the country's future, and his promotion of individualism and consumerism incompatible with republican virtue. The Founders would have found all of these near-deified Presidents to be tyrants who ruled without respect for the Constitution's limits on the powers of the federal government as a whole and the executive branch in particular. The Founders' authentic identity is much more interesting and instructive than the cartoons from historical narratives and props from political theatre.

If the Founding Fathers had any true successors, however, they were the Confederates, who followed in their footsteps by declaring independence from an old government which had exceeded its rightful powers and framing a new government of strictly limited powers. 'We recur to the compact which binds us together; we recur to the principles upon which our government was founded,' explained Jefferson Davis, bidding adieu to the Senate after learning that his State of Mississippi had seceded from the Union, 'and when you deny them, and when you deny to us the right to withdraw from a government which thus perverted threatens to be destructive of our rights, we but tread in the path of our fathers when we proclaim our independence, and take the hazard.'

These essays were originally published on the Abbeville Institute website. I would like to thank the Editor of the website, Brion McClanahan, and the Chairman of the Abbeville Institute, Donald W. Livingston, for honouring me with such an opportunity. Without that privilege, those essays and this book would not exist. The Abbeville Institute is the single greatest resource for what is true and valuable in the Southern tradition. I strongly urge you visit the website on a daily basis, attend as many events as possible, and commit to financial support. I would also like to thank Clyde N. Wilson, the Distinguished M.E. Bradford Chair of the Abbeville Institute, and Carl V. Jones, 2nd Lt. Commander of the Alabama Division of the Sons of Confederate Veterans, for recommending my writings to the Institute's website. Most importantly, however, I would like to thank my family for their support – my grandfather (to whom this book is dedicated) for passing to me his love of history; my grandmother, Lois, for encouraging me not to stop writing; my father, Stephen, for sacrificing to provide the finest education possible; my sister, Sarah, for keeping me in the twenty-first instead of the eighteenth century, and my wife, Lusine, for making me a happier and more hopeful man. Most of all, however, I would like to thank my mother, Deborah, who was not only my indispensable editor (she has faithfully edited nearly every single word which I have ever written), but also an inexhaustible source of support who keeps me from carrying the weight of the world on my shoulders.

In order to make the reading more understandable, I have taken some liberties with my quotations. In the nineteenth and especially eighteenth centuries, spelling, grammar, and capitalisation were notoriously inconsistent. I have normalised the capitalisation and corrected misspellings, though retained the traditional, beautiful English spelling (e.g. 'honour' and 'centralise' instead of 'honor' and 'centralize') which Southerners often employed before newfangled, ugly Yankee spelling took over American English. One other editorial note worth explaining is the capitalisation of words like 'States.' The States, as proper nouns, were often, but not always, capitalised. For the sake of clarity and consistency, I have capitalised all old usages of the word 'States,' and have adopted that style myself. I have also capitalised words like 'Constitution' and 'Union' when used as proper nouns, which were sometimes uncapitalised.

I. Thomas Jefferson, James Madison, & the Virginia and Kentucky Resolutions

The line of division is now the preservation of the State rights, as reserved in the Constitution, or by strained constructions of that instrument, to merge all into a consolidated government.
– Thomas Jefferson, 1823

The Gordian knot of the Constitution seems to lie in the collision between the federal and State powers, especially as eventually exercised by their respective tribunals. If the knot cannot be untied by the text of the Constitution, it ought not, certainly, to be cut by any political Alexander.
– James Madison, 1821

THE CONSTITUTIONAL DOCTRINE of States' rights is a veritable cross before a vampire to the ruling elite, officially hated as nothing more than a specious pretext for slavery and segregation, yet secretly feared as a serious threat to Washington, D.C.'s centralised power and institutionalised privilege. Arthur M. Schlesinger, Jr., the famous 'court historian' of 'Camelot' and longtime loyalist of the Kennedy family, famously dubs States' rights a 'fetish,' having more to do with 'economic interest or some other local advantage' than sincere convictions about 'constitutional construction.' According to Schlesinger, 'The pro-slavery forces sought refuge in the state rights position as a shield against federal interference with pro-slavery

1

projects.' Eric Foner, a Communist professor who has taught at academia's top universities, led academia's top societies, and won academia's top awards (and who, during the dissolution of the Soviet Union, called for President Mikhail Gorbachev to emulate President Abraham Lincoln and crush the seceding states), claims that 'the principle of state rights and minority self-determination had always been the first line of defense against Northern interference,' as well as that the choice facing Southerners was 'loyalty to the nation' or 'loyalty to slavery.' Just as Foner did not deem the Baltic states' right of self-government worthy of dignifying, so he did not deem the deeply rooted Southern creed of loyalty to one's own State (tragically expressed by Robert E. Lee when he informed his Northern friends that 'I cannot raise my hand against my home, my birthplace, my children' as well as that 'save in defence of my native State, I never desire again to draw my sword') worthy of dignifying.

Naturally, postbellum apologias by former Confederates which avow the cause of States' rights are denounced as deceitful attempts to rewrite history in accord with pathetic 'myths' fabricated to cope with the shame of defeat and sin of slavery. Instead of acknowledging that these testimonies are a valid part of the historical record and could provide clarity and context to the causes, course, and consequences of the War of Southern Independence, the victors have sought to silence the voices of the vanquished and proclaim States' rights discredited forevermore. According to the affirmative-action victim and two-time autobiographer Ta-Nehisi Coates, 'the first manifestation of what would later become a plank in the foundation of Lost Cause mythology' was when the Confederates 'came up' with the 'notion of emphasizing "states' rights" over slavery.' James M. McPherson, a Princeton professor and Pulitzer-winning historian of the War of Southern Independence (or what he smears as 'a failed rebellion to preserve slavery') scoffs at this 'Neo-Confederate orthodoxy' and 'Lost Cause mentality,' mocking it as 'the virgin-birth theory of secession: the Confederacy was not conceived by any worldly cause, but by divine principle.'

2

All of these scornful pronouncements, however, fly in the face of the facts. This essay series aims to set the story straight. The truth is that the great constitutional treatises of the Old South prove that the doctrine of States' rights was never a mere pretence for slavery, but reflected a deep passion for self-government rooted in Southern culture, as well as an earnest understanding of the Constitution rooted in Southern history. According to the scholarly, gentlemanly M.E. Bradford, States' rights were part of a Southern political tradition – a 'patrimony' and 'birthright' – dating from the foundation of the Colonies, through the independence of the States, and to the creation of the Constitution. At the crowning of the Confederate capital in Richmond, President Jefferson Davis honoured this heritage. 'The cause in which we are now engaged is the cause of the advocacy of the rights to which we were born, those for which our fathers of the Revolution bled – the richest inheritance that ever fell to man, and which it is our sacred duty to transmit untarnished to our children,' announced Davis. 'Upon us is devolved the high and holy responsibility of preserving the constitutional liberty of a free government.'

On 2 August 1864, in the midst of the War of Southern Independence, a leading Southern newspaper, the *Richmond Examiner*, insisted that States' rights were the underlying principle for which they were fighting, while slavery was merely a superficial issue:

> Mr. Davis, in a conversation with a Yankee spy...is reported by said spy to have said, 'We are not fighting for slavery; we are fighting for independence'... The sentiment is true, and should be publicly uttered and kept conspicuously in view; because our enemies have diligently laboured to make all mankind believe that the people of these States have set up a pretended State sovereignty, and based themselves upon that ostensibly, while their real object has been only to preserve to themselves the property in so many negroes, worth so many millions of dollars. The direct reverse is the truth. The question of slavery is only one

of the minor issues; and the cause of the war, the whole cause, on our part, is the maintenance of the sovereign independence of these States.

At the beginning of the struggle, and even now, to a great extent, our enemies had, and have, the ear of the world; and they have very dexterously laboured to represent us as rushing into a dreadful war on a paltry question of dollars. In the crusade they were about to make upon us, they have shown the utmost solicitude to gain for themselves, in advance, the sympathies of foreign nations, especially of England and France; and, of course, their chief means of gaining this point, consisted in representing that we had no higher or nobler cause to fight for than the possession of a certain quantity of serviceable negro flesh. Thus they knew that not only all the prevailing cants would be canted on their side, but also that a war waged to break up a free and beneficent government upon such a mean issue, would revolt all statesmen, publicists, and thinkers of high mark in every country, who have the sentiment of national dignity, and can appreciate the loftier and purer springs of human actions on the grand scale. The Yankee knew he might boldly claim the good wishes of civilised communities, so long as he could make it be believed that the only thought and care of the South was that she might keep still on her plantations so many slave hands...

The whole cause of our resistance was and is, the pretension and full determination of the Northern States to use their preponderance in the federal representation, in order to govern the Southern States for their profit, just as Austria governs Venetia, Russia governs Poland, or England governs Ireland. Slavery was the immediate occasion – carefully made so by them – it was not the cause. The tariff, which almost brought the disruption some years ago, would have much more accurately represented, though it did not cover, or exhaust, the real cause of the quarrel. Yet neither tariffs nor slavery, nor both together, could ever have been truly called the cause of the secession and the war. We refuse to accept for a cause any thing lower, meaner, smaller than that truly announced, namely, the sovereign independence of our States. This, indeed, includes both those minor questions, as well as many others yet graver and higher. It includes full power to regulate our trade for our own profit, and also complete jurisdiction over our own social and domestic institutions; but it further involves all the nobler attributes of national, and even of individual life and character. A community which once submits to be schooled, dictated to, legislated for, by any other, soon grows poor in spirit; it becomes at last incapable of producing a high style of men; its very soul withers within it; in it no genius, no art, can have its home. If they arise within its borders, they migrate to the dominant country, and seek there their career and their reward; its citizens, become a kind of half-men, feel that they have hardly a right to walk in the sun; take the lowest seats at the world's tables, and there is no man to say, friend, go up higher.

The people of Virginia do not choose to accept that position for themselves and for their children. They choose rather to die. They own a noble country, which their fathers created, exalted, and transmitted to them with all its treasures of high names and great deeds; with all its native wealth of untamable manhood. That inheritance we intend to own while we live, and leave intact to those who are to come after us. It is ours from the centre of the earth up to the heavens, with all the minerals beneath it, and all the sky above it.

It is right to let foreign nations, and 'those whom it may concern,' understand this theory of our independence. Let them understand that, though we are 'not fighting for slavery,' we will not allow ourselves to be dictated to in regard to slavery or any other of our internal affairs, not because that would diminish our interest in any property, but because it touches our independence.

As the *Examiner* explained, although the South refused 'to be dictated to' on the issue of slavery, it was the 'sovereign independence of these States' which was paramount. 'Of all the problems which beset the United States of America during the century from the Declaration of Independence to the end of Reconstruction,' agrees the renowned historian Forrest McDonald in

States' Rights and the Union: Imperium in Imperio, 1776-1876, 'the most pervasive concerned disagreements about the nature of the Union and the line to be drawn between the authority of the general government and that of the several states.' Indeed, the conflict between the North and the South over States' rights did not begin and end with Southern secession and Northern invasion; secession and war were merely the culmination of longstanding political, economic, cultural, and social/racial forces that had been dissolving the Union from the very beginning. From the foundation of the Union to its dissolution, distinguished Southern leaders and thinkers penned magnificent constitutional treatises which exhaustively established the constitutionality of States' rights and expounded upon the virtues of decentralised power in preserving the American federal republic. The aim of this essay series is to restore the greatest of these neglected and suppressed works to their rightful glory as an original and lawful American political philosophy of which the United States are in desperate need of a renaissance.

I.

Thomas Jefferson was born on 13 April 1743 in Albemarle County, Virginia. Jefferson's father, Peter, was a surveyor and cartographer who completed the Fairfax Line and extended the boundaries of Virginia and North Carolina. Jefferson was privately tutored by clergymen before attending the College of William and Mary, where he met his two mentors, the jurist George Wythe and scientist William Small – who along with Royal Governor Francis Fauquier exposed Jefferson to the Enlightenment and instilled in him his lifelong faith in the virtues of education. Growing up, Jefferson was a gay, gallant gentleman who indulged in the courtly life of the Virginian gentry, gambling on horse racing, riding on fox hunts, attending balls, and standing in weddings. When his father died, however, Jefferson developed a strict code of personal honour, inspired largely by the moral teachings of Jesus (although Jefferson held highly unorthodox/heretical beliefs, he considered himself a 'real Christian,' and he and his family were baptised, married, and buried in the Anglican/Episcopal Church). Jefferson married the lovely Martha W. Skelton and moved into his beloved Monticello (Italian for 'Little Mountain'), a project on which he worked for the rest of his life and which would become an architectural masterpiece. At Monticello, Jefferson lived comfortably on 10,000 acres with 200 slaves.

James Madison was born on 16 April 1751 in Orange County, Virginia. Madison's father, James, was a prominent planter in the Piedmont, and provided his son with the best possible education. Madison attended an elite school for young boys and benefited from a private tutor before attending the College of New Jersey (now Princeton University). Later in his life, Madison married Dolley Payne Todd, a gracious lady whose sociability later helped her husband and his friend, Jefferson, navigate the social scene in Washington, D.C. Madison lived on his ancestral estate, Montpelier, with 4,000 acres and 100 slaves.

Jefferson was elected to the House of Burgesses in 1769, allying with Patrick Henry (known as the 'Demosthenes of America'), Richard Henry Lee (also known as the 'Cicero of America'), and other 'Patriots' in the American cause. When he was still a law student, Jefferson had first encountered Henry at a Virginian convention where he declared, 'Caesar had his Brutus, Charles his Cromwell, and George the Third may profit by their example.' Henry's *Virginia Resolves*, which argued that Virginians were 'not bound to yield obedience to any law or ordinance whatsoever, designed to impose any taxation whatsoever upon them, other than the laws or ordinances of the General Assembly,' became a cornerstone of Virginian political philosophy and strategy. Henry's *Resolves* would serve as the foundation and framework for Madison and Jefferson's later doctrines of 'interposition' and 'nullification' in the *Virginia and Kentucky Resolutions*.

Jefferson began his public life as a loyal subject of the Crown who believed that 'dependence' on the mother country was best for the Colonies as long as their self-government over internal affairs was respected. As the

Parliament's policy became increasingly imperial – taxing the Colonies despite their lack of representation and thereby violating the Colonies' chartered, constitutional, and natural rights – Jefferson began to consider 'independence' from the mother country as a last resort. 'Believe me, dear Sir, there is not in the British Empire a man who more cordially loves a union with Great Britain, than I do,' explained Jefferson to an uncle, 'but by the God that made me, I will cease to exist before I yield to a connection on such terms as the British Parliament propose; and in this, I think I speak the sentiments of America.' In 1774, Jefferson authored *A Summary View of the Rights of British America*, a tract which detailed American grievances against Great Britain, pledged American allegiance to the Crown as its loyal subjects, and denied that the Parliament had any authority over the self-governing Colonies. 'The God who gave us life gave us liberty at the same time; the hand of force may destroy, but cannot disjoin them,' proclaimed Jefferson. 'This, sire, is our last, our determined resolution; and that you will be pleased to interpose with that efficacy which your earnest endeavors may ensure to procure redress of these our great grievances, to quiet the minds of your subjects in British America against any apprehensions of future encroachment, to establish fraternal love and harmony through the whole empire, and that these may continue to the latest ages of time is the fervent prayer of all British America!' The next year, Virginia's Convention sent Jefferson to Philadelphia to represent the Colony in the Second Continental Congress, despite his wishes to stay behind and participate in the momentous constitutional changes happening at home. In 1775 Jefferson and John Dickinson (a Delaware planter and Pennsylvania lawyer) co-wrote the *Declaration of the Causes of Necessity of Taking up Arms*, the militant companion to Dickinson's pacific *Olive Branch Petition*. 'Honour, justice, and humanity, forbid us tamely to surrender that freedom which we received from our gallant ancestors, and which our innocent posterity have a right to receive from us,' avowed Jefferson and Dickinson. 'With hearts fortified with these animating reflections, we most solemnly, before God and the world,

8

declare, that, exerting the utmost energy of those powers, which our beneficent Creator hath graciously bestowed upon us, the arms we have been compelled by our enemies to assume, we will, in defiance of every hazard, with unabating firmness and perseverance, employ for the preservation of our liberties; being with one mind resolved to die freemen rather than to live slaves.'

As a young man, Madison already had strong opinions on the Imperial Crisis between the American Colonies and Great Britain. Madison believed that the more the Parliament tightened its grip, the more the Colonies would slip through its fingers. 'I verily believe the frequent assaults that have been made on America, Boston especially, will in the end prove of real advantage,' observed Madison in 1773, after hearing of the Boston Tea Party. In 1774, when Virginia's Royal Governor, Lord Dunmore, seized a store of gunpowder, Madison was chosen to draft his county's commendation to Patrick Henry for leading the militia against this attempted disarmament. In addition to thanking Henry for 'your zeal for the honour and interest of your country' [i.e. Virginia – the Founding Fathers usually referred to their States as their countries], Madison added that the Parliament's recently passed 'Coercive Acts' against Massachusetts were 'a hostile attack on this and every other Colony, and a sufficient warrant to use violence and reprisal, in all cases where it may be expedient for our security and welfare.'

Although Madison was critical of Great Britain, he could also be critical of his own Colony. Madison hated the union of church and state in Virginia, where citizens were obliged to support the Anglican Church and religious dissent ('evangelical' Presbyterians, Baptists, and Methodists) was not tolerated. To Madison, the 'rights of conscience' were 'one of the characteristics of a free people,' without which freedom could not flourish. Thus, if the Colonies were to be free, then the colonists' minds must first be free, which they could never be without religious liberty. 'If the Church of England had been the established and general religion in all the Northern Colonies as it has been among us here,' Madison speculated to a

9

Pennsylvanian classmate from Princeton University, 'and uninterrupted tranquility had prevailed throughout the continent, it is clear to me that slavery and subjection might and would have been gradually insinuated among us.' Yet the grass was somewhat greener on the other side for Madison: as he and Jefferson would later learn, New England's hyper-politicised religious establishments were much more influential and intolerant than those in the South.

Following his fellow Virginian delegate Richard Henry Lee's resolutions for independence – 'that these United Colonies are, and of right ought to be, free and independent States' – Jefferson, along with a committee of Benjamin Franklin, John Adams, Richard Sherman, and Robert R. Livingston, was chosen to write the Declaration of Independence. Like the past public documents which he had drafted, Jefferson addressed the Crown (to whom the Colonies believed they owed their allegiance) and ignored the Parliament and its pretended authority altogether. Unlike his past documents, however, Jefferson's tone was no longer respectful, but defiant. 'When in the course of human events, it becomes necessary for one people to dissolve the political bands which have connected them with another, and to assume among the powers of the earth, the separate and equal station to which the laws of nature and of nature's god entitle them,' declared Jefferson, 'a decent respect to the opinions of mankind requires that they should declare the causes which impel them to the separation.' According to Jefferson, 'All men are created equal' and were 'endowed by their Creator' with the 'unalienable rights' of 'life, liberty, and the pursuit of happiness.' If a government, reasoned Jefferson, 'becomes destructive' of the ends for which it was founded – securing the unalienable rights of the people – then it was the right and duty of the people 'to alter or abolish,' or 'throw off' that government, 'and to institute new government, laying its foundations on such principles and organising its powers in such form, as to them shall seem most likely to effect their safety and happiness.' Rather than radical, this doctrine was consistent with the conventional interpretation/justification of the Glorious Revolution of 1688, when the Parliament deposed the Francophile King James II for his absolutism and Catholicism, and crowned his nephew, William III, in his place. Given the 'long train of abuses and usurpations' of the Crown against the Colonies, which Jefferson enumerated in detail – the 'design' of which was 'the establishment of an absolute tyranny over these States' – the Colonies declared themselves 'free and independent States.' Time and time again, insisted Jefferson, the Colonies had attempted compromise with the Parliament and asked the Crown to protect the rights of his loyal subjects, yet 'our repeated petitions have been answered only by repeated injury.' Such a 'tyrant' as this was clearly 'unfit to be the ruler of a free people.' Even the British people – the 'brethren' and 'common kindred' of the Americans – had betrayed 'justice and consanguinity,' and therefore were 'enemies in war, in peace friends.' Jefferson closed with a pledge among the signers of 'our lives, our fortunes, and our sacred honour.'

According to John Adams, the Massachusetts delegate who defended the Declaration of Independence in the Continental Congress – Jefferson called him 'the Colossus of Independence – American secession was 'the greatest question which was ever debated in America,' and the day on which the Lee Resolution was adopted (and thus the day that secession was actually declared), 'ought to be commemorated as the day of deliverance, by solemn acts of devotion to God Almighty.' In the twilight of their lives, having revived their friendship after years of estrangement, Jefferson reminisced with Adams over 'the flames kindled on the Fourth of July, 1776.'

In addition to writing the Declaration of Independence, Jefferson, again with Franklin and Adams, was also tasked with designing the Great Seal of the United States. Jefferson and Franklin agreed on an image of Moses parting the Red Sea, leading his people to freedom and crushing the Pharaoh, with a pillar of fire from the heavens signifying divine favour. Jefferson also proposed, for the reverse side, the figures of 'Hengist and Horsa, the [Anglo-] Saxon chiefs from whom we claim the honour of being descended, and whose political principles and form of government we have assumed.' Indeed, Jefferson was a scholar of Anglo-Saxon history and language, and firmly believed that the English political tradition originated with the Anglo-Saxons, who were, in fact, passing on the Graeco-Roman political tradition which they had learned in the Roman Empire, but which had been corrupted by the Norman conquerors. 'Has not every restitution of the ancient [Anglo-] Saxon laws had happy effects?' asked Jefferson. 'Is it not better now that we return at once into that happy system of our ancestors, the wisest and most perfect ever yet devised by the wit of man, as it stood before the eighth century?' Jefferson's belief was as mythological as historical, but history is often mythological (and vice versa). Jefferson and Franklin's seal also included the motto, 'Rebellion to Tyrants is Obedience to God.' Although the Congress did not adopt Jefferson and Franklin's motto, Jefferson made it his own and began to seal his letters with the phrase.

The Declaration of Independence was not, as Abraham Lincoln grandly argued, a 'charter of freedom' or an 'immortal emblem of humanity,' did not proclaim 'an abstract truth, applicable to all men and all times' or the 'promise that in due time the weights should be lifted from the shoulders of all men, and that all should have an equal chance,' and did not serve as 'a standard maxim for a free society' or 'a stumbling-block to the very harbingers of reappearing tyranny and oppression.' On the contrary, the Declaration was simply an act of 'secession' and 'separation from the mother country,' as Jefferson humbly referred to it in his memoirs. Rooted in the English constitutional tradition, stretching from *Magna Carta Libertatum* through the Glorious Revolution and to the Colonies' charters, the meaning of the Declaration was that all men had an equal right to govern themselves and to replace governments which were not doing their duty with new governments. 'The sacred Declaration of Independence...is to be construed by the circumstances and purposes for which it was made,' argued Lincoln's nemesis, Jefferson Davis. 'The communities were declaring their independence; the people of those communities were asserting that no man was born – to use the language of Mr. Jefferson – booted and spurred to ride over the rest of mankind; that men were created equal – meaning the men of the political community; that there was no divine right to rule; that no man inherited the right to govern; that there were no classes by which power and place descended to families, but that all stations were equally within the grasp of each member of the body politic.' Lincoln employed lawyerly sophistry and majestic rhetoric to transform the Continental Congress' act of secession into a universal manifesto of human rights: 'No matter in what shape it comes, whether from the mouth of a king who seeks to bestride the people of his own nation and live by the fruit of their labour, or from one race of men as an apology for enslaving another race, it is the same tyrannical principle.' Davis, by contrast, simply interpreted the Declaration in the historical context of the American Revolution: 'After the struggle of ages had consecrated the right of the Englishmen to constitutional representative government, our colonial ancestors were forced to vindicate that birthright by an appeal to arms.'

Jefferson's meaning was clearer in his original draft, which instead of written as, 'We hold these truths to be self-evident; that all men are created equal,' was originally written as, 'We hold these truths to be sacred and undeniable; that all men are created equal and independent.' Although Jefferson's original draft also included a condemnation of the Crown's role in slavery (which was deleted at the insistence of South-Carolinian and Georgian slave-holders along with New-England slave-traders), just a few years later, in his *Notes on the State of Virginia*, Jefferson theorized that 'the blacks, whether originally a distinct race, or made distinct by time and circumstances, are inferior to the whites in the endowments both of body and mind.' The fact is that neither Jefferson nor his compatriots in Philadelphia believed in the egalitarianism and universalism which later generations, cherry-picking lines from the Declaration and interpreting them out of context – as Abraham Lincoln did – have ascribed to them.

13

When Jefferson wrote the Declaration of Independence, Americans had long-enjoyed the rights of life, liberty, and the pursuit of happiness. Due to their proto-libertarian English political tradition, remote distance from the central government in London, and seemingly limitless western frontier, Americans were already the freest people in the world. Jefferson was not inventing new rights or experimenting with Enlightenment-era theories, but defending pre-existing rights by declaring Americans equal to as well as independent of the British. 'The meaning of this sentence is defined in its application,' Kentucky Congressman Richard M. Johnson declared of 'all men are created equal' during the Missouri Crisis, 'that all communities stand upon equality; that Americans are equal with Englishmen, and have the right to organise such government for themselves as they shall choose, whenever it is their pleasure to dissolve the bonds which unite them to another people.'

In 1775, Madison was elected to Virginia's Convention, which on 15 May 1776, resolved to adopt a declaration of rights and draft a republican constitution – the first American declaration of rights and the first such constitution in history. Madison and Jefferson took pride in the Fifteenth of May as Virginia's very own independence day, as well as in Virginia's Constitution as the first of its kind in history. 'Virginia, of which I am myself a native and resident,' boasted Jefferson, 'was not only the first of the States but, I believe I may say, the first of the nations of the earth, which assembled its wise men peaceably together to form a fundamental constitution, to commit it to writing, and place it among the archives, where everyone should be free to appeal to its text.' Madison was appointed to the committee (headed by the venerable old George Mason, who had co-authored the *Fairfax Resolves* with George Washington) which drafted the Virginia Constitution, replacing the old royal governor with an elected governor and the House of Burgesses with a bicameral legislature. Although Jefferson was in the Continental Congress at Philadelphia and was unable to return home to participate in the constitutional proceedings as he desired, he did send

Virginia's Convention a draft of a constitution, the preamble of which was ultimately included in Mason's constitution. To Jefferson, the new constitutions of the States were even more important than independence from the British Empire. 'In truth it is the whole object of the present controversy,' explained Jefferson. 'For should a bad government be instituted for us, in future it had been as well to have accepted at first the bad one offered us from beyond the water without the risk and expence of contest.' In the *Virginia Declaration of Rights*, also drafted by Mason (whom Madison would later face in the framing and ratifying of the Constitution), Madison inserted a clause strengthening the protection of religious freedom: 'That religion, or the duty which we owe to our Creator, and the manner of discharging it, can only be directed by reason or conviction, not by force or violence; and therefore, that all men are equally entitled to enjoy the free exercise of religion, according to the dictates of conscience.'

With Virginia now a free and independent State, Jefferson returned to her newfound House of Delegates with the intention of reforming the legal code to be more liberal than feudal. The law, believed Jefferson, should be written 'with a simple eye to reason, for the good of those whose government it was formed.' It was there that Jefferson and Madison were first introduced, thus beginning a friendship and political partnership that would shape the course of American history. Settling into the roles that they would play for the rest of their lives, Madison was the chief organiser behind the passage of the Statute for Religious Freedom, for which Jefferson was the inspiration and symbolic face. The bill, ending the taxation of Virginians for the support of the Episcopal Church and guaranteeing freedom of religion to all Virginians, did not pass until 1786, with Madison still a Virginia Assemblyman and Jefferson then overseas as Minister to France. Proclaiming that 'Almighty God hath created the mind free,' the bill, originally authored by Jefferson, branded official religious establishments as 'sinful and tyrannical.' In the process of passing this controversial reform, the young, upstart Madison made an enemy of the legendary Patrick Henry, whom he would again face in the debate over Virginia's ratification of the Constitution. 'I flatter myself,' Madison boasted to Jefferson, now in Paris, 'I have in this country extinguished forever the ambitious hope of making laws for the human mind.'

Jefferson, on a committee with his old mentor, the distinguished jurist George Wythe, as well another respected jurist, Edmund Pendleton, succeeded in abolishing feudalistic laws and humanising the criminal code, though his proposals for public education and the gradual abolition of slavery failed. In 1779, Jefferson was elected Governor of Virginia, a post unsuited to his intellectual disposition, but one at which he worked tirelessly, particularly in the requisition of troops and supplies for General George Washington's Continental Army. At the same time, Madison served in the Confederation Congress, also working to support General Washington and the Continental Army. In the Congress, Madison defended Virginia's territorial claims against 'misrepresentations and calumnies' and 'hostile machinations' of other envious States. During this time in the Congress, Madison also set a personal precedent which he would continue to honour for the rest of his career. Although he personally favoured a national bank, tariffs, and even a naval force to coerce States to obey the law (which, ironically, he told Jefferson would 'protect the Southern States for many years to come against the insults and aggressions of their Northern brethren'), he recognised that the Congress lacked the constitutional authority for such measures, and thus refused to exercise power he did not rightfully possess. Madison described his conflicted feelings over the national bank to Pendleton as 'the dilemma in which circumstances placed the members who felt on one side the importance of the institution, and on the other a want of power and aversion to assume it.' Meanwhile, near the end of Jefferson's term, Virginia was overrun by British forces, her government practically dissolved as officials scattered to safety, and Monticello itself menaced by marauders (his crops were burned, livestock slaughtered, and slaves captured). Despite these hardships, Jefferson faithfully discharged his duties to the end. Made somewhat of a scapegoat for the military disaster, Jefferson announced that he had 'retired to my farm, my family, and books, from which I think nothing will evermore separate me.' For the rest of his life, Jefferson ritually disavowed politics and ambition, although he could never resist what the Virginians of his class considered the duty of public service. 'In a virtuous government, and more especially in times like these, public offices are, what they should be, burdens to those appointed to them, which it would be wrong to decline, thought foreseen to bring with them intense labour, and great private loss,' Jefferson confided to his old ally, Richard Henry Lee, after his election as Governor. 'The hour of private retirement to which I am drawn by my nature with a propensity almost irresistible, will be the most welcome of my life.' Madison was dismayed at Jefferson's professed retirement. 'Great as my partiality is to Mr. Jefferson,' grumbled Madison to fellow Virginian Edmund Randolph, 'the mode in which seems to determined to revenge the wrong received from his country does not appear to me to be dictated either by philosophy or patriotism.'

Back at Monticello, Jefferson wrote *Notes on the State of Virginia*, a groundbreaking natural, cultural, and political history of his cherished homeland drawn from answers to the inquiries of a curious French diplomat. Jefferson intended his book for private circulation among his inner circle, but when foreign translations began to leak, he had it published himself. 'It can never be too often repeated, that the time for fixing every essential right on a legal basis is while our rulers are honest, and ourselves united,' Jefferson urged in support of liberalising Virginian law, worried that when the American Revolution ended the people would become complacent. 'The shackles, therefore, which shall not be knocked off at the conclusion of this war, will remain on us long, will be made heavier and heavier, till our rights shall revive or expire in a convulsion.'

Following the tragic death of his beloved wife in 1782, an empty Jefferson poured himself into his public duties. He served as a Virginia delegate to the

Confederation Congress, where he had penned the body's thankful, tearful reply to General George Washington at his resignation of command in Annapolis. 'Called upon by your country to defend its invaded rights you accepted the sacred charge,' wrote Jefferson, who praised Washington for persevering 'till these United States, aided by a magnanimous king and nation [Louis XVI and France], have been enabled, under a just Providence, to close the war in freedom, safety, and independence.' Jefferson joined with Washington 'in commending the interest of our dearest country to the protection of Almighty God' and prayed to God 'that a life so beloved may be fostered with all His care – that your days may be happy as they have been illustrious and that He will finally give you that reward, which this world cannot give.' Washington's resignation of his command, in the republican example of Cincinnatus (the Roman leader who was appointed dictator to defend the republic and returned home once the danger was defeated) and in contrast to the example of Julius Caesar (the Roman leader who seized dictatorial authority and ended the republic), symbolised the sovereignty of civil power over military power and profoundly impressed Jefferson. 'The moderation and virtue of a single character,' Jefferson later complimented Washington in private, 'has probably prevented this revolution from being closed as most others have been, by a subversion of that liberty it was intended to establish.'

Jefferson next accepted the position of Minister to France, succeeding the first American celebrity, Benjamin Franklin. In Paris, where Jefferson lived from 1784 to 1789, he negotiated a commercial treaty with Prussia, obtained commercial concessions from France for the South's tobacco trade and New England's whaling trade, and developed his idea of economic coercion as a peaceful alternative to war. Jefferson believed firmly in American friendship with France, gushing to Madison that 'its inhabitants love us more, I think, than they do any other nation on earth.' By contrast, Jefferson vented to Madison that the British were 'our natural enemies, and as the only nation on earth who wished us ill from the bottom of their souls.'

Last, but not least, Jefferson was in Paris during the early days of the French Revolution, on which he was neither among the 'left' or 'right,' but in the centre. 'The appeal to the rights of man, which had been made in the United States,' boasted Jefferson, 'was taken up by France, first of the European nations.' Disturbed by the tyranny of the *Ancien Regime,* Jefferson collaborated with liberal republicans like the Marquis de Lafayette (an aristocrat who had fought by George Washington's side and defended Virginia while Jefferson was Governor) to reform rather than replace the government. Indeed, contrasting the French political tradition of absolutist-democracy with the British-American tradition of constitutional-republicanism, Jefferson informed Madison that the French were 'not yet ripe for the blessings to which they are entitled.' Accordingly, when the Estates-General convened for the first time in almost two centuries, Jefferson put 'all the good in which the parties agree' (namely, a constitutional monarch, a national legislature, the abolition of aristocratic privileges, and the protection of civil liberties) into a charter which he advocated be adopted as a compromise. 'I think it probable,' Jefferson optimistically predicted to his protégé and fellow Virginian James Monroe, 'this country, within two or three years, be in the enjoyment of a tolerably free constitution, and that without its having cost them a drop of blood.' After the Estates-General dissolved and the king and nobility threatened force against the people (who had by then reconstituted as the National Assembly), Jefferson defended the 'legitimacy' of the riots in Paris which took over the city. 'The National Assembly now have as clean a canvas to work on here as we had in America,' pronounced Jefferson. 'I have so much confidence on the good sense of man, and his qualifications for self-government, that I am never afraid of the issue where reason is left free to exert her force.' The National Assembly adopted the *Declaration of the Rights of Man,* which Jefferson influenced, as well as a constitution along the lines of the one he had originally proposed.

When Jefferson returned to the United States, where the rising radicalism of the French Revolution became part of a propaganda war between Democratic-Republicans in the South and Federalists in the North, he protested heatedly that 'the liberty of the whole earth was depending on the issue of this contest,' and 'rather than it should have failed, I would have seen half the earth desolated.' Yet Jefferson was soon embarrassed by the diplomatic fiascos of Citizen Genet and the XYZ Affair (he himself authored the request for the ambassador's recall), disappointed by the execution of the royal family (whom he thought should have been deposed but not beheaded), and sickened by the 'horrors' of the Reign of Terror (such as the execution of class enemies and eradication of rebellious regions). 'In the end,' Jefferson reflected to Lafayette, 'the limited monarchy they had secured was exchanged for the unprincipled and bloody tyranny of Robespierre, and the equally unprincipled and maniac tyranny of Bonaparte.' Jefferson remained hopeful for the 'rights of man' in France and around the world, but he learned that colonies seceding from an empire was very different from a people overthrowing a government. As a French noblewoman reminded him, 'The characteristic difference between your revolution and ours, is that having nothing to destroy, you had nothing to injure.'

Jefferson and Madison both believed that the problem with the Articles of Confederation (a legislature of the States without a separate judiciary or executive), was that it could not even enforce its little authority. According to Jefferson and Madison, corresponding across the Atlantic Ocean, American financial credit and moral creditability was suffering abroad, while the States were defying the Confederation and feuding amongst themselves at home. Madison, in particular, who had absorbed himself in the study of books which Jefferson sent from France (what he referred to as 'literary cargo'), had composed his thoughts on the subject in two private documents, *Notes on Ancient and Modern Confederacies* and *Vices of the Political System of the United States*. Despite their agreement on the disease, however, Jefferson and Madison disagreed drastically on the cure. Jefferson desired simply amending the Confederation to grant a few new powers. Whatever the Confederation's flaws, Jefferson still considered its government a 'good, old, and venerable fabric' and 'the best existing or that ever did exist.' To Jefferson, the Confederation should be reformed without altering its federal foundation. 'To make us one nation as to foreign concerns and keep us distinct in domestic ones,' Jefferson recommended to Madison, 'gives the outline of the proper division of powers between the general and particular governments [i.e. the States].' By contrast, Madison rejected the 'individual independence of the States,' preferring 'due supremacy of the national authority' and only keeping the States 'so far as they can be subordinately useful.' When Madison informed Jefferson of his plans for a new constitution – including separation of legislative, executive, and judicial powers as well as a national 'negative' over State laws – Jefferson endorsed the former as 'just and necessary,' but rejected the latter. 'Prima facie, I do not like it,' Jefferson bluntly replied. 'This proposes to mend a small hole, by covering the entire garment.' Jefferson probably had Madison in mind when he acknowledged to another Virginian, 'I do not go as far in the reforms thought necessary as some of my correspondents in America.'

In their Transatlantic correspondence, Jefferson and Madison disagreed not just on the form of government, but on the role of government as well. What Madison viewed as the misrule of the Confederation convinced him that the role of government was to provide 'stability' and 'energy' as well as to prevent 'factions' of majorities from tyrannising minorities. 'The great desideratum in government,' Madison told Jefferson, 'is so to modify the sovereignty as that it may be sufficiently neutral between different parts of society to controul one part from invading the rights of another, and at the same time sufficiently controulled itself from setting up an interest adverse to that of the entire society.' According to Madison, power, whether in the hands of the majority or a monarchy, was prone to abuse and must be limited. 'Wherever the real power in a government lies, there is the danger of oppression,' Madison explained to Jefferson. 'Wherever there is an interest and power to do wrong, wrong will generally be done.' Jefferson, however, trusting 'the good sense of the people,' did not trust the government with the power to restrain the will of the majority, believing that this would lead to the very tyranny which Madison hoped to prevent. 'I own that I am not a friend to a very energetic government,' Jefferson informed Madison. 'It is always oppressive.' Jefferson conceded that the Confederation lacked power, or 'energy,' which was indeed an 'inconvenience' in some circumstances, but cautioned that the other extreme of 'absolute governments' and 'armed force' resulted in 'the effect of the bayonet constantly held at the breast of every citizen...which resembles very much the stillness of the grave.' Between the crimes from an excess of liberty and the crimes from an excess of power, avowed Jefferson, it was the latter which was 'most numerous, most oppressive on the mind, and most degrading to the dignity of man.' Jefferson and Madison's interpretations of Shays' Rebellion (an anti-tax, anti-debt uprising in New England which frightened many Americans into supporting a stronger central government, especially a separate executive branch) illustrated the political differences between the two. 'I hold it that a little rebellion now and then is a good thing,' the contemplative Jefferson shared with the anxious Madison, 'and as necessary in the political world as storms in the physical.' Madison, by contrast, considered Shays' Rebellion 'perfidious' and the rebels themselves a 'diseased part' of the American polity, demanding 'every concession in favour of stable government not infringing upon fundamental principles, as the only security against an opposite extreme.' In short, while Madison reasonably believed that 'if men were angels, no government would be necessary,' Jefferson also reasonably wondered what 'angels in the forms of kings' would be 'trusted with the government of others' if mankind 'cannot be trusted with the government of himself.' It was the South-Carolinian statesman, John C. Calhoun, who would reconcile these two seemingly irreconcilable viewpoints of minority rights and majority rule – who the paleo-conservative sage Richard M. Weaver described as 'a bridge between the old and new schools of Southern political thought.'

Jefferson may not have been bothered by Shays' Rebellion, but Madison was right that such an uprising 'contributed more to that uneasiness which produced the Constitution and prepared the public mind for general reform.' Madison was instrumental in organising support in Virginia for the Constitutional Convention and convincing the retired George Washington lend his prestige to the constitutional movement by heading the Virginia delegation. In the summer of 1787, the men who would become the Framers – 'an assembly of demigods,' in Jefferson's glowing opinion to John Adams – gathered in Philadelphia, commissioned by their States to reform the Articles of Confederation in accord with the Confederation Congress' recommendation. Madison asked Edmund Randolph, the Governor of Virginia, to open the Convention with a presentation of his plan for a national, consolidated government, knowing that it might be better-received from an established figure as opposed to a youthful reformer. Although Randolph obliged, Madison ultimately spoke about two-hundred times over the next few months, in addition to taking voluminous notes on the debates and proceedings. Randolph proposed fifteen resolutions (the 'Virginia Plan'), the centerpiece of which was a 'national legislature' with the powers 'to legislate in all cases to which the separate States are incompetent...to negative all laws passed by the several States, contravening in the opinion of the national legislature the articles of union; and to call forth the force of the union against any member of the union failing to fulfill its duty under the articles thereof.' According to Randolph, 'A union of the States merely federal will not accomplish the objects proposed by the Articles of Confederation, namely common defence, security of liberty, and general welfare,' and therefore 'a *national* government ought to be established consisting of a *supreme* legislature, executive, and judiciary.' Having seized the initiative and set the agenda, Madison initially succeeded in getting the Convention to pass most of the resolutions of the Virginia Plan. His momentum faltered, however, when small States (Maryland, Delaware, and New Jersey) and large States (Virginia, Pennsylvania, and Massachusetts) clashed over whether the people of the States or the State governments would elect the national legislature and whether States' representation in the national legislature would be apportioned equally or according to population – in other words, whether the government would be federal or national. Delaware delegate John Dickinson, noting that 'the happiness of the country required considerable powers to be left in the hands of the States' and hoping that 'each State would retain an equal voice at least in one branch of the national legislature,' urged Madison to compromise, but Madison, aware that any concession to the States would dilute his theory and vision, was overriding in his tactics and, ultimately, overreaching in his aims. Connecticut delegates Roger Sherman and Oliver Ellsworth proposed a compromise of proportional representation in one house of the legislature and equal representation in the other, but this was rejected, despite Sherman's plea that 'the smaller States would never agree to this plan on any other principle than an equality of suffrage in this branch.' The only point which Madison did concede was 'the practicability, the justice, and the efficacy' of the coercion of a State. 'A union of the States containing such an ingredient seemed to provide for its own destruction,' admitted Madison. 'The use of force against a State, would look more like a declaration of war, than an infliction of punishment, and would probably be considered by the party attacked as a dissolution of all previous compacts by which it might be bound.'

Once the Virginia Plan had been discussed in full, New-Jersey delegate William Paterson countered with resolutions for a 'purely federal' alternative to the national Virginia Plan. 'You see the consequence of pushing things too far,' the elder Dickinson chided the youthful Madison. 'Some of the members from the small States wish for two branches in the general legislature, and are friends to a good national government; but we would sooner submit to a foreign power, than submit to be deprived of equality of suffrage in both branches of the legislature, and thereby be thrown under the domination of the large States.' According to Paterson, 'The States stood on the footing of equal sovereignty…and we have no power to vary the idea of equal sovereignty.' If the 'balance of equality' were destroyed, warned Paterson, then 'you endanger the rights of the lesser societies by the danger of usurpation in the greater.' The New Jersey Plan rallied opposition to the Virginia Plan and divided the Convention. Madison, dismissing the New Jersey Plan as 'a pertinacious adherence to an inadmissible plan,' insisted that 'the States never possessed the essential rights of sovereignty' and that 'they ought to be placed under the controul of the general government – at least as much so as they formerly were under the King and British Parliament.' New-York delegate Alexander Hamilton proposed a new constitution of his own which 'reduced' and even 'extinguished' the States more than Madison's Virginia Plan. 'No amendment of the Confederation leaving the States in possession of their sovereignty,' asserted Hamilton, 'could possibly answer the purpose.' Hamilton, who admitted that his plan and the Virginia Plan were 'remote from the idea of the people' and that 'the Jersey Plan is perhaps nearest their expectation,' did not intend for his plan to be taken seriously, but was hoping to reposition the New Jersey Plan as extreme and the Virginia Plan as moderate. Massachusetts delegate Rufus King took Madison and Hamilton's radical views a step further, claiming that 'none of the States are now sovereign or independent' and that 'consolidation is already established.' Maryland delegate Luther Martin, who had mourned that 'the language of the States being *sovereign* and *independent*, was once familiar and understood, though it seemed now so strange and obscure,' countered that 'when the States threw off their allegiance on Great Britain, they became independent of her and each other.' According to Martin, the States had 'united and confederated for mutual defence, and this was done on principles of perfect reciprocity' and the States 'would now again meet on the same ground.' Against the Virginia Plan and for the New Jersey Plan, Martin avowed that 'if we cannot confederate on just principles, I will never confederate in any other manner.' Faced with plans for consolidated governments and even proposals for the coercion of the States, Madison's fellow Virginia delegate, George Mason (deemed 'the wisest man of his generation' by Jefferson), declared that 'not withstanding [my] solicitude to establish a national government, [I] never would agree to abolish the State governments, or render them absolutely insignificant.' Mason held that the States 'were as necessary as the general government, and [I] would be equally careful to preserve them.' Amidst all this acrimony, North-Carolina delegate William Blount pessimistically (and presciently) predicted in a letter home that 'we shall ultimately end not many years just separate and distinct governments perfectly independent of each other.'

Pennsylvania delegate Benjamin Franklin, who had earlier called for each day's session to begin with prayer in hopes of saving the Convention, proposed a compromise between the Virginia and New Jersey plans: one house of the legislature would be elected by the people of the States with each State represented according to population, and the other would be elected by the State legislatures with each State represented equally. When the delegates agreed that Franklin's proposal should be considered in a committee, Madison sensed that he was losing controul of the Convention and opposed the committee, though to no avail. After breaking for Independence-Day festivities, the committee introduced a more detailed version of Franklin's compromise. In an outburst, Pennsylvania delegate Gouverneur Morris sneered that States' rights were the 'bane of this country,' threatening that 'we cannot annihilate, but we may take out the teeth of the serpents,' as well as that 'if persuasion does not unite...the sword will,' thereby prompting New-York delegates Robert Yates and John Lansing to leave the Convention in protest. In the ensuing debate over legislative representation, Northern and Southern delegates stumbled upon the ominous subject of sectional differences. 'It seemed now to be pretty well understood that the real difference of interests lay, not between the large and small but between the Northern and Southern States,' observed Madison. Despite the strenuous objections of Madison and other proponents of the Virginia Plan, the Convention ultimately passed the committee's compromise. South-Carolina delegate John Rutledge, who would ultimately chair the committee which composed the text of the Constitution, quelled discussion of adjournment. 'I can assure you, gentlemen, that I have been obliged to sacrifice much that I have held dear,' Rutledge reminded the delegates. 'However, when I have been tempted to reduce our joint actions to a nullity by consulting only my own desire I have said, "Is it not better than I should sacrifice one prized opinion than that all of us should sacrifice everything we might otherwise gain?"' The Convention, which had already been in session for a month and a half, would remain for another two months, but the crucial division between the small States and the large States, as well as between the principles of State sovereignty and national supremacy, was overcome. Madison's ambitious proposals for proportional representation in both houses of the national legislature, unlimited authority for the national legislature, and the national legislature's 'negative' over State laws were all defeated – even the word 'national,' on the motion of Oliver Ellsworth, was specifically struck from the Constitution! 'I hazard an opinion,' the defeated Madison vented to Jefferson, 'that the plan, should it be adopted, will neither effectually answer its national object nor prevent the local mischiefs which everywhere excite disgusts against the State governments.' Madison is often dubbed the 'Father of the Constitution,' yet while the debate was established on his terms, the final product was hardly what he had originally intended. Indeed, Madison graciously demurred from the title, adding that the Constitution was 'the work of many heads and many hands' – namely, the heads and hands of others.

Jefferson, still serving in France during the summer of 1787, was apprehensive about the Constitution, especially the glaring absence of a bill of rights. 'I confess there are things in it which stagger all my dispositions to subscribe to what such an assembly has produced,' Jefferson exclaimed to John Adams of his 'assembly of demigods.' Jefferson feared that the Constitutional Convention was overreacting to relatively minor incidents, such as Shays Rebellion, and thus 'in the spur of the moment…setting up a kite [a bird of prey] to keep the hen yard in order.' To Madison, Jefferson politely complimented the Constitution as 'a good canvas, on which some strokes only want retouching,' particularly 'a bill of rights…to guard the people against the federal government.' While Jefferson agreed with the Federalists that 'all is reserved in the case of the general government which is not given, while in the particular ones [i.e. States] all is given which is not reserved' was a sound legal principle, he countered pragmatically that such an legalistic argument would be a mere *gratis dictum* [i.e. not legally binding] without the same 'express' protection which States' rights had in the Articles of Confederation. 'A bill of rights is what the people are entitled to against every government on earth, general or particular [i.e. federal or State],' Jefferson insisted to Madison, 'and what no government should refuse, or rest on inferences.' Despite his concerns about the Constitution, Jefferson was ultimately 'neutral' on the question of the States' ratification – neither a Federalist nor an Anti-Federalist. 'It is my principle that the will of the majority should always prevail,' Jefferson assured Madison. 'If they approve the proposed Convention in all its parts, I shall concur in it cheerfully, in hopes that they will amend it whenever they shall find it work wrong.' Personally, Jefferson hoped that the Constitution would be ratified by nine States and rejected by four, thus putting it into effect while also requiring amendments for a bill of rights. 'We shall thus have all that is good,' Jefferson explained to Madison of this strategy, 'and cure its principal defect.' Although Jefferson did not endorse the Constitution altogether, he was nevertheless proud of 'the example of changing a constitution by assembling the wise men of the State, instead of assembling armies' and 'a government reformed by reason alone without bloodshed.' Although Jefferson was suspicious of the new government without a bill of rights, he predicted to

Madison that as long as the people preserved their independent way of life and improved their education, 'our governments shall remain virtuous for many centuries.'

Despite his disappointment in Philadelphia, Madison meant to make the best of the Constitution and to present it as what it was, not twist it into what he wanted it to be. Although it was far from what he had initially desired, Madison supported the Constitution 'because I thought it safe to the liberties of the people, and the best that could be obtained from the jarring interests of the States, and the miscellaneous opinions of politicians.' Just as Solon believed that the laws he had established for the Athenians were 'the best they were able to receive,' Madison believed that the Constitution was the best possible change under the circumstances. While finishing his term in the Confederation Congress, Madison honed his arguments for ratification in *The Federalist*, a series of pro-Constitution essays co-written with fellow Federalists Alexander Hamilton and John Jay and published in New York City. Three of Madison's most famous arguments from *The Federalist* were that the new government would be 'partly federal, partly national,' with the States reserving to themselves whatever powers they did not delegate to the government and enumerate in the Constitution; that large republics would minimise the power of 'factions,' or tyrannous majorities (an original idea contrary to the consensus among political philosophers, such as the Baron de Montesquieu, that republics must be small); and that the powers of the federal branches would 'check' and 'balance' the powers of the others. 'Is it not the glory of the people of America, that, whilst they have paid a decent regard to the opinions of former times and other nations, they have not suffered a blind veneration for antiquity, for custom, or for names, to overrule the suggestions of their own good sense, the knowledge of their own situation, and the lessons of their own experienced?' asked Madison in the *Federalist*. 'To this manly spirit, posterity will be indebted for their possession, and the world for the example, of the numerous innovations displayed on the American theatre, in favour of private rights and public happiness.'

When Madison returned home and headed to Richmond for Virginia's Ratification Convention, the road loomed long and hard. Virginia's political elite was divided on the Constitution, with the formidable five-time former Governor and popular tribune Patrick Henry, the venerable lawgiver George Mason, and the American Cicero Richard Henry Lee (who was serving in the Confederation Congress and could not attend) in firm opposition (even Governor Edmund Randolph had refused to sign the Constitution in Philadelphia and remained uncertain). In addition to Madison, Virginian Federalists featured personages no less honourable, such as the war heroes George Washington (who did not attend the Convention, but was still an overruling influence) and Henry Lee III, as well as the jurists George Wythe and Edmund Pendleton. According to the Virginian Anti-Federalists, the Constitution was a betrayal of the American Revolution: there was no crisis worthy of replacing the Articles of Confederation with a bigger, stronger government when the specific shortcomings of the Articles could be easily amended. Madison denounced such fears as demagoguery and the Anti-Federalists themselves as demagogues, but Henry, speaking before the Convention, believed himself to be 'a servant of the people of this commonwealth...a sentinel over their rights, liberty, and happiness.' This public servant and sentinel of freedom perceived in the Constitution 'a revolution as radical as that which separated us from Great Britain,' but instead of a revolution which would free Americans, a revolution which would enslave Americans. Henry warned that if Virginia ratified the Constitution, 'our rights and privileges' would be 'endangered,' and 'the sovereignty of the States' would be 'relinquished.' Henry scoffed at the Constitution's 'ridiculous' checks and 'specious' balances, arguing that 'there will be no checks, no real balances in this government.' Henry also feared that the Northern majority which would controul the new government would tyrannise the Southern minority, 'laying what taxes they please, giving themselves what salaries they please, and suspending our laws at their pleasure.' Pointing out that if Virginia ratified the Constitution, 'we shall then be taxed by those who bear no part of the taxes themselves, and who consequently will be regardless of our interest in imposing them on us,' Henry asked, 'How can the Southern members prevent the adoption of the most oppressive mode of taxation in the Southern States, as there is a majority in favour of the Northern States?' This Northern majority, continued Henry, would not construe the Constitution conservatively, as the States intended, but would simply 'construe it as they please,' and 'among ten thousand *implied powers* which they may assume, they may, if we be engaged in a war, liberate every one of your slaves if they please.' Like Jefferson, Madison, and many of the Founding Fathers from the South, Henry was against slavery, but was against Northern interference even more. 'As much as I despise slavery, I see that prudence forbids its abolition,' admitted Henry. 'I deny that the general government ought to set them free, because a decided majority of the States have not the ties of sympathy and fellow feeling for those whose interest would be affected by their emancipation.' Despairing that Virginians were placing far too much faith in the virtue of mankind and forgetting mankind's fallen nature, as well as trusting theoretical checks and balances over a tangible bill of rights, Henry urged his countrymen to 'guard with jealous attention the public liberty' and to 'suspect everyone who approaches that jewel.' Henry mocked what he viewed as the Federalists' perverse refusal to accede to a bill of rights. 'A bill of rights may be summed up in a few words. What do they tell us?' asked Henry. 'That our rights are reserved,' he answered. 'Why not say so? Is it because it will consume too much paper?' Henry was equally scornful of the compromise to amend the Constitution after its ratification. 'You agree to bind yourselves hand and foot – for the sake of what?' snorted Henry. 'Of being unbound,' he answered. 'You go into a dungeon – for what? To get out.'

In debating Henry and the Anti-Federalists in Richmond, Madison nobly conceded to the Constitution which the Philadelphia Convention had framed on paper rather than the Constitution he had framed in his mind. Madison countered that rather than forming an unchecked, unbalanced government, the powers of the federal government would be 'enumerated' to 'defined and limited objects, beyond which it cannot extend its jurisdiction.' In addition, federal powers would not pose a threat to the sovereignty of the States, but be limited to 'external objects' such as foreign relations and interstate trade, while the States retained 'those great objects which immediately concern the prosperity of the people.' Madison denied that the North would economically exploit the South, claiming instead that the general welfare meant 'the collective interest of the Union,' not the 'local views' of one section over another. Madison acknowledged that because the agrarian South imported more of its manufactures than the North, taxes on imports (also known as tariffs) would impose 'a disproportion of the burdens...on the Southern States,' but reminded the Virginians that the Constitution provided for other forms of taxation which would 'lessen that inequality.' Assuring the Virginians that any Northern proclamation emancipating Southern slaves would be a 'usurpation of power,' Madison insisted that 'there is no power to warrant it' and that 'such an idea never entered into any American breast, nor do I believe it ever will.' Furthermore, Madison was confident that 'the weight of the population will be to the southward,' preventing the possibility of the North tyrannising and terrorising the South. Madison rejected the Anti-Federalists' suspicion that the federal government would 'do every mischief they possibly can, and that they will omit to do every possible good which they are authorised to do.' At the Constitutional Convention Madison had observed, 'The truth was, that all men having power ought to be distrusted to a certain degree,' and at Virginia's Ratification Convention Madison continued, 'We do not depend on their virtue, or put confidence in our rulers, but in the people who are to choose them.' Lastly, facing demands for a bill of rights, Madison reiterated that a bill of rights was unnecessary and dangerous: 'Unnecessary, because it was evident that the general government had no power but what was given it, and the delegation alone warranted the exercise of power – dangerous, because an enumeration which is not complete, is not safe.'

In the end, Virginia's Ratification Convention narrowly approved the Constitution, 89 to 79, with resolutions asserting State sovereignty and conservative constructionism, as well as a list of recommended amendments for a bill of rights. These resolutions and recommended amendments, along with similar resolutions from other States like Massachusetts, New York, and South Carolina (as well as Rhode Island and North Carolina, which initially refused to ratify the Constitution), were the basis for the amendments which formed the Bill of Rights. What was peculiar about the ratification debate in Virginia (and, in fact, everywhere else) was that the Federalists almost completely conceded the argument to the Anti-Federalists. While there was a broad consensus among Federalists and Anti-Federalists concerning the powers of the government and the rights of the people, the contention between the two concerned whether the Constitution would preserve and protect this small-f federal and small-r republican consensus. In a sense, then, it was the Anti-Federalists, who by forcing the Federalists to fight on their terms, won the ratification debate. Throughout his life, Madison rejected the 'error' of 'ascribing to the intention of the Convention which framed the Constitution, an undue ascendancy in expounding it,' stressing that it was actually the 'State conventions which gave it all the validity and authority it possesses.' In other words, it was the intent of State conventions such as Virginia's (which actually enacted into law what the Constitutional Convention merely drafted) that mattered the most, not the personal opinions of individual Philadelphia framers.

As soon as Jefferson returned to Virginia from France in 1789, he learned that President George Washington had appointed him Secretary of State in the first government under the Constitution. Jefferson reluctantly accepted the position out of a sense of public duty and personal loyalty to Washington. When Governor Patrick Henry prevented the General Assembly from electing Madison to the Senate, Madison won election to the House of Representatives, where he was discouraged to see factions – 'contentions first between Federal and Anti-Federal parties, and then between Northern and Southern parties' – in spite of his theory that 'factious tempers' and 'local prejudices' would wane in the new American republic. Despite his personal reservations, out of a sense of duty and political necessity Madison spearheaded amendments to the Constitution which would become the Bill of Rights. 'The conventions of a number of States having at the time of their adopting the Constitution,' the forgotten preamble to the Bill of Rights explained, 'expressed a desire, in order to prevent misconstruction or abuse of its powers, that further declaratory and restrictive clauses should be added: and as extending the ground of public confidence in the government, will best insure the beneficent ends of its institution.' With Jefferson in the Cabinet and Madison in the Congress, the two Virginians led the opposition to the policies of Alexander Hamilton, a Revolutionary-War veteran trusted by President Washington and the Secretary of the Treasury. Jefferson was initially unfamiliar with Hamilton (though he quickly soured on him after being 'duped' into supporting the nationalisation of State debts in exchange for relocating the Capitol from Philadelphia to the Potomac River), but Madison and Hamilton had been fellow Federalists during the campaign for the Constitution. Unlike Hamilton, however, Madison was committed to upholding the Constitution as framed and ratified, even if it conflicted with his own opinions. 'Whatever might have been the opinions entertained in forming the Constitution,' reflected Madison many years later, in stark contrast with Hamilton's approach, 'it was the duty of all to support it in its true meaning, as understood by the nation at the time of its ratification.'

Jefferson and Hamilton were polar opposites, as different in appearance and demeanor as they were in principles and policies. Jefferson, the tall, reserved patrician and philosopher from the Virginian gentry, supported a conservative construction of the Constitution, the sovereignty of the States, *laissez-faire* economics, and an alliance with France (or, more realistically, neutrality). Hamilton, the short, aggressive bastard from the West Indies, supported a liberal construction of the Constitution, national supremacy, mercantilist economics, and an alliance with Great Britain. 'I consider the foundation of the Constitution as laid on this ground: "That all powers not delegated to the United States, by the Constitution, nor prohibited to it by the States, are reserved to the States or to the people,"' argued Jefferson in a report to President Washington against Hamilton's proposed national bank. 'To take a single step beyond the boundaries of thus drawn around the powers of Congress, is to take possession of a boundless field of power, no longer susceptible to definition.' In addition to its unconstitutionality, Jefferson considered Hamilton's whole financial system parasitic and corrupt. 'A system had there been contrived, for deluging the States with paper money instead of gold and silver, for withdrawing our citizens from the pursuits of commerce, manufactures, buildings, and other branches of useful industry, to occupy themselves and their capitals in a species of gambling, destructive of morality, and which had introduced its poison into the government itself,' Jefferson informed Washington. Furthermore, Hamilton's financial system – which formed a cartel of Northern banks to act as a national bank and taxed Southern agriculture to subsidise Northern industries and fund Northern public works – ultimately enriched the North at the South's expence. 'Whenever Northern and Southern prejudices have come into conflict,' Jefferson reminded Washington, 'the latter have been sacrificed and the former soothed.' Because of Hamilton's financial system, Jefferson warned Washington that the 'monarchical Federalists' had 'adopted the very construction of the Constitution, of which, when advocating its acceptance before the tribunal of the people, they declared it unsusceptible,' and that 'Anti-Federal[ist] champions,' such as Patrick Henry, had been 'strengthened in argument by the fulfillment of their predictions.' To one of these former Anti-Federalists, fellow Virginian George Mason, Jefferson confided that 'the only correction of what is corrupt in our present form of government' would be the 'augmentation' of Southern 'agricultural

35

representation' against the Northern 'stock-jobbers.' Jefferson also resented Hamilton's 'interferences' in the State Department and 'conferences' with the British and French, in which Hamilton undermined the United States by leaking administration secrets in order to thwart Washington and Jefferson's foreign policy and advance his own agenda. When Hamilton suggested, probably ironically, that the English Constitution's corruption made it 'the most perfect constitution of government ever devised by man' and that 'the greatest man that ever lived was Julius Caesar,' Jefferson's worst fears of a Tory who believed 'in the necessity of either force or corruption to govern men' were confirmed. Overall, Jefferson reviled Hamilton as 'a man whose history, from the moment history can stoop to notice him, is a tissue of machinations against the liberty of the country which has not only received and given him bread, but heaped honours on his head.' The conflict between the liberal-republican Jefferson and the statist-nationalist Hamilton drew battle lines in American politics which have endured ever since.

The division of his Cabinet distressed President Washington, who played the father figure to the two unruly young men and urged them to reconcile their differences for the good of the American republic. 'I will frankly and solemnly declare, that I believe the views of both of you to be pure and well-meant, and that experience only will decide with respect to the salutariness of the measures which are the subjects of dispute,' Washington assured Jefferson. 'I have a great, a sincere esteem and regard for you both, and ardently wish that some line could be marked out by which both of you could walk.' Despite the paternal Washington's pleas for 'mutual yieldings' between Jefferson and Hamilton, their principles and personalities proved utterly irreconcilable. After Jefferson's early retirement, political and personal disagreements estranged him from Washington, as they did Washington from many of his old Virginian friends.

Meanwhile, Madison, whether advising the President, speaking in the Congress, or writing in the press, was diligently organising opposition to the

Hamiltonian agenda. When President Washington was debating whether to sign the bill chartering a national bank, he requested that Madison draft him a veto address to read before the Congress. 'I object to the bill because it is an essential principle of the government that powers not delegated by the Constitution cannot be rightfully exercised; because the power proposed by the bill to be exercised is not expressly delegated; and because I cannot satisfy myself that it results from any express power by fair and safe rules of implication,' Madison wrote for Washington, continuing that the national bank was 'unequal between the public and the institution in favour of the institution,' creating a financial class above the citizenry based on patronage and privilege rather than merit. In the Congress himself, Madison blasted the bank bill, forcefully concluding 'that the power exercised by the bill was condemned by the silence of the Constitution; was condemned by the rule of interpretation arising out of the Constitution; was condemned by its tendency to destroy the main characteristic of the Constitution; was condemned by the expositions of the friends of the Constitution, whilst depending before the public; was condemned by the apparent intention of the persons which ratified the Constitution; was condemned by the explanatory amendments proposed by Congress themselves to the Constitution; and [I hope] that it would receive its final condemnation by the vote of this House.'

To counter the Federalist party organ, the *Gazette of the United States*, Jefferson and Madison founded the *National Gazette*, to which Madison was a prolific and potent contributor. In a typical essay titled, 'The Union: Who Are Its Real Friends?' Madison charged that those 'who would force on the people the melancholy duty of choosing between the loss of the Union, and the loss of what the Union was meant to secure,' were, in fact, the enemies of the Union. 'The real friends to the Union,' countered Madison, were those 'who are friends to the authority of the people, the sole foundation on which the Union rests,' 'who are friends to liberty, the great end for which the Union was formed,' 'who are friends to the limited and republican system of government,' 'who are enemies to every public measure that might smooth the way to hereditary government,' and 'who considering the public debt as injurious to the interests of the people, and baneful to the virtue of the government, are enemies to every contrivance for unnecessarily increasing its amount, or protracting its duration, or extending its influence.' The irony of Madison and Hamilton, who just a few years earlier had written together as *Publius*, now writing against one another as *Helvidius* and *Pacificus*, respectively, was not lost on anyone. When asked by a young protégé why he deserted his friend and fellow Federalist, Hamilton, Madison replied, 'Colonel Hamilton deserted me, from his wishing to administer the government into what he thought it ought to be; while, on my part, I endeavored to make it conform to the Convention that produced and recommended it, and particularly by the State conventions that adopted it.' Indeed, Madison and Hamilton both knew that in the Constitutional Convention, the power to charter corporations like a national bank had been decisively rejected and that tariffs for revenue rather than protectionism were what was intended and expected. Nevertheless, Hamilton won over President Washington and fastened his financial and foreign policies upon the young American republic.

Jefferson and Madison both convinced a weary George Washington to serve an additional term as President, impressing upon their fellow Virginian that it was his immense prestige which held the already-divided Union together. Jefferson had advised him that 'North and South will hang together, if they have you to hang on,' and Madison had commended him for 'conciliating and uniting all parties under a government which had excited such violent controversies and divisions.' When Washington retired in 1796, however, the Federalist John Adams was elected President, and Jefferson, the symbol of the growing Democratic-Republican Party (what he regarded as 'the Southern interest,' but which also had key support in Northern States like Pennsylvania and New York), elected Vice President. During the Adams Administration, while war between Great Britain and France wracked

Europe, warmongering wracked the young American republic. Under the pretence of preparing for an imagined French invasion, the Federalists created a crisis of fear which they exploited to justify heavy taxes, high expenditures and debt, a standing army, the repression of civil liberties, and the abrogation of their treaty with France. President Adams, who paraded about in a military uniform despite never having served and insisted on enforcing courtly customs in the new government, warned of terrorism and treason among the Democratic-Republicans, but Jefferson and Madison believed that it was the Federalists who were truly terrorising the people and betraying the American Revolution. 'Their system is professedly, to keep up an alarm,' Jefferson sighed to Madison, who wisely replied, 'Perhaps it is a universal truth that the loss of liberty at home is to be charged to provisions against danger real or pretended from abroad.'

It was amid the hysteria and paranoia of this 'Quasi-War' that the controversial Alien and Sedition Acts were passed, empowering the President to deport foreigners at will and to arrest citizens for criticising the federal government (except, curiously, the Vice President). The Federalist Party, which Jefferson now referred to as the 'war party,' was indeed becoming frighteningly militant and statist. 'He that is not for us is against us,' threatened the official Federalist newspaper. 'It is patriotism to write in favour of our government – it is sedition to write against it.' Jefferson and Madison were appalled by these laws, which violated core American principles such as States' rights, civil liberties, and the separation of powers. Furthermore, and perhaps most frighteningly to Jefferson and Madison, the Federalists were specifically targeting Democratic-Republican public figures, including journalists like Benjamin Franklin Bache (editor of the *Philadelphia Aurora*) and politicians like Albert Gallatin (a Swiss immigrant to Pennsylvania and party spokesman on economics). Jefferson described the Acts to Madison as 'so palpably in the teeth of the Constitution as to show they mean to pay no respect to it' and suspected that they were actually 'an experiment on the American mind, to see how far it will bear an avowed violation of the Constitution.' Since the Congress had passed the Acts, the President was enforcing the Acts, and the Supreme Court was upholding the Acts, the States were, as Jefferson put it, 'the last ditch' of defence.

In 1798, driven into this last ditch, Jefferson and Madison authored the *Virginia and Kentucky Resolutions*, which declared that the States were the sovereign creators of a constitutional compact; that as sovereigns the States possessed the right and duty to judge the constitutionality of the acts of their subordinate creature, the federal government; that unconstitutional acts of the federal government had no legal authority; and that, accordingly, Virginia and Kentucky did not recognise the Alien and Sedition Acts as law within their jurisdictions. Jefferson firmly believed that the *Resolutions* 'saved the Constitution at its last gasp.' Secrecy was paramount, as Jefferson and Madison were both subject to punishment under the Sedition Act for writing against the Adams Administration; as Vice President, Jefferson himself could have been accused of treason. Accordingly, Jefferson and Madison's correspondence for this period is unusually sparse. 'I know not which mortifies me most,' Jefferson complained to his friend and ally, fellow Virginian John Taylor of Caroline, 'that I should fear to write what I think, or my country bear such a state of things.' As a result of this secrecy, Madison's authorship was not revealed until 1809, and Jefferson's until 1821. A year after the adoption of the *Resolutions*, Madison wrote the *Report on the Virginia Resolutions* rebutting common objections to the *Resolutions*, such as the particularly persistent notion that the Supreme Court was 'the sole expositor of the Constitution, in the last resort.' According to Madison, 'The [Virginia] *Resolution* supposes that dangerous powers, not delegated, may not only be usurped and executed by the other departments, but that the judicial department also may exercise or sanction dangerous powers beyond the grant of the Constitution; and, consequently, that the ultimate right of the parties to the Constitution [i.e. the States] to judge whether the compact has been dangerously violated, must extend to violations by one delegated authority, as well as by another; by the judiciary, as well as by the executive, or the legislature.' Madison's *Report* became as celebrated as the original *Resolutions* themselves, all of which together constituted the 'Principles of '98,' a cornerstone of American (and especially Southern) political philosophy and constitutional doctrine during the Antebellum Era.

Jefferson's invocation of States' rights was not a mere tactic, but one of his longstanding political principles. Jefferson had always believed that in order to balance power in the Union, the States must vigilantly defend their rights from usurpation. 'It is important to strengthen the State governments,' Jefferson advised the Virginian ratifier, Archibald Stuart, in 1791, 'and as this cannot be done by any change in the Federal Constitution (for the preservation of that is all we need contend for) it must be done by the States themselves, erecting such barriers at the constitutional line as cannot be surmounted either by themselves or by the general government.' After the establishment of the First Bank of the United States, Jefferson recommended to Madison in 1792 that any Virginians who served on the unconstitutional bank 'shall be adjudged guilty of high treason and suffer death accordingly.' According to Jefferson, such Draconian justice was 'the only opposition worthy of our State' and 'would bring the general government to respect the counter-rights of the States.' Later, when a federal grand jury in Richmond indicted Jefferson's own Congressional representative for seditious libel (he was guilty of criticising President Adams' Francophobic foreign policy), Jefferson urged the General Assembly to punish the jurors. 'It is of immense consequence that the States retain as complete authority as possible over their own citizens,' Jefferson urged the Revolutionary-War veteran and Anti-Federalist James Monroe in 1797. Jefferson increasingly viewed the Congress as a 'foreign legislature' to the States. Thus, by 1798, Jefferson was perfectly consistent when he told Madison that what was needed against the Alien and Sedition Acts was a 'proper direction of the local force.' Jefferson, however, was not yet willing to consider secession, as he explained to John Taylor of Caroline shortly before the passage of the Alien and Sedition Acts. 'It is true that we are

41

completely under the saddle of Massachusetts and Connecticut, and that they ride us very hard, cruelly insulting our feelings as well as exhausting our strength and substance,' admitted Jefferson. 'A little patience, and we shall see the reign of witches pass over, their spells dissolve, and the people, recovering their true sight, restore their government to its true principles.' To Jefferson, preserving the rights of the States went hand in hand with preserving the Union, but after the Federalist tyranny of the Quasi-War, the divided reaction from other States to the *Virginia and Kentucky Resolutions* (one half opposed them and the other half did not), and the threat of American civil war (to strengthen the federal government, Hamilton wanted to 'make its existence a question of force' and 'put Virginia to the test of resistance'), Jefferson reaffirmed that self-government was ultimately paramount to the Union. Thus, just over a year after his optimistic letter to Taylor, Jefferson confided to Madison that Virginia and Kentucky should 'express in conciliatory and affectionate language our warm attachment to the union with our sister States,' but to add that they were also 'determined...to sever ourselves from that union we so much value, rather than give up the rights of self-government which we have reserved, and in which alone we see liberty, safety and happiness.' Although, Jefferson, after conferring with Madison, conceded that 'we should never think of separation but for repeated and enormous violations,' he did not and would never deny the right of secession – that is, the right of declaring independence.

When President Adams learned of the secret agenda of Alexander Hamilton and the 'Essex Junto' (his derisive term for a faction of arch-Federalists from New England), he pronounced Hamilton 'stark mad,' ridiculed the Essex Junto's fear of Virginia as a sign of 'weakness,' and thwarted their plot to seize power under the pretence of war by reopening diplomacy with France. 'He knows nothing of the character, the principles, the feelings, the opinions and prejudices of this nation,' Adams sniffed at Hamilton. 'If Congress should adopt this system, it would produce an instantaneous insurrection of the whole nation from Georgia to New Hampshire.' President Adams' principled defiance of his party and rescue of the American republic from the road to civil war was not enough to save his administration, however, much less the Federalist Party. In 1800, those States which had either supported the *Virginia and Kentucky Resolutions* or stayed silent prevailed over those which had opposed them, electing Jefferson to the presidency and the Democratic-Republicans to the Congress, thus beginning a 'Virginia Dynasty' which would dominate the American republic for the next generation. In later years, Jefferson remembered the Federalist downfall and the Democratic-Republican triumph as 'the Revolution of 1800...as real a revolution in the principles of our government as that of 1776 was in its form.'

Jefferson's First Inaugural Address was a call for unity between Federalists and Democratic-Republicans and appeal to common ground. 'Let us, then, with courage and confidence,' Jefferson announced, 'pursue our federal and republican principles, our attachment to union and representative government.' After this sincere invocation, Jefferson reviewed what he considered 'the essential principles of our government,' which he defined as peace and free trade with the world, the respective separation of powers between the States and the Union into domestic and foreign spheres, free elections, a military of citizen-soldiers, low taxes and expenditures, freedom from debt, and the civil liberties protected in the Bill of Rights. Jefferson recounted the 'blessings' upon the American republic – independence from world conflict, a frontier free for posterity, a society of opportunity and ability, as well as a Christian culture and society – 'What more is necessary to make us a happy and prosperous people?' asked Jefferson. 'A wise and frugal government, which shall restrain men from injuring one another, shall leave them otherwise free to regulate their own pursuits of industry and improvement, and shall not take from the mouth of labour the bread it has earned,' he answered.

With republican stalwarts like Nathaniel Macon (a widely respected Revolutionary-War veteran from North Carolina) as Speaker of the House, John Randolph of Roanoke (a scion of one of Virginia's 'First Families,' one of America's most passionate and principled statesmen, as well as a spellbinding orator) as Chairman of the House and Ways Committee, and Abraham Baldwin (a Revolutionary-War chaplain, Georgia delegate to the Constitutional Convention, and founder of the first State-chartered public university in the American republic), Jefferson cut Federalist taxes and expenditures, paid down the national debt, reduced the military to peacetime levels, and pardoned those convicted under the soon-to-expire Alien and Sedition Acts. To Jefferson, that government which governed best was that which governed least. 'A noiseless course, not meddling with the affairs of others, unattractive of notice, is a mark that society is going on in happiness,' Jefferson believed. 'If we can prevent the government from wasting the labours of the people, under the pretext of taking care of them, they must be happy.' Randolph of Roanoke concurred, describing Jefferson's early presidency as 'the true republican interlude in American government.'

Jefferson continued his opposition to Alexander Hamilton's national bank, which he described as an institution of 'the most deadly hostility existing against the principles and form of our Constitution,' responsible for 'supplanting precious metals by a paper circulation.' In Jefferson's view, the national bank had not only debased the currency and profited from the debt, thereby depressing the economy (particularly agriculture, which paid the highest price for inflation), but also corrupted the Congress, thereby threatening the integrity of republicanism itself. According to Jefferson, 'I deem no government safe which is under the vassalage of self-constituted authorities, or any other authority than that of the nation.' Unfortunately, although Jefferson told his Treasury Secretary, Albert Gallatin, that he wished to 'make a beginning towards an independent use of our own money,' the Democratic-Republican Congress could not abolish Hamilton's handiwork, which had already taken root in the economic and political system. 'When the government was first established, it was possible to have kept it going on true principles, but the contracted half-English, half-lettered ideas of Hamilton destroyed that hope in the bud,' fumed Jefferson. 'We can pay off his debt in 15 years, but we can never get rid of his financial system.' At the same time, Federalist-appointed judges controulled and corrupted the judiciary, undermining the plain meaning of the Constitution with partisan rulings known today as 'constitutional law.' For the rest of his life, Jefferson scorned the judiciary as 'a corps of sappers and miners, steadily working to undermine the independent rights of the States and to consolidate all power in the hands of that government in which they have so important a freehold estate,' national banks as 'more dangerous than standing armies,' and a national debt as 'swindling futurity on a large scale.'

Jefferson put an end to the aggression of the Barbary States, North-African pirates who had been demanding tribute from governments with ships sailing the Mediterranean Sea and even enslaving captured American sailors. 'We took the liberty to make some enquiries concerning the ground of their pretensions to make war upon nations who had done them no injury, and observed that we considered all mankind as our friends who had done us no wrong, nor given us any provocation,' Jefferson and John Adams had relayed home of a meeting with a Tripolitan ambassador while they were serving as foreign ministers. 'The ambassador answered us that it was founded on the laws of their Prophet; that it was written in their Koran; that all nations who should not have acknowledged their authority were sinners; that it was their right and duty to make war upon them wherever they could be found, and to make slaves of all they could take as prisoners; and that every Musselman [Muslim] who was slain in battle was sure to go to Paradise.' When Jefferson became President he refused to pay tribute to Tripoli, and the Pasha retaliated by declaring war on the United States. Jefferson, recognising that as President he was 'unauthorised by the Constitution, without the sanction of Congress, to go beyond the line of defence,' only dispatched a small squadron to defend American ships and sailors in the Mediterranean Sea. Although he desired 'measures of offence' against the pirates (which he received in the form of various statutes authorising specific, limited military action), Jefferson admitted that the power to declare war was 'confided by the Constitution to the legislature exclusively.' As Jefferson had earlier observed to Madison, 'We have already given in example one effectual check to the dog of war by transferring the power of letting him loose from the executive to the legislative body.'

One of the strangest episodes of Jefferson's presidency was the Yazoo Land Scandal. When the citizens of Georgia discovered that their legislature had accepted bribes from speculators to sell their public lands in the west (known then as the Yazoo territory and which are now Alabama and Mississippi) for pennies on the dollar, they promptly voted out almost the entire legislature and peremptorily repealed the law. When the speculators and their clients objected that Georgia must honour her contracts, Georgia countered that fraudulent contracts were invalid, and a federal commission was then established to resolve the claims. Madison and the other members of the executive branch on the commission recommended that Georgia sell the Yazoo territory to the United States and let the latter assume legal liability for the claims. When the commission's claims came before the Congress, John Randolph of Roanoke broke with the Jefferson Administration and had them voted down. The Yazoo speculation, insisted Randolph, was a fraud which Georgia had the right to invalidate and with which the federal government had no right to interfere. 'Gentlemen not only annihilate this act without a scruple,' exclaimed Randolph, 'they declare as subversive the rights of Georgia, and with them, of every State in the Union.' Randolph continued to block the Yazoo settlement until the Supreme Court, in another coup of constitutional law, circumvented the Congress and bogusly interpreted the Contract Clause to protect fraudulent contracts. Randolph, however, never let the 'Yazoo men' live down the shame, singling them out on Capitol Hill with his bony finger and shouting 'Yazoo!'

The greatest triumph of Jefferson's presidency was the Louisiana Purchase, which doubled the territory of the United States, acquired navigation of the Mississippi River (a source of sectional friction since the Confederation), averted war with France (a rich, powerful empire ruled by the ambitious, aggressive Napoleon Bonaparte), and silenced the warmongering Federalists (who were attempting to reclaim power by pandering to militant American frontiersmen) – and all for a pittance and without a single drop of blood! Jefferson had successfully steered the American republic between the Scylla and Charybdis of the 'maniac Federalists' and the 'gigantic power' of Napoleonic France. 'The world will here see such an extent of country under a free and moderate government as it has never yet seen,' beamed Jefferson. New-England Federalists feared that the new Western States which would be formed from the Louisiana Territory would taint the Anglo-Saxon and English-speaking polity with foreign blood and tongues, predominate over the original thirteen Eastern States, and dissolve the Union if sectional interests clashed. In protest of these possibilities, New-England Federalists grumbled about seceding themselves, but Jefferson saw nothing to fear in multiple American unions spread across the continent. 'Whether we remain in one confederacy, or break into Atlantic and Mississippi confederacies, I believe not very important to the happiness of either part,' admitted Jefferson. 'Why should we take sides with our Atlantic rather than Mississippi descendants?' he asked. 'It is the elder and younger son differing. God bless them both and keep them in the Union, if it be for their good, but separate them, if it be better.' Indeed, as early as 1776, Jefferson proposed that all new Colonies formed from Virginia's western territory be 'free and independent of this Colony and of all the world.' Later, in 1786, after the Jay-Gardoqui Treaty (which proposed to trade away Southern navigation of the Mississippi River for shipping concessions to New England), Jefferson anticipated that the Western States might one day choose to separate from the Eastern States. 'The moment they resolve to do this, the point is settled,' held Jefferson. 'A forced connection is neither our interest nor within our power.' To Jefferson, these separate unions of 'free and independent Americans, unconnected with us but by ties of blood and interest, and employing like us the rights of self-government' would form an 'empire of liberty.'

Trouble soon emerged out west, however. In 1805, Jefferson was notified of a conspiracy by his former Vice President, the vainglorious Aaron Burr, to raise a rebellion in the Western States and conquer Mexico from the Spanish Empire. Despite this brazen act of treason, Jefferson reacted with restraint, refusing to suppress civil liberties or install military dictatorships over the civil governments of the suspected States, and simply issued orders for Burr's arrest. The loyalty of the Western States (none joined the conspiracy) and Burr's quick capture by the Western authorities greatly cheered Jefferson. 'The hand of the people has given a mortal blow to a conspiracy which in other countries would have called for an appeal to arms, and has proved that government to be the strongest of which every man feels himself a part,' Jefferson congratulated the Ohio Governor after Burr was arrested. 'It is a happy illustration, too, of the importance of preserving the State authorities all that vigour which the Constitution foresaw would be necessary, not as only for their own safety, but for that of the whole people.'

The greatest failure of Jefferson's presidency was the Embargo Act. British harassment of American shipping, including the impressment of American sailors, had become increasingly aggressive, but Jefferson hoped that his theory of 'peaceable coercion' (what he earlier described to Madison as 'showing that nations may be brought to justice by appeals to their interests as well as by appeals to arms') would be an effective alternative to war. Madison agreed that between 'submission or war,' an embargo allowed the United States to 'a happy recourse for avoiding both.' Indeed, the Colonies' policy of non-importation with Great Britain had pressured the Parliament to make concessions in policy if not principle. Jefferson firmly believed that if not for the 'little selfish minority' of New England (which resisted the embargo and threatened to secede from the Union), the United

States could have broken the 'tyrant of the seas' and established American commercial independence. 'The embargo appears to be approved even by the Federalists of every quarter except yours,' Jefferson grumbled to his former Attorney General, then serving as the Massachusetts Governor. 'The alternative was between that and war, and in fact, it is the last card we have to play short of war.'

The most underrated aspect of Jefferson's presidency was the abolition of the Transatlantic slave trade. After the failure of his first two attempts to abolish slavery in Virginia, Jefferson grew pessimistic. 'I have long since given up the expectation of any provision for the extinguishment of slavery among us,' Jefferson admitted to a Quaker friend, though he maintained that 'should an occasion ever occur in which I can interpose with decisive effect, I shall certainly know and do my duty with promptitude and zeal.' Such an occasion occurred in 1808, the first year that the slave trade was eligible for national abolition. Virginia had originally opposed any extension of the slave trade at the Constitutional Convention, with Virginia delegate George Mason – enraged at the dark bargain between the South and the North to exchange the slave trade for commercial regulation – warning that 'every master of slaves is born a petty tyrant' as well as that slaves 'bring the judgment of Heaven on a country.' Despite Mason's principled stand, South Carolina and Georgia (i.e. buyers of slaves) agreed with New England (i.e. sellers of slaves) to extend the slave trade by twenty years. 'If the Southern States were let alone they will probably of themselves stop importations,' suggested South-Carolina delegate Charles Pinckney. Indeed, by 1808, every State (except, ironically, South Carolina) had abolished the slave trade. 'I congratulate you, fellow citizens, on the approach of the period of which you may interpose your authority constitutionally, to withdraw the citizens of the United States from all further participation in the violations of human rights which have been so long continued on the unoffending inhabitants of Africa,' Jefferson encouraged the Congress in his annual address, 'and which the morality, the reputation, and the best interests of our country have long been eager to prescribe.' Soon after, Jefferson happily signed the abolition of the slave trade into law, outlawing American complicity in the shipment of African captives purchased from African warlords across the Atlantic Ocean.

As his second term ended, Jefferson repealed the failed embargo and headed home to Monticello, never to return north of the Potomac. There, Jefferson finished his days growing close with his family, entertaining hosts of admiring pilgrims, and maintaining a copious correspondence which reached around the world. Years before, Jefferson had mused that 'all my wishes end where I hope my days will end, at Monticello,' and now he was finally home for good. 'Within a few days I retire to my family, my books, and farms; and having gained the harbour myself, I shall look to my friends still buffeting the storm, with anxiety indeed, but not envy,' sighed Jefferson. 'Never did a prisoner, released from his chains, feel such relief as I shall on shaking off the shackles of power.' When Jefferson arrived home, he was moved to find the citizens of his county there to welcome him. 'Of you, then, my neighbors, I may ask, in the face of the world, "Whose ox have I taken, or whom have I defrauded?" asked Jefferson. "Whom have I oppressed, or of whose hand have I received a bribe to blind mine eyes therewith?" On your verdict I rest with conscious security.'

In 1809, Madison followed Jefferson as President. Madison's First Inaugural Address was an affirmation of Democratic-Republican principles, full of Jeffersonian phrases such as: 'To foster a spirit of independence too just to invade the rights of others, too proud to surrender our own, too liberal to indulge unworthy prejudices ourselves, and too elevated not to look down upon them in others; to hold the Union of the States as the basis of their peace and happiness; to support the Constitution, which is the cement of the Union, as well in its limitations as in its authorities; to respect the rights and authorities reserved to the States and to the people as equally incorporated with and essential to the success of the general system.' Madison's presidency was defined by the War of 1812, which resulted from the British policies of interdiction and impressment that Jefferson had tried to stop with his embargo. Unless the Parliament's orders authorising these aggressions were repealed, Madison instructed his Minister to Great Britain, 'war is inevitable.' Madison, like Jefferson, wished to avoid war, but the pressure from the forceful 'War Hawks' (young Scotch-Irish from the backcountry who demanded 'submission or war') overpowered the moderate Madison. In a war message to the Congress, Madison admitted that while 'a state of peace toward Great Britain' existed in the United States, 'a state of war against the United States' existed in Great Britain. Madison added, however, that the Constitution entrusted the Congress rather than the President with the power to declare war, and so requested that the Congress make such a declaration rather than he act unilaterally. 'Whether the United States shall continue passive under the progressive usurpations and these accumulating wrongs, or, opposing force to force in defence of their national rights, shall commit a just cause into the hands of the Almighty Disposer of Events, avoiding all connections which might entangle it in the contests or views of other powers, and preserving a constant readiness to concur in an honourable reestablishment of peace and friendship, is a solemn question which the Constitution wisely confides to the legislative department of the government,' Madison informed the Congress. 'In recommending it to their early deliberations, I am happy in the assurance that the decision will be worthy of the enlightened and patriotic councils of a virtuous, a free, and a powerful nation.' Tragically, when the Congress declared war, the Parliament had just repealed its orders two days earlier; due to the delays of Transatlantic communication, it was too late.

The war started badly for the United States: patriotic American militiamen were no match for professional British veterans from the Napoleonic Wars. Washington, D.C. was sacked and razed; even the White House itself was burned, though Madison's papers and Gilbert Stuart's classic portrait of George Washington were saved thanks to Dolley Madison's forethought. Fortunately, at the Battle of Baltimore, a land and sea campaign which culminated with the bombardment of Fort McHenry (where the American national anthem, 'The Star-Spangled Banner,' was written), the British invasion was stopped. To Jefferson, down home in Monticello, the War of 1812 appeared to be a moral as well as a military disaster. 'Farewell all hope of extinguishing the public debt! Farewell all visions of applying the surplus revenue to the improvements of peace, rather than the ravages of war!' cried Jefferson. 'Our enemy has indeed the consolation of Satan on removing our first parents from Paradise; from a peaceful and agricultural nation he makes us a military and manufacturing one.' Upon learning that the Library of Congress had been burned by the British, Jefferson (who had once admitted, 'I cannot live without books') offered his own considerable collection to the federal government. As with Jefferson's earlier embargo, New-England Federalists resisted Madison's war, not just refusing to fight, but actively aiding the enemy and again threatening to secede from the Union. 'No foreign foe has broken my heart,' confessed Madison. 'To see the Capitol wrecked by the British does not hurt so deeply as to know sedition in New England.' Despite this massive treachery, Madison and the Democratic-Republicans did not restrict civil liberties as President Adams and the Federalists had done during the Quasi-War. 'Of all the enemies to public liberty, war is, perhaps, the most to be dreaded, because it comprises and develops the germ of every other,' Madison reflected years earlier. 'No nation could preserve its freedom in the midst of continual warfare.'

Jefferson was disgusted with New England's 'apostacy,' branding her Federalist Party a 'parricide party,' 'venal traitors,' and 'the Marats, the Dantons, and the Robespierres of Massachusetts' for making threats during wartime. He also delighted in his sectional rival's 'humiliation' when the whole scheme backfired, relishing the thought of high and mighty New England crawling back to the United States, forced to admit that 'her Southern brethren are somewhat on a par with her in wisdom, in information, in patriotism, in bravery, and even in honesty, although not in psalm-singing.' The War of 1812 ended with a mere return to the *status quo antebellum*, yet General Andrew Jackson's spectacular victory at New Orleans saved American pride and Madison's presidency. According to Jefferson, the war had accomplished the 'good' of 'assuring to the world, that although attached to peace from a sense of its blessings, we will meet war when it is made necessary.'

In 1816, Madison enacted a protectionist tariff into law to secure American commercial independence and renewed the charter of the national bank out of deference to its twenty-year existence – two measures that he had opposed from Alexander Hamilton yet now somewhat awkwardly supported himself. Jefferson, who reluctantly conceded to temporary tariffs and internal improvements to help the North recover from the damage which embargoes and war had done to her shipping industry, despaired at America's transformation from an agrarian-republican society of farms and freeholds to an industrial-democratic society of cities and corporations. Jefferson was beginning to realise that while 'commercial avarice and corruption' infested the North (and especially New England, which he had long scorned for her 'perversity of character'), the South remained 'the last asylum and bulwark' of 'the principles of free government.' Jefferson wished to 'confederate with those alone which are for peace and agriculture [as opposed to] unlimited commerce and war,' adding, 'If any State in the Union will declare that it prefers separation...to a continuance in union...I have no hesitation in saying, "Let us separate."' Madison's last act as President was the veto of the Bonus Bill, an internal-improvements programme (i.e. 'public works') financed by the national bank. In characteristic fashion, Madison personally supported the bill, yet recognised that it was unconstitutional and so refused to sign it into law. 'Believing that the permanent success of the Constitution depends on a definite partition of powers between the general and State governments, and that no adequate landmarks would be left by the constructive extension of the powers of Congress as proposed in this bill,' explained Madison, 'I have no option but to withhold my signature from it.'

Jefferson and Madison, back in what they considered their 'country,' Virginia, worked to restore their plantations, which embargoes, war, and neglect (and soon the bank-driven Panic of 1819) had impoverished. As part of his lifelong passion for education reform, intended to instill the virtues necessary for self-government and free Virginians from 'dark Federalist mills of the North,' Jefferson convinced the General Assembly to charter a State university (the University of Virginia) and recruited professors at home and abroad to come teach at his new institution. To prevent the growing body of constitutional law (that is, the liberal rulings of the Marshall Court) from corrupting the minds of young Virginians, Jefferson prepared a political curriculum of John Locke, Algernon Sidney, the Declaration of Independence, *The Federalist*, and the *Report on the Virginia Resolutions*, which he forwarded to Madison for his approval. Madison, no doubt honoured to see his name appear twice in Jefferson's curriculum, agreed, suggesting that Washington's farewell address be added as well. 'This institution will be based on the illimitable freedom of the human mind,' boasted Jefferson. 'For here we are not afraid to follow truth wherever it may lead, nor to tolerate any error so long as reason is left free to combat it.' Jefferson and Madison served as the University's first two Rectors.

Jefferson and Madison were both disturbed by the Missouri Crisis, in which the admission of Missouri to the Union was contested by Northern Federalists on the grounds that her constitution permitted slavery. These two elder statesmen viewed this sudden attack on slavery as a partisan ploy to divide the dominant Democratic-Republicans along sectional lines – uniting the Northern majority against the Southern minority – and not as a genuine anti-slavery movement. 'The Federalists completely put down, and despairing of ever rising again under the old division of Whig and Tory,' observed Jefferson, using the terminology of the American Revolution to denote the two parties, 'devised a new one, of slave-holding and non-slaveholding States, which, while it had a semblance of being moral, was at the same time geographical, and calculated to give them ascendancy by debauching their old opponents to a coalition with them.' Madison shared his opinion with President James Monroe: 'I find the idea is fast spreading that the zeal with which the extension, so-called, of slavery is opposed, has, with the coalesced leaders, an object very different from the welfare of the slaves, or the check to their increase; and that their real object is, as you intimate, to form a new state of parties founded on local instead of political distinctions; thereby dividing the [Democratic-] Republicans of the North from those of the South, and making the former instrumental in giving to the opponents of both an ascendancy over the whole.'

Jefferson and Madison did not take the Federalists' stance seriously – 'a mere party trick' and 'false front' they quipped respectively – but they did take the threat it posed to the Union seriously. Jefferson described the emerging conflict between the North and the South as 'a fire bell in the night' and 'the knell of the Union' – foreboding terms indeed. 'The Missouri question aroused and filled me with alarm,' admitted Jefferson. 'The old schism of Federal[ist] and [Democratic-] Republican, threatened nothing because it existed in every State, and united them together by fraternism of party, but the coincidence of a marked principle, moral and political, with a geographical line once conceived, I feared, would never more be obliterated from the mind, that it would be recurring on every occasion, and renewing irritations, until it would kindle such mutual and mortal hatred as to render separation preferable to eternal discord.' Madison explained that while political parties were a necessary evil in popular government, broad-based national parties (such as the Democratic-Republicans) 'strengthen the Union of the whole,' but narrowly based sectional parties (such as the Federalists), forced the 'great repulsive masses' of opposing sections into 'awful shocks against each other.' Madison advised President Monroe against compromise, insisting that there was no intention among the men who framed and ratified the Constitution to interfere with slavery and reminiscing about the 'sense of equity' and 'spirit of mutual concession' which prevailed during the Founding Era. Mourning the division of the

Union between the North and the South, Jefferson accused the Federalists of committing 'suicide on themselves' and 'treason against the hopes of the world' by politicising slavery, concluding that the American Revolution had ultimately been in vain. 'I regret that I am now to die in the belief that the useless sacrifice of themselves, by the generation of '76, to acquire self-government and happiness to their country, is to be thrown away by the unwise and unworthy passions of their sons,' mourned Jefferson, 'and that my only consolation is to be that I live not to weep over it.'

Although large, lifelong slave-holders themselves, Jefferson and Madison were impassioned, eloquent enemies of slavery, which they not only regarded as physically and morally abusive to slaves, but also morally corrosive to masters. Jefferson made clear his opposition to slavery in his Revolutionary-era emancipation proposals in Virginia's General Assembly and his commentary in *Notes on the State of Virginia*. 'Can the liberties of a nation be thought secure when we have removed their only firm basis, a conviction in the minds of the people that these liberties are the gift of God? That they are not to be violated but with his wrath?' asked Jefferson. 'Indeed I tremble for my country when I reflect that God is just: that his justice cannot sleep forever.' After the American Revolution, Madison emancipated his body servant in the name of 'that liberty for which we have paid the price of so much blood, and have proclaimed so often to be the right and worthy pursuit of every human being,' and argued during the Constitutional Convention, 'We have seen the mere distortion of colour made in the most enlightened period of time, a ground of the most oppressive dominion ever exercised by man over man.' Jefferson and Madison both understood that abolishing slavery was an enormous challenge – in Jefferson's famous phrase, 'We have the wolf by the ear, and we can neither hold him, nor safely let him go. Justice is in one scale, and self-preservation in the other' – and so insisted that any plan of emancipation must be, as Madison put it, 'gradual, equitable, and satisfactory to the individuals immediately concerned, and consistent with the existing and durable prejudices of the nation.'

'I can say with conscious truth that there is not a man on earth who would sacrifice more than I would to relieve us from this heavy reproach, in any *practicable* way,' explained Jefferson. To Jefferson, 'practicable' meant the 'expatriation' of freed slaves to foreign colonies or the 'diffusion' of slaves into the Territories, which would relax racial tensions where the slave population was most-concentrated as well as ease the progress of emancipating and integrating enslaved Africans into a society of independent, individualistic Americans. Jefferson added that barring slavery from the Territories would not free any slaves (but merely keep them penned up in the South where their welfare worsened) and that allowing slavery in the Territories would not add to the total number of slaves (but simply diffuse the pent-up slave population). 'All know that permitting the slaves of the South to spread into the West will not add one being to that unfortunate condition,' Jefferson tried to convince the anti-slavery Marquis de Lafayette, 'that it will increase the happiness of those existing, and by spreading them over a larger surface, will dilute the evil everywhere, and facilitate the means of finally getting rid of it, an event more anxiously wished by those on whom it presses than by the noisy pretenders to exclusive humanity.' Jefferson and Madison both desired for the slaves to be freed, but held that due to 'the real distinctions which nature has made,' along with 'prejudices entertained by the whites' and 'recollections by the blacks of the injuries they have received,' this was only possible through 'diffusion' in the Territories or 'colonisation' in a foreign country. 'The two races cannot coexist, both being free and equal,' argued Madison. 'The great *sine qua non*, therefore, is some external asylum for the coloured race.' Or, as Jefferson put it, while 'nothing is more certainly written in the book of fate than that these people are to be free,' it was no less certain 'that the two races, equally free, cannot live in the same government.' Madison, who served as President of the American Colonisation Society, was optimistic about the future of emancipation, especially after the General Assembly (led by Jefferson's grandson and future Confederate colonel, Thomas Jefferson Randolph) debated emancipation from 1831 to 1832. 'Many circumstances at the present moment seem to concur in brightening the prospects of the Society,' beamed Madison, 'and cherish the hope that the time will come when the dreadful calamity which has so long afflicted our country and filled so many with despair, will be gradually removed and by means consistent with justice, peace, and the general satisfaction.' Colonisation was widely considered the most enlightened solution to the problem of slavery, and Antebellum-American figures as diverse as John Marshall, James Monroe, Andrew Jackson, Henry Clay, Daniel Webster, and Abraham Lincoln were, along with Madison, members of the ACS.

Although Jefferson and Madison were both adamantly against slavery, they were equally against the politicisation of slavery – that is, the external interference with the internal affairs of a State – which they regarded as self-serving, self-righteous, and ultimately self-destructive. The legality of slavery was, as Jefferson put it, 'the exclusive right of every State, which nothing in the Constitution has taken from them and given to the government,' and thus any attempt to prohibit slavery in new States was an unconstitutional 'act of power.' Unlike Jefferson, Madison lived long enough to witness the dawn of radical abolitionism in the North, which rejected their conservative plans of colonisation or diffusion and demanded immediate abolition at all costs, even/especially if it meant a race war. For refusing to compromise, preaching hatred of the South, and forcing slave-holders onto the defensive, Madison condemned 'modern abolition' as counterproductive – aborting the progressive Southern anti-slavery movement and fomenting the reactionary Southern pro-slavery movement. 'To it alone we owe not only the lamentable arrest of onward emancipation,' sighed Madison, 'but till it intruded, no Governor in Carolina extolled slavery as a happy balance of her government, no Virginia professor vindicated its moral advantages.'

When John Adams' son, John Quincy Adams, was elected President in 1824, he proposed a neo-Federalist programme of internal improvements, protectionist tariffs, and national banking (dubbed the 'American System' by the upcoming Kentucky Senator Henry Clay).' In response, Jefferson authored a reaffirmation of the 'Principles of '98' – the *Solemn Declaration and Protest of the Commonwealth of Virginia*. According to Jefferson, the Constitution was a 'compact' between the States, each of which united into a 'single' government on 'foreign' affairs but remained 'independent' on 'domestic' affairs. Jefferson denounced the taxes and internal improvements of the American System, which encroached on the domestic affairs of the States, as 'usurpations...against which, in point of right, we do protest as null and void, and never to be quoted as precedents of right.' To demonstrate her loyalty to the Union, however, Jefferson offered that Virginia would acquiesce to such 'assumptions of power' and even assent to constitutional amendments authorising the assumed powers. Jefferson warned, however, that while a 'separation' in the Union would be 'among the greatest calamities,' the 'greatest' would be 'submission to a government of unlimited powers.' If this ever became the question, then Jefferson concluded that 'further forbearance could not be indulged.' The reasoning and recommendation of Jefferson's *Declaration and Protest* was similar to John C. Calhoun's *South Carolina Exposition and Protest*, published just a few years later in response to a heavy tariff signed into law by President Quincy Adams. When Jefferson asked Madison for his opinion on the *Declaration and Protest*, Madison replied in characteristic fashion that it was unnecessary and risky. 'It may be well, at least, to know the weakness of the proposition, in and out of Congress, before any irrevocable decision be had at Richmond,' suggested Madison. 'Should any strong interposition there be ultimately required, your paper will be a valuable resort.' Jefferson obliged and did not press the *Declaration and Protest* any further, but remained despondent about the future of the American republic nonetheless.

In addition to the sectionalisation of politics and politicisation of slavery – 'a question of power' to the North, but 'a question of existence' to the South – another of Jefferson's fears was the 'silent descent' of the States into the 'gulf of consolidation.' To Jefferson, all three branches of the federal

59

government (especially John Marshall's Supreme Court) were conspiring against the States to usurp their rights and powers. 'It is not by the consolidation or concentration of powers, but by their distribution that good government is effected,' observed Jefferson. 'Were not this great country already divided into States, that division must be made that each might do for itself what concerns itself directly and what it can do so much better than a distant authority.' According to Jefferson, 'When all government, domestic and foreign, in little as in great things, shall be drawn to Washington as the centre of all power, it will render powerless the checks provided of one government on another and will become as venal and oppressive as the government from which we separated.' Jefferson warned that 'giving to the federal member of the government, by unlimited constructions of the Constitution, a controul over all the functions of the States, and the concentration of all power and authority at Washington' was merely monarchy by another name – perhaps 'monocracy.' Noting that the Anti-Federalists had originally opposed the Constitution because of 'the jealousy and fear of every State being subjected to the other States in matters merely its own,' Jefferson argued that not a single State 'would have agreed to the Constitution had it given all powers to the general government,' and continued that there was no 'reason to believe the States more disposed now than then to acquiescence in this general surrender of all their rights and powers to a consolidated government, one and undivided.'

Jefferson, who had once quipped, 'Were we directed from Washington when to sow and when to reap, we should soon want bread,' scorned the newfound 'National Republicans' and their schemes of economic planning. 'Having nothing in them of the principles of '76,' accused Jefferson, the National Republicans, 'now look back to a single and splendid government of an aristocracy, founded on banking institutions and monied incorporations under the guise and cloak of their favoured branches of manufactures, commerce, and navigation, riding and ruling over the plundered ploughman and beggared yeomanry.' According to Jefferson, the

States were besieged by a consolidated government, sectionalised politics, and liberal constitutionalism. 'I see,' worried Jefferson to fellow Virginian and staunch Democratic-Republican William B. Giles, 'with the deepest affliction, the rapid strides with which the federal branch of our government is advancing towards the usurpation of all the rights reserved to the States, and the consolidation in itself of all powers, foreign and domestic, and that too by constructions which leave no limits to their powers.' Secession, concluded Jefferson, may be Virginia's only hope. 'We must have patience and long endurance with our brethren,' urged Jefferson, 'and separate from our companions only when the sole alternatives left are a dissolution of our Union with them, or submission to a government without limitation of powers.' If the question ever did come down to an unlimited government in Washington, D.C. or the right of a State to govern herself, then Jefferson held that 'there can be no hesitation.'

Madison shared Jefferson's concerns for the future of small-f federalism in the American republic – or, as he put it, 'the true balances of power, on which must depend the success and permanency of the federal republic, the best guardian, as we believe, of the liberty, the safety, and the happiness of man.' Like Jefferson, Madison was particularly concerned with the liberal constructionism of Chief Justice John Marshall. 'It is to be regretted that the Court is so much in the practice of mingling with their judgments pronounced, arguments and reasonings of a scope beyond them; and that there is often an apparent disposition to amplify the authorities of the Union at the expence of those of the States,' Madison told Virginia judge and fervent Democratic-Republican Spencer Roane. 'It is of great importance as well as of indispensable obligation, that the constituted boundary between them should be impartially maintained.' Madison held that neither the framers at the Constitutional Convention nor the ratifiers at the State conventions 'anticipated...that a rule of construction would be introduced as broad and pliant as what has occurred,' and added that 'the avowal of such a rule' would have 'prevented its ratification.' Madison was more optimistic about the future of small-f federalism than Jefferson, however, believing that without 'some change in the character of this nation,' the 'violations of the rights and authorities of the States' passed by the Congress and affirmed by the Supreme Court would not be *durable.*' Madison cited the 'Principles of '98' and the 'Revolution of 1800' as an example: 'In the case of the Alien and Sedition Laws, which violated the general *sense* as well as the *rights* of the States, the usurping experiment was crushed at once, notwithstanding the cooperation of the federal judges with the federal laws.'

On 4 July 1826 – the fiftieth anniversary of the Declaration of Independence – Jefferson died; John Adams, with whom he had reconciled in his old age, died later that same day. In the last letter he ever wrote, Jefferson regretfully declined an invitation to celebrate Independence Day with the citizens of Washington, D.C. 'I should, indeed, with peculiar delight, have met and exchanged there congratulations personally with the small band, the remnant of that host of worthies, who joined with us on that day, in the bold and doubtful election we were to make for our country, between submission or the sword,' reflected Jefferson, 'and to have enjoyed with them the consolatory fact, that our fellow citizens, after half a century of experience and prosperity, continue to approve the choice we made.' According to Madison, Jefferson 'lives and will live in the memory and gratitude of the wise and good, as a luminary of science, as a votary of liberty, as a model of patriotism, and as a benefactor of humankind.'

Between 1828 and 1833, when South Carolina nullified the Tariff of Abominations and civil war nearly erupted, Nullifiers and Unionists looked to Madison for legitimacy. To the dismay of the Nullifiers, Madison denied that the 'Principles of '98' justified the so-called Carolina Doctrine, and went to great lengths to explain that the *Virginia and Kentucky Resolutions* and *Report on the Virginia Resolutions* did not really mean what they seemed to mean. According to Madison, Virginia and Kentucky had declared 'that the States, as parties to the constitutional compact, had a right and were bound, in extreme cases only, and after a failure of all efforts of redress under the forms of the Constitution, to interpose in their sovereign capacity, for the purpose of arresting the evil of usurpation, and preserving the Constitution and Union.' Yet South Carolina, continued Madison, was asserting 'that in a case of not greater magnitude than the degree of inequality in the operation of a tariff in favour of manufactures, she may of herself finally decide, by virtue of her sovereignty, that the Constitution has been violated, and that if not yielded to by the federal government, though supported by all the other States, she may rightfully resist it and withdraw herself from the Union.' Although Madison argued that 'the right of nullification meant by Mr. Jefferson is the natural right which all admit to be a remedy against insupportable oppression,' as well as that 'there is nothing which excludes a natural right in the States individually, more than in any portion of an individual State, suffering under palpable and insupportable wrongs, from seeking relief by resistance and revolution,' he denied that South Carolina's grievances qualified as 'insupportable oppression' and that the States could remain in the Union while resisting federal law. 'A separation from the Union, not a resistance to its authority while remaining in it,' was Madison's solution. While Madison recognised the right of a State to secede from the Union, he added that 'a rightful secession requires the consent of the others, or an abuse of the compact, absolving the seceding party from the obligations imposed by it.' It is curious that Madison, who was so concerned for minority rights under majority rule and the preservation of the Union, strenuously disavowed a civil and peaceable (if somewhat cumbersome) means of protecting minority rights within the Union and instead endorsed outright revolution.

To the upcoming generation of Southerners, who had taken the 'Principles of '98' to heart and had honestly attempted to put Jefferson and Madison's doctrines into practice, Madison's repudiation felt like a betrayal. For his part, Madison was intensely fearful for the fate of the Union, especially because of 'the insidious exhibitions of a permanent incompatibility between the South and North,' and so, in the counterweight role which he always played as a statesman, reinterpreted the *Virginia and Kentucky Resolutions* in an attempt to neutralise what he saw as the danger of disunion. Balancing the extremes was why Madison sought to correct the errors of the leading figures in the Tariff Crisis, telling South-Carolina Senator Robert Y. Hayne that a State could not 'nullify' a federal law on her own, Kentucky Senator Henry Clay that his American System favoured 'one part of the community...at the expence of the other,' and Massachusetts Senator Daniel Webster that the Union was not one nation indivisible but a 'compact' between sovereign States. In the *Federalist*, Madison had theorised that the larger the scope of a republic, the smaller the danger of factions. As a result, perhaps Madison was blinded to the fact that in spite of his theory, a faction of the North over the South was emerging within the Union. As John C. Calhoun, the South-Carolinian statesman and architect of the Carolina Doctrine who attributed his understanding of the Constitution to Madison's *Report on the Virginia Resolutions*, remarked of the elder Madison, 'I must think, that Mr. Madison, in his old age, returned to the old consolidation notions of his early days; and has given a construction to his celebrated *Report* hard to be reconciled with its language, or the history of the times; and let me add, which strips it of most of its value.'

Jefferson had long desired to amend the Virginia Constitution to be more liberal than feudal. In 1776, while serving in the Second Continental Congress, Jefferson sent a draft of such a constitution to Virginia's Convention, but George Mason's draft had already been adopted. Jefferson's draft would have appointed the House of Delegates by county population (instead of equal representatives per county) and extended suffrage to all free white men. By 1829, western Virginians sought such Jeffersonian reforms so that their growing population would be better-represented in the State legislature. To settle this intrastate conflict, another constitutional convention was assembled in Richmond, along the lines of the conventions of 1776 and 1788. Madison, hoping for all Virginians to have 'a sufficient stake in the public order,' proposed reapportionment according to county population and suffrage for all economically independent white men. John Randolph of Roanoke, that old-fashioned champion of the Old Dominion's old guard, rose to challenge 'the all-pervading principle that numbers, and numbers alone, are to regulate all things in political society,' and to warn that 'governments are like revolutions: you may put them in motion, but I defy you to controul them after they are in motion.' Pointing out that numbers were what made the Northern oppression of the South possible in the Missouri Crisis and the tariff bills of the 1820s, Randolph asked, 'Shall we in Virginia introduce this deadly principle into our own government?' Randolph refused to bow to a 'Robinhood society' or 'King Numbers.' As a result of the opposition marshaled by Randolph, Virginia's Convention rejected Madison's proposal and compromised instead. As with the Yazoo scandal, Randolph had foiled Madison again.

James Madison died on 28 June 1836, the last member of America's true greatest generation – the Founding Fathers. The faculty of the University of Virginia, where Madison had been serving as rector, sent their condolences to his wife, Dolley: 'On the services of this illustrious man it is unnecessary to dwell; for what American does not know the parts which James Madison acted in the public councils of his country? And what Virginian needs to be reminded of the unrivalled force of his tongue and his pen in defending her most cherished principles?' According to Jefferson, Madison was 'the greatest man in the world.'

II

In the summer of 1798, Jefferson and Madison appear to have met at Monticello and strategised against the tyrannical Federalist regime. After conferring with one another as well as with a close circle of Virginians, Jefferson and Madison secretly authored the *Virginia and Kentucky Resolutions*, assertions of States' rights and denunciations of the Alien and Sedition Acts. Madison wrote on behalf of Virginia, the most prestigious

State in the Union and an old dominion of republicanism. John Taylor of Caroline, a close friend of Jefferson's, introduced Madison's resolutions in the Virginia legislature, where they were adopted on 24 December 1798. Jefferson originally wrote on behalf of North Carolina, but was persuaded that Kentucky, an independent-spirited frontier State ceded from Virginia herself, would be more receptive. John Breckenridge, the relative of another of Jefferson's close friends, introduced Jefferson's resolutions in the Kentucky legislature, where they were adopted on 16 November 1798. Luigi Marco Bassani, an intellectual historian who authored a study of Jefferson's political philosophy, identifies the *Resolutions* as 'the fountainhead of states' rights doctrine.' Kevin R.C. Gutzman, an expert on Madison and Jefferson, describes the *Resolutions* as 'touchstones of future state and Southern sectionalism,' quoting a Virginia ratifier who claimed that the *Resolutions* were 'an appeal to the real laws of our country.' According to one of Jefferson's best biographers, Merrill D. Peterson, the *Resolutions* were 'a vigorous defense of the principles of freedom and self-government under the United States Constitution,' which in time became the 'sacred texts' of the 'political religion' of the Old South, and built up Jefferson's reputation as 'the Father of State Rights.'

'Resolved, that the several States comprising the United States of America are not united on the principle of unlimited submission to their general government,' began Jefferson with a bang. When the States ratified the constitutional compact, continued Jefferson, they 'constituted a general government for special purposes,' and 'delegated to that government certain definite powers, reserving, each State to itself, the residuary mass of right to their own self-government.' Jefferson cited the Tenth Amendment as express affirmation of the 'general principle' that the States retained any and all powers which they had not delegated to the federal government and enumerated in the Constitution: 'The powers not delegated to the United States by the Constitution, nor prohibited to the States, are reserved to the States respectively, or to the people.' According to Jefferson, if the federal government ever encroached upon the States' reserved powers, such an unconstitutional usurpation of power would not be binding upon the States. 'Whensoever the general government assumes undelegated powers,' declared Jefferson, 'its acts are unauthoritative, void, and of no force.'

Jefferson claimed that each State 'acceded' to the constitutional compact as an 'integral party' and denied that the federal government was solely entrusted with interpreting the Constitution or limiting its own authority. 'The government created by this compact was not made the exclusive or final judge of the extent of the powers delegated to itself,' reasoned Jefferson, 'since that would have made its discretion, and not the Constitution, the measure of its powers.' The States, however, as the sovereign parties to the constitutional compact, not only had the right to determine the constitutionality of federal laws (here, Jefferson was drawing from the established 'compact law' of the eighteenth century), but also to nullify whatever laws they determined to be unconstitutional. 'As in all other cases of compact among powers having no common judge,' explained Jefferson, 'each party has an equal right to judge for itself, as well of infractions as of mode and measure of redress.'

By 'nullification,' Jefferson meant exactly what he had already advised Virginia to do against early encroachments: declare that the law was unenforceable within the State's jurisdiction and that any attempted enforcement would be punished as an act of treason against the State. Jefferson's 'mode and measure of redress' for the States, therefore, was similar to the methods by which the Colonies had resisted British tyranny: refusing to comply with British taxes, cutting off British trade, and forcing the resignation of British agents. This time, however, the 'foreign legislature' was in Philadelphia, not London.

After establishing the rights of the States in the constitutional compact, Jefferson applied those principles to the issue at hand: the assault on civil liberties in the Alien and Sedition Acts. Jefferson started with the Sedition Act. 'No power over the freedom of religion, freedom of speech, or freedom of the press, being delegated to the United States by the Constitution, nor prohibited by it to the States,' reasoned Jefferson, 'all lawful powers respecting the same did of right remain, were reserved to the States, or the people.' Thus, any federal laws violating those basic freedoms were unconstitutional usurpations of undelegated, unenumerated powers. In fact, Jefferson noted that the First Amendment specifically protected those very freedoms from the federal government, 'thereby guarding, in the same sentence, and under the same words, the freedom of religion, of speech, and of the press, insomuch that whatever violated either throws down the sanctuary which covers the others.' Jefferson insisted that even 'libels, falsehood, and defamation, equally with heresy and other false religion, are withheld from the cognizance of federal tribunals.' Nevertheless, in the name of fighting seditious libel, the Sedition Act had 'abridged' the freedom of speech and the freedom of the press. Therefore, Jefferson concluded that the Sedition Act was 'not law, but is altogether void, and of no force.'

Proceeding to the Alien Act, Jefferson asserted that foreigners were 'under the jurisdiction and protection of the laws of the State wherein they are,' and that 'no power over them has been delegated to the United States, nor prohibited to the individual States.' Thus, any federal interference with foreigners 'assumes powers over alien friends not delegated by the Constitution.' Jefferson further argued that for the President 'to remove a person out of the United States who is under the protection of the law, on his own suspicion, without jury, without public trial, without confrontation of the witnesses against him, without having witnesses in his favour, without defence, without counsel,' violated the Fifth Amendment, which provided that 'no person shall be deprived of life, liberty, or property without due process of law.' Thus, Jefferson concluded that the Alien Act was also 'not law, but altogether void and of no force.'

According to Jefferson, because the Alien and Sedition Acts violated the civil liberties protected under the First and Fifth Amendments, as well as the reserved powers of the States protected under the Tenth Amendment, they were therefore 'unauthoriative, void, and of no force' – in other words, nullified.

Jefferson warned that liberally interpreting the General Welfare Clause and Necessary and Proper Clause so as to grant implied powers to the federal government 'goes to the destruction of all limits prescribed to their powers by the Constitution.' Jefferson held that those clauses were 'meant by the instrument to be subsidiary only to the execution of limited powers,' and 'ought not to be so construed as themselves to give unlimited powers, nor a part be so taken as to destroy the whole residue of the instrument.' In other words, the General Welfare Clause and Necessary and Proper Clause were not delegations of power themselves, but rather explanations of why and how the delegated powers should be exercised.

Jefferson avowed that Kentucky was 'faithful to the compact' as it was first founded – a Union of 'peace, happiness, and prosperity of all the States' – but added that 'to take from the States all the powers of self-government and transfer them to a general and consolidated government without regard to the special delegations and reservations solemnly agreed to in that compact' was a betrayal of that very same Union. In other words, while Kentucky was indeed loyal to the original Union, she would 'submit to undelegated, and consequently unlimited power in no men, or body of men on earth.'

If the federal government abused its delegated powers, then the people could simply choose new elected officials, admitted Jefferson, but if the federal government usurped undelegated powers, then he held that 'a nullification of the act is the rightful remedy.' Jefferson argued that 'every State has a natural right in cases not within the compact (*casus non foederis*) [i.e. 'case not for the alliance,' an eighteenth-century diplomatic term regarding something outside the terms of a compact between sovereigns] to nullify of their own authority all assumptions of power by others within their limits.' If the States were deprived of this sovereign right, then they would fall 'under the dominion, absolute and unlimited, of whatsoever might exercise this right of judgment for them.' Since the Congress was not a party to the constitutional compact, but merely a 'creature' created by the States in that compact, Jefferson deduced that it and its 'assumptions of power' should be 'subject...to the final judgment of those by whom and for whose use itself and its powers were all created.'

Jefferson unleashed his formidable powers of logic and language against the tyranny of the Alien and Sedition Acts. These usurpations consolidated the roles of 'accuser, counsel, judge, and jury' in the President, 'whose suspicions may be the evidence, his order the sentence, his officer the executioner, and his breast the sole record.' According to Jefferson, 'the barriers of the Constitution' were 'swept from us all' and 'no rampart now remains against the passions and the power of a majority of Congress.' Jefferson noted the acts turned many peaceable, law-abiding citizens into 'outlaws' simply for exercising their First Amendment rights, and feared that anyone who dared to 'reclaim the constitutional rights and liberties of the States and people' would be persecuted by the ruling Federalist Party. The 'friendless alien' targeted by the Alien Act was merely the 'safest subject of a first experiment' which would set a precedent eventually turning citizens themselves into the President's 'prey.' Jefferson realised that it was imperative for the States to take a stand for their rights now, at an early stage in the history of the American republic, in order to prevent civil war and tyranny. 'Unless arrested at the threshold,' warned Jefferson, these acts of usurpation would 'drive these States into revolution and blood,' subverting 'republican government' for government 'by a rod of iron.' Thus, resolved Jefferson, 'In questions of power, then, let no more be heard of confidence in man, but bind him down from mischief by the chains of the Constitution.'

In the end, just as Jefferson feared, the States failed to make an authoritative statement against federal usurpation at the threshold, culminating in a revolution which drowned the Union in blood and replaced republican government with a rod of iron.

Jefferson called on Kentucky's 'co-States' to adopt resolutions of their own, declaring that the Alien and Sedition Acts were 'seizing the rights of the States, and consolidating them in the hands of the general government, with a power assumed to bind the States (not merely as cases made federal *casus foederis*), but in all cases whatsoever, by laws made, not with their consent, but by others against their consent.' Jefferson's use of the infamous language of the Parliament's 'Declaratory Act' – 'a power...to bind the States...in all cases whatsoever' – was deliberate and unmistakable: the Federalists were the Tories, the Democratic-Republicans the Patriots, and the war no less than a Second American Revolution.

'Resolved, that the General Government of Virginia doth unequivocally express a firm resolution to maintain and defend the Constitution of the United States, and the Constitution of this State, against every aggression, either foreign or domestic,' announced Madison more mildly but no less meaningfully than Jefferson. Because of Virginians' 'warm attachment to the Union of the States...it is their duty to watch over and oppose any infraction of those principles which constitute the only basis of that Union,' assured Madison.

According to Madison, the Constitution was a compact between sovereign States, which delegated limited powers to the federal government enumerated in the Constitution. 'This Assembly doth explicitly and peremptorily declare,' wrote Madison, 'that it views the powers of the federal government, as resulting from the compact, to which the States are parties.' These powers were 'limited by the plain sense and intention of the instrument constituting the compact,' and were 'no further valid than they are authorised by the grants enumerated in that compact.' In other words, the powers delegated to the federal government by the States were limited to those which were enumerated in the Constitution. If the federal government ever violated the constitutional limits on its power, however, then the States must invoke their sovereignty and unite against encroachment. 'In the case of a deliberate, palpable, and dangerous exercise of other powers, not granted by the said compact,' argued Madison, 'the States who are parties thereto, have the right, and are in duty bound, to interpose for arresting the progress of the evil, and for maintaining, within their respective limits, the authorities, rights, and liberties pertaining to them.'

Madison lamented 'sundry instances' of the federal government's attempts 'to enlarge its powers by forced constructions of the constitutional charter which defines them.' Twisting the General Welfare Clause and Necessary and Proper Clause into expansive conferrals of implied powers rather than a mere introduction to and/or explanation of the enumerated powers undermined the whole point of having a written constitution in the first place. 'Implications have appeared of a design to expand certain general phrases (which having been copied from the very limited grant of power, in the former Articles of Confederation were the less liable to be misconstrued) so as to destroy the meaning and effect, of the particular enumeration which necessarily explains and limits the general phrases,' objected Madison. Unchecked and uncontrolled, this liberal construction of the Constitution would ultimately 'consolidate the States by degrees, into one sovereignty, the obvious tendency of which would be to transform the present republican system of the United States, into an absolute, or at best a mixed monarchy' (by 'monarchy,' Madison meant an executive branch which coerced and corrupted the other branches of government, not necessarily a king).

Today, as Madison's Anti-Federalist foes had prophesied at Philadelphia and Richmond, these twin terrors of 'general welfare' and 'necessary and proper' are routinely and unreflectively cited as justification for whatever the Congress, the President, and the Supreme Court desire, with no regard for the enumerated powers whatsoever. Madison, who knew as much about the Constitution as any man, denied that there was even authority to build roads and canals under these clauses, yet now bailouts for bankers whose bets blew up in their faces, subsidies for abortionists who sell the body parts of dismembered fetuses, or arms deals with foreign states which sponsor jihadism, are taken for granted and considered untouchable.

Of all the usurpations up until that time, Madison regarded the Alien and Sedition Acts as the absolute worst. 'The General Assembly doth particularly protest against the palpable and alarming infraction of the Constitution, in the two late cases of the "Alien and Sedition Acts,"' declared Madison. According to Madison, 'uniting legislative and judicial powers to those of the executive, subverts the general principles of free government.' In other words, making the President the judge, jury, and executioner, as the Alien Act did over foreigners in the United States, undermined the essential system of checks and balances between the federal branches and made the President a monarch in all but name. Furthermore, Madison continued, the usurpation of undelegated, unenumerated powers subverted 'the particular organisation and positive provisions of the federal Constitution.' Aggression against freedom of speech and the press 'ought to produce universal alarm,' warned Madison, for 'the right of freely examining public characters' and 'the free communication of the people thereon' was 'the only effectual guardian of every other right.' Madison noted that Virginia, as a condition of ratifying the Constitution, had stipulated that 'the liberty of conscience and of the press cannot be cancelled, abridged, restrained, or modified by any authority of the United States,' and had recommended that the federal government affirm these basic freedoms in what ultimately became the First Amendment. 'It would be a reproachful inconsistency, and criminal degeneracy,' charged Madison, 'if an indifference were now shown to the most palpable violation of one of the rights thus secured, and to the establishment of a precedent which may be fatal to the other.'

Madison reiterated that while Virginia bore the 'truest anxiety for establishing and perpetuating the Union of all,' she equally valued 'scrupulous fidelity to that Constitution, which is the pledge of mutual friendship, and the instrument of mutual happiness.' That is, the Union without the Constitution was not just meaningless to Virginia, but dangerous. Madison closed by appealing 'to the like dispositions of the other States, in confidence that they will concur with this commonwealth in declaring, as it does hereby declare, that the acts aforesaid, are unconstitutional; and that the necessary and proper measures will be taken by each, for cooperating with this State, in maintaining the authorities, rights, and liberties, referred to the States respectively, or to the people.'

III

Jefferson and Madison did not devise the *Virginia and Kentucky Resolutions* as provisional defences of civil liberties or weapons in a partisan struggle with the Federalists, as it is fashionably but unfoundedly asserted nowadays, but derived them from the principles and intentions of those who framed and ratified the Constitution. 'The Virginia and Kentucky Resolutions should not be understood as the invention of distraught minds faced with extraordinary circumstances,' argues historian Kevin R.C. Gutzman. 'Although the situation faced by the Virginia [Democratic-] Republican high command at the end of the 1790s was urgent, the twin enunciations of the [Democratic-] Republican constitutional position adopted by the Virginia and Kentucky legislatures corresponded closely to the explication of the Federal Constitution offered by Virginia Federalists in the Richmond Ratification Convention of 1788.' The Resolutions and the 'Principles of '98' were the first systematic statement of the constitutional doctrine of States' rights in American history, and would influence and inspire Americans throughout the Antebellum Era. As late as 1860, for instance, the Northern and Southern factions of the Democratic Party were pledging allegiance to 'the Principles of 1798' as 'one of the main foundations of our political creed.' The 'Principles of '98' were particularly popular in the Old South, however, and became the constitutional cornerstone of a political tradition which had always placed organic 'society' above artificial 'government' and believed in bottom-up rather than top-down power. Indeed, Jefferson and Madison became the professed heroes, and the 'Principles of '98' the professed credo, of many Southern statesmen, as well as the subject of many Southern toasts. 'State Rights and State Remedies, as interpreted by Mr. Jefferson, and as contained in the Virginia and Kentucky Resolutions, the rock of our political salvation,' cheered the quintessential Southern statesman, John C. Calhoun in 1834. 'State Rights was the most marked peculiarity of the politics of the Southern people,' reflected Richmond editor Edward A. Pollard in his unapologetic apologia of the Lost Cause of the Confederacy. The *Resolutions*, continued Pollard, were the 'the textbook of State Rights.'

Confusing the integrity of the Constitution with the authority of the federal government, Ron Chernow, the best-selling biographer of George Washington and Alexander Hamilton, claims that Jefferson and Madison's 'radical doctrine of states' rights...effectively undermined the Constitution' and concludes that the Principles of '98 did damage that was 'deep and lasting, and was a recipe for disunion.' Fearing the simple decentralisation of power more than the suppression of basic civil liberties, award-winning historian Garry Wills argues that Jefferson and Madison's 'nullification effort, if others had picked it up, would have been a greater threat to freedom than the misguided [Alien and Sedition] laws, which were soon rendered feckless by ridicule and electoral pressure.' Popular radio host and fervent neo-conservative Mark Levin often sputters against modern-day nullifiers as 'Neo-Confederates' and cries, 'Didn't we fight a civil war over this?' at news of nullification – apparently unaware of the compliment he is paying Johnny Reb by recognising the distinguished lineage of his defeated but not dishonoured cause (for it was not just Jefferson and Madison's physical descendants who donned the butternut and grey and hoisted the Stars and Bars, but their spiritual descendants as well). What these sophists and demagogues fail to understand is that the Union and liberty are not, despite Massachusetts Senator Daniel Webster's majestic peroration in 1830, 'now and forever, one and inseparable.' Rather, as South-Carolina Senator Robert Y. Hayne countered, the Union is 'founded on the Constitution,' and does not transcend the purposes for which it was founded: justice, peace, and liberty among the States. 'The gentleman is for marching under a banner studded all over with stars, and bearing the inscription *Liberty* and *Union*,' replied Hayne. 'Ours, Sir, is the banner of the Constitution, the twenty-four stars are there in all their undiminished lustre, on it is inscribed, *Liberty – the Constitution – Union*.' In the *Resolutions* (one of the many subjects which the two orators debated), Webster saw a threat to the Union as an end in itself, ultimately leading to 'disunion' and 'civil war.' Hayne, however, saw the only hope for preserving the ends for which the Union was founded, leading to 'a free, a happy, a united people.' Although who won the battle in the Senate was disputed, it is indisputable that Webster, with the strength of over two million Yankee troops, would win the war.

II. St. George Tucker & *View of the Constitution of the United States*

'For the Constitution of the Union is the source of all the jurisdiction of the national government; so that the departments of that government, can never assume any power, that is not expressly granted by that instrument, nor exercise a power, in any other manner than is there prescribed. This is, indeed, a short, clear, and comprehensive exposition of the principles of a limited government, founded upon compact between sovereign and independent States.'
– St. George Tucker, 1803

TO MOST HISTORIANS, the constitutional doctrine of States' rights is nothing more than a treasonous smokescreen for the evil agenda of slavery. William K. Scarborough, a historian from the University of Southern Mississippi and a past president of the St. George Tucker Society, declares States' rights to be 'simply a philosophical justification for the more fundamental institutions of slavery and segregation.' The irony that St. George Tucker, Scarborough's society's namesake, was a Virginia jurist who systematised the implicit, incipient understanding of States' rights into a constitutional doctrine while simultaneously advocating for emancipation, was apparently lost on this prestigious professor. William C. Davis, a historian from the Virginia Polytechnic Institute and a three-time winner of

77

the Jefferson Davis Award, declares of the Confederates, 'Slavery, and not states' rights, really lay at the heart of their movement.' According to Davis, who enjoys using puns to put down the South in his book titles, States' rights were just a 'shadow issue' for slavery. Most historians would not be caught dead dismissing primary sources and claiming that major historical events on the scale of the War of Southern Independence have one and only one cause – indeed, such revisionism and fundamentalism is ideological and even conspiratorial – although when it comes to the Old South, the more simplistic and sinister the theory, the better.

This essay series aims to set the story straight. The truth is that the great constitutional treatises of the Old South prove that the doctrine of States' rights was never a mere pretence for slavery, but reflected a deep passion for self-government rooted in Southern culture as well as an earnest understanding of the Constitution rooted in Southern history. According to the scholarly, gentlemanly M.E. Bradford, States' rights were part of a Southern political tradition – a 'patrimony' and 'birthright' – dating from the foundation of the Colonies, through the independence of the States, and to the creation of the Constitution. At the crowning of the Confederate capital in Richmond, Virginia, President Jefferson Davis honoured this heritage. 'The cause in which we are now engaged is the cause of the advocacy of the rights to which we were born, those for which our fathers of the Revolution bled – the richest inheritance that ever fell to man, and which it is our sacred duty to transmit untarnished to our children,' announced Davis. 'Upon us is devolved the high and holy responsibility of preserving the constitutional liberty of a free government.'

St. George Tucker and his essay, *View of the Constitution of the United States*, published in 1803, are the subjects of this essay.

I

St. George Tucker was born on 10 July 1752, in the British colony of
Bermuda. The Tuckers were a mercantile family with shipping interests
across the Atlantic seaboard. Planning to strengthen his family's influence
throughout the British Empire, Tucker's father, Colonel Henry, sent his son
to Virginia in 1772 to study law at the College of William and Mary. Henry,
Jr., Tucker's older brother, informed him that he was embarking into 'the
grand theatre of the world,' and encouraged him to bring 'credit and
reputation' to himself, but 'honour to their family' above all else. Tucker's
father reminded him that 'the smallest deviation' from 'honour and virtue'
led to 'unhappy consequences.' At William and Mary, Tucker was a member
of the Flat Hat Club, a fraternity of young Virginian revolutionaries
including Thomas Jefferson. Under the instruction of Jefferson's mentor,
George Wythe, Tucker passed the bar in 1774, after which he visited relatives
in New York, Pennsylvania, and South Carolina. Upon returning to Virginia,
unfortunate turns of events seemed to have ruined Tucker's prospects. The
American embargo against Great Britain – in protest of taxation without
representation and the violation of colonial self-government – threatened
his family's mercantile business. Furthermore, the Royal Governor of
Virginia, the detested Lord Dunmore, had dissolved the Virginia House of
Burgesses and closed the Virginian courts, rendering Tucker's law licence
and clerkship worthless. When the legislature convened in defiance of
Dunmore, the unemployed Tucker happened to be observing the
proceedings, and it was his recollection of Patrick Henry's 'Liberty or Death'
oration which preserved it for posterity as the watchwords of the American
Revolution:

> It is vain, sir, to extenuate the matter. Gentlemen may cry, peace,
> peace – but there is no peace. The war is actually begun! The next
> gale that sweeps from the north will bring to our ears the clash of
> resounding arms! Our brethren are already in the field! Why stand
> we here idle? What is it that the gentlemen wish? What would they

have? Is life so dear, or peace so sweet, as to be purchased at the price of chains and slavery? Forbid it, Almighty God! I know not what course others may take, but as for me, give me liberty or give me death!

Despite the threat to their material interests, the Tuckers sided with the American Colonies out of principle. 'I think the Colonies ought to hazard everything rather than submit to slavery,' declared Tucker's father, 'for if the Parliament of Great Britain has a right to dispose of the American's property as they please, call it by what name you will, there can be no greater marks of slavery.' Tucker's father asked his son to inform Virginia's leaders that Bermudians 'wish well the American cause.' He even led a raid on a store of British gunpowder, which he smuggled to the Colonies. Tucker was soon recalled to Bermuda, where he and his brother smuggled supplies past the British blockade into the newly free and independent Virginia and South Carolina.

While in Virginia arranging another smuggling operation, Tucker met Frances B. Randolph, the widow of John Randolph. The two met in a thanksgiving church service for the monumental American victory at Saratoga; for Tucker, it was love at first sight. In marrying Frances, Tucker married into one of Virginia's wealthy and powerful 'First Families,' ensuring that his 'golden dreams of Virginia' would finally come true. In 1779, Tucker enlisted in the Virginia militia, receiving a major's commission due to his newfound connections. Tucker, an amateur poet from childhood to old age, composed a poem titled 'Liberty' commemorating the American Revolution and exhorting the United States not to decline and fall into empire:

> *If Liberty thy board shall deign to grace*
> *And smiling Peace adorn thy humble cot,*
> *Columbia, thus, shall live to deathless fame,*
> *Unrivall'd by Rome, or Britain's vaunted name!*

Tucker fought at the Battle of Guilford Courthouse, where he was wounded and promoted to lieutenant colonel. At the Siege of Yorktown, Tucker was asked to join General Thomas Nelson's staff as a French translator. General George Washington, who received Lord Cornwallis' surrender at Yorktown and thus made American independence a *fait accompli*, left an enormous impression on Tucker. 'Acknowledgements to this protector, their deliverer, and to the Savior of their Country,' Tucker gushed to his wife, 'implore an uninterrupted profusion of blessing on the head of the glorious and immortal WASHINGTON!' In another poem, 'Fairy Hill,' a fantastical retelling of the American Revolution, Tucker celebrated American victory and looked to the future with high hopes:

> *Since Tyranny's banish'd this happy domain,*
> *And Mars with his terrors hath quitted the plain,*
> *Gentle Peace far and wide shall her banners display,*
> *And Liberty heighten the joys of each day,*
> *While trumpet proclaims the glad tidings around,*
> *Let the mountains and valleys re-echo the sound.*
> *That America's free, let each heart, and each voice*
> *In unison should, and in concert rejoice;*
> *For virtue rever'd and wisdom renown'd,*
> *May her States still with freedom and glory be crown'd*
> *May this Union be stronger cemented each year,*
> *And the rage of old time ne'er the fabric impair.*

At the dawn of American independence, Tucker was a well-respected veteran and well-off member of the Virginian gentry. He sought to establish himself as a Virginia planter, acquiring large tobacco plantations, pursuing scholarly pursuits befitting a gentleman, and hosting company at Matoax, the ancestral Randolph estate along the Appomattox River. Tucker wrote a poem, 'Ode for the Fourth of July, 1784,' which he explained was intended to 'commemorate that important event...to felicitate ourselves on the attainment of that state of political happiness, which has been the consequence of the Revolution; and finally to recommend peace and union, as the only means of continuing to ourselves, and our posterity, the enjoyment of those blessings which seem to have been derived to the people of the United States from the peculiar bounty of Providence.' In his ode, Tucker captured the optimism and idealism of the Revolutionary generation:

> *Ever venerate the plough;*
> *Thick the moral virtues sow;*
> *Elevate the human mind;*
> *Teach the love of all mankind!*
> *Justice, equal hold thy scales;*
> *Commerce, spread thy swelling sails,*
> *And to distant nations bear,*
> *That which plenty gives to spare.*

Partly as a result of independence from Great Britain, the once-lucrative tobacco market depressed and never fully recovered, ruining many members of the highly indebted Virginian gentry. At the same time, under the Articles of Confederation, States were levying tariffs on one another, inflating their currencies, and violating property rights by allowing debtors to stiff creditors. With a merchant's mind, Tucker believed that the loose Union needed to be tightened in order to enact a uniform commercial policy. Tucker caught the eye of James Madison with a 'sensible pamphlet' he wrote on this subject. 'A sensible Federal[ist] and skilled in the art of commerce,' according to Madison, Tucker was elected to represent Virginia at the Annapolis Convention, the forerunner to the Constitutional Convention in Philadelphia. The duty of the American citizen, argued Tucker, was now 'to advance the interest of his native country, to promote her happiness, to raise her consequence among the nations, and to defend her from foreign influence and insult, as well as from intestine jars [a Shakespearean phrase meaning internal discord], and the machinations of domesticated enemies.'

Great Britain, however, was the United States' 'natural enemy,' nursed a 'vindictive jealousy' towards her former Colonies, and ruled supreme as 'mistress of the ocean.' Trade was 'the barometer of power,' and Great Britain's policy was 'to undermine, or engross the trade of every other nation.' In order to obtain commercial independence from Great Britain, and thus secure political independence, the United States required a uniform commercial policy leveraging British desire for American exports against the American desire for access to British ports. 'The establishment of our independence calls upon us to act with the provident circumspections and foresight of a nation laying the foundation of its future character,' concluded Tucker. 'The only means by which nations can rise into consequence, are, by their arms, or by their commerce. The genius, constitution, and situation of America preclude every idea of the former, while naturally prompt her to resort to the latter: so long, therefore, as the dominion of the sea shall be worth contesting, commerce will be found the only road, by which America can arrive at opulence and power.' Tucker's proposal of commercial pressure on Great Britain became a key element of Jefferson and Madison's future foreign policy.

Despite his participation in the Annapolis Convention, Tucker was not sent to the Constitutional Convention. Like many Virginians, Tucker initially opposed the Constitution, believing that the Convention had exceeded its authority in proposing a new form of government instead of simply amending the Confederation, as well as objecting to the absence of a bill of rights. Tucker eventually accepted the Constitution (apparently persuaded by the arguments of the sort that appeared in James Madison and Alexander Hamilton's *Federalist* essays), although not without reservations – stemming mainly from the likelihood that it would provide for the recovery of American debts to the British. 'You will have heard that the Constitution has been adopted in this State; that event, my dear children, affects your interest more nearly than that of most others,' Tucker told his stepsons. 'The recovery of British debts can no longer be postponed, and there now seems to be a moral certainty that your patrimony will all go to satisfy the unjust debt from your papa to the Hanbury's [a London bank].' Indeed, in marrying Frances, Tucker did not just inherit Randolph's land and slaves, but his sizable debts and three stepsons. Seeing that the days of the Virginian gentry were numbered, Tucker encouraged his children to rely on their own merit rather than status and land. 'If there was a period in the history of man which demonstrated the necessity of man's being able to place his reliance on *himself*, the last thirty years may be considered as furnishing the most awful and instructional lessons upon that head,' lectured Tucker. 'Your sole dependence must be on your own personal abilities and exertions.' To support his family, Tucker sold much of his property (including the majestic Matoax), invested in Virginian banks and land companies, relocated to a townhome in Williamsburg, and resumed the practice of law.

After moving to Williamsburg, Tucker was appointed to the Virginia General Court in 1786 and in 1789 was named Rector (the highest academic official) of his alma mater, William and Mary, as well as President of the Board of Visitors. In 1790, Tucker resigned the presidency to accept the position of law professor at William and Mary, replacing his former mentor, George Wythe. His classes, which he insisted on teaching from home in order to have access to his personal library, soon became famous. As part of his reevaluation of the Virginian way of life, Tucker also reevaluated the cornerstone social and economic institution of slavery. To his students, Tucker asked if there was 'due consistency between our avowed principles and our practice' when it came to slavery. According to Tucker, 'Whilst America hath been the land of promise to the Europeans, and their descendants, it hath been the vale of death to millions of the wretched sons of Africa.' Tucker held that out of 'a recognition of the first principles of the law of nature,' as enunciated in the Declaration of Independence, whites must regard blacks as 'our fellow men.' The slave revolt in the French colony of Santo Domingo, in which the slaves responded to their emancipation by the idealistic revolutionaries in Paris by massacring the white population, shook Tucker to his core. Tucker became convinced that Virginians must be proactive in abolishing slavery before they met the same fate, and was confident that 'a very large majority of the slave-holders among us would cheerfully concur in any feasible plan for the abolition of it.'

Tucker supported the Constitution in the hope that it would bring law and order to the American republic, but was disappointed in the rise of sectionalism, factionalism, and corruption which broke out during the 1790s. Tucker was particularly troubled by Treasury Secretary Alexander Hamilton's financial programme of national banks, national debt, paper money, heavy taxes, and high expenditures, which he feared promoted bribery and speculation as well as reestablished British mercantilism in the United States. Tucker composed a number of pointed poems at Alexander Hamilton, John Adams, and other Federalists, which were published in the opposition newspaper, the *National Gazette*. Tucker mocked Hamilton as 'Atlas' on a 'paper throne,' Federalist Congressmen as Hamilton's 'faithful janissaries' [the castrated guard of the Ottoman sultan], and mourned that 'Liberty' had become a 'castoff mistress.' Tucker diagnosed 'assumption, bank-script, [and] foreign loans' to the American republic as what 'small-pox,' 'yellow-fever,' and 'leprosy' were to the human body. 'The public credit to increase, It tax'd us without ending,' Tucker rhymed of the Congress, 'But lest the public debt should cease, devis'd new ways of spending.' The Federalists' attachment to the mother country, Great Britain, over their wartime ally, France, was a case of 'false friends prefer'd to true ones.' Tucker mocked President Adams' arrogance, gibing that perhaps Braintree, Adams' hometown, was the new home of the Biblical Tree of Knowledge. In a pamphlet which might have been written at the request of opposition leaders Thomas Jefferson and James Madison, Tucker demolished the Jay-Grenville Treaty, which put British interests ahead of American, subjected American ships to British interdiction and impressment, alienated the United States from France, and usurped the role of the judiciary by creating extralegal commissions to resolve British claims. 'As a treaty of AMITY,' fumed Tucker, 'it is partial and defective; as a treaty of COMMERCE, it is not reciprocal; as a treaty of NAVIGATION, it is humiliating; and it is, in other respects, destructive to the prosperity, security, and independence of the United States; and subversive of the CONSTITUTION.' Tucker tried to have a play of his, 'Wheel of Fortune' (in which the Southern protagonist, 'Freeman,' and the Northern antagonists, 'Shee,' 'Transfer,' 'Buckeye,' and 'Prig' debate the political issues of the 1790s), produced in the capital city of Philadelphia, but it was considered too pointed in its satirisation of leading Federalists. Tucker would have agreed with Jefferson's biting remark that 'men who were Samsons in the field and Solomons in the council...have had their heads shorn by the harlot England.'

Tucker also fiercely opposed the Alien and Sedition Acts, which respectively authorised the President to deport foreigners at will and criminalised criticism of the government. Tucker taught his students at William and Mary that these acts threatened the civil liberties of the people as well as the rights of the States. Writing to his Congressman in 1798, Tucker took him to task for supporting the hated Acts. According to Tucker, under British law, colonial law, and the Constitution, 'aliens' were equally entitled to the due process of law. To illustrate his point, Tucker suggested that the word 'persons' should be substituted for 'aliens' in the Alien Act. With such a substitution, the Alien Act was plainly 'the most abominable engine of oppression and tyranny that ever was conceived by the most arbitrary despot that ever swayed the sceptre in the old world,' making the President 'more absolute than the Grand Seignior [the Ottoman sultan], more tyrannical than the Mamelukes of Egypt [a Turkish warrior caste], and more terrible than the hydra-headed Directory of France [the latest revolutionary government in Paris].' Tucker continued that criticising the government – 'to assert that Mr. Adams...affects the style and mimics the etiquette of a crowned head; that in his political writings he is an advocate for monarchy; that in his administration he has taken care to advance and provide for his own family, friends, and adherents,' he swiped – may be false, but it was by no means 'sedition.' The Sedition Act replaced the freedom of speech and the freedom of the press, 'consecrated' under the First Amendment, with Great Britain's infamous 'Star Chamber.' Again, to illustrate his point, Tucker suggested that the word 'speak' be substituted for 'seditious libel' in the Sedition Act. With this revealing substitution, the Sedition Act clearly threatened to turn 'the most enlightened nation upon earth to a nation of mutes and slaves.' Tucker would have agreed with Thomas Jefferson's later justification of why, as President, he refused to enforce those laws and pardoned those convicted under the Adams Administration: 'I discharged every person under punishment or prosecution under the Sedition Law, because I considered and now consider that law to be a nullity as absolute as if Congress had ordered us to fall down and worship a golden image; and that it was as much my duty to arrest its execution in every stage, as it would have been to have rescued from the fiery furnace those who should have been cast into it for refusing to worship their image.'

In 1789, Jedidiah Morse, a Connecticut Federalist and preacher, published *American Geography*, a survey of the United States from a Yankee perspective. According to Morse, New England was industrious, intelligent, and virtuous, while the rest of America south of the Hudson River became a veritable heart of darkness. While other Northern States such as New York, Pennsylvania, and New Jersey were inferior for their Dutch, German, and Scotch-Irish, the Southern States were inferior for their Africans, who corrupted the morals and manners of Southern whites. When Morse reached Williamsburg, he sneered, 'Everything in Williamsburg appears dull, forsaken, and melancholy – no trade – no amusements, but the infamous one of gaming – no industry, and very little appearance of religion.' Tucker rose to defend his home against Morse, whom he remarked was 'without one generous sentiment, was never seduced from his road by *love* or *pity*; and sorry am I to add, that even the allurements of *truth* appear to have been equally ineffectual.' If Morse found Williamsburg to be a 'ruined village,' perhaps it was because it was still recovering from 'the ravages of war' and 'the devastation of fire' suffered during the American Revolution. Far from lacking religion, Williamsburg was home to the Bishop of the Episcopal Diocese of Virginia, two other Episcopal ministers, a Supreme-Court Justice, the Chancellor of Virginia, and an Episcopal church with an organ where the people gathered each Sunday. Perhaps if Morse had visited Williamsburg for more than a couple days, suggested Tucker, he could have seen a church service. Regarding the charge of gambling, Tucker avowed that he had never witnessed any serious gambling in Williamsburg, except among wayfarers like Morse in local taverns, and was confident that Williamsburg was as 'exempt from the vice of gambling' as anywhere else. 'A more unprovoked attack, I believe, has rarely been made,' concluded Tucker, who was hailed throughout Virginia for his public letter. 'To be sure, how many dirty efforts are made these Northern cattle to reduce the consequence of Virginia,' grumbled John Tyler, Sr., an Anti-Federalist delegate to Virginia's Ratification Convention and father of a future President of the United States. 'Every circumstance of human life (both civil and political) proves how unfit the States were for such a Union as ours,' continued Tyler, comparing the Union to an unhappy marriage in need of a divorce.

In 1796, Tucker published *A Dissertation on Slavery*, a conservative plan of gradual emancipation, which he submitted to the General Assembly. 'The representatives of a free people...who have declared that all men are by nature equally free and independent, cannot disapprove an attempt to carry so incontestable a moral truth into practical effect,' argued Tucker. Virginia's peremptory rejection of his proposal disheartened Tucker, although later slave revolts forced Virginia to take the issue seriously and revisit Tucker's idea. For what it was worth, Thomas Jefferson (who had himself proposed a similar plan after Virginia had declared her independence) agreed with Tucker. 'As to the mode of emancipation, I am satisfied that it must be a matter of compromise between the passions and prejudices and the real difficulties, which will each have their weight in that operation,' Jefferson encouraged Tucker, 'but if something is not done, and soon done, we shall be the murderers of our own children.' Tucker despaired of the failure of his 'utopian idea,' but he was pleased at least to see slavery's paternalistic reformation. 'The treatment of slaves is infinitely more humane than before the Revolution,' Tucker later observed. Without a general programme of emancipation, Tucker believed that continued enslavement was more benevolent than private manumissions, pointing out that the lives of such freedmen would be 'a hundred times harder than that to which they have been...accustomed.' According to historian Clyde N. Wilson, 'Perhaps the most important things about Tucker's essay for later times are the following: it shows the potential in the South for constructively addressing the most difficult issue in American society before it became necessary to defend against outside control; and, it demonstrates that Tucker's state rights understanding of the Constitution is not merely a rationalization in defense of slavery.'

Tucker was a personal friend and political ally of Thomas Jefferson, a fellow Virginian, revolutionary, and republican. Tucker celebrated the triumph of the Democratic-Republican Party over the Federalists in 1800, which in his opinion prevented the dissolution or consolidation of the Union. 'I do most sincerely rejoice in the termination of a contest which threatened the peace if not the existence of the Union,' Tucker breathed in relief. 'My most cordial congratulations on the triumph of the Democratic [Republican] representatives in Congress, and their constituents, over the tools of faction, the advocates of monarchy, the blind adorers of Britain, and the props of her influence, and the misguided zeal of many well-meaning citizens, supposing themselves exclusively Federalists.' As the students of William and Mary paraded through Williamsburg in celebration of Jefferson's victory, Tucker, as Rector of the college, invited them into his home for a toast 'to the health of the President-elect.' As a jab at the ousted Federalists, most of whom were New Englanders, Tucker composed several mocking poems to be sung to the tune of 'Yankee Doodle.'

Tucker's two most famous sons – his stepson, John Randolph of Roanoke, and his second-born, Nathaniel Beverly Tucker – became 'Tertium Quids,' a minority of Democratic-Republicans who sharply opposed the Jefferson and Madison administrations for straying from their professed liberal-republican principles. 'The principles of the [Democratic-] Republican Party...what are they?' asked Randolph as President James Madison stumbled into the War of 1812. 'Love of peace, hatred of offensive war; jealousy of the State governments towards the general government, and of the influence of the executive government over the coordinate branches of that government; a dread of standing armies; a loathing of public debt, taxes, and excises; tenderness for the liberty of the citizen; jealousy, Argus-eyed jealousy, of the patronage of the President,' he answered. 'From these principles,' Randolph concluded solemnly, 'what desertions have we not witnessed?' Beverly Tucker loved and respected his 'noble' father, Tucker, yet was more influenced by his older half-brother, Randolph, complimenting him as a man of 'integrity, fidelity, independence, courage, and magnanimity,' and his 'Spartan Band' of Tertium Quids as men of 'firmness and decision,' as opposed to the 'imbecility and distraction' of the other Democratic-Republicans. Despite the passionate, principled opposition of his sons, Tucker staunchly defended Jefferson and Madison from the attacks of the Federalists and the Tertium Quids. In fact, Tucker even wrote a pamphlet warmly praising the Louisiana Purchase, which he confessed made him so happy that he felt like bursting into song! Tucker rejoiced that the French threat had been neutralised and that the navigation of the Mississippi River with the port of New Orleans had been acquired 'without bloodshed.' To Tucker, the Louisiana Purchase was 'the most momentous object which has been achieved' since American independence. 'Never since the commencement of mankind did any civilised nation possess so advantageous a position,' beamed Tucker. 'Never was there a people who had their happiness so much in their own power.' Tucker anticipated that the 'treasure' of the vast Louisiana Territory would not simply be settled by

American freemen, but could also be used to resettle Indians, freed slaves, and criminals. This, Tucker freely admitted, was another 'utopian idea.'

As a judge, Tucker was known for his formal manner and strict rulings. Tucker worried that the egalitarianism and individualism of the American Revolution (and, in fact, the Enlightenment itself) was backfiring, creating a litigious and demagogic society rather than a just and enlightened one. Courts were 'places of general resort for the idle and dissipated' and men 'of inferior pretensions to the confidence of the people' were elected to office over men whose 'minds had been properly enlightened by study and application.' According to Tucker, 'We have refined upon the words philosophy, philanthropy, and the rights of man, until we are in real danger of that system of anarchy with which the adversaries of a republican government reproach it.' In 1803, Tucker was appointed to the Virginia Court of Appeals, replacing the venerable jurist Edmund Pendleton. There, Tucker feuded with Spencer Roane, who resented Tucker for his formalism and whom Tucker resented for outside political activism unbecoming of a judge. When Roane physically accosted Tucker, Tucker demanded an apology which he did not receive. In 1810, Tucker resigned his prestigious position and foreswore any further public service. 'No man in public life can promise himself any portion of *real* happiness,' vented Tucker, 'and I am not patriot enough to sacrifice *that*.'

Tucker ardently supported the War of 1812, seriously distrusting Great Britain and accusing her of trying to reconquer her former Colonies. 'Britain is the natural enemy of our liberty and independence,' Tucker had often observed. 'She must necessarily be the same to our political advancement in every instance.' Frustrated with his sons' opposition to war on the suspicion that it would create a tyrannous federal government, Tucker wrote a play, 'The Patriot Rous'd,' a story about the boys of 'Colonel Trueman' imprisoned aboard a British ship, and the machinations of the British characters, 'Lawless' and 'Townly.' Tucker spoke through Colonel Trueman, an old American patriot: 'I have shunn'd crowds, and avoided public places and public offices; I have endeavored to forget my hatred and resentment to that oppressive and insolent nation, whose tyranny drove us into war, and whose wrongs toward us have only multiplied, under the pretext of a peace, which she never observed.' The play ended with a call to arms:

> *Be not blind to freedom's claims!*
> *Be not deaf to war's alarms!*
> *Raise ye! Quick to arms!*
> *Rouse! And drive your foes away!"*

Tucker was embittered by New England's refusal to contribute troops, cooperation with the enemy, and threats of secession, which he considered nothing less than 'sedition' and a 'revolt' in the midst of a war. 'I look forward to a dissolution of the Union as an event not far off,' admitted Tucker. Specifically, Tucker feared 'a general insurrection of slaves' along with 'the separation of the States, and perhaps the subjugation of the Southern part of the Union.' Tucker took up his poet's pen to mock New England's politicised pulpit and its pretended piety (what Thomas Jefferson derided as 'priestcraft' and 'lawcraft'):

> *Since we are Slaves to Jemmy MADISON,*
> *O make us free,*
> *That evermore we may be glad,*
> *O L[ord] to follow thee.*
>
> *But if, O L[ord] it be thy will,*
> *We shall not rule this nation;*
> *At least our ardent prayers fulfill*
> *By speedy separation.*
>
> *Then loud Hosannahs shall we sing*
> *To Thee L[ord] G[od] of Hosts.*
> *When thou has granted us a king,*
> *With honours, wealth, and posts.*

After the War of 1812, Tucker wrote another play, 'The Patriot Cool'd,' a celebration of American victory and condemnation of Northern treachery. 'Are not the Yankees quietly looking on whilst our invaders have possessed themselves of a large portion of their country?' Trueman asked. Unlike the American Revolution, when Southerners rushed to the aid of the invaded, occupied North, the bonds of the Union were now beginning to fray. 'We were then united in our hearts,' mourned Trueman. 'We are now a divided people.' Reflecting the differences becoming clear between the North and the South, Tucker's play featured honourable, amiable Southerners ('Colonel Trueman' and 'Major Friendly') and 'Pedlar,' an ambitious, avaricious Yankee. For good measure, Tucker included 'Doctor Quid' and 'Major Grumble' (for the anti-war, anti-Madison 'Tertium Quids'). Again, Tucker spoke through Colonel Trueman: 'Old, and decrepit, and useless, I now am to my country, my soul exults in the hope that she will finally triumph over our haughty, tyrannical, and bloodthirsty enemy ... Spirit of immortal Washington! Descend upon [the Americans], and lead them on to victory!'

From 1819 to 1821, Northern Congressmen demanded that the Territory of Missouri abolish slavery before she could be admitted to the Union as a State. Tucker agreed with Thomas Jefferson and James Madison (Southern slave-holders who dearly longed for the States to abolish slavery but strictly maintained that slavery was a right of the States) that the Congress had 'no right to prohibit it.' During the Missouri Crisis, Tucker revised his *Dissertation on Slavery*, proposing that freedmen be resettled on homesteads west of the Mississippi River. Tucker hoped 'to emancipate the slave, and afford him an asylum against poverty and wretchedness, without inviting him to stay within the territories of the United States, if he can find a happier or more comfortable situation in any other country.' After the failure of his Revolutionary-era emancipation plan, Tucker and his family became more conservative and less liberal on the issue of slavery – particularly as Northerners politicised the problem. 'These Yankees have almost reconciled me to negro slavery,' exclaimed Randolph of Roanoke. 'I am persuaded that the cause of humanity to these unfortunates has been put back a century, certainly a generation, by the unprincipled conduct of ambitious men, availing themselves of a good will as well as of a fanatical spirit in the nation.'

Tucker died on 10 November 1827. In the years following his death, the unlettered Andrew Jackson would win the presidency in the first populist election, an abominable new tariff would further saddle the burdens of the Union on the South and send the benefits to the North, South Carolina would take the 'Principles of '98' farther than they had ever gone before in nullifying the tariff, and President Jackson would threaten civil war against South Carolina to enforce the tariff. All of these events and more would have distressed the conservative Tucker, perhaps confirming his gnawing fear that the American Revolution had ultimately been in vain. According to Clyde N. Wilson, Professor Emeritus of the University of South Carolina, Tucker was 'the judge of Jeffersonian democracy' and 'the exponent of Jeffersonian republicanism, or what has been called "South Atlantic republicanism," in contrast to the commercial republicanism of New England that has since the Civil War been taken to be the only true form of American philosophy.'

II

Although Tucker's courses at William and Mary were based on Sir William Blackstone's voluminous legal commentaries, Tucker believed that his students required formal education in the American and Virginian evolutions of British law. Blackstone's commentaries, which invaluably organised the mass of unwritten British common law into a written collection, nevertheless included monarchical and aristocratic elements which the American republic had repudiated. To teach his students the principles of American constitutional law, Tucker annotated Blackstone with commentaries of his own. At first, Tucker simply read his annotations to his classes, but in 1803, after encouragement from his friends, he published his commentaries, including appended essays such as *View of the Constitution of the United States* and *Of the Constitution of Virginia*. Tucker's commentaries were the first systematic analysis of American constitutionalism in history and were widely accepted as authoritative – even cited by the Supreme Court in many significant rulings. The paleo-conservative godfather Russell Kirk calls Tucker's edition of Blackstone 'the Bible of every Virginian lawyer,' and the historian Clyde Wilson describes Tucker's *View* as 'an important piece of constitutional history and a key document of Jeffersonian republicanism.'

Tucker split his *View of the Constitution of the United States* into two sections: the first analysed the basic nature of the Constitution and the Union which it created, and the second how power was divided between the States and the federal government.

'The Constitution of the United States of America,' began Tucker, 'is an original, written, federal and social compact, freely, voluntarily, and solemnly entered into by the several States of North America, and ratified by the people thereof, respectively; whereby the several States, and the people thereof, respectively, have bound themselves to each other, and to the federal government of the United States; and by which the federal government is bound to the several States, and to every citizen of the United States.' Tucker thankfully delved into the meaning of each of these terms – compact, federal, social, original, written, free, voluntary, solemn, and bound – which may seem foreign today but which were familiar in Tucker's time.

A 'compact,' according to Tucker, was distinguished from a 'charter' or 'grant,' since the latter were acts between superiors and inferiors. Yet States were all equal to one another, and as equal parties to the compact, each State was entitled to benefit equally from the Constitution. 'Here the contracting parties ... as States, in their political capacity and character ... are all equal,' explained Tucker. 'Nor is there anything granted from one to another: each stipulates to part with, and to receive the same thing, precisely, without any distinction or difference in favour of any of the parties.' The benefits which the States expected to receive from the Constitution were listed prominently in its Preamble: 'to establish justice, and ensure domestic tranquility, between them; to provide for their common defence, against foreign force, or such powerful domestic insurrections as might require to aid to suppress them; to promote their general welfare; and to secure the blessings of liberty to the people of the United States, and their posterity.' This was the true meaning of the Preamble's oft-quoted, oft-misunderstood phrase – 'a more perfect union.'

While a compact was an agreement between equal parties, a 'federal compact' occurred when 'several sovereign and independent States may unite themselves together by a perpetual confederacy, without each ceasing to be a perfect State.' Tucker simply recognised what was, in his time (before the rise of legalistic, mystic, Lincolnite more-perfect-unionism in America) plain as day: the States were sovereign, independent political entities and separate, distinct societies. Indeed, Tucker described Virginia as a 'sovereign and independent State' in the opening sentence of his commentary! Tucker considered this 'separate organisation' of the States, along with the integrity of 'every power, jurisdiction, and right' which they had reserved for themselves, as essential to the 'nature of the compact.' As long as the States existed, held Tucker, 'the Union is in fact, as well as in theory, an association of States, or, a confederacy.'

Tucker credited the Baron de Montesquieu with the concept of a 'confederate, or federal republic,' which he defined as a form of government 'for extending the sphere of popular government, and reconciling internal freedom with external security.' Although the conversion of the United States from the Articles of Confederation to the Constitution strengthened the powers of the federal government, Tucker (who was reform-minded yet initially skeptical about ratification) maintained that it did not fundamentally alter the federal relations between the States. Tucker explained that the Constitution was not a repudiation of Montesquieu's principles, but a mere 'expansion' of those principles to fix particular problems under the Confederation. 'In the new government, as in the old,' assured Tucker, 'the general powers are limited, and ... the States, in all unenumerated cases, are left in the enjoyment of their sovereign and independent jurisdictions.'

Tucker believed that the Tenth Amendment 'fully confirmed' this conservative construction of the Constitution and prevented 'misconstruction and abuse' of the federal government's enumerated powers in the Constitution. As Thomas Jefferson remarked, 'The States supposed that by their Tenth Amendment, they had secured themselves against constructive powers.' In fact, to Tucker, the liberal construction of implied powers in the Constitution was contrary to basic legal principles. 'The powers delegated to the federal government being all positive, and enumerated, according to the ordinary rules of construction, whatever is not enumerated is retained,' Tucker argued. 'For *expressum facit tacere tacitum* [i.e. that which is expressed makes that which is implied to cease] is a maxim in all cases of construction: it is likewise a maxim of political law, that sovereign States cannot be deprived of any of their rights by implication; nor in any manner whatever by their own voluntary consent, or by submission to a conqueror.'

When arguments of implication proved unavailing against the South, the North resorted to conquest to force the South to submit.

Although the Constitution was a 'social compact' in that it was ratified only upon the consent of the people, it remained 'strictly federal' in that the people were not one nation, under God, indivisible, but composed of sovereign and independent States which assented of their own accord. 'Upon these grounds,' by which Tucker meant the social character of the compact, 'a considerable alarm was excited in the minds of many, who considered the Constitution as in some danger of establishing a national or consolidated government, upon the ruins of the old republic.' Quoting extensively from one of James Madison's *Federalist* essays (a series of pro-ratification essays originally published with Alexander Hamilton and John

Jay in New York City), Tucker answered that 'although the Constitution would be founded on the assent and ratification of the people of America...that assent and ratification was to be given by the people, not as individuals composing one entire nation; but as composing the distinct and independent States, to which they respectively belong.' According to Madison, 'That it will be a federal and not a national act...the act of the people, as forming so many independent States, not as forming one aggregate nation, is obvious from this single consideration, that it is the result neither from the decision of a majority of the people of the Union, nor from a majority of the States.' Tucker held that the fact that the Constitution was ratified separately by each State in a convention, rather than by the Philadelphia Convention or in a national referendum, clearly proved that the Constitution was a federal and not a national compact. Tucker admitted that if the Constitution were ever construed to be 'an act of the people' instead of an act of the States, then 'an interpretation that would tend to the annihilation of the States, and their authority' would prevail, but he doubted that these well-documented truths could ever be denied. Yet, that was exactly what Northern more-perfect-unionist revisionists such as Justice Joseph Story would legitimise with ingenious interpretations, Senator Daniel Webster would popularise with rousing rhetoric, and President Abraham Lincoln would ultimately seal with blood and iron.

By 'original compact,' Tucker meant that 'whatever political relation existed between the American Colonies, antecedent to the revolution, as constituent parts of the British Empire, or as dependencies upon it ... was completely dissolved and annihilated from that period.' In other words, the States were completely free, with nothing left over from their time as Colonies in the British Empire binding them together. Tucker traced the origin of State sovereignty to the Declaration of Independence itself. 'From the moment of the Revolution,' explained Tucker, 'they became severally independent and sovereign States, possessing all the rights, jurisdiction, and authority, that other sovereign States, however constituted, or by whatever title denominated, possess; and bound by no ties but of their own creation, except such as all other civilised nations are equally bound by, and which together constitute the customary law of nations.' Contrary to the tortuous theories of Northern more-perfect-unionist revisionists like Webster, Story, and Lincoln, the Declaration of Independence was not an act of union among the States, but a collective act of separation from the British Empire. The 'first act of union' (the Articles of Confederation, ratified in 1781) took place five years after the States had declared their independence. The second act of union, the Constitution, simply expanded upon the principles of its predecessor. Since the compact was original, Tucker asserted that the federal government generally had no constitutional authority over the 'municipal law' (that is, local law) of the States. 'No case of municipal law can arise under the Constitution of the United States, except such as are expressly comprehended in that instrument,' argued Tucker. 'For the municipal law of one State or nation has no force or obligation in any other nation; and when several States, or nations unite themselves together by a federal compact, each retains its own municipal laws, without admitting or adopting those of any other member of the Union, unless there be an article expressly to that effect.' The few instances in which the federal government did have authority over the States' laws, however, must be construed conservatively. 'Otherwise,' Tucker warned, 'the gradual and sometimes imperceptible usurpations of power, will end in the total disregard of all its intended limitations.'

Despite the fact that the federal government has little to no authority over the States' laws, the nominally pro-legalisation Obama Administration threatened Colorado and Washington (which legalised marijuana in statewide referenda) with violent enforcement of federal law – a total disregard of all the Constitution's limitations if there ever were one. As George Mason, the chief framer of Virginia's constitution and bill of rights, warned at the Constitutional Convention, 'The most jarring elements of nature, fire and water themselves, are not more incompatible than such a mixture of civil liberty and military execution.'

That the Constitution was 'written' was immensely important to Tucker. Like all liberal republicans of the age, Tucker believed in the 'social contract,' the idea that to secure the benefits of 'civil society' (i.e. 'the peaceful possession of property, a method of obtaining justice with security, and in short, a mutual defence against all violence from without') people implicitly assented to some form of government. This history was idealised, of course, for no government has ever been formed in such a way, but liberal republicans like Tucker believed that it was important to provide at least a theoretical basis for government. Tucker noted, however, that the American republic was unique from other 'social contracts' in that her constitutions were written and adopted by the people, as opposed to the British system of unwritten precedents and assumed consent. In the American constitutions, the 'unalienable' sovereignty of the people was recognised, while governments were relegated from sovereigns to 'servants and agents.' Furthermore, the government's rightful role in society was spelled out in a document which any citizen (not just legal scholars like him) could understand. 'The advantages of a written constitution, considered as the original contract of society must immediately strike every reflecting mind,' avowed Tucker. 'Power, when undefined, soon becomes unlimited; and the disquisition of social rights where there is no text to resort to, for their explanation, is a task equally above ordinary capacities, and incompatible with the ordinary pursuits, of the body of the people.' As an example of the heavy limits which the Constitution placed upon the federal government – 'to guard against encroachments on the powers of the several States' – Tucker cited the Ninth and Tenth Amendments. 'The sum of all which appears to be,' explained Tucker, 'that the powers given to the federal government, are, in all cases, to receive the most strict construction that the instrument will bear where the rights of the States or of the people, either collectively, or individually, may be drawn in question.' Thomas Jefferson told George Washington that this principle formed the 'foundation' of the Constitution.

According to Tucker, the fact that the Constitution was ratified by the States 'freely,' 'voluntarily,' and 'solemnly,' was essential to the nature of the Union it created. The compact was 'free' because it was based upon consent, not coercion. The compact was 'voluntary' because the idea of a new constitution came from separate acts of the State legislatures. The compact was 'solemn' because it was framed by a convention of delegates from the States and finally ratified by popular conventions of the States. To illustrate how the States freely, voluntarily, and solemnly enacted the Constitution into law, Tucker cited Virginia's act of ratification, in which she stipulated that she retained her sovereignty and reserved the right of secession, issued a bill of rights and recommended constitutional amendments, many of which were ultimately adapted into the Bill of Rights.

Since the States created the federal government when they ratified the Constitution, Tucker rejected as illogical the ludicrous claim that the federal government was a party to the Constitution. 'The federal government can, in no possible view,' Tucker protested, 'be considered as a party to a compact made anterior to its existence, and by which it was, in fact, created.' In fact, as the 'creature' of the Constitution, the federal government was 'bound' to its creators, the States, its entire existence depending entirely on their consent. 'Having no existence but under the Constitution,' Tucker explained, 'nor any rights, but such as that instrument confers; and those rights being in fact duties; it can possess no legitimate power, but such as is absolutely necessary for the performance of a duty, prescribed and enjoined by the Constitution.'

'The Constitution of the United States,' concluded Tucker, 'then being that instrument by which the federal government has been created; its powers defined, and limited; and the duties, and functions of its several departments prescribed; the government, thus established, may be pronounced to be a confederal republic, composed of several independent, and sovereign democratic States, united for their common defence, and security against foreign nations, and for the purposes of harmony, and mutual intercourse between each other; each state retaining an entire liberty of exercising, as it thinks proper, all those parts of its sovereignty, which are not mentioned in the constitution, or act of union, as parts that ought to be exercised in common.' The Constitution could be amended, noted Tucker, but any amendment required the 'assent of the body politic of the States.'

Tucker closed the first section of his commentaries with a philosophical question. 'That mankind have a right to bind themselves by their own voluntary acts, can scarcely be questioned: but how far have they a right to enter into engagements to bind their posterity likewise?' asked Tucker, echoing Thomas Jefferson's famous musing to James Madison. 'Are the acts of the dead binding upon their living posterity, to all generations; or has posterity the same natural rights which their ancestors have enjoyed before them? And if they have, what right have any generation of men to establish any particular form of government for succeeding generations?' To Tucker, the 'fundamental principle' of 'the consent of the governed,' as enunciated in the Declaration of Independence, provided the solution to this apparent problem. Since 'government derives its just authority from the consent of the governed,' if posterity no longer consented to the constitution of their forefathers, then it was free 'to alter or abolish it, and to institute new government.' Until another free, voluntary, solemn act, however, Tucker affirmed that the Constitution 'must be received, respected, and obeyed among us, as the great and unequivocal declaration of the will of the people, and the supreme law of the land.'

In the second section of his commentaries, Tucker analysed the constitutional division of power between the States and the federal government, as well as the constitutional division of power among the federal branches. To Tucker the division of powers between the States and the federal government was as important of a safeguard to liberty as the checks and balances within the federal government. In general, Southerners like Tucker placed their trust in the 'separation of powers,' or political decentralisation, while Northerners tended towards 'checks and balances' in the centre – counterweights as opposed to a clockwork. As Thomas Jefferson put it, 'The true barriers of our liberty in this country are our State governments; and the wisest conservative power ever contrived by man is that of which our Revolution and present government found us possessed.'

Before analysing what powers were delegated to the federal government, Tucker thought it was necessary to reiterate the reserved powers of the States, which he did by the example of his own Virginia. Alongside her federal relations with other States in the Union, Virginia was a self-governing 'representative democracy,' as her constitution (the first written constitution in America and in the world) and bill of rights made clear:

> In the Commonwealth of Virginia, the constitution, which is the fundamental law of the republic, hath been shown to be the act of the people. The establishment of this constitution was an immediate act of sovereignty by them. They declared that all power is vested in and consequently derived from the people. That magistrates are their trustees and servants, and at all times amenable to them. That government is instituted for the common benefit, protection, and security of the people. That no man or set of men are entitled to exclusive or separate emoluments or privileges but in consideration of public services. That the people have a right to uniform government; and, that no free government, or the blessings of liberty, can be preserved to any people but by a firm adherence to justice, moderation, temperance, frugality, and virtue; and by frequent recurrence to fundamental principles. This is the principle of democracy.

In declaring her independence and establishing her constitution (which Virginia, along with many other States, did by herself before their delegates signed the Declaration of Independence), Tucker claimed that Virginia rose from the status of a subject Colony to that of a 'sovereign and independent

State...equal to any other state or nation, being sovereign and independent' (indeed, Tucker's friend, Thomas Jefferson, referred to Virginia as a 'nation' and 'country' to Americans and foreigners alike). When Virginia formed a 'federal alliance' with the other States in the Articles of Confederation, Tucker noted that 'she expressly retained her sovereignty and independence.' According to Tucker, Virginia acted on the belief that 'a number of independent States may unite themselves by one common bond or confederacy, for the purposes of common defence and safety, and for the more perfect preservation of amity between themselves, without any of them ceasing to be a perfect, independent, and sovereign State, retaining every power, jurisdiction, and right, which it has not expressly agreed shall be exercised in common by, the confederacy of the States.' In the Constitution, however, there was no such 'express reservation' of State sovereignty as existed in the Articles, which Tucker noted was 'a subject of considerable alarm, and discussion, among those who were opposed to everything that resembled, or might hazard, a consolidation of them [the States].' Tucker quelled these concerns by referring to another *Federalist* essay, this one by Alexander Hamilton. According to Hamilton, sovereignty could only be delegated in express terms and not by implication. 'An entire consolidation of the States into one complete national sovereignty, would imply a complete subordination of all the parties; and whatever power might remain in them would be altogether dependent on the general will,' Tucker quoted Hamilton. 'But as the plan of the Convention aims only at a partial union, the State governments will clearly retain all the rights of sovereignty, which they had before and which are not by that act [the Constitution] exclusively delegated to the United States.' Of course, repeated Tucker, the Tenth Amendment 'confirmed' that the States did indeed retain their sovereignty under the Constitution. 'The right of sovereignty,' asserted Tucker, paraphrasing the Tenth Amendment, 'in all cases not expressly ceded to the United States by the Constitution, or prohibited by it to the several States, remains inviolably, with the States, respectively.'

According to Tucker, the federal government's powers pertained to foreign affairs such as war, peace, and commerce. 'The federal government, then, appears to be the agent through which the united republics communicate with foreign nations, and with each other,' explained Tucker. States remained in charge of their internal affairs – 'domestic economy,' as well as 'domestic peace, happiness, or prosperity' – and were responsible for protecting the person and property of their citizens. As Thomas Jefferson proclaimed in his First Inaugural Address, while the federal government was 'the sheet anchor of our peace at home and safety abroad,' the States were 'the most competent administrations for our domestic concerns and the surest bulwarks against anti-republican tendencies.'

Today, of course, the States have been reduced to mere administrative provinces of the all-controlling, all-planning, all-seeing, all-knowing supreme government centered in Washington, D.C. – 'Mordor on the Potomac,' in the colourful phrasing of the paleo-conservative commentator Mike Church.

Tucker recognised that secession was a right of the States, avowing that the Union was 'not a flame by which they have been consumed, nor a vortex in which they are swallowed up.' Based on Virginia's act of ratification, Tucker explained that 'their submission to its operation is voluntary...each is still a perfect State, still sovereign, still independent, and still capable, should the occasion require, to resume the exercise of its functions, as such, in the most unlimited extent.' Of course, Tucker hoped that the 'the dissolution of the bonds of Union' and 'a resumption of the rights of sovereignty by the several States [or] the exercise of the rights of sovereignty by the States individually' would never come. To Tucker, the dissolution of the Union would be 'an event which no good citizen can wish, and which no good, or wise administration will ever hazard.'

Nevertheless, Tucker agreed with Thomas Jefferson that the only evil greater than the Union's dissolution would be its consolidation. 'If ever this vast country is brought under a single government, it will be one of the most extensive corruption, indifferent and incapable of a wholesome care over so wide a spread of surface,' warned Jefferson. 'This will not be borne, and you will have to choose between reformation and revolution.'

To prevent the necessity of secession, Tucker wholeheartedly supported the 'removing and punishing' (i.e. impeachment) of politicians guilty of 'corruption and mal-administration,' both of which were vices if left 'unchecked' could culminate in dissolution. 'The aggregate of mankind understand their own interest and their own happiness better than any individual,' claimed Tucker. 'They can never be supposed to have resigned their right of judging for themselves to any set of men whatsoever; it is a right which can never be voluntarily resigned, though it may be wrested from their hands by tyranny, or violated by the infidelity and perfidy of their servants.'

If the conniving neo-conservatives and neo-liberals of the Bush, Clinton, and Obama administrations are not one day held accountable for lying the country into wars for Israeli and Saudi agendas, then 'corruption and mal-administration' will indeed be 'unchecked' and the people will appear to have indeed 'resigned their right of judging for themselves.' As Tucker's stepson, Randolph of Roanoke, put it, 'They who, from indifference, or with their eyes wide open, persist in hugging the traitor to their bosom...deserve to be slaves, with no other music to soothe them but the clank of the chains which they have put on themselves and given to their offspring.'

While the House of Representatives, where each State's Congressmen were proportional to her population, represented the people, the Senate represented the States, which was why each State had an equal number of Senators irrespective of her population. 'The Senate are chosen to represent the States in their sovereign capacity, as moral bodies, who as such are all equal,' explained Tucker. 'The smallest republic, as a sovereign State, being equal to the most powerful monarchy upon earth.' Tucker considered State equality 'one of the happiest traits' of the Constitution, for it prevented a majoritarian tyranny of larger States over smaller States. 'Without this equality,' held Tucker, 'the Union could not, under any possible view, have been considered an equal alliance between equal States.' Tucker, however, doubted that the United States would exceed half of their current size, and thus did not foresee how incompatible the sections of the Union and oversized its government would become. 'Government, to be safe and free, must consist of representatives having a common interest and a common feeling with the represented,' argued Randolph of Roanoke. 'No government extending from the Atlantic to the Pacific can be fit to govern me or those whom I represent.'

After these general observations about the relationship between the States and the federal government, Tucker analysed the constitutional powers of each federal branch.

Beginning with the legislature, Tucker discussed the limitations on its taxing powers. Since the Constitution was a compact between equals from which all parties were entitled to equal benefits, 'indirect' taxes (extracted from the people by an intermediary, e.g. customs) were required to be uniform throughout the United States, and 'direct' taxes (extracted directly from the people by the government, e.g. capitation) were required to be proportionate to the population of each State. Tucker realised, however, that despite the required uniformity of indirect taxation, economic differences within the Union made this mandate chimerical. 'The inequality of indirect taxes, among States, as well as among individuals, is perfectly unavoidable,' Tucker predicted. 'It may in time become so great as to shift all the burdens of government from a part of the States, and to impose them, exclusively, on the rest of the Union.' Tucker noted that this shift was already taking place between the North and the South. The industrial North was beginning to produce manufactures which the agrarian South was already importing from Europe in exchange for exports of cash crops. 'The Northern States, for example, already manufacture within themselves, a very large proportion, or perhaps the whole, of many articles which in other States are imported from foreign parts, subject to heavy duties,' observed Tucker. Since federal taxes

107

were predominantly levies on imports ('tariffs') the South therefore paid the bulk of federal taxation. 'They [the Northern States] are consequently exempted,' Tucker continued, 'in the same proportion, from the burden of duties paid on these articles.' In fact, far from paying taxes, the North was actually paid by taxes, as tariffs forced up the prices of her foreign competition and freed Northern industries to inflate their own prices accordingly. 'Hence a considerable inequality already exists between the contributions from the several States,' argued Tucker. 'This inequality daily increases, and is indeed daily favoured, upon principles of national policy: for whenever any species of manufacture becomes considerable in the United States, it is considered proper to impose what are called protecting duties, upon foreign articles of the same kind.'

Randolph of Roanoke described the tariff as 'an immense tax on one portion of the community to put money into the pockets of another,' based on the principle that 'a bare majority may oppress, harass, and plunder the minority at its pleasure.' Tucker's second-born son, Nathaniel Beverly Tucker, a young Tertium Quid who later became one of the first Fire-Eaters, predicted in an early science-fiction novel, *The Partisan Leader*, that the Southern States would ultimately secede from the Union in protest of the tariff's suppression of their commerce and redistribution of their wealth. During the War of Southern Independence, Beverly Tucker's book was reprinted in New York with the subtitle 'The Key to the Disunion Conspiracy.'

Concerning the legislature's power of borrowing money, Tucker approved of public debt as a temporary expedient during times of extreme emergency, such as war – which was, to Tucker, an evil to be avoided at all costs. Taxes required to finance a war would be 'miserable' and 'oppressive,' but debt could ease the burden over time. 'On the other hand,' cautioned Tucker, sniping at Alexander Hamilton's famous phrase that a public debt is a public blessing, 'where loans are voluntarily incurred, upon the principle that public debt was a public blessing, or to serve the purposes of aggrandising a few at the expence of the nation, or of strengthening the hands of the government (or more properly, those of a party grasping at power, influence, and wealth), nothing can be more dangerous to the liberty of the citizen, nor more injurious to remotest posterity, as well as to present generations' (the current on-books national debt of $19 trillion and off-books national debt of $222 trillion would have been utterly unfathomable to Tucker). Furthermore, under the Constitution, the legislature had the power only to coin money and regulate its value. According to Tucker, this meant exactly what it said: 'regulating the alloy and value of coin struck by their own authority,' not a national bank pumping out trillions of dollars in unbacked paper money in the form of credit. Tucker would have been shocked to learn that the federal government would one day be printing worthless paper (not 'coining' real money from gold or silver) to finance its own ballooning debt. Indeed, Tucker judged the national bank of his day, the First Bank of the United States (a harmless puppy compared to the ravenous wolf that is today's Federal Reserve), to be utterly unconstitutional. Between today's national debt and today's national bank, Tucker would not deem the modern United States worthy of the names 'republic' or 'democracy.'

'To preserve [our] independence, we must not let our rulers load us with perpetual debt,' warned Thomas Jefferson of debt and banks. 'We must make our election between economy and liberty or profusion and servitude.'

Tucker, like most of the liberal republicans of the Founding generation, and unlike today's pinheaded 'patriots' (or as Randolph of Roanoke put it, 'the pseudo patriot...he who wishes to ride on the surface of the billow of his own breath'), deplored war. Tucker condemned war as 'the extremes of human misery and iniquity,' and 'the sufferings and calamities of mankind, resulting from the ambition, usurpation, animosities, resentments, piques, intrigues, avarice, rapacity, oppressions, murders, assassinations, and other crimes, of the few possessing power.' The power to declare war was simply too terrible to entrust to one man, especially since kings, presidents, and other executives were prone to conflate their personal interests in power and glory with their country's national interests in peace and prosperity. Therefore, the power to declare war belonged solely to the legislature; the executive could only command troops in time of war, but never start a war himself. 'The power of declaring war,' explained Tucker, 'with all its train of consequences, direct and indirect, forms the next branch of the powers confided to Congress; and happy it is for the people of America that it is so vested.' Tucker believed that the people preferred peace to war, and thus the legislature would act as a deterrent against its outbreak. 'War would be banished from the face of the earth,' averred Tucker, 'were nations instead of princes to decide upon their necessity.'

Beginning with Abraham Lincoln's unilateral invasion of the Confederacy, Presidents have been usurping the Congress' constitutional authority and forcing the United States into horrendous wars which could, should, and would have been avoided if power had remained with the people.

The legislature was authorised to make whatever laws were 'necessary and proper' for the exercise of its constitutional powers. Alexander Hamilton and the Federalists, after lying about their intentions in order to trick the States into ratifying the Constitution, seized on this Necessary and Proper Clause with a 'design' to justify a sweeping array of powers never, ever considered by the men who framed and ratified the Constitution. For instance, in one of his *Federalist* essays in 1788, Hamilton claimed that the Necessary and Proper Clause pertained only to 'certain specified powers,' but in 1791, in a report to President George Washington, Hamilton claimed that the Necessary and Proper Clause pertained to 'implied powers,' too. Tucker countered that the 'plain import' of this clause was to affirm 'incidental or instrumental powers,' not serve as a 'pretext for an assumption of power not specified in the Constitution.' According to Tucker, 'It neither enlarges any power particularly granted, nor is a grant of new powers to Congress, but merely a declaration, for the removal of all uncertainty, that the means of carrying into execution those otherwise granted, are included in the grant.' Tucker gave two examples to illustrate the difference between necessary and proper powers and unnecessary and improper powers. In the first case, the President had the power to make treaties, and according to a treaty with Algiers, the United States were obligated to pay her annual tribute. The President, however, had no power to levy a tax to pay this tribute. It was 'necessary and proper,' therefore, for the Congress to execute the treaty by collecting the tax and making the appropriation. In the second case, infringing upon the right to bear arms for the purpose of preventing insurrection would not be 'necessary and proper,' as resorting to such a means would assume a power which was reserved by the States and expressly protected by the Second Amendment. 'This construction of the words "necessary and proper,"' concluded Tucker, 'is not only consonant with that which prevailed during the discussions and ratification of the Constitution, but is absolutely necessary to maintain their consistency with the peculiar character of the government, as possessed of particular and defined powers, only; not of general and indefinite powers vested in ordinary governments.' So long as men honoured their oaths of office and obeyed their conscience, Tucker believed that the Necessary and Proper Clause would actually be a 'powerful and immediate check' on the legislature. Without men of integrity, however, the clause would be perverted 'to destroy the effect of the particular enumeration of powers, by which it explains and limits them.' In other words, if the legislature were free to read 'implied powers' into that clause, then all constitutional limits on federal power would be essentially voided.

Today, men and women without any sense of honour or conscience controul the Congress, and accordingly, they recognise no limit on their power and acknowledge no loyalty to their constituents. Political parties controul the Congress and special interests and pressure groups controul the parties, the combined effect of which makes a mockery of representation.

Despite his belief in the virtues of the Constitution, Tucker was skeptical that any constitution could ever limit a government. 'All governments have a natural tendency towards an increase, and assumption of power,' observed Tucker, 'and the administration of the federal government has too frequently demonstrated that the people of America are not exempt from this vice in their Constitution.' Ultimately, Tucker believed that only the people could protect their lives, liberties, and property by holding the government to the Constitution. 'We have seen that parchment chains are not sufficient to correct this unhappy propensity,' admitted Tucker. 'They are, nevertheless, capable of producing the most salutary effects; for, when broken, they warn the people to change those perfidious agents, who dare to violate them.' Some priggish libertarians deride the Founding Fathers for supposedly falling for the fallacy that constitutions alone can limit government, without realising that they understood perfectly well that in the end, the people (or, more specifically, the States), were the ones who must turn parchment chains into power. This was what Randolph of Roanoke meant when he exclaimed that he had 'no faith in parchment ... no faith in the abracadabra of the Constitution,' but rather 'faith in the power of that Commonwealth [Virginia], of which I am an unworthy son.'

Tucker then examined all of the specific restrictions on legislative power in the Constitution and the Bill of Rights, a charter of traditional English liberties which Americans had seceded from the British Empire in order to protect and preserve for posterity.

The Congress could not suspend *habeas corpus* except for the sake of public safety during rebellion or invasion. According to Tucker, a writ of *habeas corpus* – by which a judge orders the government to bring a prisoner to court to determine whether his imprisonment is lawful – was 'the great and efficacious remedy provided for all cases of illegal confinement.' Just as *habeas corpus* could only be suspended in Great Britain by the Parliament – 'it has been done so several times of later years, both in England and in Ireland, to the great oppression of the subject,' noted Tucker – so *habeas corpus* in the United States could only be suspended by the Congress. Even then, the Congress' power to suspend *habeas corpus* was limited only to times of insurrection or invasion. If *habeas corpus* were suspended 'under any other circumstances, whatever might be the pretext,' Tucker held that such a suspension would be 'unconstitutional' and should be 'disregarded' by judges.

During the War of Southern Independence, President Abraham Lincoln unilaterally suspended *habeas corpus* in order to imprison anti-war dissidents, including journalists, elected officials, and other public figures. When Chief Justice Roger B. Taney did his duty as Tucker recommended, ruling against this executive usurpation and issuing a writ of *habeas corpus* for the political prisoner John Merryman (a pro-Confederate Marylander), the President refused to obey the Chief Justice and even considered having him arrested for treason.

To Tucker, the 'establishment clause' of the First Amendment preserved the separate integrity of church and state and prohibited the ancient union of throne and altar – nothing more, nothing less. Referring to the 'numberless martyrdoms and massacres which have drenched the whole earth, with blood, from the first moment that civil and religious institutions were blended together,' Tucker argued that 'to separate them by mounds which can never be overleaped, is the only means by which our duty to God, the peace of mankind, and the genuine fruits of charity and fraternal love, can be preserved.' The First Amendment, therefore, had nothing to do with banishing religious expression from the public square; its aim was to prevent the federal government from establishing the sort of government-supported churches as had been abolished in the South but remained in power in New England.

As the Internet makes it practically impossible to controul information, 'intelligence officials' distinguished for their unintelligence demand that the 'freedom of speech' clause of the First Amendment no longer apply to everyone – namely public watchdogs independent of the lapdog media who bring to light what they would rather keep in the dark. Fortunately for the freedom of speech, Tucker insisted that 'the right of the people to inquire into, censure, approve, punish or reward their agents according to their merit, or demerit ... by speaking, writing, printing, or by any other mode of publishing' was 'unlimited.' The free speech of the people and the freedom of the press were absolutely vital in a democratic republic. Indeed, Tucker described the freedom of speech as 'one of the great bulwarks of liberty,' only denied by 'despotic governments.'

Tucker praised the Second Amendment, which protected the right to bear arms, as 'the true palladium of liberty.' According to Tucker, self-defence was a natural right, violated only by governments for the consolidation of power over the people. 'The right of self-defence is the first law of nature,' asserted Tucker. 'In most governments it has been the study of rulers to confine this right within the narrowest limits possible.' More so than any other European people, the English were accustomed to bearing arms and serving in the militia, and in the American Colonies (where the constant threat of Indian raids and slave revolts made militia service mandatory), bearing arms became even more embedded in the culture than in the mother country. In England, the Stuart kings had attempted to disarm their subjects, and during the Revolutionary War, men like 'Colonel Tucker' resisted similar attempts to disarm the colonists. Both attempted disarmaments resulted in reaffirmations, in bills of rights, of the necessity of an armed populace for internal peace and external defence. Along those lines, in the *Federalist*, James Madison described how a State, with her armed militias, 'forms a barrier against the enterprises of ambition, more insurmountable than any which a simple government of any form [i.e. a single national government] can admit of.' Tucker continued to explain that the combination of a standing army (a permanent military of professional soldiers) and popular disarmament would leave the people powerless and defenceless in the event of emergencies. 'Wherever standing armies are kept up, and the right of the people to keep and bear arms is, under any colour or pretext whatsoever, prohibited,' warned Tucker, 'liberty, if not already annihilated, is on the brink of destruction.' Tucker preferred the Anglo-

American tradition of the militia (a temporary military of civilian-soldiers) to a standing army (a permanent military of professional soldiers), holding that the former would be loyal to the people while the latter would be loyal to the government. Virginia had hailed the militia in her Declaration of Rights as 'the proper, safe, and natural defence of a free State,' noted Tucker, and even the United States had upheld the militia in their Second Amendment as 'necessary to the security of a free State.' In modern militaristic America, however, the standing army has become a symbol of freedom rather than a symbol of despotism. Perhaps such a militia is no longer realistic today, but the United States can come close to this original ideal by scaling back their foreign entanglements and shoring up safety and freedom in their homeland.

According to Tucker, the Fourth Amendment's protection against 'searches and seizures' without a warrant was a right which 'cannot be too highly valued by a free people.' Tucker defined Anglo-American jurisprudence (or, as he put it, the 'principles of the only preventive justice known to American jurisprudence') to be the rights of *habeas corpus* (i.e. 'you may have the body,' meaning 'the body of law' preventing arbitrary arrest and imprisonment). Tucker continued with the Fifth and Sixth Amendments, which made many key civil liberties, such as due process of law and the 'inestimable' right of a jury trial, 'a fundamental law of the government of the United States.'

These protections of civil liberties were thoroughly English in their origin, in some cases dating back to 1689 and the *Declaration of Right* or even 1215 and the *Magna Carta Libertatum*. Indeed, although it is popular to view the Founding Fathers as historically transcendent figures, it is impossible to understand them, and the revolutionary events from 1763 to 1789, without also understanding their fundamentally conservative English heritage and identity. Far from enlightened lawgivers philosophising about the role of government and divining new universal truths, the Founders, virtually all of whom were 'White Anglo-Saxon Protestants,' had inherited a constitutional order which they adapted to their time and place – an order which included traditions and institutions such as representative government, mixed government, limited government, and republican government. Well-aware that their revolutionary and constitutional principles derived at least as much from the customs and charters of their age-old Anglo-Saxon ancestors as the salons of the Enlightenment, the Founders declared independence because the British government had refused to respect those ancestral rights, and afterwards established a constitution and bill of rights modeled after those of the English. Even Thomas Jefferson, one of the most Enlightenment-influenced and Anglophobic Founders, described American ideas of government as 'more peculiar than those of any other nation in the universe ... a composition of the freest principles of the English Constitution, with others derived from natural reason.'

Since all federal powers were 'either expressly enumerated, or necessary and proper to the execution of some enumerated power,' the Ninth Amendment, which held that the enumeration of particular rights in the Constitution should not be construed to deny any of the other unenumerated rights reserved by the people, thereby required that 'every power which concerns the right of the citizen, must be construed strictly, where it may operate to infringe or impair his liberty; and liberally, and for his benefit, where it may operate to his security and happiness, the avowed object of the Constitution.' Tucker continued that the Tenth Amendment likewise required that the benefit of the doubt be given to the rights of the States, which were the source of the unenumerated rights in the Ninth Amendment. 'Every power which has been carved out of the States,' explained Tucker, 'who, at the time of entering the confederacy, were in full possession of all the rights of sovereignty, is in like manner to be construed strictly, whenever a different construction might derogate from the rights and powers, which by [the Tenth Amendment] are expressly acknowledged to be reserved to them respectively.' Together, the Ninth and Tenth Amendments not only overcame the Federalists' objection that a bill of rights would be 'unnecessary' and 'dangerous,' but also, more than anything else in the Constitution, established the division of power between the States and the federal government. 'To preserve the liberty, and to promote the happiness of the people of the United States,' explained Tucker, the States delegated to the federal government power over 'objects which relate only to the common interests of the States, as composing one general confederacy,' and reserved to themselves power over 'whatever may affect, or promote its domestic peace, happiness, or prosperity.' Although the Constitution placed checks and balances on the federal government, the strongest safeguards of the 'great and essential rights of the people' were States' rights.

Unlike the other amendments, which guaranteed traditional English rights and liberties, these guarantees of conservative constructionism and small-f federalism were thoroughly American in their origin. Given that disputes between the former Colonies and the Parliament over constitutional gray areas had recently resulted in a revolution, the American Constitution was much more black and white than the English.

After completing his analysis of the legislature (by far the most powerful and prestigious branch of the federal government), Tucker proceeded to the executive. The modern chief executive – a trumped-up 'leader of the free world,' swaggering celebrity, busybody, and bully ramming through laws at home and picking fights abroad – bears no resemblance to Tucker's humble magistrate. In fact, Tucker denied that the executive had any 'powers' of his own, instead preferring to call them 'duties.' The executive, as the servant of the legislature, had the duty to uphold the law, serve as commander-in-chief in times of duly declared war, and make treaties and various appointments with the approval of the Senate. Aside from issuing pardons, the executive had very little authority of his own outside of wartime. Tucker, however, still suspected that this was too much power for one man, and personally favoured a Senatorial committee of executives drawn from different sections of the country – a proposal drawn from classical antiquity which the South-Carolinian statesman John C. Calhoun would later revive. Tucker preferred the self-possessed President Thomas Jefferson (who traveled about Washington, D.C. on foot, delivered addresses to the Congress in writing in order to avoid the English custom of the Crown dictating to the Parliament, lived peacefully among two-hundred slaves, and practiced country manners at official events) to the self-absorbed President Adams (who rode about the capital in a carriage, fortified his home in fear of mobs, and insisted on English-style courtly manners at official events).

Last, but not least, Tucker finished his commentaries with the judiciary. Tucker had great confidence in the 'calm, temperate, upright, and independent' federal judiciary as 'a necessary check upon the encroachments, or usurpations' from the legislature or executive. According to Tucker, the secure tenures of judges ensured their independence, freeing them from the 'sword' of the executive or the 'purse' of the legislature. The jurisdiction of the judiciary covered all cases arising under the Constitution or federal law, but Tucker was not opposed to the idea of 'judicial review,' either. 'If the legislature should pass a law dangerous to the liberties of the people,' held Tucker, 'the judiciary are bound to pronounce, not only whether the party accused hath been guilty of any violation of it, but whether such a law be permitted by the Constitution.' Tucker certainly did not envision the Supreme Court as a judicial oligarchy legislating from the bench – the unelected, unaccountable nine-man legislature that it is today – but as a guardian of the Constitution striking down federal usurpations of power.

Tucker's view of the Supreme Court mirrored that of Thomas Jefferson, who at the dawn of the American republic believed that the judiciary was 'a body, which if rendered independent, and kept strictly to their own department merits great confidence for their learning and integrity,' yet had come to fear the judiciary by the twilight of his life, warning that 'the power of declaring what the law is, *ad libitum* [i.e. at one's pleasure], sapping and mining, slyly, and without alarm, the foundations of the Constitution, can do what open force would not dare to attempt.'

Tucker trusted the judiciary to rule on the constitutionality of federal law, a responsibility which he regarded as a 'bulwark provided against undue extension of the legislative power.' Like Thomas Jefferson and James Madison, however, Tucker objected to the absurdity of trusting the federal government to be the sole judge of the extent of its own powers. In the Southern political tradition, a single authority could not hold sole power; power must be divided and decentralised. Tucker endorsed the right of the States to interpret the Constitution for themselves and 'interpose' between their citizens and federal government when all checks and balances in the federal government failed them, specifically citing Madison's *Virginia Resolutions* and the 'Principles '98.' 'In case of a deliberate, palpable, and dangerous exercise of other powers, not granted by that compact,' argued Tucker, quoting the *Resolutions*, 'the States, who are parties thereto, have the right, and are in duty bound, to interpose, for arresting the progress of the evil, and for maintaining within their respective limits, the authorities, rights, and liberties appertaining to them.' Virginia, Tucker continued to quote from the *Resolutions*, 'protested against the palpable, and alarming infractions of the Constitution...and which, by uniting legislative and judicial powers to those of executive, subverts the general principles of a free government, as well as the particular organisation, and positive provisions of the Federal Constitution.' In other words, if the checks and balances within the federal government ever failed to protect the States from unconstitutional usurpations of power, then the States, as the sovereign parties to the Constitution, were entitled and obligated to protect their rights on their own.

As Thomas Jefferson urged, 'If the Congress fails to shield the States from dangers so palplable and imminent, the States must shield themselves and meet the invader foot to foot.'

Tucker acknowledged that the Supremacy Clause of the Constitution seemed to consolidate all authority in the federal government, reducing the States to its subjects, but he clarified that the clause only applied to laws which were constitutional, not just any law passed by the Congress and signed by the President. 'A law limited to such objects as may be authorised by the Constitution, would, under the construction of this clause, be the supreme law of the land,' explained Tucker, 'but a law not limited to those objects, or not made pursuant to the Constitution, would not be the supreme law of the land, but an act of usurpation, and consequently void.' Tucker doubted that the 'positive, enumerated, defined, and limited' powers of the federal government, pertaining mainly to war and peace, could ever collide with the negative, unenumerated, indefinite, and unlimited powers of the States, pertaining mainly to 'domestic concerns.' Tucker reiterated his confidence that the Tenth Amendment made this division of delegated federal powers and reserved State powers clear. Of course, nowadays, old expressions like 'don't make a federal case out of it' and 'it's a free country,' which Tucker would have appreciated, are now meaningless – everything is now a federal case and it is no longer a free country!

Tucker closed his commentary with a call for constructive criticism of the Constitution. 'Attached from principle, and confirmed in that attachment from past experience, to a *federal* union of the American States, and to the principles of a democratic government,' Tucker admitted of his own biases, 'I have probably regarded with a jealous eye those parts of the Constitution which seem to savor of monarchy or aristocracy, or tend to a consolidated, instead of a federal union of the States.' In the eighteenth century, of course, 'jealousy' did not mean 'envy,' but rather 'suspicion.' John Dickinson, the famed 'Pennsylvania Farmer' renowned as the 'Penman of the Revolution,' defined 'jealousy' in his famous essays against the Townshend Acts: 'That every free State should incessantly watch, and instantly take alarm on any addition being made to the power exercised over them.' Charles Carroll of Carrollton, the Catholic Marylander hailed as an 'American Cicero' and the 'Last of the Romans,' argued that the English Constitution, which served as the model for the American, was 'founded on jealousy and suspicion,' and defined those terms as 'the most watchful care and strictest vigilance.'

Tucker explained that unlike the *Federalist*, which although an 'elaborate and masterly discussion of the Constitution,' were pamphlets arguing for the ratification (and thus did not address its 'defects' with the 'equal candour' with which it addressed its 'eminent advantages'), he was committed to fully discussing 'excellencies' and 'defects' of the Constitution. 'A sincere attachment to the former will always lead an ingenuous mind to a candid investigation, and correction of the latter,' quipped Tucker. 'To shut our eyes against this inestimable advantage which we possess, beyond any other nation in the universe, would be an unpardonable act of ingratitude to that divine being, under whose providence we have accomplished the great work of our independence, and the establishment of free government, in every State, and a Union of the whole upon such a solid foundation, as nothing but our own folly, or wickedness, can undermine.'

III

In supporting the doctrine of State' rights in his writings, teachings, and rulings, St. George Tucker was not merely reinterpreting the Constitution in order to defend slavery. Instead, he was, in the fashion of Blackstone, systematising and codifying what was already understood and accepted about the Constitution when it was framed in Philadelphia and ratified in Richmond. Indeed, the doctrine of States' rights was not Tucker's mere theory or opinion, but a plain historical fact. That self-evident truth was why Tucker quoted extensively from primary sources such as the *Federalist* essays, the records of Virginia's Ratification Convention, and the *Virginia Resolutions*. Indeed, quoting James Madison's *Report on the Virginia Resolutions*, Tucker insisted that 'the construction which prevailed during the discussions and ratifications of the Constitution' was 'absolutely necessary to maintain their consistency with the peculiar character of the government, as possessed of particular and definite powers only, not of the general and indefinite powers vested in ordinary governments.'

121

James Madison, one of the chief Federalists behind the Constitutional Convention, returned home to Virginia from Philadelphia in disappointment, having desired a supreme national government with plenary authority and the power to overrule State laws, but instead receiving a limited federation of sovereign States with enumerated powers. A man of integrity, however, Madison resolved to present the Constitution as it was, not the Constitution as he wanted. In New York City, Madison had honed his case for the new Constitution in his *Federalist* essays with Alexander Hamilton – who was, by contrast with Madison, a scoundrel perfectly willing to make promises about the Constitution he had no intention of keeping. According to Madison, the General Welfare Clause did not contain any implied powers beyond those enumerated. 'For what purpose could the enumeration of particular powers be inserted, if these and all others were meant to be included in the preceding general power?' asked Madison. The Necessary and Proper Clause only authorised the Congress to take common-sense measures to enact its enumerated powers into law; it did not authorise any powers which were not enumerated. 'No part of the power is unnecessary or improper for accomplishing the necessary objects of the Union,' explained Madison. In the event of any 'ambitious encroachments of the federal government on the authority of the State governments,' the States would make 'common cause' and 'repel the danger,' even if it meant 'a trial of force.' Sensitive to States' vigilance for their rights, Madison maintained that while powers of the federal government would be 'few and defined,' those of the States would remain 'numerous and indefinite.' Furthermore, Madison assured that the States would not sacrifice their sovereignty in ratifying the Constitution and that the Union would be consensual rather than coercive. 'Each State,' maintained Madison, 'ratifying the Constitution, is considered a sovereign body, separate of others, and only to be bound by its own voluntary act.'

Madison had heard from fellow Federalists in Virginia that his essays' 'greatness is acknowledged generally' and had influenced several prominent

Virginians to change their minds. Nevertheless, the road to ratification in Richmond was rough; the political elite was divided on the issue, with the venerable George Mason and the legendary Patrick Henry leading the conservative opposition, known as 'Anti-Federalists' (who were, indeed, against the big-f Federalists, but not against small-f federalism). Mason, who had attended the Constitutional Convention, had come home early in protest, declaring, 'I would rather chop off my right hand than put it to the Constitution as it now stands.' Henry, although elected to the Convention, had declined to attend, exclaiming, 'I smelt a rat!' The Anti-Federalists feared that the powers delegated to the new government were too open to interpretation and prone to abuse, and would ultimately lead to a consolidated, Northern-controulled national government usurping the rights of the States and oppressing the South. As the largest and most prestigious State, Virginia's course of action would determine the fate of the Constitution.

Virginia's Convention opened on 2 June 1788, and continued to meet six days a week until 27 June. After some formalities, Henry and Mason opened fire against the Federalists. 'What right had they to say, *We, the People?*' demanded Henry. 'Who authorised them to speak the language of, *We, the People*, instead of *We, the States?*' According to Henry, 'If the States be not the agents of this compact, it must be one great consolidated national government of the people of all the States.' Henry argued that the Constitution sacrificed the liberty won in the American Revolution for money and power. 'When the American spirit was in its youth, the language of America was different: liberty, sir, was then the primary object,' cried Henry. 'But now, sir, the American spirit, assisted by the ropes and chains of consolidation, is about to convert this country into a powerful and mighty empire.' Mason warned that the new government would be 'paramount to, and in every respect more powerful than, the State governments,' and thus would eventually 'annihilate totally' the States. 'Is it to be supposed that one national government will suit so extensive a country, embracing so many climates, and containing inhabitants so very different in manners, habits and customs?' asked Mason. 'It is ascertained by history, that there never was a government, over a very extensive country, without destroying the liberties of the people.' According to Mason, 'The very idea of converting what was formerly a confederation, to a consolidated government, is totally subversive of every principle which has hitherto governed us.'

After Mason and Henry's opening salvo, the Federalists countered that the rights of the States would be respected under the Constitution. Madison answered that 'We, the People' meant 'not the people as composing one great body, but the people as composing thirteen sovereignties,' that the federal government would only have 'legislative powers on defined and limited objects, beyond which it cannot extend its jurisdiction,' that the States would remain the people's source of 'political existence,' and that 'the patriotism of the people' would be 'a sufficient guard to their liberties.' Noting the absence of a bill of rights, Henry reminded the Convention that the 'implication' of American rights in the British Empire was the 'source of dissension' which resulted in revolution. Henry insisted that a bill of rights was 'indispensably necessary,' particularly 'a general positive provision ... securing to the States and the people, every right which was not conceded to the general government.' Challenging Henry, 'Light Horse' Henry Lee III (hero of the American Revolution and father of future Confederate hero Robert E. Lee), asserted 'the principle that all power is in the people, and that rulers have no powers but what are enumerated in that paper.' Whenever the constitutionality of a power was disputed, Lee claimed that the solution was simple: 'Is it enumerated in the Constitution? If it be, it is legal and just. It is otherwise arbitrary and unconstitutional.' Regarding a bill of rights, Lee held that since the federal government would only possess 'certain defined powers,' the proposal was 'folly.' Edmund Randolph (the Governor of Virginia and a framer in Philadelphia), concurred with Lee, explaining that 'every power not given by this system is left with the States.' According to Randolph, the best limit on the federal government was 'the express enumeration of its powers,' not a bill of rights. To illustrate the intention of the Necessary and Proper Clause, another Federalist, George Nicholas, asked that if such a clause followed each enumerated power – 'that they should have the power to make laws to carry that power into execution' – whether that would amount to any implied powers. 'This clause only enables them to carry into execution the powers given them, but gives them no additional power,' Nicholas concluded. Nicholas also rejected the idea of a bill of rights, arguing that if a 'disputed right' were not 'enumerated,' then 'Congress cannot meddle with it.' When Nicholas speculated that political dominance in the Union would eventually shift from the North to the South, Mason exclaimed, 'A very sound argument indeed, that we should cheerfully burn ourselves to death in hopes of a joyful and happy resurrection!' Mason requested amendments 'as will point out what powers are reserved to the State governments, and clearly discriminate between them, and those which are given the general government, so as to prevent future disputes and clashing of interests.' Madison elaborated that the federal government's powers would concern 'external objects' such as war and peace, but that the States would keep for themselves 'those great objects which immediately concern the prosperity of the people.' John Marshall, future Chief Justice of the Supreme Court, denied that the federal government would have 'power to make laws on every subject' and 'go beyond the delegated powers.' According to Marshall, 'If they were to make a law not warranted by any of the powers enumerated, it would be considered by the judges an infringement of the Constitution which they are to guard [and] they would declare it void.' In sum, the Federalists, confident that the Constitution would always be conservatively construed, believed that the rights of the States and the interests of their section were implicitly protected, but the Anti-Federalists, suspecting that the Constitution would not always be conservatively construed, warned that the rights of the States and the interests of their section should be explicitly protected.

After much debate, Nicholas suggested that the Anti-Federalists' concerns about what Henry denounced as a constitution 'incompatible with the genius of republicanism...no checks, no balances,' be guarded against in Virginia's instrument of ratification. Instead of simply voting 'aye' or 'nay' on the Constitution itself, the delegates would vote on a resolution holding 'that every power not granted thereby, remained at their will.' According to Nicholas, just as thirteen men entering into a contract would be bound by a single man's declaration 'that he understands its meaning, signification, and intent to be, what the words of the contract plainly and obviously denote; that it is not to be construed so as to impose any supplementary condition upon him, and that he is to be exonerated from it, whensoever any such imposition shall be attempted,' so would a similar declaration from Virginia be 'binding' on the other twelve States and the new government which they were creating. Madison preferred this 'general negation' over a bill of rights, which he considered 'unnecessary' and 'dangerous.' Randolph had 'no objection,' either, noting that 'as this style of ratification would manifest the principles on which Virginia adopted it, we should be at liberty to consider as a violation of the Constitution, every exercise of power not expressly delegated therein.' Even with Nicholas' compromise, however, the Virginians only narrowly ratified the Constitution 89 to 79.

'We the delegates of the people of Virginia,' read Nicholas' act of ratification, 'do in the name and on behalf of the people of Virginia, declare and make known that the powers granted under the Constitution, being derived from the people of the United States, may be resumed by them whensoever the same shall be perverted to their injury or oppression, and that every power not granted thereby remains with them and at their will.' The Virginians also attached a bill of rights and a number of recommended amendments to their act of ratification, the first of which asserted, 'That each State in the Union shall respectively retain every power, jurisdiction, and right which is not by this Constitution delegated.' According to historian Kevin R.C. Gutzman, this instrument of ratification, with its reservation of

State sovereignty and recommendation of amendments, was soon 'elevated by Virginia's moderate Federalists and [Democratic-] Republicans alike to the position of the Rosetta Stone of American constitutionalism, the first article of the Jeffersonian republican faith.'

By 1861, after the national consolidation and sectional conflict which the Anti-Federalists had prophesied came to a crossroads, a new generation of Virginians assembled at another convention in Richmond to debate secession from the Union to which their forebears had acceded. Earlier, Virginia had taken the lead in the pursuit of compromise between the North and the South, calling upon her sister States to hold a Peace Convention in Washington, D.C., just as she had called upon them to hold a Constitutional Convention in 1787. Even when the Peace Convention failed to find a compromise which the Republican Party would accept, the Secession Convention still voted against a resolution for 'an ordinance resuming the powers delegated by Virginia to the federal government.' At the same time, however, the Secession Convention adopted other resolutions declaring that Virginia shared the grievances of the South against the North, asserting the right of the States to secede from the Union, and opposing war on the Confederacy. Drawing from their Ratification Convention, the Virginians maintained that when the States adopted the Constitution, they did so as 'independent sovereignties,' and thus it was the 'duty' of the federal government to 'respect the rights of the States and the equality of the people thereof.' Next drawing from the Declaration of Independence, the Virginians recognised 'the American principle that government is founded in the consent of the governed [and] the right of the people of the several States of this Union, for just causes, to withdraw from their association under the federal government with the people of the other States, and to erect new governments for their better security,' and, accordingly, refused to agree to anything 'for the purpose of subjugating the people of such States to the federal authority.' The Virginians hoped that 'an adjustment may be reached by which the Union may be preserved in its integrity,' but in the meantime expected a 'pacific policy' toward the Confederacy – specifically, that no provocations would be made under the pretext of reinforcing the forts or collecting the tariff. The Virginians warned that any attempt by the federal government to start a war would be regarded as 'aggressive and injurious to the interests and offensive to the honour of this Commonwealth.'

When President Abraham Lincoln, under the very pretexts of reinforcing the forts and collecting the tariff which the Secession Convention had suspected, successfully provoked the Confederacy into firing the first shot at Fort Sumter, Virginia erupted with a fervour for Southern independence. When news of the battle reached Richmond, an artillery battery fired a hundred-gun salute and a crowd at the capital building lowered the Stars and Stripes and raised the Stars and Bars. Despite this patriotic ardour, it was Lincoln's unilateral declaration of war on the Confederacy and calling of troops for an invasion which was the final cut, convincing the Virginians that the Union could no longer be saved and that secession was their only hope. 'Your object is to subjugate the Southern States, and a requisition made upon me for such an object – an object, in my judgment, not within the purview of the Constitution or the Act of 1795 – will not be complied with,' a shocked John Letcher, Virginia's Governor, replied to the War Department. 'You have chosen to inaugurate civil war, and having done so, we will meet it in a spirit as determined as the administration has exhibited towards the South.' Two days after Lincoln's proclamation, Virginia's Secession Convention, which had previously voted decisively against secession 45 to 88, now voted decisively for secession 88 to 55 – an act which was then decisively approved in a popular referendum, 132,201 to 37,451. According to the act of secession, Virginia would 'repeal the ratification of the Constitution' and 'resume all the rights and powers granted under the Constitution.' In their act of secession, the Virginians recalled the terms of their act of ratification: 'That the powers granted under the said Constitution, were derived from the people of the United States, and might be resumed whensoever the same should be perverted to their injury and oppression.' The federal government, averred the Virginians, had indeed 'perverted said powers, not only to the injury of the people of Virginia, but to the oppression of the Southern slave-holding States.'

Following in their fathers' footsteps, the sons of Washington, Jefferson, Henry, Mason, and Lee declared 'liberty or death,' and pledged 'their lives, their fortunes, and their sacred honour' to the cause of independence. Shortly after the final vote, John Tyler, Jr. (a former President and delegate to the Secession Convention whose father had been an Anti-Federalist at the Ratification Convention and whose son would carry the colours of his regiment at Gettysburg), gave a triumphant speech reviewing 'all the struggles of our race for freedom, from *Magna Carta* to the present day,' avowing that 'at no period in our history were we engaged in a more just and holy effort for the maintenance of liberty and independence,' and pledging that if Virginians continued to do their Christian and patriotic duty, then 'the same benign Providence which favoured the cause of our forefathers in the Revolution of 1776, would again crown our efforts with similar success.' Thus, Virginia left the Union freely, just as she had first entered, but when she returned, it was by force – a fate which Tucker, the Judge of Jeffersonian democracy, never imagined in his darkest dreams.

III. John Taylor of Caroline & *Construction Construed and Constitutions Vindicated*

If the Constitution is an opaque body, the United States whilst groping about in the dark, will be as likely to stumble upon the witch – despotism – as the goddess – liberty. In one instance, however, it is luminous. As its own existence depended upon the Union, so the preservation of the Union, must have been the first object of its care. On which side of the question ought a federal construction to make its effort? One roots the fraternity of the States in the immutable principles of justice. The other commits it to the animosities of partiality, and the fluctuations of expedient. One removes, the other nurtures the causes of civil dissension. Can a construction be true, which is founded in immorality – engenders corruption – fosters political hatred – weakens the Constitution in its most essential principle, and endangers the Union itself? As a political and constitutional principle, which all republicans admit to be orthodox and fundamental, is the basis of my construction, it seems to be founded on a rock.
– John Taylor of Caroline, 1795

STATES' RIGHTS MAY HAVE BEEN what Thomas Jefferson called 'the foundation of the Constitution' as well as a 'check' and 'counterpoise' to the 'engulfing power' of consolidated government, and what James Madison called 'sure guardians of the people's liberty,' but modern, mainstream historians would have you believe that this constitutional doctrine was nothing more than a wicked creed cooked up by a few corrupt slave-holders.

For instance, a review of *The Liberal Republicanism of John Taylor of Caroline*, an intellectual biography, refers to Taylor's 'opprobrium' as the 'premier states' rights philosopher.' It would have been news to Taylor, who wrote brilliant books and pamphlets on everything from the Constitutional Convention to the rulings of the Supreme Court, that there was any opprobrium to such a title. According to Bertram Wyatt-Brown, a historian from the University of Florida who delights in deconstructing 'Southern honor,' States' rights were merely the 'rationale' with which the South 'presented' her 'paramount' interest – slavery. 'Enough has been said about states' rights to require no elaboration here,' sniffs this past president of the Southern Historical Association and St. George Tucker Society.

This essay series aims to set the story straight. The truth is that the great political treatises of the Old South prove that the constitutional doctrine of States' rights was never a mere pretence for slavery, but reflected a deep passion for self-government rooted in Southern culture as well as an earnest understanding of the Constitution rooted in Southern history. According to the scholarly, gentlemanly M.E. Bradford, States' rights were part of a Southern political tradition – a 'patrimony' and 'birthright' – dating from the foundation of the Colonies, through the independence of the States, and to the creation of the Constitution. At the crowning of the Confederate capital in Richmond, President Jefferson Davis honoured this heritage. 'The cause in which we are now engaged is the cause of the advocacy of the rights to which we were born, those for which our fathers of the Revolution bled – the richest inheritance that ever fell to man, and which it is our sacred duty to transmit untarnished to our children,' announced Davis. 'Upon us is devolved the high and holy responsibility of preserving the constitutional liberty of a free government.'

John Taylor of Caroline and his book, *Construction Construed and Constitutions Vindicated*, published in 1820, are the subjects of this essay.

I

John Taylor was born on 19 December 1753, in Caroline County, Virginia. His father died at a young age, and his widowed mother sent him to live with his uncle, the self-made jurist Edmund Pendleton. Taylor started his education at a small school with other future Virginia leaders like James Madison. Taylor graduated from the College of William and Mary in 1770, at a time when the faculty was bitterly divided between Whigs and Tories over the American Colonies' conflict with Great Britain. Taylor studied law under Pendleton, one of the finest legal mentors in all of Virginia, and began practicing in 1774. Pendleton was also an active figure in Virginia politics, and when he was elected to the Continental Congress in 1775, he brought Taylor with him to Philadelphia. News of the Battle of Lexington and Concord gripped the Congress, and Taylor repeated stories of the British 'plundering and laying waste to the country,' the 'utmost humanity and tenderness' of the Americans to the wounded British, and all that the Americans were doing 'in defence of LIBERTY.'

Taylor was a veteran of the American Revolution, serving intermittently from 1775 to 1781. Although Taylor began as a quartermaster, he took part in the effort to overthrow the British government in Virginia and in the recapture of the Tory hotbed of Norfolk. In 1776, thanks to Pendleton's influence, Taylor was appointed judge advocate of the Virginian troops in the Continental Army and major of a regiment known as 'Congress' Own.' To outfit himself for the war, Taylor sold his patrimony in exchange for soon-to-be-worthless paper money and headed north to the front, where he would remain for three long, hard years. There, Taylor fought in the botched Battle of Staten Island, the bloody Battle of Brandywine Creek, and joined in the 'chimerical' Canadian campaign. Taylor deplored the corruption of the Continental Congress, '(except those from Virginia), a set of rude, covetous, ignorant, selfish rabble,' as well as the Continental Army, 'a collection of naked, undisciplined bandits, and the officers (except General Washington), poor, cowardly mechanics.' According to Taylor, the soldiers were either

133

'mercenaries' from New England, 'Tories' from the Middle States, or 'undisciplined' Southerners. 'Hope for the best, but at the same time fear for the worst,' admitted Taylor. 'I wish, I wish from my soul we had more Virginias than one, but as we have not, the honour of preserving America must be acquired by one alone.' Taylor was disillusioned with the army, but not the cause. 'As long as I am in the army and there is a possibility of battle,' Taylor wrote home, 'I will be ready to give my assistance.' Eventually, however, over General Washington's protests, Taylor resigned and returned to Virginia.

In 1779, Taylor resumed his law practice and was elected to the House of Delegates. Taylor prepared Virginia for war by forming the Board of War (an executive council which assisted the Governor) and reorganising her militia, in which he himself was elected a lieutenant colonel. Taylor and his legion of militiamen mustered into service in the spring of 1781, just as Lord Cornwallis was invading Virginia. Under the command of the Marquis de Lafayette, Taylor scouted and skirmished with the hated Hessians (German mercenaries infamous for their brutality) in the weeks leading up to Cornwallis' surrender at Yorktown. In addition to preparing Virginia for war and serving in the war himself, Taylor authored a remonstrance to the Congress condemning the North for abandoning the South to the British after the South had fought to free the North. 'We accompanied our Northern allies during almost every progressive stride it made, where danger seemed to solicit our ardour,' Taylor fumed, 'but when we came to look for our Northern allies, after we had thus exhausted our powers in their defence...they were not to be found.' Taylor pointed out that Georgia, South Carolina, North Carolina, and Maryland had fallen, and that Virginia alone stood against the British in the South. While Virginia 'impoverished by defending the Northern department, exhausted by the Southern war, now finds the whole weight of it on her shoulders,' the North was seeking economic relief from the Continental Congress. Taylor called on the North to do her duty, and fortunately, the Continental Army (along with the

French) did eventually save the day. Even then, Southerners like Taylor noticed that there were no Northern regiments among the Continentals.

Taylor strengthened Virginia for the sake of the war effort, but was against strengthening the Continental Congress (not wanting more of the misrule he witnessed in the Continental Army) and resisted a constitutional amendment to allow the Congress to levy tariffs as well as any infringement upon Virginia's vast western territory. 'Should Congress assume a jurisdiction, and arrogate to themselves a right of adjudication, not only unwarranted by, but expressly contrary to the fundamental principles of the Confederation, superseding or controulling the internal policy, civil regulations, and municipal laws of this, or any other State,' read a remonstrance which Taylor signed, 'it would be a violation of public faith, introduce a most dangerous precedent, which might hereafter be urged to deprive of territory or subvert the sovereignty and government of any one or more of the United States, and establish in Congress a power which, in process of time, must degenerate into an intolerable despotism.' Naturally, then, in 1788, Taylor was an Anti-Federalist, opposed to the proposed Constitution without amendments safeguarding civil liberties and the rights of the States. Taylor might have even been elected to Virginia's Ratification Convention (where he could have voiced his objections alongside his friend, fellow Revolutionary-War veteran, and future President James Monroe), but declined due to the fact that he would have to campaign for election against his brother. 'He had objections to the Federal Constitution, as who had not?' summarised Edmund Pendleton, who was a Federalist himself. 'But when ratified, he has ever considered it as fixing a rule of conduct to the whole society, governors and governed; and holds it to be a sacred duty in himself and every other citizen to watch over and guard it from violations by their several agents in the administration: being wisely hostile to the project of one general consolidated government for the whole United States, he has been particularly attentive to the strides of the federal government, which encroached upon the reserved rights of the State governments, and tended to their annihilation.'

Taylor's law practice became one of the most successful in Virginia. Along with the land grants he received for his military service, Taylor plowed the profits from his practice into Virginia and Kentucky soil, establishing himself as a great planter. He and his wife, Lucy Penn (a daughter of John Penn, a North-Carolinian signer of the Declaration of Independence), lived at Hazelwood, a plantation along the Rappahannock River, with about 3,000 acres and 150 slaves. Taylor loved to entertain, and hosted company in fine, warm fashion – authentic Southern hospitality. As a lawyer, Taylor sparred with the likes of Edmund Randolph (the future first Attorney General) and John Marshall (the future Chief Justice of the Supreme Court). Taylor's most famous case, however, was *Hylton v. United States* (1796), the first time the constitutionality of a federal law was challenged before the Supreme Court. Alexander Hamilton (the evil genius of the Federalist Party) represented the government in the case. Taylor argued that the carriage tax was unconstitutional, as it was a direct rather than an indirect tax, and therefore must be apportioned among the States. 'If without apportionment among the States, by the rule of the census, Congress can tax the drink, the food, the clothing and all necessaries, raised or kept by individuals for their own ease and subsistence, without limitation, is there any real restriction on their power of taxation?' asked Taylor. The Constitution's requirement that direct taxes be apportioned among the States, just as indirect taxes be uniform among the States, was meant to preserve the 'equality' of the States. Once the burdens and benefits of the Union became unequal among the States, and the 'government of equality' became one of 'aristocracy,' then the Union would divide and dissolve. 'If oppressed,' predicted Taylor, 'States will combine – the grand divisions of Northern and Southern will retaliate as majorities or ministers fluctuate – and a retaliation between nations, invariably ends in a catastrophe.' Indeed, Taylor stressed that if the Congress could overrule the Constitution, then 'democratic republicanism' was dead.

Taylor mocked the 'political catechumen' of his opponents: 'What is the Constitution? "A majority of Congress." What is federalism? "Passive obedience to that majority." What is Union? "Unequal taxation." What is an energetic government? "A standing army." What is good order? "Tactics."' Taylor lost the case, but history would prove his point.

Once the Constitution was ratified and the new federal government inaugurated, Alexander Hamilton, President George Washington's ambitious and arrogant Treasury Secretary, began pushing a financial programme which Southerners like Taylor found antithetical to their liberal-republican philosophy and adverse to their agrarian way of life. The federal government would assume the States' wartime debts, levy excise taxes (such as the carriage tax) to pay the assumed debts, incorporate a national bank to loan the government money, and subsidise domestic industries. The Southern States, however (and especially Virginia), had already paid most of their debts, and the financiers who would own the bank were centered in the North, meaning that the burdens of Hamilton's system would fall on the South and the benefits on the North. In 1790, Patrick Henry, in the tradition of his *Stamp Act Resolves* – a tradition which would be continued by Thomas Jefferson and James Madison in 1798 – introduced a resolution to the General Assembly declaring Hamilton's plan for the nationalisation of the States' debts 'repugnant to the Constitution, as it goes to the exercise of power not *expressly* granted to the general government.' After adopting Henry's Revolutionary-style resolution, the General Assembly adopted a memorial comparing Hamilton's economic policies to British mercantilism. 'In an agricultural country like this,' protested the Virginians, 'to erect, and concentrate, and perpetuate, a large monied interest in opposition to the landed interest, is a measure which [we] apprehend must, in the course of human events, produce one or other of two evils: the prostration of agriculture at the feet of commerce, or a change in the present form of federal government fatal to the existence of American liberty.' Thus, when Taylor was elected to replace the retiring Senator Richard Henry Lee in 1793, he was determined to defend Virginia and defeat Hamilton. Taylor authored two pamphlets, *An Enquiry into the Principles and Tendency of Certain Public Measures* and *Definition of Parties or the Political Effects of the Paper System Considered*, exposing the unconstitutionality and corruption of what Taylor labeled Hamilton's 'plot.' The two foremost Virginians in the new government, Jefferson and Madison, who were sowing the seeds of opposition to the Federalist Party, had Taylor's pamphlets published and distributed. According to Taylor, the national bank would inflate the currency by loaning paper money to the federal government, thus creating a national debt, and to repay this debt to the bank the government would have to levy new taxes, thus saddling the people with a perpetual cycle of inflation, debt, and taxes. Taylor warned that 'a design for erecting aristocracy and monarchy, is subsisting – that a *money impulse*, and not the *public good*, is operating on Congress; and that taxes are imposed upon motives, other than the general welfare.' Taylor pointed out that the Congress not only had no power to establish a national bank, but also no power to print money – only to coin money. In the event of such a usurpation, Taylor admitted that the people could simply elect new leaders, but suggested that the States themselves 'have at least as good a right to judge of every infraction of the Constitution, as Congress itself.'

Taylor resigned from the Senate in 1794 and was chosen as a presidential elector for Thomas Jefferson in 1796. That same year, when he was reelected to Virginia's General Assembly despite having declined to stand for election, he agreed that 'in a democratic society...every individual is bound to serve the community if required by the public will.' During the Quasi-War with France, as the Federalists levied heavy new taxes and began building an ominous standing army, Taylor feared a conspiracy to install a British-style monarchy under the guise of national security. 'Should we get embroiled with France, the simple question for the States to determine, will be, whether it will be better to submit to an immovable fixation of our monarchy for the sake of the Union: or to break the Union for the sake of destroying our monarchy,' proclaimed Taylor. 'In the first case, the Union will exist, but upon principles which will oppress human nature – in the other a renovation of it may take place upon principles which may generate the public good.'

When a Virginia Congressman who had criticised the Francophobic foreign policy of President John Adams was indicted by a federal court for seditious libel, Taylor led the General Assembly in passing resolutions denouncing this violation of free speech and the rights of the States. The Alien and Sedition Acts, however, which authorised the President to deport foreigners without due process and criminalised criticism of the government, were the last straw. In a letter to his friend and ally, Thomas Jefferson, Taylor raised the possibility of Virginia and North Carolina seceding from the Union. 'The Southern States must lose their capital and commerce,' worried Taylor. 'America is destined to war – standing armies – and oppressive taxation.' Jefferson, as sanguine as ever, rejected the idea of secession at the present time, confident that the Federalists would soon be voted out of office once the taxes to pay for their militarism took their toll on the people. Taylor responded that the 'party spirit' in the United States was 'geographical,' and that a change in parties in a corrupt system would simply result in the South oppressing the North just as badly as the North had oppressed the South. To Taylor, a mere 'change in tyrants' would be no different than 'the lucid intervals of a madman.' It was the system, Taylor impressed upon Jefferson, not any particular party or President, which needed to be changed if possible or resisted if necessary. Taylor added that such resistance must be more than 'constitutional paper vetoes,' which were worthless, but 'a solid check, so woven into the form of government, as to be incapable of separation from it.' Taylor again suggested that 'the right of the State governments to expound the Constitution might possibly be made the basis of a movement towards its amendment,' and that 'the people in State conventions, are incontrovertibly the contracting parties, and possessing the infringing rights, may proceed by orderly steps to attain the object.'

In 1798, Taylor introduced the *Virginia Resolutions* to the House of Delegates. The *Resolutions*, authored by James Madison (Thomas Jefferson authored their companion, the *Kentucky Resolutions*), claimed that the Constitution was a compact between the States, that the States as parties to that compact had the right and duty to judge the constitutionality of federal laws for themselves, accordingly declared the Alien and Sedition Acts unconstitutional, and called on other States to join with Virginia. In the ensuing legislative debate, Taylor defended the *Resolutions*. 'A concentration of power in the hands of one individual tends to enslave others; a concentration in the hands of Congress tends to enslave the States,' warned Taylor. 'This oppression and concentration will bring revolution unless the States redress the balance.' If it were true that 'every government inherently possesses the powers necessary for its own preservation,' argued Taylor, then that principle applied to the States as well, which must stand up for their rights against the government which they formed for themselves. If they did not, continued Taylor, 'the inevitable consequence must be a consolidation of these States into one great sovereignty, which will, from its vast extent, as inevitably settle with rapidity into a monarchy, and like all other great empires, it must resort to those oppressions to support itself, which make the cup of life bitter to man.'

The reaction to the *Virginia and Kentucky Resolutions* was generally divided along sectional lines: the half of the States above the Mason-Dixon Line in opposition, the half below not in opposition. Massachusetts, Connecticut, New York, Rhode Island, and New Hampshire unanimously opposed the *Resolutions*, objecting that 'State legislatures are not the proper tribunals to determine the constitutionality of the laws of the general government' and holding that the Alien and Sedition Acts were 'not only constitutional, but expedient and necessary.' Other States, such as Maryland, Delaware, and Vermont simply found the *Resolutions* to be 'unwise and impolitic.' South Carolina was sympathetic to the *Resolutions*, with a Democratic-Republican General Assembly and Governor, but the legislative session ended before she could respond. North Carolina's Democratic-Republican House of Commons labeled the Acts 'a violation of the principles of the Constitution' which should be 'repealed without delay,' but her Federalist Senate rejected this resolution. Pennsylvania and New Jersey were unable to respond to the *Resolutions* either way due to intense disagreement within their legislatures. Georgia and Tennessee unanimously supported the *Resolutions*, passing resolutions of their own calling for the repeal of the Alien and Sedition Acts. Tennessee's General Assembly labeled the Acts 'opposed to the Constitution' as well as 'impolitic, oppressive, and unnecessary.' According to Georgia's General Assembly, 'If the American government had no greater hold on the people's allegiance and fidelity, than those Acts, it would not rest on that firm foundation which the committee hope and trust it does and ever will, on the affections of the citizens over whom it presides; riveted by the acts of a wise and virtuous administration.' Those States which either did not oppose or supported the *Resolutions* would go on to vote out the Federalists and vote in the Democratic-Republicans in the 'Revolution of 1800' – the very first peaceful transfer of power between parties in a republic.

Taylor celebrated Thomas Jefferson's election to the presidency in 1800 and the overall triumph of the newfound Democratic-Republican Party, but reminded the President that good government was based on principles, not personality. So as to ensure that his presidency had a lasting legacy of liberty, Taylor recommended to Jefferson that he champion the constitutional amendments which the aged Edmund Pendleton had listed in his recent pamphlet, "The Danger Not Over." Pendleton's recommended amendments included stricter accountability for all federal branches of government, a 'check upon the abuse of public credit, which, though some instances useful, like fleets and armies, may, like those, be carried to extremes dangerous to liberty and inconsistent with economical government,' an explicit definition of which powers were prohibited to the federal government 'as to defy the wiles of construction,' as well as an explicit delineation of 'the distinct powers of the *general* and *State* governments.' In 1803, Taylor was appointed to finish the term of a deceased Senator, but refused to stand for reelection, vowing that he would decline even 'a seat in heaven.' Taylor spearheaded the Senate's approval of the Twelfth Amendment, which simplified presidential elections, and the Louisiana Purchase, a treaty which the Senate could ratify or reject. Federalists objected that the new territory would primarily strengthen the South and taint their White Anglo-Saxon Protestant polity with Creoles and Catholics, as well as facetiously claimed that President Jefferson had no constitutional authority to acquire new territory. Taylor's defence, however, was ingenious. The means of acquiring territory, he reasoned, were war, purchase, or treaty, all of which were reserved to the States under the Articles of Confederation but prohibited to States under the Constitution. The federal government, however, not only had the powers of war, purchase, and treaty, but also the right to controul territory. Thus, reasoned Taylor, since the federal government had the right to controul territory as well as all the powers of acquiring territory previously reserved to the States (a power covered under the President's power to negotiate treaties and the Senate's power to ratify or reject those treaties), the acquisition of the Louisiana Territory was therefore constitutional.

As Thomas Jefferson campaigned for his second term, Taylor was chosen as an elector and wrote a pamphlet commending his first term. Taylor applauded the cutting of taxes and expenditures, scaling back of the standing army in favour of the militia, eliminating useless offices, and paying down the national debt. However, like fellow Virginian John Randolph of Roanoke, who compared Jefferson's two terms to Pharaoh's dream of the lean kine consuming the fat kine, Taylor was ultimately disappointed in Jefferson's presidency, regretting that while he had successfully treated the symptoms of the disease in the federal government, he had failed to cure the disease along the lines that he and Edmund Pendleton had proposed. 'Had the present administration done something for principle,' ranted Taylor, 'by overturning the Sedition-Law construction of the Constitution – or by shortening the Senate's tenure – or diminishing the President's patronage – or by making that office rotary, it would have invigorated principle to struggle for honest government, far beyond the exploits of diminishing the public debt, and coextensively increasing it by purchasing Louisiana.' While Taylor remained personally loyal to Jefferson, he suspected that the influence of the former Federalist, James Madison, was why Jefferson had not championed any constitutional amendments sealing the 'Principles of '98' and the 'Revolution of 1800' into law. 'I really believe it is owing to him,' Taylor grumbled of Madison, 'that all of Mr. Jefferson's great principles not to be found in our policy, are to die with him, and perhaps to be lost forever.'

In the presidential election of 1808, Taylor endorsed James Monroe over James Madison, believing the former a firmer republican and a more seasoned statesman. Indeed, given the brewing conflict with Great Britain and France over American maritime rights, and the retaliatory embargo which Jefferson imposed and Madison favoured maintaining, various Federalists and Democratic-Republicans preferred Monroe as an anti-war alternative to the heir apparent, Madison. In the *Spirit of 76*, a campaign newspaper for Monroe, Taylor called for Democratic-Republican unity, but defended the role of the Tertium Quids, a minority faction of conservatives within the party. Since 'majority republicanism is inevitably, widely (though not thoroughly) corrupted with ministerial republicanism' (that is, pragmatic rather than principled politics), the duty of 'a true minority man' was to hold the party accountable, or 'to unveil ministerial republicanism, and to awaken honest majority republicanism.' Taylor professed that he was 'destined to live and die a republican minority man.' Ultimately, Madison was elected President and Monroe elected Governor of Virginia, though Madison later appointed Monroe as his Secretary of State. Madison's presidency was defined by the War of 1812, which Taylor derided as a 'metaphysical war, a war not for conquest, not for defence, not for sport,' but 'a war for honour, like that of the Greeks against Troy,' as well as a war which 'may terminate in the destruction of the last experiment in favour of free government.' In other words, the War of 1812 was the result of party pride and nationalism and would permanently ratchet up the powers of the federal government. Taylor urged peace, though he did not actively oppose the war as did the Federalists in New England. After the Treaty of Ghent ended the war with a return to the *status quo antebellum*, Taylor remarked that 'the general joy on a barren, though an honourable peace, arose from the general, though secret, dislike of the war.' Taylor remained supportive of Monroe's presidential ambitions (and Monroe was eventually elected twice, following the two-term Virginian Presidents, Jefferson and Madison), but he joked to Monroe that 'by casting my vote, carried a hundred miles in a snowstorm, my confidence in you would be most confoundedly diminished, and I would instantly join again the republican minority.' Taylor was truly a minority man.

As a liberal republican, Taylor viewed slavery as an evil, but as a Southern slave-holder, he viewed emancipation as an even greater evil, and concluded that slavery, as a problem which only slave-holders understood and were thus entitled to solve, should be reformed but could not be abolished. 'The fact is that negro slavery is an evil that the United States must look in the face,' asserted Taylor. 'To whine over it, is cowardly; to aggravate it, criminal; to forbear to alleviate it, because it cannot be wholly cured, foolish.' Furthermore, added Taylor, the present generation of Southerners was not responsible for 'stealing and transporting negroes from Africa' (a crime which he noted had been the business of New England), and therefore should not be demonised for the way of life that it had inherited. 'The French Revolution, bottomed upon as correct abstract principles and sounder political hopes, turned out to be a foolish and mischevious speculation,' argued Taylor. 'What then can be expected from making republicans of negro slaves and conquerors of ignorant, infuriated barbarians?' Indeed, the slave revolt of Santo Domingo, in which the newly emancipated slaves responded to French egalitarianism by exterminating the French colonists, convinced Taylor and virtually all Southerners that 'two nations of distinct colours and features' could not coexist without one enslaving or exterminating the other. 'Were the whites of Santo Domingo morally bound to bring on themselves the massacre produced by the liberation of their slaves?' asked Taylor. 'Is such a sacrifice of freemen to make freemen of slaves, virtuous or wicked?' Just as the French Revolution 'attempted to make freemen of the people of France' (but, in the end, 'pronounced that they were incapable of liberty'), so the French Revolution also 'attempted to compound a free nation of black and white people in St. Domingo' (but, in the end, 'pronounced that one colour must perish'). Taylor dismissed Northerners as 'religious and philosophical Quixotes' who did not take such realities into account. Besides, pointed out Taylor, emancipation without equality (a prospect for which there was virtually no public support in the North or the South) meant that freedmen would become a dangerous underclass, just as they had in Santo Domingo. 'Cut off from most of the rights of citizens, and from all the allowances of slaves,' warned Taylor, freedmen would not only be 'driven into every species of crime for subsistence; and destined to a life of idleness, anxiety, and guilt,' but also would 'constitute the most complete instrument for invasion or ambition, hitherto forged throughout the entire circle of human folly.' Taylor, a model planter, denied that slavery was abusive and oppressive, instead insisting that it was paternalistic. 'To me it seems,' argued Taylor, taking exception to Thomas Jefferson's claim that slavery had a de-humanising and de-civilising effect on whites as well as blacks, 'that slaves are too far below, and much to in the power of the master, to inspire furious passions; that such are nearly as rare and disgraceful towards slaves as towards horses; that slaves are more frequently the objects of benevolence than of rage; and hardly ever suffered to tyrannise over them; that they open instead of shut the sluices of benevolence in tender minds; and that fewer good public or private characters have been raised in countries enslaved by some faction of particular interests, than in those where personal slavery existed.' When Northerners, seeking to block the admission of slave-holding States to the Union, objected that slavery was incompatible with republican government, Taylor countered that every republic in history had been a slave-holding nation, particularly the Antebellum American ideals of Greece and Rome. 'Slavery was carried farther among the Greeks and Romans than among ourselves,' Taylor noted, 'and yet those two nations probably produced more great and good patriots and citizens, than, probably, all the rest of the world.' Taylor worried that one day Northern slave-traders would brand Southern slave-holders as tyrants for defending themselves against their insults and aggressions. 'If self-preservation shall force the slave-holders into stricter measures of precaution than they have hitherto adopted,' worried Taylor, 'those who shall have driven them to these measures, by continually exciting their negroes to cut their throats, will accuse them of tyranny with as little reason, as the prosecutors of the slave trade accuse them of negro stealing.'

The Missouri Crisis, in which Federalists protested Missouri's admission to the Union on the grounds of its slave-holding constitution, was the first time slavery had been on the federal agenda since the abolition of the Transatlantic slave trade. Northerners claimed that if Missouri were admitted to the Union, 'the scale of political power will preponderate in favour of the slave-holding States' and the West would be 'blackened' rather than 'filled with a race of free white men.' Southerners such as President James Monroe claimed in turn that the exclusion of Missouri was 'an effort to give such a shape to our Union, as would secure the dominion over it, to the [North-] Eastern section' and pointed out that Northerners 'did not hesitate to avow that it was a contest for power only, disclaiming the pretext of liberty, humanity, etc.' Taylor agreed with Thomas Jefferson that 'the Missouri question is for power' – a 'mere party trick' on the part of the Federalists to divide the Democratic-Republicans on a sectional issue. Taylor identified the forces behind the Missouri Crisis as 'a temporary impression concerning slavery' (i.e. religious and philosophical Quixote-ism) along with an agenda of 'contriving laws for making one portion of the Union tributary to another' (i.e. neo-Hamiltonian mercantilism) and began speculating about the prospects of a 'Southern confederacy.' According to Taylor, 'the fanatical crisis, the avaricious crisis, and the geographical crisis' threatened 'to convert a hatred of slavery into a veneration for exclusive privilege, taxation, and inflamed geographical parties.'

As early as 1794, after a disagreement with John Adams over a hereditary executive and life appointments for the legislature, and a perusal of Adams' book, *A Defence of the Constitutions of the Government of the United States of America*, Taylor conceived of writing a book of his own refuting Adams' 'monarchism.' Taylor wrote in such a 'wild, desultory, careless way,' however, that his book, *An Inquiry into the Principles and Policy of the Government of the United States*, was not completed until 1804 and published until 1814. According to Taylor, Adams 'paid too much respect to political skeletons, constructed with fragments torn from monarchy, aristocracy, and democracy...and too little to the ethereal moral principles, alone able to bind governments to the interest of nations.' Shortly before completion, Taylor anonymously sent his *Inquiry* section by section to Adams. Upon reading the anonymous letters, Adams remarked that 'the Honourable John Taylor of Virginia, of all men living or dead, first occurred to me.' Thomas Jefferson, who also received advance copies of the *Inquiry*, congratulated Taylor for having 'completely pulverized' Adams' political philosophy. Taylor and Adams, old adversaries though older friends, began a correspondence and reconciled their differences – much like Jefferson and Adams later in their lives. According to the Progressive-school historian, Charles A. Beard, Taylor's *Inquiry* 'deserves to rank among the two or three really historic contributions to political science which have been produced in the United States.'

Taylor loathed the snake pit of politics and loved his pastoral idyll of Hazelwood. 'Mother Earth offers to her children subsistence and repose, of which it seems to be their great business to rob each other,' Taylor explained to the likeminded Thomas Jefferson during one of his precious retirements. 'It was foolish of me to leave the bosom which has nurtured me for the sake of exposing my own to the unfraternal shafts of all the wicked passions.' Taylor shared in the Southern creed, drawn from the English political tradition, that an agrarian life cultivated the virtues necessary for independence (i.e. republicanism and liberty), but an urban, industrial life cultivated vices which led to dependence (i.e. tyranny and slavery). In early eighteenth-century Great Britain, the Whigs, or 'Country Party,' opposed the Prime Minister's policy of consolidating loyalty to the Crown by creating a 'Court Party' based on pensions and positions. Only those men who were of independent means, concluded the Country Party, could resist the 'corruption' of the Court Party and pursue their own happiness freely. In Colonial America, where the Whigs were extremely influential in the formation of liberal republicanism, Southerners came to view their agrarian lifestyle as the fulfillment of the ideal of independence and the pursuit of happiness. Thus, according to Taylor, agriculture was 'a system which sheds happiness, plenty, and virtue all around,' but industry a system 'which fosters vice, breeds want, and begets misery.' Jefferson gave this creed its most famous expression in his *Notes on the State of Virginia.* 'Those who labour in the earth are the chosen people of God, if ever He had a chosen people, whose breasts He has made His peculiar deposit for substantial and genuine virtue,' declared Jefferson. 'Dependence begets subservience and venality, suffocates the germ of virtue, and prepares fit tools for the designs of ambition.' According to historian Forrest McDonald in *Novus Ordo Seclorum: the Intellectual Origins of the Constitution*, in the 'agrarian republicanism' of the Jeffersonian South, 'virtue, independence, liberty, and the ownership of unencumbered real property were inextricably bound together...ownership of land begat independence, independence begat virtue, and virtue begat republican liberty.' Taylor, who had devised methods to restore the exhausted Virginia soil and to improve the efficiency of plantations, was widely regarded as the foremost agricultural scientist of his time. He served as president of several agricultural societies and shared his ideas in person and in print, especially through essays compiled in another book, *Arator*.

Indeed, Taylor boasted that he would rather serve as President of the Virginia Agricultural Society than as President of the United States. Taylor considered agrarianism and liberty as so inextricably intertwined that in tilling his fields he was performing an even greater public service than holding office. 'There is a spice of fanaticism in my nature upon two subjects,' Taylor confessed to Jefferson, 'agriculture and republicanism.'

In the final four years of his life, Taylor wrote three brilliant political treatises responding to the rising tide of more-perfect-unionism and sectionalism. In 1816, President James Madison enacted a protectionist tariff into law and reinstated the national bank, and the Congress passed an internal-improvements bill – three policies that Southerners considered oppressive and unconstitutional. The Supreme Court, under the leadership of Chief Justice John Marshall, overturned the rulings of State Supreme Courts in *Martin v. Hunter's Lessee* (1816), *McCulloch v. Maryland* (1819), and *Cohens v. Virginia* (1821). Combined with the Missouri Crisis, Taylor foresaw America's federal republic descending into a national despotism and sectional strife. In his three books, Taylor valiantly but vainly sought to stem the tide of consolidation. *Construction Construed and Constitutions Vindicated*, published in 1820, dismantled Marshall's ruling in *McCulloch*. *Tyranny Unmasked*, published in 1822, demolished the policy of protectionist tariffs. *New Views of the Constitution*, published in 1823, delved into the recently published records of the Constitutional Convention to determine the correct interpretation of the Constitution. Thomas Jefferson lent his immense prestige to Taylor's writings. 'Col. Taylor and myself have rarely, if ever, differed in any political principles of importance,' announced Jefferson, who endorsed Taylor's views as 'the true political faith, to which every catholic [i.e. liberal-minded] republican should steadfastly hold.'

In 1822, Taylor was once more summoned to the Senate against his will. Although his health was failing and he could barely walk, Taylor was determined to do his duty and went to Washington, D.C., where he was disgusted with the consolidation and corruption that he encountered.

According to Taylor, 'federal geographical patronage' (that is, the redistribution of wealth from the South to the North), was reducing the States to 'insignificant corporations.' Furthermore, the Congress was 'filled with a multitude of beggars all roaring out "give me money, or let me keep what I have stolen,"' with Congressmen casually voting for such claims without even reviewing them. With his old-fashioned views, as well as his old-fashioned manner and attire, Taylor seemed like a ghost from the past in the changing times. As the sympathetic John Randolph of Roanoke quipped, Taylor's clothes 'will be rather nearer the fashion of the day than his principles.'

When the Congress attempted to raise tariff rates and fund the repairs of roads and canals, the wizened Taylor rose to make the case for small-f federalism and small-r republicanism one last time. Taylor asserted that internal improvements (public-works projects which were located largely in the North) would 'inflame geographical interests' and destroy 'the outworks by which the Constitution is defended.' Internal improvements were a local responsibility, not a national responsibility, insisted Taylor, and if the Congress abandoned the general welfare for specific sectional interests, real representation was no longer possible. 'It is obvious that, wherever, the exercise of local internal powers begins, representation ends,' explained Taylor, 'because Congress, acting by a majority, without fellow feeling, can never constitute a representation of the geographical interests and climates at the extremities of the United States, North or South, East or West.' Taylor refuted all of the legal arguments for internal improvements, such as that they were authorised under the powers of war and taxation. 'Thus all minor powers are assumed by these two greater powers, and the States possess no reserved powers, unless such as are of greater magnitude than those of war and taxation,' remarked Taylor of this artful argument. 'Thus a complete subjection is substituted for the sovereignty of the States.' Protectionist tariffs, continued Taylor, were 'merely a tribute to capitalists' and 'a copy of the English combination between the government and the capitalists.' By taxing the imported manufactures on which Southerners relied, protectionist tariffs enriched a parasitic class in the North at the expence of the productive agricultural section of the South. Indeed, noted Taylor, Southerners complained of 'legislative frauds, by which our property to a great extent, and theirs to some amount, is transferred from poverty to affluence – from labour to ease – and from industry to idleness.' Taylor also refuted the legal argument that the constitutional power to regulate commerce authorised protectionism, countering that this construction was incompatible with the required uniformity of tariffs among the States as well as the equality of the States. 'The uniformity required in the imposition of imports and other taxes corresponds with a construction of this word (commerce) which leaves unimpaired the local justice and security intended to be established by this uniformity,' charged Taylor, 'and visibly interdicts the destruction of one of the plainest principles of our Federal Union, by giving to a single word, used in a particular case, and limited to a special application, a meaning which would obliterate substantially the uniformity required, and expose the members of the Union to the frauds and oppression which this rule was intended to prevent.' According to Taylor, the tariff bill 'is not a tariff bill to encourage manufactures,' but 'a bill of bargains, to enrich a pecuniary aristocracy.' Last, but not least, Taylor predicted that the consolidation of power in Washington, D.C., through laws such as the tariff and internal improvements, spelled doom for the American federal republic. 'Under our Constitution, neither territories nor representation were intended to be consolidated; or law, geographically partial, to be enacted,' warned Taylor. 'It was never intended that the West should be the guardian of the East, nor the North of the South, nor that the specious but false idea of a national representation should be used to abolish a real representation, upon which a republican government must be founded, or finally cease to exist.'

Taylor died on 21 August 1824, happily away from Washington, D.C., and at home in Hazelwood. He was given a soaring eulogy in the *Richmond*

Enquirer. 'The great lawyer – the profound politician – the friend of the Constitution in its original purity – he who served as a member of the State legislature in the dark days of '98 and '99 – who formerly shone as a member of the United States Senate, and who has been dotted anew with the confidence of Virginia in the same high capacity – he, who both by precept and example has scattered a flood of light over agriculture, the staple occupation of this people, "the chosen people" of the land, has suddenly descended to the tomb, "full of years and full of honour!"' waxed the editor, Thomas Ritchie. 'Let Virginia weep over the ashes of the illustrious patriot.' A colleague of Taylor's in the Senate, Thomas Hart Benton of Missouri, paid him a noble tribute. 'I can hardly figure to myself the ideal of a republican statesman more perfect and complete than he was in reality: plain and solid, a wise counsellor, a ready and vigourous debater, acute and comprehensive, ripe in all historical and political knowledge, innately republican – modest, courteous, benevolent, hospitable – a skillful, practical farmer, giving his time to his farm and his books when not called by an emergency to the public service – and returning to his books and his farm when the emergency was over,' reflected Benton. 'He belonged to that constellation of great men which shone so brightly in Virginia in his day, and the light of which was not limited to Virginia, or our America, but spread through the bounds of the civilised world.' The Pulitizer-winning historian Gordon S. Wood, author of *The Creation of the American Republic, 1776-1787* and *Empire of Liberty: A History of the Early Republic, 1789-1815*, dubs Taylor 'the philosopher of agrarian republicanism,' 'the conscience of the [Democratic-] Republican Party,' and a man who 'brilliantly expressed the conception of American politics that had emerged from the Revolutionary era.' The distinguished Southern scholar, M.E. Bradford, in an introduction to a new edition of *Arator*, describes Taylor as 'the classic figure of "old republican" theory: the exemplar of an almost Roman *virtus*, the Virginia Cato, who soldiers, enforces the law, writes in its defense and of the life it secures, and serves the state well when called to office because he has something better to do – because there are lands and people of whose good he is a faithful steward.'

II

Taylor wrote *Construction Construed and Constitutions Vindicated* in opposition to the troubling trends of his time – 'political combinations' of 'parasitical privileges' corrupting the common sense of the Constitution with 'the instrumentality of inference, convenience, and necessity.' These honeyed words, to Taylor, were poisoned. Specifically, Taylor was worried about the growing power of the Supreme Court over the Constitution, a national bank, protectionist tariffs, and internal improvements. These problems had ended the short-lived, so-called 'Era of Good Feelings,' and initiated an open struggle for power between the North and South. Although he hoped it would be published anonymously, Taylor was eventually forced to reveal his identity as the author. Thomas Ritchie, the editor of the Jeffersonian *Richmond Enquirer*, wrote a glowing preface to the book. 'The period is, indeed, by no means an agreeable one,' began Ritchie, who described a situation of 'gloom' and 'apathy' in the United States, in which 'the very sound of State rights is scarcely ever heard among them; and by many of their eminent politicians, it is only heard to be mocked.' Ritchie held, however, that 'a good citizen will never despair of the republic,' and heralded Taylor as such a citizen. 'Penetrated by the conviction, that the Constitution is in danger; that the balance has seriously inclined towards the side of consolidation,' continued Ritchie, 'he comes forward to commune with his countrymen, and to state to them frankly his impressions and his fears.' According to Ritchie, 'If there be any book that is capable of rousing the people, it is the one before us.' Thomas Jefferson described the book as 'the most logical retraction of our governments to the original and true principles of the Constitution creating them, which has appeared since the adoption of the instrument,' and recommended that 'every State in the

153

Union should give a copy to every member they elect, as a standing instruction, and ours should set the example.'

Taylor was a clearer and more consistent thinker than Thomas Jefferson, but as a writer, Taylor had none of what John Adams described as Jefferson's 'felicity of expression.' Taylor's writing style is indeed more lawyerly than popular, often burdened with repetitive arguments and archaic language, though it is also filled with brilliant imagery and amusing digressions. In *The Liberal Republicanism of John Taylor of Caroline*, intellectual historians Garrett Ward Sheldon and Charles William Hill describe Taylor's writing style as 'unfortunate,' and claim that it is one of the reasons he has been overlooked both then and now. Randolph of Roanoke, renowned for his wit and wisdom and who praised Taylor's principles as 'the only bond of union among republicans,' exclaimed after reading the *Inquiry into the Principles and Policy of the Government of the United States*, 'For Heaven's sake, get some worthy person to do the second edition in English!' Taylor himself acknowledged that his writing contained 'a multitude of angles and windings,' but explained that 'mine is a sort of metaphysical world over which the plastick power of the imagination is unlimited.' Taylor's style is more suited to the tongue than the pen, and is reminiscent of sitting in a rocker on a front porch, sipping whiskey and smoking a pipe while listening to a wise (if sometimes long-winded) old uncle impart his experience.

Taylor believed that the 'principles of our revolution' were the keys to unlocking the meaning of the Constitution. 'These are the keys of construction,' avowed Taylor, 'and the locks of liberty.' Any accurate interpretation of the Constitution, held Taylor, must be rooted in an understanding of what the Americans had fought for in the first place. According to Taylor, 'freedom of property' was one of the chief motives of the American patriots. 'It was tyrannical in the English government, said the Colonies, to insist upon taking away their property, and giving it to placemen and pensioners; and they very justly considered life and liberty so intimately connected with property, that the rights of the latter could not be invaded, without invading the other rights also,' explained Taylor. 'They fought for a revolution, and established governments to secure all three of these natural rights, because a loss of one was equivalent to a loss of all, in a national view.' Thus, life, liberty, and property were the principles of the American Revolution.

Although the American Revolution was fought for the rights of life, liberty, and property, one look at Washington, D.C. – 'a government accoutered in the complete panoply of fleets, armies, banks, funding systems, pensions, bounties, corporations, [and] exclusive privileges' – convinced Taylor that these rights were no longer safe. 'We are exchanging the pure principles of the Revolution,' warned Taylor, 'for the garbage of aristocracy, and compromises with venality.' Taylor compared the contest for power between political parties to a kaleidoscope, 'which at each revolution exhibits new scenes of glittering delusions, whilst the pebbles from which they are reflected, remain substantially the same.' Taylor worried that if 'pecuniary combinations' of industrialists and bankers were construed to be constitutional, then they would clamp down on the people as a permanent parasitic class. 'Legislatures will become colleges for teaching the science of getting money by monopolies or favours,' predicted Taylor, 'and the deluge of laws will become as great in the United States, as was once the deluge of papal indulgences in Europe for effecting the same object.' To prevent this regression from the principles of the American Revolution, Taylor noted that the framers and ratifiers of the Constitution had placed strict limitations on federal powers and totally reserved whatever powers they did not delegate. 'A greater mass of these evils was foreseen by the framers of the Union,' explained Taylor, 'and attempted to be avoided, by restricting the powers given to Congress, and by retaining to the States those powers united with the local interests, habits, and opinions of each State.'

Taylor denied that freedom was found in any particular form of government and held that tyranny was intrinsic to government in any form. 'To contend for forms, only,' quipped Taylor, 'is to fight for shadows.' Taylor

155

considered the extent to which governments upheld their duty to protect life, liberty, and property, rather than the form by which they were organised, to be the true measure of their value. Taylor pointed out that governments were not *teleocratic* ends in themselves, but *nomocratic* means instituted to achieve certain ends, and should be judged on the merits. 'If the acts of a monarchy, aristocracy, and democracy are the same,' Taylor argued, 'these forms of government are to a nation essentially the same also.' The American Revolution, according to Taylor, was fought over the fundamental question of the rightful role of government, not for one form of government over another. 'The United States,' remarked Taylor, 'did not go to war for nothing but forms.' Indeed, the Democratic-Republican, Unitarian Thomas Jefferson and the Federalist, Catholic Charles Carroll, who agreed on very little, agreed that '173 despots would surely be as despotic as one,' and that 'one tyrant is better than twenty,' respectively. To Taylor, then, the best way to secure life, liberty, and property was not to trust any particular form of government, but to identify and restrain the causes of tyranny in government in general. 'If we ascertain the quality in human nature, from which political evil has chiefly proceeded under every form of government, this quality is the cause which can corrupt every form,' explained Taylor, 'and instead of amusing ourselves with these new forms, not to be confided in, it behooves us to search for a remedy, able to remove or controul the cause itself.' That corrupting quality, according to Taylor, was 'avarice' and 'ambition.'

There were two types of constructions of the Constitution: one of 'common sense' which appealed to 'understanding,' another of tortuous reasoning which appealed to 'prejudice or self-interest.' Taylor insisted that the latter, which he called a 'pernicious species of construction,' was refuted by the Constitution's 'specifications and restrictions' on power. To the people, the construction of the Constitution should be 'a science to preserve the rights of mankind,' but to governments, constructions were 'an art for extending their own power.' What distinguished the United States, however, was that the people were free to construe written constitutions for their governments, rather than governments construing constitutions for themselves as in Great Britain. 'In all except our own, the people have nothing to do with it,' noted Taylor, 'but ours is modeled with an intention that they should have much to do with it.'

Taylor was wary of using the term 'sovereignty' to describe the status of the people of the States in the Union. He recognised that the term's intentions were good (it was meant to signify 'the right of self-government'), but preferred the terminology in the Declaration of Independence of 'free and independent States,' along with the Constitution's 'limitations, restrictions, balances, and divisions of power,' as safer and sounder. The nebulous term 'sovereignty' was far too subjective and open to interpretation and distortion, worried Taylor. Indeed, Taylor feared that this powerful term (originally a religious term for the absolute authority of God over creation, 'impiously assumed by kings,' and maintained out of 'imitation and ignorance') could be misconstrued to apply to the government instead of the people, thus reversing the American people's liberation from the tyranny of 'sovereign' rulers. 'Chastened down to the signification of a natural right in nations to institute and limit their own governments, it only embraces the principle by which every social liberty can be established,' Taylor acknowledged of 'sovereignty' as a term. 'Extended to the idea of power in governments to regulate conscience or distribute property,' he continued, 'it includes the principle by which social liberty is destroyed.' Despite his reservations, Taylor acknowledged that 'sovereignty' had become synonymous with 'self-government,' and conceded to employ the term 'in accordance with the common language.'

Although everyone knew that the Union was formed by 'We, the people of the United States,' there was a serious political debate over whether 'We, the people of the United States' meant 'the associated inhabitants of each State, or the unassociated inhabitants of all the States.' In other words, was the United States one nation among one people or a republic between the people

157

of the States? 'No people or community has ever been composed in the United States except by the inhabitants of each State, associating distinctly from every other State, by their own separate consent,' answered Taylor. To modern Americans, indoctrinated to believe in 'one nation, under God, indivisible, with liberty and justice for all,' a debate of 'nations' versus 'federations,' may seem like meaningless quibbling over semantics, hopelessly antiquated, and even 'unpatriotic.' To Founding Fathers like Taylor, however, this was a question of vital importance. 'By this new doctrine,' Taylor warned of more-perfect-unionist revisionism, 'the checks provided to controul the powers of government of the Union are ingeniously evaded.' The 'melting down' of the 'body politicks' of the States into 'one great nation' would result in the consolidation of power and the loss of life, liberty, and property. In a republic between sovereign, self-governing 'body politicks,' however, power would be decentralised, and life, liberty, and property protected. 'Now as an effective sovereignty of the people can only result from their having constituted themselves into a civil society, and [the people of the nation, as opposed to the people of the States] having never done so,' Taylor pointed out, 'an acknowledgment of a sovereignty which does not exist, only annuls that which does; and escapes altogether from any species of loyalty to this superior authority.' That is, pretending that the one people of one American nation (an 'imaginary body politick') were sovereign while denying the sovereignty of the people of the States (effective 'body politicks') would free the federal government from any 'controul or modification.' According to Taylor, 'Not a single one of the United States [the plural form was common among the Founders] would have consented to have dissolved its people, to have reunited them into one great people, and to have received State governments or unrestricted legislation from this great people, so ignorant of local circumstances, and so different in local habits.'

Proving that the Constitution was ratified by the States, not one people, and that the Union was a federal republic of sovereign States, not one nation, was a paltry task for an old Jeffersonian like Taylor. Taylor dismissed the more-perfect-unionist revisionism of men like Chief Justice John Marshall as 'an attempt to construe away a fact, known to everybody,' and either a case of 'playing the fool' or 'playing the knave.' The constitution of each State referred to herself as a separate 'civil society' with the inalienable right of self-government. For example, Taylor's own Virginia called herself a 'free State,' proclaiming that 'all power is derived from the people.' Massachusetts, who had already twice threatened to secede from the Union at the time of Taylor's writing, concurred with Virginia: 'The people of this commonwealth have the sole right of governing themselves as a free, sovereign, and independent State.' It was the States which sent delegates to represent them at the Constitutional Convention, and the States which separately ratified the Constitution in popular conventions back home. It was the States which elected Representatives, Senators, and Presidents, each with their own individual suffrage laws. Last, but not least, it was the States which possessed the power to amend the Constitution and dissolve the Union. 'Thus,' reasoned Taylor, 'a supremacy of the States, not only over Congress, but over the whole Constitution, is twice acknowledged; first, by their power over the legislative and executive departments instituted for executing the Union; and secondly, by their power over the Union itself.' Even the name 'United States,' or 'people of the United States,' indicated that the Union was a republic of separate States, not one nation. 'The plural "States" rejects the idea, that the people of all the States considered themselves as one State,' argued Taylor. 'The word "united" is an averment of pre-existing social compacts, called States.' Taylor also noted that the term 'union' was never applied to governments established among individuals by social contract. 'I do not recollect that a single compact between individuals, for the establishment of a government, has ever been called a union.' Unions, according to Taylor, were 'agreements between independent States.' As if all of this were not obvious enough, the Ninth and Tenth Amendments (which, taken together, explained that the enumeration of particular rights should not be misconstrued as to imply that other unenumerated rights were not reserved and that the States reserved to themselves any powers which they did not delegate to the federal government or prohibit to themselves) firmly established that the States created the Union and remained sovereign within the Union. 'The precision of these expressions,' noted Taylor, 'is happily contrived to defeat a construction, by which the origin of the Union, or the sovereignty of the States, could be rendered at all doubtful.'

'The government of each State is, and is to be, sovereign and supreme in all matters that relate to the whole,' John Dickinson, Delaware delegate to the Constitutional Convention, explained to his fellow countrymen in 1788, 'and it will be their own fault if the several States suffer the federal sovereignty to interfere in things of their respective jurisdictions.'

According to Taylor, the 'division and limitation of power' was 'vitally important to our system of government.' In the past, explained Taylor, the people were subordinate to the government – 'pedestals' to the 'splendid statues' of government. All of the various forms (or 'natural principles') of government – monarchy, aristocracy, democracy – struggled for power, but all were 'founded in the principle of subordination to unlimited power,' and therefore all were a 'scourge to mankind.' Without any division or limitation of power, these sovereigns began reigning so oppressively and abusively (as did King John I in the early thirteenth century and the Stuart dynasty throughout the seventeenth century) that the people (in this case, the barons and the burgesses) established, by force, 'a remedy for the defects of each, from the mixture of all' (embodied in documents such as *Magna Carta Libertatum* and the Glorious Revolution). Taylor's brief political history of mankind was, in fact, mainly a brief history of the English Constitution – a body of precedents formed from historical experience which balanced power by mixing monarchy (the King), aristocracy (the Lords), and democracy (the Commons) into one government. The same was also true of the Roman Constitution, another model constitution to the Americans, which had balanced power between the aristocratic patricians and the democratic plebeians (the Tarquin kings having been overthrown) by mixing them together in one republican government. 'It was seen and admitted, that the formation of a government, after the model of an army, by a series of subordination from a king to a constable, from a general to a corporal, made tyrants and slaves,' explained Taylor, 'and checks and balances were contrived to prevent both consequences by poising the three supposed natural principles against each other, fraught with coordinate, distinct, and independent powers.' While this 'mixed government,' forged by centuries of rebellions, reforms, regicides, and revolutions, did indeed represent progress – the Baron de Montesquieu acknowledged the English Constitution to be the best in the world – Taylor stressed that it was still founded on 'the error of maintaining absolute power in the government, and inflicting absolute submission on the people,' and so the people (or, at least, intellectuals) continued searching for a 'better remedy.'

While the political philosophy that governments be made subordinate to the people and that the people be made sovereign had taken root in Great Britain (Taylor cited the classical-liberal luminary John Locke as an example), Taylor noted that it was the American Revolution which catapulted these liberal-republican theories into the field. 'The natural right of self-government, and the consequent rights of dividing and limiting power, might have slept forever in theory, except for the American Revolution,' boasted Taylor, 'which seems to have been designed by Providence for the great purpose of demonstrating its practicability and effects.' Unlike previous revolutions, which had merely established one form of government over another, the American Revolution overturned the tradition of mixed government and established a new principle of government altogether. 'Far from allowing sovereignty to governments or confiding our rights to a balance between arbitrary and artificial political principles, we were obliged to feel and to act upon the genuine and natural principle of self-government,' explained Taylor, 'and to vindicate these rights by creating coordinate and collateral political departments invested with limited powers; instead of that absolute power, so highly pernicious in the hands of any one of the three ancient principles, and so far from being made harmless by their mixture.'

The American division of power which Taylor referenced was one of many American adaptations of the English political tradition – the tradition which the American Colonies inherited from their mother country, including unique ideas of government such as representation, rule of law, separation of powers, checks and balances (especially on the executive branch), and bills of rights. Indeed, the newly free and independent American republic was not an intellectual construct, conceived in the minds of philosophers and dedicated to propositions, but an organic outgrowth of English civilisation – an 'Anglo-American' civilisation so to speak. 'We are descended from a people whose government was founded on liberty: our glorious forefathers of Great Britain made liberty the foundation of everything,' Patrick Henry declared at Virginia's Convention. 'That country is become a great, mighty, and splendid nation; not because their government is strong and energetic, but, sir, because liberty is its direct end and foundation.' According to Henry, 'We drew the spirit of liberty from our British ancestors: by that spirit we have triumphed over every difficulty.'

Taylor identified two divisions of power in the United States: one between the people and their State governments, and another between the States and the federal government. 'The first division of power we have established according to this new policy, consists of the limited rights delegated by the people to their governments or trustees; and all of the residue of the attributes of sovereignty, retained, as not having been delegated by the people,' explained Taylor. 'Our second division of power, also unknown to the English system, is that between the governments of the States and the government of the Union.' Whether in ancient Greece and Rome or in Great Britain, Taylor admitted that, historically, divisions of power had resulted in 'perpetual and violent collisions,' as the English Civil War would attest (and later, unimaginably to Taylor, the American Civil

War), but added that the cause of those conflicts was the fact that power was divided among the monarchic, aristocratic, and democratic branches of a sovereign government, all of which were struggling for supremacy over one another. 'The object of our wise and good patriots, was to reap the benefits and avoid the evils arising from a division of power,' explained Taylor. Accordingly, 'the right of the people to alter, abolish, and institute governments, as to them shall seem most likely to effect their safety and happiness,' as proclaimed in the Declaration of Independence, revoked sovereignty from the government and recognised it in the people. The people would divide power among State governments and the federal government, which instead of struggling amongst themselves for power would actually limit the power of one another. 'By the authority of the right of self-government, we have with great deliberation established divisions of power, created political departments subordinate to the people, defined the functions of each, and prescribed to individuals and the inferior officers of each, the obedience respectively due to these departments,' boasted Taylor. 'Of this improved system for dividing and limiting power, we took a hint from the balances between monarchy, aristocracy, and democracy, as established, not by a deliberative choice, but by violence; but whilst we adhered to the principle practised by this triumvirate for self-preservation, we applied it to the preservation of the general liberty, by creating coordinate and collateral political departments, with distinct powers, for the special design of making them mutual checks upon each other.' To Taylor, the right of self-government was absolutely essential in distinguishing the American division of power from the English division of power. 'By virtue of this right,' reiterated Taylor, 'the people of each State established certain coordinate divisions of power, without investing one with a supremacy over the others; and by virtue of the same right, solemnly asserted in that sacred instrument, the same people uniting with each other, established other coordinate divisions of power, still excluding an investiture of one, with a supremacy over the others.'

According to Taylor, the American Colonies had always accepted that under the English Constitution the Parliament had authority over the foreign affairs of the British Empire, including the Colonies, but argued that they retained authority over their own domestic affairs. The Parliament, however, claimed that its power over foreign affairs 'implied' other powers over domestic affairs, such as levying taxes on the Colonies, regulating the commerce of the Colonies, and stationing a standing army in the Colonies. 'It would be absurd to allow powers, and withhold any means necessary or proper to carry them into execution,' argued the Parliament, to which the Colonies objected, 'It would be more absurd to limit powers, and yet concede unlimited means for their execution, by which the internal supremacy, upon which their liberty and happiness depended, though nominally allowed, would be effectually destroyed.' The Colonies made the case for everything, from chartered rights to constitutional rights to natural rights, yet the Parliament 'closed the debate, by declaring that it had a right to legislate over the Colonies in all cases whatsoever.' After imposing some 'trifling taxes...as an entering wedge into the colonial claim of local supremacy, to be gradually driven up to the head,' the Parliament attempted to trick the Colonies into conceding to its supremacy by artificially lowering the price of taxed tea through a royally chartered monopoly. 'But the Colonies,' beamed Taylor, 'too wary to be caught by a gilded hook, detected, resisted, and defeated the artifice.'

The division of power between the States and the federal government was a continuation of the Colonies' old relationship with the Parliament in their newfound federal republic. 'During, and soon after a war, firmly waged for eight years, to resist a right to legislate for them locally and internally, inferred from parliamentary sovereignty or supremacy,' argued Taylor, 'the Colonies or States, constructed two unions, and established in both a division of power, bearing a strong similitude to that upon which they were willing to have continued their union with England.' Just as the Colonies had claimed their sovereignty in domestic affairs against the Parliament, Taylor claimed that so the States retained their sovereignty in domestic affairs against the federal government. 'The extent of our country was so great, and its former division into distinct States so established, that we thought it better to confederate as to foreign affairs only,' explained Thomas Jefferson. 'Every State retained its self-government in domestic matters, as better-qualified to direct them to the good and satisfaction of their citizens, than a general government so distant from its remoter citizens and so little familiar with the local peculiarities of the different parts.' Indeed, Taylor argued that the Colonies' reasons for dividing power between themselves and the Parliament likewise justified a strict division of power between the States and the federal government: after all, a domestic tyranny could be just as oppressive as a foreign one. 'Many of the arguments which convinced the Colonies of the necessity for such a division in relation to England, apply forcibly to the government of the Union,' noted Taylor. 'A supremacy of London or Washington, however more direful to liberty at one place, would not be divested of terrors at the other.'

Although there were some similarities between the Colonies' old relationship with the Parliament and the States' new relationship with the federal government, there were also important differences. While the Crown had chartered the Colonies, the federal government did not charter the States. In fact, it was the States which had chartered the federal government, so to speak. In that sense, then, the States had an even stronger claim to self-government against their creature, the federal government, than the Colonies against their creator, the Crown. 'Had the Colonies, under their charters from the King of England, claimed a supremacy over the Parliament,' quipped Taylor, 'their pretension would have been equivalent to a claim of supremacy by the government of the Union over the States.' Unfortunately, what Taylor regarded as preposterous – the federal government's pretension to supremacy over the States – is now no longer a laughing matter.

For the federal government to claim that it possessed 'implied' powers over the States was akin to the Parliament's tyrannous claims of supremacy over the Colonies. Taylor compared such a specious claim to the purchaser of a house claiming all of the seller's personal property as an 'implied' part of the contract. 'The grant of a charter implies the retention of every power not granted, just as a deed of gift or sale for a portion of an estate leaves unimpaired the title of the owner to the portion he does not convey away,' argued Taylor. 'A conveyance of part does not entitle the grantee to take more, or the whole of the residue if he pleases.' In other words, the States – 'the true owners of a great fee simple estate' who 'created the division of power between the government of the Union, and the State governments' – reserved for themselves whatever rights they did not delegate to the federal government and enumerate in the Constitution. 'If one trustee,' warned Taylor, continuing his analogy, 'can by construction or by force, despoil the other of his portion, he will become so rich as to be able to betray his trust, and deprive the owner of the part of his own estate retained.' In order to prevent the federal government from usurping these reserved rights, Taylor argued that it was imperative for the States to resist both covert and overt forms of federal encroachment. 'The great extent of the United States will not admit both of a central supremacy, and of a free form of government,' concluded Taylor. 'The preservation of liberty must depend on the division of power between the State and federal governments.'

By 1865, Taylor's free form of government would be in ruins, the Confederate States which made a final stand against central supremacy in Washington, D.C., burned and bled into submission.

Taylor considered property 'the chief hinge on which social happiness depends.' By property, Taylor certainly did not mean the Yankee idolisation of Mammon – he considered 'avarice' and 'ambition' to be terrible vices – but of property's connection with the vital rights of life and liberty. 'The rights to life, liberty, and property, are so intimately blended together, that neither can be lost in a state of society without all,' observed Taylor. Since these

166

rights were all united, the acceptance of one logically entailed the acceptance of all. Likewise, a violation of one of those rights was ultimately a violation of them all. Any government which recognised the rights of life and liberty, but did not respect the right of property, was hypocritical. 'In the civilised world, property is the franklin for conducting the electrical stream, either of liberty or of slavery, to invigorate or to degrade mankind,' argued Taylor. 'If therefore in exercising the right of self-government, and in vindicating the sovereignty of the people, we have left a sovereign power over property, in the hands either of the State governments or the government of the union, all our work will be fruitless; because we shall have placed in the hands of power the instrument with which it can root out any restriction however carefully planted.' According to Taylor, 'This error is the rock upon which most republican governments have split.' When the government had the power to prey upon property, parasitic 'combinations' proliferated around it, lobbying for 'patronage' and leeching off the property of the people, along with their lives and liberties. While the 'unconcealed despotism' of a government with sovereign power over the persons and property of its subjects was no longer 'openly avowed,' Taylor insisted that it was still 'indirectly practised.' Under such a government, elections, remarked Taylor, were mere ruses to 'render the sovereignty of the government over property still stronger; and harder to transmute from being an instrument for inflicting private misery, into one for securing national happiness.' In other words, elections deceived the people into believing that they were sovereign, when in reality they were merely voting for which masters would enslave them. 'Thus,' quipped Taylor, 'the pretext of publick good is made into a mask with which to hide publick oppression.'

Taylor did not want the revolutionary rallying cry of 'no taxation without representation' to be taken out of context. 'In contending that our property could not be taken from us without our consent by our representatives,' he explained, 'it was admitted, whilst we spoke in reference to the English system of government, that it might be both taken and expended by our representatives, without restriction.' After declaring independence from the British Empire, however, the Americans clarified their intentions, crowning the people as sovereign and dethroning their governments as subordinate. 'When we separated from that government,' he continued, 'this admission, suggested by the wish for a compromise, was renounced by the adoption of forms of government founded in the principles, that sovereignty resided in the people, and that these governments were their trustees.' In other words, representative governments (even the State governments, delegated with far more power by their people) were not sovereign; only the people were sovereign. 'The powers not delegated by the people to the State governments, are as undoubtedly reserved to them, as the powers not delegated to the government of the United States,' argued Taylor. 'The exercise of any undelegated power by either, under a belief that it will advance the publick good, is unconstitutional in both cases; because a right to seek for the publick good, without our constitutional limits, involves a power of finding publick harm.' According to Taylor, transferring sovereignty from the British government to the State governments or federal government would 'subvert the great principle (the sovereignty of the people) upon which our political superstructure is founded' and 'repass the Rubicon, after we had gotten safely over it.'

Having delineated the basic principles of the American federal republic – the sovereignty of the people of the States, a division of power between the States and the Union, a conservative construction of the Constitution, and a liberal-republican government limited to the role of protecting property – Taylor then deftly applied them to current events. First and foremost in Taylor's sights was the ruling of *McCulloch v. Maryland*. This infamous case began when the Baltimore branch of the Second Bank of the United States refused to pay Maryland's taxes on its banknotes. Maryland took the national bank to court, where her old Anti-Federalist attorney general, Luther Martin, argued that because she and her sister States had neither surrendered their power of taxation nor delegated the power to charter a corporation in the

Constitution, her tax was not just constitutional, but the bank itself was actually unconstitutional. Martin knew firsthand that the States had never delegated this power to the Congress, as he was a Maryland delegate to the Constitutional Convention where that power was specifically considered and rejected. James Madison himself, who took copious notes on the proceedings, 'well-recollected that a power to grant charters of incorporation had been proposed in the general convention and rejected.' Although the State court upheld Maryland, the Supreme Court, led by Chief Justice John Marshall, struck her down, setting Constitution-shattering precedents which haunt the United States to this day. Ironically, as a young delegate at Virginia's Ratification Convention in 1788, Marshall had remarked, 'I hope that no gentleman will think that a State will called at the bar of the federal court.' Of course, in *McCulloch*, Marshall not only called Maryland to the bar of the federal court, but also ruled against her!

Specifically, Marshall asserted that under the Necessary and Proper Clause, the federal government was vested with 'implied powers' beyond its enumerated powers: unlimited 'means' for limited 'ends.' Incorporating a national bank, argued Marshall, though not strictly a delegated power, was a legitimate means in the execution of the ends of taxation and expenditure, both of which were delegated powers. This liberal construction of the Constitution came straight out of Treasury Secretary Alexander Hamilton's reports to President George Washington, written to counter Secretary of State Thomas Jefferson's conservative reports. Jefferson had strictly reasoned, 'To take a single step beyond the boundaries of thus drawn around the powers of Congress, is to take possession of a boundless field of power, no longer susceptible to definition,' but Marshall (and Washington) had found Secretary Hamilton's looser reasoning that 'if the end be clearly comprehended within any of the specified powers, and if the measure have an obvious relation to that end, and is not forbidden by any particular provision of the Constitution, it may safely be deemed to come within the compass of the national authority,' more persuasive. Furthermore, continued Marshall in *McCulloch*, since the Supremacy Clause made federal law superior to State law, Maryland had no right to interfere with the operations of the national bank or defy the federal government at all. Marshall's *McCulloch* ruling enshrined Hamiltonian liberal constructionism into 'constitutional law,' a growing body of court rulings increasingly contrary to what James Madison and Thomas Jefferson held as the true meaning of the Constitution: the intent of the ratifying States as expressed in their sovereign conventions.

Taylor's objections to this ruling were so extensive that he devoted five whole chapters (about one-third of the book) to its systematic demolition. Taylor viewed the ruling as extraordinarily duplicitous and accused Marshall of talking out of both sides of his mouth – paying homage to sound principles while advancing fraudulent ones. Taylor considered this trick to be analogous to currency counterfeiting – 'the art of melting up brass with gold.' Thomas Jefferson had his cousin, Marshall, and rulings such as *McCulloch v. Maryland*, in mind when he described the federal judiciary as 'an irresponsible body (for impeachment is scarcely a scarecrow), working like gravity by night and day, gaining a little today and a little tomorrow, and advancing its noiseless step like a thief over the field of jurisdiction until all shall be usurped from the States and the government be consolidated into one.'

The essence of Taylor's view of Marshall's ruling in *McCulloch v. Maryland* is summarised below:

> The essential conclusion of this opinion is, that an absolute sovereignty as to means does exist, where there is no sovereignty at all as to ends. This doctrine seems to me, to be evidently inconsistent with the principle of dividing, limiting, balancing, and restraining political powers, to which all our constitutions have unequivocally resorted, as the only resource for the preservation of a free form of government. If the means to which the government of the Union may resort for executing the powers

confided to it, are unlimited, it may easily select such as will impair
or destroy the powers confided to the State governments.

To Taylor, Marshall's reasoning of 'means' and 'ends' mirrored the
Parliament's assertion of unlimited power over the Colonies during the
Imperial Crisis: the federal government would have the right 'to legislate
over the States in all cases whatsoever.' Taylor warned that allowing the
federal government to decide for itself what 'means' were necessary and
proper for the execution of its enumerated powers, or 'ends,' would open up
a Pandora's box of unchecked, uncontroullable power. 'Like a fine lady
admiring a casket of jewels,' smirked Taylor, the federal government would
very easily find its heart's desire to be necessary and proper. In short,
McCulloch v. Maryland was a repudiation of the American Revolution: where
the Redcoats had failed, Federalist judges had succeeded.

When the States ratified the Constitution, explained Taylor, they
delegated particular ends to the federal government and reserved the rest to
themselves. While these divided State and federal ends would oppose one
another, in order to keep the government limited, they should never
encroach upon one another, as Marshall did in McCulloch v. Maryland. 'The
ends with which these governments are respectively entrusted, are allowed
to have been exclusively bestowed, and neither could constitutionally use its
legitimate ends, to defeat or absorb the legitimate ends assigned to the
other,' argued Taylor. 'So far the array of ends against ends appears to have
been placed by the Constitution on equal ground, and this equality justifies
the inference, that a mutual check upon the exercise of political power by
each government was intended.' Although the Constitution was 'positive
and explicit' in dividing the ends between the States and the federal
government, it was 'silent' regarding the means of executing the ends. Taylor
accused Marshall of trying to twist this silence into an unlimited reservoir of
power, or 'implied means,' for the federal government. 'This silence is
attempted to be exclusively appropriated to the government of the Union, so

that by the instrumentality of a monopoly of means, it may supplant and destroy the equality of ends plainly established by the Constitution, subdue the State ends by the appendages of the Union ends,' warned Taylor, 'and thus effectually overturn by implied means, our whole positive division of ends, made for the purpose of limiting, checking, and moderating power.' According to Taylor, 'As ends may be made to beget means, so means may be made to beget ends, until the cohabitation shall rear a progeny of unconstitutional bastards, which were not begotten by the people; and their rights being no longer secured by fixed principles, will be hazarded upon a game at shuttlecock with ends and means, between the general and State governments.'

Taylor scoffed at Marshall's reasoning that implied powers must exist because there was no clause in the Constitution which explicitly prohibited them. There was also no clause, he retorted, which established such a thing as implied powers, either, and there was certainly no clause allowing for alleged implied powers to override the actual division of power between the Union and the States. Since the Constitution was a compact of enumerated or 'marked' powers, however, a clause prohibiting implied powers would have been irrelevant and redundant. For good measure, however, Taylor observed that the Tenth Amendment, which held that all powers not delegated in the Constitution were reserved by the States, was, in fact, the very prohibition of implied powers which Marshall claimed did not exist.

Taylor was suspicious of Marshall's 'sophistical' discussion of the 'sovereignty' of the federal and State governments in their 'spheres of action.' The people of the States were the only sovereign 'body politick,' Taylor reiterated. If governments rather than the people were sovereign, then power would be unlimited and the Constitution a dead letter. Advancing under the cover of means for ends, the division of power between the States and the federal government would be surrendered. Thus an object of the first necessity or convenience, that of a free, moderate, and limited form of government, might be sacrificed for such pitiful objects, called objects of necessity or convenience, as transmitting the publick money by banks, staying judgments and executions, making a road or canal, creating fraudulent corporations, and absolving their great wealth from taxation, whilst very poor people are contributing to the support of government,' predicted Taylor. 'Usurpation begins with weaving a shroud for the support of free principles by the woof and warp of little conveniences and pretended necessities, and ends by inflicting the slavish quietism of a perfect subordination.' To illustrate this important point, Taylor told a story of a lady who wanted a new house, but could only convince her husband to repair the old one. The 'ingenious' lady gradually altered the house, carefully measured so as not to alert her husband to her true design. When the work was done, he found that she had, bit by bit, changed their old house into an entirely new one. Taylor suspected that rulings such as McCulloch v. Maryland would have the same insidious effect on the Constitution. 'Thus the indefinite attributes of a sovereignty of spheres, will gradually usurp and supplant the attributes of the sovereignty of the people,' warned Taylor. 'The old principle of limited ends will be thrown out of the window by the new principle of unlimited means.'

'It is a question of supremacy,' pronounced Marshall, a pompous phrase which annoyed Taylor to no end. Taylor surmised that since Marshall and the defunct Federalist Party were unable to refute the self-evident sovereignty of the people of the States at the polls, they had, in the courts, resorted to a ludicrous construction of the Supremacy Clause out of desperation. The Declaration of Independence declares the Colonies to be free and independent States; the constitutions of many States assert the sovereignty of the people; and sovereignty has hitherto been considered as the highest political degree,' argued Taylor. 'In that sense it has been claimed, held, and exercised by the people of every State in the Union from the Revolution to this day.' According to Taylor, 'The attempt made by the court to transplant sovereignty from the people of each State, by whom it has been and may be exercised, to the people of the United States, by whom it never has been nor can be exercised, under our present system of government, might fail of success; and therefore a new mode of destroying the sovereignty of the people is resorted to.' Marshall ruled that the Supremacy Clause made federal law 'supreme' to State law, but what the Supremacy Clause actually stated was that 'the Constitution,' along with all laws and treaties 'made in pursuance thereof' were 'the supreme law of the land.' In other words, only constitutional laws were supreme. 'Both the laws and treaties to be supreme must, therefore, be made in conformity with the powers bestowed, limited, and reserved by the Constitution,' reasoned Taylor, 'and by these we must determine whether a law or treaty has been constitutionally made, before the question of its supremacy can occur.' The Constitution encompassed the entire system of government in America – 'both State and federal, by delegating and reserving powers' – so describing it as the supreme law of the land was indeed correct. It was, however, the Constitution which was supreme, not federal law. Despite Taylor's refutation of Marshall's spurious claim, the crude notion that 'federal law trumps State law' remains firmly embedded in constitutional law.

Taylor denied that the Supreme Court ('supreme' insofar as its supremacy to other 'inferior' federal courts) even had jurisdiction over State law, the Constitution containing no such delegation of power. 'The constitutionality of State laws cannot be legitimately decided by the federal courts,' claimed Taylor, 'because they are not a constituent part of the State governments, nor have the people of the State confided to them any such authority.' Just as federal legislation had no supremacy over State legislatures, Taylor claimed that so the federal judiciary had no authority over the State judiciary. Taylor warned that the federal government (particularly the unelected and unaccountable judiciary) would expand this usurped power to 'modify' State laws which conflicted with its own laws. As Thomas Jefferson put it, 'The opinion which gives to the judges the right to decide what laws are constitutional and what are not, not only for themselves in their own sphere of action, but for the legislature and executive also in their spheres, would make the judiciary a despotic branch.' The division of power between the States and federal government would be 'idle' and 'insignificant' if the federal government could directly interfere in the States' internal affairs. If the federal government could strike down Maryland's tax (taxation being a reserved power of the States) then the rest of the States' reserved powers were also vulnerable. 'The supremacy of Congress and of the Court, in alliance also, has declared war against the sovereignty of the States,' observed Taylor, 'but how it will terminate, is hidden in the womb of time.'

How this war ended – the defeat of State sovereignty, the death of a quarter of Southern men, the defilement of Southern women, the destruction of two-thirds of Southern wealth, and the disintegration of Southern society – would have left the quick-witted, self-possessed Taylor speechless and shaken.

Nullification was Taylor's antidote to Marshall's poisonous doctrine of federal supremacy. Today, nullification is taboo, derided as a 'racist' antique of the Old South (as so many ideas, individuals, and institutions are in attempt to conceal the truth and value they have to offer), but in Taylor's time, nullification was much more commonplace. In 1765, 1767, and 1773 the American Colonies had, in effect, nullified the Stamp Act, the Townshend Acts, and the Tea Act by refusing to comply with British taxes, cutting off commerce with Great Britain, and forcing the resignation of British agents. In 1793, Georgia nullified the ruling of the Supreme Court in *Chisholm vs. Georgia*. In 1798, Virginia and Kentucky nullified the Alien and Sedition Acts. In 1809, Massachusetts and Connecticut nullified a federal embargo. In 1832, South Carolina would nullify the 'Tariff of Abominations.' From 1854 to 1858, Wisconsin, Connecticut, Rhode Island, Massachusetts, Michigan, Maine, and Kansas would effectively nullify the Fugitive Slave Act of 1850. Each of these acts resulted in some form of success, ranging from compromises to constitutional amendments. Indeed, up until the triumph of national supremacy and the defeat of State sovereignty in the War of Southern

Independence, nullification cropped up in all sections of the American republic for a variety of reasons – the States interpreting the Constitution for themselves (i.e. governing themselves) and pushing back against an overreaching federal government. By contrast, now all of 'The Land of the Free and the Home of the Brave' bends the knee to Washington, D.C., no matter how outrageous or oppressive its orders.

As Thomas Jefferson, the author of nullification, observed to Taylor in the midst of the Crisis of 1798, 'It is a singular phenomenon that while our State governments are the very best in the world, without exception or comparison, our general government has, in the rapid course of nine or ten years, become more arbitrary and has swallowed more of the public liberty than even that of England.'

Before the formation of the Union, noted Taylor, the States were sovereign, or 'supreme.' United, the States never surrendered their sovereignty to the federal government, but delegated limited powers enumerated in the Constitution, while reserving the rest of their rights to themselves. In the powers which the States delegated to the federal government, the federal government was supreme. Likewise, in all the powers reserved to the States, the States remained supreme. Thus, the States and the federal government were each supreme in their respective spheres; the delegation of some powers to the federal government did not amount to a delegation of the whole. 'By recognizing the supremacy transferred,' argued Taylor, 'it was not intended to destroy the portion of supremacy not transferred.' The States alone had supremacy over the rights which they reserved to themselves, just as the federal government had supremacy over the rights which the States had delegated to it. 'Hence it results, that the right of construing the Constitution within their respective spheres, is mutual between the State and general governments,' he deduced, 'because the latter have no supremacy over the State powers retained, and the former no supremacy over the federal powers delegated.' Therefore, the States, as supreme in their own spheres, were entitled and obligated not only to construe the Constitution for themselves as it pertained to their reserved rights, but also to resist federal encroachment of any of their reserved rights. 'Unconstitutional judgments, like unconstitutional laws,' averred Taylor, 'are null and void, and both courts are mutually bound by their oaths to the Constitution, and have a mutual right to resist and defeat, by every means in their power, unconstitutional laws falling within their respective jurisdictions.'

Thomas Jefferson once sent Taylor, a fellow nullifier, a poem which held that what constituted a State was men who did their duty and defended their rights:

> *What constitutes a State?*
> *Not high-raised battlements, or labour'd mound,*
> *Thick wall, or moated gate;*
> *Not cities proud, with spires and turrets crown'd;*
> *No: men, high-minded men;*
> *Men, who their duties know;*
> *But know their rights; and knowing, dare maintain.*
> *These constitute a State.*

Taylor acknowledged that if the federal government did not enjoy 'unlimited, unchecked supremacy in construing the Constitution,' then 'clashing constructions will ensue.' To Marshall, this would have been unthinkable, unimaginable lawlessness. If constitutional, declared Marshall, the actions of Maryland were capable of 'prostrating' the federal government 'at the foot of the States.' Taylor retorted that the federal government was already prostrated before the States as their creation and that prostrating a government exceeding the legal limitations on its power was a virtue rather than a vice. Furthermore, the paramount political ideal in America was not the uniformity of 'union,' but the liberty of self-government. The choice, held Taylor, was between abandoning the division of power for the sake of uniform construction or preserving the division of power in spite of clashing constructions. While the problems of clashing constructions were conjectural and trivial, Taylor pointed out that the terror of a supreme government able to construe the extent of its own power was factual and terrible. 'It is very true, that the federal and State courts may occasionally carry on little wars with the weapons called injunction and *habeas corpus*,' noted Taylor, 'but then these weapons cannot shed blood, confiscate property, nor burn hereticks, as supremacy has frequently done.'

When the Constitution was ratified by the States, it was understood that power would be separated between the States and the federal government, and that the former would be the chief restraint on the latter. 'How can this feature of our political system, so highly eulogised in the Federalist, be preserved,' asked Taylor, 'if the means for giving it efficiency should be taken away from these same State legislatures, by investing the federal judges with a supreme power over these means?' Indeed, Marshall's liberal construction left the States impotent and the federal government omnipotent.

Marshall asserted that even though the States (or, in his view, the collective people of the American nation) never delegated the power to incorporate a national bank to the federal government, the General Welfare Clause and Necessary and Proper Clause gave it the right to incorporate a bank anyway. One of the chief bones of contention of Anti-Federalists like Taylor, who opposed replacing the Articles of Confederation with the Constitution, were these clauses, the ambiguity of which they rightly insisted would be manipulated to justify the usurpation of powers supposedly reserved to the States. The Federalists, of course, assured them that this would and could never happen (to Taylor, however, McCulloch was 'proof' of the Federalists' 'real intention').

'The defence against the charge founded on the want of a bill of rights, presupposed...that the powers not given were retained; and that those given were not to be extended by remote implications,' argued James Madison against liberal constructionism in the first Congress' debate on incorporating a national bank. 'The explanations in the State conventions all turned on the same fundamental principle, and on the principle that the terms necessary and proper gave no additional powers to those enumerated.'

Today, if the politicians in Washington, D.C. are ever pressed to defend the constitutionality of one of the myriad bills written by their cronies that they never even read before voting into law, they mindlessly invoke the General Welfare Clause. One particularly dimwitted Congressman decreed that 'ObamaCare' was constitutional under 'The Good and Welfare Clause,' which was simply his constitutionally illiterate way of saying that the General Welfare Clause authorises the Congress to do whatever it wants. When asked the same question, the Speaker of the House simply squawked, 'Are you serious?' It is sometimes difficult to tell whether the ruling class is simply stupid or seriously sinister.

Perhaps on one wild and crazy night in Philadelphia, the framers, after overindulging in Samuel Adams' homebrew, decided that even though they had been painstakingly debating the delegated powers which would be enumerated in the Constitution, they should also add a clause granting unlimited powers to the new government. 'Had they done so, no specification of federal power would have been necessary,' observed Taylor, 'and if they do so, the subsequent specifications mean nothing.' This belief in the General Welfare Clause as some sort of genie which exists to grant the every wish of the Congress stems from Marshall's contrived construction in *McCulloch v. Maryland*, an unpleasant outgrowth which Taylor tried to nip in the bud.

Taylor despised the 'artifice' of construing the General Welfare Clause beyond the few enumerated powers in the Constitution. Such a liberal construction, held Taylor, rendered the Constitution so loose as to be 'unintelligible,' reducing it to 'a reservoir of every meaning for which its expounder may have occasion.' In other words, under such a construction, the Constitution would mean whatever those in power wanted it to mean, which defeated the whole purpose of placing constitutional limits on those in power in the first place. According to Taylor, the meaning of the General

179

Welfare Clause was limited to the powers delegated by the States to the federal government and enumerated in the Constitution. The federal government was to use these enumerated powers to provide for the 'common defence' and promote the 'general welfare,' but the General Welfare Clause itself was not a delegation of any power. It was, explained Taylor, 'introductory,' not 'decretal' – 'the ends in view are recited, and then follow the means for effecting those ends.' Furthermore, 'general welfare,' meant 'external objects, or objects common to all the States, as to which a consentaneous interest and feeling would prevail,' not a controversial measure favoured by a narrow majority, nor a bonanza to bring home the bacon to every Congressional district.

'The general purposes themselves were limited and explained by the particular enumeration subjoined,' continued James Madison against liberal constructionism in the debate on a national bank. 'To understand these terms in any sense, that would justify the power in question, would give to Congress an unlimited power; would render nugatory the enumeration of particular powers; would supersede all the powers reserved to the State governments.'

Taylor noted that the Necessary and Proper Clause applied only to the 'foregoing powers' enumerated in the Constitution. The federal government was permitted to make laws which were necessary and proper for the execution of the delegated powers enumerated in the Constitution, nothing more. Like the General Welfare Clause, the Necessary and Proper Clause was not a grant of power in itself, but an explanation of how the delegated powers should be enacted. For example, since the federal government had the constitutional power to levy customs taxes, it would therefore be necessary and proper to build customs houses and employ customs officers. It would not, however, be necessary and proper to incorporate a national bank, with a plethora of new powers unrelated to collecting customs, under the pretence of managing the customs revenue. Because there would be no limit to the powers which the federal government might claim were necessary and proper in relation to the constitutional powers of war, commerce, and taxation, only a conservative construction of the Necessary and Proper Clause, limited to the foregoing powers, was consistent with the Constitution. 'In short, this mode of construction completely establishes the position, that Congress may pass any internal law whatsoever in relation to things, because there is nothing with which war, commerce, and taxation may not be closely or remotely connected,' concluded Taylor, thereby stripping the States of 'their whole wardrobe of rights' and reducing them to 'naked political skeletons.' As Taylor put it, 'I see no end to the power of necessity, armed with supremacy...Necessity, inference, and expediency never fail to beget an endless successive progeny.'

'The plain question, divested of verbal evolutions,' sighed Taylor, 'is, whether Congress are invested with the supreme power of altering or mending the Constitution, should they imagine it to be expedient?' Taylor speculated that if the federal government could construe away the checks and collisions of the Constitution as Marshall had done, then there was nothing stopping one federal branch from finding it necessary and proper to overthrow the other federal branches as well as the State governments. 'If the inconvenience of collisions between coordinate political departments begets a necessity for the supremacy of one; and this necessity will justify its assumption, the scheme of checks and balances is entirely chimerical, and a political fabric built upon that theory must fail,' noted Taylor. 'A supreme power able to abolish collisions, is also able to abolish checks, and there can be no checks without collisions.' Collisions, therefore, were not a sign of dysfunctional 'gridlock,' but rather a sign that checks and balances were working as intended.

Taylor adamantly denied that establishing a national bank was necessary and proper for the execution of any delegated power, even under Marshall's liberal construction. Marshall claimed that a national bank was 'convenient, useful, and essential to fiscal operations.' Taylor countered that the question was not whether a bank was beneficial for the 'fiscal operations' of the government (for controul over the currency and higher tax revenues were certainly good for the government), but whether a national bank was beneficial for the people. First, by inflating the money supply, a national bank depreciated the currency, thereby 'aggravating' price levels and spending patterns. Second, a depreciated currency was worth less in international markets, making imports more expensive. Third, by loaning money to the government, a national bank saddled the posterity with debt and taxes beyond their consent and perhaps even their resources. Fourth, fractional-reserve banking (inflating the economy with artificial credit by pyramiding loans atop reserves, which Taylor seems to have figured out before most) was 'fraudulent' and a 'falsehood.' As soon as the people realised that a bank's loans exceeded its reserves, and that it therefore could not meet its obligations to all of its depositors, 'a heavy shock of factitious misfortunes' would ensue as depositors rushed to claim their deposits. Indeed, writing in the aftermath of the Panic of 1819, which ruined many of his fellow planters, Taylor was painfully aware of the damage that the boom-bust cycle could do to the economy. Lastly, the example of exempting wealthy and powerful bankers from punishment for their crimes would demoralise the people and corrupt the virtue necessary to maintain republican government. 'Can these be preserved,' asked Taylor of republican virtues, 'by investing corporate bodies with the privileges of committing remediless frauds, of laughing at detection, and of retaining the pillage?' Taylor went so far as to compare a national bank to the Devil himself, ruining his victims with the very temptations by which he ensnared them. 'Fiscal operations are the means by which civilised nations are oppressed and enslaved,' concluded Taylor. 'If a government may do whatever it pleases to think "convenient, useful, or essential in the prosecution of fiscal operations," however inconvenient, useless, and injurious to a nation, and however detrimental to the morals, interest, and happiness of individuals, it is difficult to conceive of any limitations by which it can be restrained.'

Taylor scoffed at Marshall's reliance on 'the frippery of precedents' in *McCulloch v. Maryland*, as if two wrongs somehow made a right. The Supreme Court was not sovereign, so it did not have the right to issue precedents dictating how the Constitution was to be construed. Only the people of the States were sovereign, and only they had the authority to make such determinations. If the federal government could expand its power by its own precedents, then there would no longer be any real limitations on its power. 'What should we say to a husband, who should surrender the custody of his wife to a set of professed rakes?' asked Taylor. 'That which ought to be said of a nation, which entrusts its constitution to the care of precedents.'

'If you comply with the Act, by using stamped papers, you rivet perpetual chains upon your unhappy country,' the renowned 'Pennsylvania Farmer' John Dickinson warned the colonists of the Stamp Act in 1765. 'You unnecessarily, voluntarily establish the detestable precedent, which those who have forged your fetters ardently wish for, to varnish the future exercise of this new claimed authority.' In 1767, against the Townshend Acts Dickinson again warned that 'the late act of Parliament is only designed to be a precedent, whereon the future vassalage of these Colonies may be established.' According to Dickinson, 'Here may be observed, that when any ancient law or custom of Parliament is broken, and the Crown possessed of a precedent, how difficult a thing it is to restore the subject again to his former freedom and safety.'

'A phalanx of words have been enlisted to assail the plainest portions of the Federal Constitution,' Taylor concluded *of McCulloch v. Maryland*. To Taylor, McCulloch was nothing more than 'artificial phraseology,' which he defined as 'the vocation of stripping evils of unseemly attire in order to dress them more handsomely, or of subjecting the Federal Constitution to the needles of verbal embroiderers, in obedience to the saying, "the tailor makes the man."' Taylor was confident that this plain truth would cut through the 'fine webs' spun by Marshall – that the people would not be bamboozled by such sophistry. Given that McCulloch is now taught to students of history and law as Gospel truth, Taylor appears to have overestimated the republican virtues of future Americans, who have indeed proven themselves unworthy sons and cuckolded husbands.

In 1820, most federal tax revenue came from taxes on imported manufactures, also known as tariffs (an income tax, although collected illegally during the so-called 'Civil War,' was not constitutional until 1913). The Constitution required that taxes only be levied for the collection of revenue and that indirect taxes such as tariffs be uniform among the States, yet while the North was profiting handsomely, the South was paying a heavy price. The South was an agricultural economy with little domestic industry, trading her cash crops (cotton, tobacco, rice, and sugar) for European manufactures. In fact, Southern cash crops comprised almost all of American exports. The North, by contrast, was a nascent industrial economy with little to no foreign trade. As a result of these differing economies, federal tariffs fell on the trade-dependent South the hardest, burdening her with higher taxes on imported manufactures and higher prices on domestic manufactures. All told, the South was paying the bills of Washington, D.C., as well as subsidising the bottom lines of government-dependent Northern industries. In 1816, Southerners such as John C. Calhoun had generously consented to protectionist tariffs to help Northerners repair the damage done to their economy during the War of 1812, as well as to secure American commercial independence. By 1820, however, it was becoming clear to Southerners like Taylor that Northerners were not interested in temporary aid for postwar recovery, but rather a scheme of permanent privilege and economic exploitation. To Taylor, this alleged 'American System' was equivalent to 'a right to distribute wealth and poverty, gain and loss, between occupations and individuals.'

Taylor espoused the liberal-republican philosophy that the purpose of government was to protect mankind's natural rights. 'Man, by nature, had two rights,' claimed Taylor, 'to his conscience, and to his labour; and it was the design of civil society to secure these rights.' Free men, of course, had an equal right to their conscience and labour. 'Equal laws, and equal rights in its citizens,' were what distinguished liberty from tyranny. While some sacrifice of the 'freedom of labour' in the form of taxation was considered necessary for public use, taxation for private use – taking from some and giving to others – was abhorrent in a free society, no different from theft in practice and principle. The natural rights of labour, in subjecting themselves to contributions for the support of civil government, never meant to acknowledge themselves to be the slaves of a despotick power,' argued Taylor. In Europe, governments divided and ruled by pitting 'religious sects' against each other; in America, it was 'occupations' (that is, class warfare).

Taylor found the argument for protectionist tariffs absurd, comparing it to the scene from *Don Quixote* in which Sancho is deceived that he will be happier and healthier if he declines food and drink. Taylor, echoing the English economist David Ricardo, explained that each economy had its own comparative advantage in producing certain goods, and that trading those goods was mutually beneficial for all economies involved. Tariffs, quipped Taylor, were equivalent to 'bartering comforts for deprivations,' while trade was equivalent to 'bartering comforts for comforts.' Indeed, enriching some at the expence of others, thus infringing on a man's right to labour, ultimately infringed on his very life. 'It is an evasion of the right to live, to take away the products of labour by which man lives, and to give them to other men,' remarked Taylor. 'If a government can take some, it may take all; and bad governments, by this species of tyranny, do often starve men to death.' Taylor would have been sickened, though not surprised, at the mass-starvation, mass-disease, and mass-murder under the totalitarian regimes of the twentieth century.

Ambitious and avaricious minority interests, which Taylor labeled 'combinations,' had always been devising schemes for the government to oppress the majority for their own profit. 'An encouragement of manufacturers' was simply the latest 'nominal modification' of this age-old 'tyrannical principle.' What difference, asked Taylor, did a man's occupation

185

make concerning his natural rights? Whether a farmer, manufacturer, merchant, lawyer, or doctor, all free men had an equal right to the fruits of their labour and their property. 'It is equality of rights, and nothing else, which constitutes a free, fair, and mild government,' claimed Taylor.

Protectionist tariffs were not only unjust, argued Taylor, but also unconstitutional. Since the Constitution created a federal government between separate, equal States instead of a national government over one people, its powers pertained only to the States, not 'persons and things.' Tariffs, however, targeted some individuals, interests, and sections of the Union for exploitation and others for enrichment. The General Welfare Clause, far from granting unlimited power to the federal government, actually limited the government to laws which benefited all States equally, yet tariffs were inherently unequal in their economic effect. 'Congress can only impose taxes, constitutionally, for the defence and welfare of the States,' asserted Taylor, 'and an imposition of taxes for the purpose of enriching one State, one interest, or one individual, at the expence of another State, another interest, or another individual, is as unconstitutional as it is adverse to the freedom and fairness of exchange.' Taylor quoted Alexander Hamilton in the *Federalist*, detailing how the prospective federal government would have no authority to promote any industry over another. 'Exorbitant duties on imported articles tend to render other classes of the community, tributary, in an improper degree, to the manufacturing classes,' explained Hamilton, creating 'inequality, between the manufacturing and non-manufacturing States.' Once the Constitution was ratified, however, Hamilton (another lying Federalist, as Taylor saw it) came out in favour of the very tariffs he disclaimed as oppressive and discriminatory. 'What a whimsical thing is party politicks!' scoffed Taylor.

The federal government's constitutional power to 'regulate commerce' was frequently trotted out as a legal justification for protectionist tariffs. Yet, the power to regulate commerce and the power of taxation were separately defined and limited in the Constitution. The power to regulate commerce could not be intended to convey to Congress an indefinite power of taxation,' noted Taylor, 'because a definite power of taxation had already been expressed.' By the Constitution, direct taxes had to be apportioned among the States, indirect taxes had to be uniform among the States, taxes on exports were prohibited, and no preferential treatment could be given to the ports of one State over those of others. Protectionist tariffs, argued Taylor, violated each of these restrictions. First, although tariffs were indirect taxes in form, they were direct taxes 'in fact,' and thus should be apportioned among the States according to their population. Because the Southern States comprised a minority of the population of the United States, the Northern States would have to pay their fair share for the expensive government they were enjoying for free. Second, European consumers of American exports often paid in kind (i.e. with exports of their own rather than cash). By taxing the medium of exchange in American trade, exports fell as if taxed directly. If anything, then, tariffs were a 'double tax,' depressing the price of what Americans were selling abroad and inflating the price of what they had to buy at home. Third, protectionist tariffs amounted to preferential treatment for ports. The whole point of protectionist tariffs was to force up the price of imports so that Americans (particularly import-consuming Southerners) would be forced to substitute higher-priced Northern manufactures for the lower-priced European imports. The Northern ports benefited from this government-engineered draining of money across the Mason-Dixon Line, not because it promoted the general welfare, but because it was from those ports where many Northern manufactures were shipped to the South.

Although the amount of 'verbal subterfuges' by which the federal government attempted to usurp power and violate liberty was overwhelming, Taylor was confident that the Constitution, properly construed, could guard against them all. 'Man's foresight cannot anticipate all the artifices of ambition and avarice,' admitted Taylor, 'but the restrictive clauses of the Constitution, compared the limited powers bestowed, demonstrate an abhorrence of the idea, that the federal government should have a power of bestowing preferences of any kind upon States, districts, or occupations.'

Taylor was especially appalled that those who paid the price of protectionist tariffs were primarily poor farmers in the North as well as the South. 'Morality may calmly disapprove of the rich plundering the rich,' exclaimed Taylor, 'but humanity shrinks with no little impression of abhorrence, from the idea of the rich plundering the poor.' To Taylor, the rich and powerful preying on the poor was 'worse than fraud,' and was, in fact, 'grinding oppression.' Taylor saw through the protectionists' profession that high tariffs helped the 'manufacturing poor' and strengthened the economy as nothing more than a 'flimsy pretence' to justify their tariff-protected monopolies over the domestic market. 'To tax one poor man for the benefit of another, each having no other capital, but his natural ability to labour, in its degree oppression, is the same to the sufferer, as if the tax had been appropriated to the rich; but the distinction is of no consequence, because the fact upon which it is surmised does not exist,' argued Taylor. 'The whole community, poor and rich, is taxed by the protecting-duty system...it is a tax upon the poor and rich of the whole community, all being consumers, for the exclusive benefit of one rich occupation.' According to Taylor, 'This is aristocracy in its worst character.'

At the time Taylor was writing, the longstanding political, economic, cultural, and social/racial differences between the North and the South, previously the source of secret suspicions, were turning into open hostilities. Taylor blamed this growing sectionalism on 'combinations,' by which he meant factions of rich and powerful 'capitalists' relying on government-granted privileges. 'Combinations have hitherto succeeded by deluding particular States into an opinion, that they would be benefitted by serving under the banners of mercenary self-interest,' observed Taylor. Yet Taylor insisted that the North and the South were not foes, but friends. Their economies were complementary, each specialising in what it produced best and engaging in tariff-free interstate trade. It was the 'monied interest,' a wealthy and powerful faction of bankers and industrialists, which exploited their differences and divided them against each other. 'An intercourse upon fair and equal terms, between the sections of the Union, founded in an exchange of agricultural labour for naval, commercial, and manufactural, is the basis of mutual prosperity,' argued Taylor, 'and utterly distinct from the speculations of a monied interest, whose prosperity is founded in principles, always hostile to the interest of labour.' Indeed, most Northerners did not even benefit from the 'American System' which they supported! While the productive Northern and Southern people paid the price of these policies, a parasitic paper-aristocracy reaped the profits. 'The policy of fostering combinations by federal laws, has undoubtedly transferred, and continues to transfer, a considerable portion of the profits of labour, from one portion of the Union to another,' explained Taylor, 'not to enrich the people generally of the receiving States, but to amass great capitals for a few individuals residing in them; towards which all the States must contribute, and by which is artificially reared a monied interest at the expence of the whole community.'

The machinations of this monied interest, claimed Taylor (which had 'deluded' the Northern States onto its side), had 'already produced awful calculations in reference to a dissolution of the Union.' The rise of a 'geographical majority' of North over South was the harbinger of disunion, avowed Taylor, as the South, like her revolutionary forefathers, would never submit to the usurpations over her life, liberty, and property which such a majority aimed to impose. For now, Taylor cautioned, the North and the South were fighting with pens, but soon they may be fighting with swords. The prospect of civil war pained Taylor, who desperately maintained that Northerners and Southerners were not enemies, but allies, and had no real reason to fight in the first place. 'For what are the States going to disunion, and for what are they going to war amongst themselves?' asked Taylor. 'To create and establish a monied sect, composed of privileged combinations, as an aristocratic oppressor of them all,' he answered bitterly. The mercantilist, militaristic, maniacal Republican Party which took over the American federal republic and transformed her into a national democracy through corruption, consolidation, and conquest, was the consummation of the 'monied interest' which Taylor sensed in the shadows.

The unnecessary, avoidable economic conflict between the North and the South which Taylor deplored culminated with the presidential election of the Republican Abraham Lincoln, a self-professed 'Old Henry Clay Tariff Whig.' The Republicans, hoping to win the swing States of Pennsylvania and New Jersey, proposed the highest-ever tariff increase, tripling the average rate. The Congressmen who introduced the bill, Justin S. Morrill and Thaddeus Stevens, handsomely profited from the bill's protection for their private investments. South Carolina and six other Lower-South States had already seceded (which, ironically, by removing their Congressmen from Capitol Hill, was what made the passage of the bill possible), but Virginia and five other Upper-South States were still debating their future in the Union. 'For what purpose does the Yankee want power? What do they do with power?' asked Leonard Stout Hall, representing Wetzel County at Virginia's Secession Convention. 'The very first thing they do is to pass a Morrill tariff bill for the purpose of robbing and plundering the South,' he answered. 'Look at the condition of this general government,' remarked Pittyslvania County's William M. Tredway. 'In the hands of utterly incompetent, corrupt men from the highest to the lowest, so stupid, so utterly blind to the true principle upon which a government ought to be administered, and so hungry for spoils, the first thing they have done is to pass that iniquitous Morrill tariff bill – a bill by which it was intended to plunder the South.' According to Halifax County's James C. Bruce, 'If the South were true to itself, it would require the North to give up its tariff policy, and give us free trade; but instead of that they give us the Morrill Tariff.' Declaring slavery and the tariff the two 'fundamental questions' dividing the North and the South, former President John Tyler, Jr., representing Charles City County, argued that 'the tariff law which has been lately passed,' the Morrill Tariff, proved that Virginia was 'manacled, in the power of that majority without restraint.' Shortly before his unilateral proclamation of war against the Confederacy, Lincoln explained to three separate delegations from the Upper South (two from Virginia and one from Maryland) that he could not afford to let the South (upon which the federal government relied for taxes and Northern industry relied for profits) go in peace. 'What, then, would become of my tariff?' exclaimed Lincoln. 'If I do that, what would become of my revenue?' Taylor would have wept to have encountered such rank Yankee ambition and avarice in the midst of a national crisis.

In 1821, Missouri and Maine were admitted to the Union on a compromise in Congress. When Missouri petitioned Congress for admission to the Union, the House of Representatives voted for the abolition of slavery within Missouri as a precondition for statehood. When the Senate rejected the House's precondition, statehood stalled and tempers flared. The 'Missouri Compromise' broke the deadlock, dividing slavery in the Territories along the 36°30 latitude, permitting it southward and prohibiting it northward. The attempt to block the admission of Missouri on an alleged objection to slavery was not an act of humanity, however, but a political calculation. The Northern-based Federalists had been irrelevant for twenty years and counting, having lost the last four presidential elections to a Virginian of the Southern-based Democratic-Republican Party (the next year, they would go on to lose another) and been reduced to a minority in the Congress. Since the people had decisively rejected their neo-Hamiltonian agenda of a supreme national government, standing armies, heavy taxes, high subsidies for domestic industries, national banks, and a permanent debt, the desperate Federalists decided to divide the Union along the line of slavery, hoping to subvert the Democratic-Republicans and exclude new Southern States from the Union at the same time, all the while cloaking their political aspirations with moral pretension. Taylor regarded the 'spectacle of slavery' as a 'cunning device' to unite the North against the South, but urged

Northern Democratic-Republicans to remember that 'those who forget their own pockets during a fray often lose their money.'

'The idea of a balance of power between two combinations of States, and not the existence of slavery,' protested Taylor, 'gave rise to this unfortunate, and I shall endeavor to prove, absurd controversy.' Taylor vividly compared the Missouri Crisis to the three witches of *Macbeth*, casting the ingredients 'ambition, avarice, exclusion, privileges, bounties, pensions, and corporations,' disguised as 'slavery,' into a cauldron of 'United States' while chanting their curse, 'Double, double, toil and trouble, fire burn, and cauldron bubble.'

A balance of power belonged between hostile nations like Great Britain and France, objected Taylor, but not confederated States. Any struggle for power was doomed to end tragically, as the losing side would eventually attempt to free itself from the grasp of the winner. If the Congress would simply do its duty and confine itself to the powers 'common to all,' insisted Taylor, then there would be no reason for 'combinations' of States to form against each other in the first place. 'The extreme anxiety to obtain a preponderance,' Taylor pointed out, 'acknowledges a thorough conviction on both sides and that it will sacrifice the interest of some States and individuals to advance that of others.' To Taylor, the very idea of dividing the Union along the line of slavery seemed unnatural. 'Climate, proximity, and navigation' were the only 'natural causes' which could separate States into different sections, yet the States were all too diverse for such a division to take place. Even the closest sister States of any section, such as Maine and Ohio, or Maryland and Missouri, did not all share all of the same interests. 'Slave-holding' and 'non-slaveholding' States were artificial distinctions which forced two sections which were otherwise at peace into 'combinations' against each other.

Taylor saw the Missouri Crisis as a dangerous advance in a 'succession of events' of national supremacy against State sovereignty. First, the federal assumption of the State debts begat the national debt, which in turn begat the national bank, which in turn begat a privileged position for financiers and industrialists. Now came the 'idea of using slavery as instrument for effecting a balance of power,' leading to 'new usurpations of internal powers over person and property' which would ultimately 'beget a dissolution of the Union.' Taylor compared this creeping consolidation of power to the Serpent's corrupting presence in the Garden of Eden. 'If the division of powers between the State and federal governments be rooted out of the Federal Constitution, and the freedom of labour or of property should be lost, by the temptations of the two devils, avarice and ambition, to induce legislatures to meddle with forbidden fruit,' warned Taylor, 'the essence of our political system will be destroyed, and with it our vaunted residence in a region of political felicity.'

As if it were not enough that it portended a sectional conflict which could lead to the dissolution of the Union, Taylor pointed out that the Missouri Compromise also happened to be unconstitutional. First, States were prohibited from forming agreements or compacts with other States, yet the compromise was obviously such an agreement. 'Is not the Missouri agreement or compact, a positive violation of this plain prohibition, and supposing no other argument existed, clearly unconstitutional from this single consideration?' marveled Taylor. 'It is a compact or agreement by one half of the States with the other half.' Second, it had been 'definitively disposed of by the federal compact' that the legality of slavery was an internal affair of each sovereign State. 'A Southern majority in Congress has no right to compel the Northern States to permit slavery,' insisted Taylor, 'nor a Northern majority to compel the Southern States to abolish it, because it is a subject of internal State regulation prohibited to Congress, and reserved to the States.' Slavery and emancipation, Taylor held, 'belong to the local powers reserved to the States.' Third, the federal government only had the authority to 'admit' new States to the Union, not to 'modify' them. If Congress was not allowed to meddle in the internal affairs of 'old States,' then it was equally forbidden from meddling in the internal affairs of 'new

States.' Fourth and finally, the federal government was obliged to guarantee a republican government for each State. The essence of republicanism was 'representation,' yet the Congress was already interfering with Missouri's internal affairs before she was even represented in the Congress.

Taylor counseled caution in freeing the slaves, pointing to the catastrophic failure of emancipation in the French colony of Santo Domingo. 'Liberty, equality, and fraternity' were bestowed upon the French slaves by fiat, and the result was the total slaughter of the white population (as well as much of the mixed-race population by the pure-blooded Africans) and the crushing defeat of an army Napoleon Bonaparte dispatched to quell the rebellion. 'An intemperate zeal, united with an ignorance of local circumstances,' warned Taylor, 'had to bewail the massacre of about forty thousand white men, women, or children, of about thirty thousand mulattoes, after they had united with the blacks in that atrocity, of about one hundred thousand of the blacks themselves, and of dividing the residue into tyrants, and slaves.' Taylor hoped that the United States would learn from France's mistake and follow a more conservative course in emancipating their slaves. After all, emancipation was already growing organically in the South without any outside interference from the North. 'A reformation of longstanding evils is best affected by slow remedies,' pled Taylor, 'and the progress made by the States themselves towards diminishing this, shews that they may be trusted with confidence in an affair of their own, of which they are the best and rightful judges.' Indeed, ten years later, Taylor's Virginia would seriously debate emancipating her slaves – an act which would have led the way among the Southern States – and if not for the terrible timing of a gruesome slave revolt and the outbreak of abolitionist agitation, may very well have embarked on such a course.

If Northern States could exclude Southern States from admission to the Union, then Southern political power would wane while Northern political power waxed. 'The ends to be effected,' explained Taylor, 'are a monopoly of the office of government, and of the partialities of Congress.' Even if the

North gained controul of the federal government, Taylor was sure that her victory would prove bittersweet. Although the North would 'absorb the office of government, and the favours of Congress' to 'gratify the avarice and ambition of a few individuals among them for a short space,' such oppression would drive the South out of the Union, thus killing the goose that laid the golden egg. Taylor believed that a Union controulled by national parties drawn from every section would be stronger than a Union controulled by sectional parties tyrannising each another. Taylor ominously threatened that if 'the danger to the slave-holding States' continued, then they may 'put the subject of slavery to rest' by resorting to 'the natural right of self-defence,' which was 'a right, anterior to every political power whatsoever.'

According to Taylor, James Madison and Alexander Hamilton, writing in the Federalist, assured their readers that 'in the division of powers between the federal and State governments, the largest share had fallen to the latter.' Yet whatever the men who framed and ratified the Constitution had agreed to on paper, it had clearly failed in practice, as the federal government's 'capacity for augmentation' had proven. 'Most or all of the measures complained of as unconstitutional, have originated with Congress,' noted Taylor, 'and a capacity for augmentation naturally encroaches.' This augmentation of federal power and encroachment upon State sovereignty should 'awaken the vigilance of those who think, that federalism is indispensable for the good government of so large a country as the United States.' Taylor defined 'federalism' as a 'positive confederation of a family of States,' stressing that federalism was a bottom-up rather than a top-down system of government. 'Federalism cannot exist without confederates, and confederates are inefficient without power.' If the financiers and industrialists (whom Taylor mocked as 'eleemosynarians' for their hypocritical advancement of private interests in the name of the public good) controulled the federal government instead of the States, then small-f federalism and small-r republicanism were dead. Since the States were the pillars of the federal government, weakening the States' power would ultimately weaken the federal government as well. 'If these props fall, a very different power from that Congress will spring from the ruins,' worried Taylor. At the same time, while the States offered the federal government honest 'friendship,' and were a sort of 'federal militia fighting without pay,' the 'eleemoysynarians' were little more than 'mercenary troops, sure to desert unless allowed to plunder.' Taylor stressed that 'the notion of a contest for power between the federal and State government' had no rational basis, but had 'originated from sounds without sense, or from artifices without honesty.' According to Taylor, the federal government must choose 'whether to appease its old friends, the States, or to cling to its courtiers, the eleemoysynarians,' and the States must choose 'whether an imitation of the federal eleemoysynarian system, or a cultivation of the publick good, will by economy and justice, contribute most to their preservation.' At the same time, concluded Taylor, the North, in driving the South to disunion, must choose 'whether an animal, created with a number of legs, would act wisely in cutting off one half, from a notion that it would walk better with half than with all.'

III

In 1794, a curious meeting took place between John Taylor of Caroline and two New Englanders in the Senate. Taylor related the details of the meeting to James Madison, the Jeffersonian opposition leader in the House of Representatives. When Taylor announced his intention to resign from the Senate, Rufus King of Massachusetts, a former framer at the Constitutional Convention, invited him to a committee room 'to converse with him seriously and candidly upon a very important subject.' Given the fierce Southern opposition which Virginia had led against the Northern-based Federalist Party, King was convinced that 'it was utterly impossible for the Union to continue.' According to King, 'The Southern and [North-] Eastern people thought quite differently,' and as a result, the Southern opposition had 'clogged and counteracted' all of the Federalists' policies. Soon 'the Southern interest would prevail' in the Congress, but the North would 'never submit to their politicks,' either. Thus, concluded King, 'a dissolution of the Union by mutual consent, was preferable to a certainty of the same thing, in a less desirable mode.' Then, in what Taylor figured was staged, Oliver Ellsworth of Connecticut, another framer from the Constitutional Convention, entered the room and agreed with King, both pressing upon Taylor that 'fixing the outlines of a separation' should be done peacefully while it was still possible, and speculating that the 'line of division' could be anywhere from the Potomac River to the Hudson River.

Taylor responded that while he appreciated his colleagues' candour, he disagreed that the Union had to be dissolved. It was political parties which divided the Union, held Taylor, not an actual 'material contrariety of interests.' Taylor continued that the national debt was 'the great cause of these parties,' with the emerging Democratic-Republicans suspecting that the Federalists were 'determined to use this debt as a political machine, and to counteract its payment,' and the Federalists suspecting that the Democratic-Republicans would 'destroy' the debt (and thus American national credit) by repudiation. If the two parties could 'remove these mutual suspicions,' then it would 'give new vigour to the Union.' Of course, if it did come down to disunion, agreed Taylor, 'an amicable separation was certainly preferable.' King adamantly rejected Taylor's suggested compromise, insisting that 'there were other essential subjects of difference between the extremities of the Union, besides the debt.' The North and the South 'had never and would never think alike.' King accused his fellow framer, James Madison, the leader of the Southern opposition, of 'some deep and mischievous design,' and 'saw no remedy but a dissolution of the Union.' Taylor asked King what he thought the other differences between the parties were and if 'any alternative preferable to a dissolution of the Union, could not be hit upon.' King refused to elaborate – significantly, nothing was said of slavery, the supposed source of all differences between the North and the

South – reiterating that 'the only remedy for the political dissensions, was a dissolution of the Union.' In his letter to Madison, Taylor remarked that since King and Ellsworth knew that he was an Anti-Federalist they must have assumed he was 'secretly an enemy to the Union' and was a 'fit instrument' for their 'design to break the Union.' Although Taylor was not yet ready to dissolve the Union, he did distrust Northern leaders of harbouring some plot 'to bring the South to their terms.'

James Madison, reading Taylor's letter, must have worried for the fate of the Union, for he was aware that there was strong sentiment for secession in the South as well. 'To disunite is dreadful to my mind, but dreadful as it is, I consider it a lesser evil than union on the present conditions,' the Henry Lee III, the Revolutionary-War hero and father of future Confederate hero Robert E. Lee, had informed Madison. 'I had rather myself submit to all the hazards of war and risk the loss of everything dear to me in life, than to live under the rule of a fixed insolent Northern majority.' Convinced that 'no policy will be adopted by the Congress which does not more or less tend to depress the South and exalt the North,' Lee put the question bluntly to Madison: 'Is your love for the Constitution so ardent as to induce you to adhere to it though it should produce ruin to your native country?'

By 1865, the Union had indeed been shattered, as Rufus King and Oliver Ellsworth had predicted to Taylor, but had been hammered back together by blood and iron, which none of these Founding Fathers ever expected or desired. The North, as Taylor had suspected, had indeed brought the South to her terms: the 'rebels' had been forced to adopt new State constitutions, written by their conquerors, abolishing slavery and disavowing secession. In that year, another Taylor had another curious meeting with other Northerners, though under far different and darker circumstances. General Richard Scott Taylor, a distant descendant of John Taylor of Caroline, was in command of 10,000 Confederate soldiers in Alabama. Taylor had received news of General Robert E. Lee's surrender at Appomattox and President Abraham Lincoln's assassination in Washington, D.C., but despite these events, Taylor told his 'gallant, faithful men' that 'granting the cause for which we had fought to be lost, we owed it to our own manhood, to the memory of the dead, and to the honour of arms, to remain steadfast to the last.' When Taylor heard of General Joseph E. Johnston's surrender at Bentonville, however, he decided that the time had come. On 4 May 1865, Taylor surrendered to General Edward R.S. Canby, the 'urbanity' of whom made a profound impression on him. Taylor recalled the contrast between the Federals and the Confederates, the former in 'full fig' (ceremonial dress) the latter in 'rusty suits' (battle-worn uniforms). After the terms were finalised, Canby hosted a feast where Taylor was reunited with some of his old Northern friends. When the Federal band struck up, 'Hail, Columbia,' Canby ordered that they play, 'Dixie' instead, out of respect to their former foe, but Taylor politely declined. 'I insisted on the first, and expressed a hope that Columbia would be again a happy land, a sentiment honoured by many libations.'

Unfortunately, 'there was, as ever, a skeleton at the feast' – a German officer who had immigrated to the United States during the war. 'With the strong accent and idioms of the Fatherland,' recalled Taylor, the German 'comforted me by assurances that we of the South would speedily recognise our ignorance and errors, especially about slavery and the rights of the States, and rejoice in the results of the war.' Canby tried to silence the sneering officer, but to no avail. 'I apologised meekly for my ignorance,' Taylor retorted, 'on the ground that my ancestors had come from England to Virginia in 1608, and, in the short intervening period of two hundred and fifty-odd years, had found no time to transmit to me correct ideas of the duties of American citizenship. Moreover,' Taylor continued, 'my grandfather, commanding the 9th Virginia Regiment in our Revolutionary army, had assisted in the defeat and capture of the Hessian [i.e. German] mercenaries at Trenton, and I lamented that he had not, by association with these worthies, enlightened his understanding.' With a thin smile, the German assured Taylor that he would be happy to instruct him, and indeed, thenceforth the United States have been the nation-state of Otto Van Bismarck, not the federal republic of George Washington. Taylor, for his part, was being modest: he might also have mentioned his father, former President Zachary Taylor, or his distant ancestor, John Taylor of Caroline, who as much as any man stood for what the American federal republic was meant to be and what the Confederacy had defended to the death.

IV. Abel Parker Upshur & *A Brief Enquiry into the Nature and Character of the Federal Government*

I confess that it seems to me exceedingly clear, that our Constitution is most worthless and tyrannical, if the usurpations of those who administer it, cannot be resisted by any means short of revolution. I have always considered the reserved powers of the States, as the only real check upon the powers of the federal government; and I have always considered it, not only the right, but the imperious duty of the States, so to apply that check, as not to dissolve the Union.
– Abel Parker Upshur, 1833

TODAY, THE CONSTITUTIONAL doctrine of States' rights is remembered, if it is remembered at all, as a legalistic excuse for the preservation of slavery – a part of the past best forgotten. 'Everything else – states' rights, Southern self-government, Southern honor, white supremacy, the "Southern way of life" as a whole – served, grew out of, required, or derived its meaning from chattel slavery,' sweepingly concludes Bruce Levine, a historian at the University of Illinois. Taking seriously what Southerners said about States' rights, Levine continues, is nothing more than 'sepia-tinged nostalgia for the Old South.' James M. McPherson, a Pulitzer-winning historian from Princeton University, claims that masking slavery with an 'alternative explanation,' such as constitutional or cultural differences between the North and the South, was merely a 'psychological necessity' on the part of racists and rebels with a guilty conscience. 'States' rights, or sovereignty, was always more a means than an end, an instrument to achieve a certain goal more than a principle,' McPherson argues. 'In the antebellum South, the purpose of asserting state sovereignty was to protect slavery from the potential hostility of a national majority against Southern interests – mainly slavery.' Indeed, it is *de rigueur* among modern historians to discount whatever Southerners said about politics, economics, or culture as a false front for the ulterior motive of slavery – as if Southerners were not perfectly clear and candid about slavery elsewhere and required codewords to communicate!

This essay series aims to set the story straight. The truth is that the great political treatises of the Old South prove that the constitutional doctrine of States' rights was never a mere pretence for slavery, but reflected a deep passion for self-government rooted in Southern culture as well as an earnest understanding of the Constitution rooted in Southern history. According to the scholarly, gentlemanly M.E. Bradford, States' rights were a part of the Southern political tradition – a 'patrimony' and 'birthright' – dating from the foundation of the Colonies, through the independence of the States, and to the foundation of the Constitution. At the crowning of the Confederate capital in Richmond, President Jefferson Davis honoured this heritage. 'The cause in which we are now engaged is the cause of the advocacy of the rights to which we were born, those for which our fathers of the Revolut

ion bled – the richest inheritance that ever fell to man, and which it is our sacred duty to transmit untarnished to our children,' announced Davis. 'Upon us is devolved the high and holy responsibility of preserving the constitutional liberty of a free government.'

Abel P. Upshur and his book, *A Brief Enquiry into the Nature and Character of the Federal Government*, published in 1840, are the subjects of this essay.

I

Abel P. Upshur was born on 17 June 1790 on Virginia's Eastern Shore, a small strip of land between the Chesapeake Bay and the Atlantic Ocean. Upshur, son of a prominent family in this isolated corner of the country, attended Yale College and the College of New Jersey (now Yale University and Princeton University, respectively), but was expelled from the latter after leading a student rebellion which threatened to shut down the school. At Upshur's hearing, college officials compared the school administration to civil government, arguing that both were owed absolute obedience. Upshur disputed this comparison, retorting that if the people were 'dissatisfied with the government' then they 'have a right to resist or even to overthrow it.' Upshur studied the law privately and was admitted to the bar in 1810. He opened his own law firm in Baltimore, but returned to Virginia after his father's death, where he briefly volunteered in the War of 1812. Back home, his new law practice flourished and he became active in Virginia politics, serving as a legislator, attorney, and judge. Upshur and his family divided their time between his father's old plantation, 'Vauclause,' and his wife's home in Baltimore.

At first, Upshur followed his father into Virginia's distinguished Federalist elite, but the growing political, economic, cultural, and social/racial conflict between the North and the South (underscored during the War of 1812, when the Federalists in New England actively resisted the American war effort in the South, implicitly sided with the British, and openly threatened to secede from the Union) pushed him out of the disgraced and declining party. 'Why should Virginia,' asked Upshur in 1824, referring to tariff and internal-improvement bills that would cost the South the most, 'hitherto distinguished alike for the soundness of her views and the greatness of her talents sink to thee second or third rank in the Confederacy [a common Southern term for the United States]?' Although Upshur espoused the Jeffersonian view of States' rights, the former Federalist could never bring himself to join the egalitarian Democratic-

Republicans or the even more populist Democrats, and eventually settled in the Whig Party, a new party nominally born in opposition to the tyrannical President Andrew Jackson. The name 'Whig' came from Great Britain, where it was the name of a party which opposed the absolute monarchism of the Tory Party and established many political principles which proved key to the American Revolution. During the American Revolution, revolutionaries referred to themselves as 'Whigs' and loyalists as 'Tories,' and Thomas Jefferson later applied these terms to describe the Democratic-Republicans and the Federalists. While most self-professed American Whigs, like Henry Clay, Daniel Webster, and young Abraham Lincoln, were actually Tories merely opposed to executive absolutism in a President of the opposing party, Upshur was a principled Whig opposed to executive absolutism in any party or person. Upshur stressed that while the presidency was created with a man of George Washington's integrity and nobility in mind – 'first in war, first in peace, and first in the hearts of his countrymen,' according to his famous eulogy by Robert E. Lee's father – Washington was dead and had no worthy successors, hence executive power must be vigilantly watched and controlled.

At Virginia's Convention of 1829-30, to which he was a delegate from his little corner of the Old Dominion, Upshur was against amending the constitution to increase the legislative representation of the young, upcoming west against old, established east. Since the east owned most of the property and paid most of the taxes, argued Upshur, it was entitled to a greater share in the government. 'Shall he who possesses no property be permitted to dictate laws for regulating the property of others?' asked Upshur. 'Shall he who pays no taxes be permitted to pass laws taxing others?' As Upshur saw it, only a government comprised of a freeholding yeomanry and gentry (in other words, landowners) was responsible enough to rule. This propertied class had produced public-spirited statesmen like George Washington, who had always governed for the good of the whole rather than for their own class, and Upshur saw no reason to change what did not require reform. Upshur also opposed the so-called 'rights' of majority rule and equality, arguing that just as 'no one man can claim a natural right to rule over another,' so 'no ten men can claim a natural right to rule over any nine men.' The only equality which Upshur recognised was the equal right not to be ruled by other men. Upshur agreed with another conservative delegate at Virginia's Convention, the bizarre yet brilliant John Randolph of Roanoke, who memorably decried mere majority rule as 'King Numbers' and opined that *'change is not reform.'*

The evolution of Upshur's view of slavery mirrored that of most Southerners during the Antebellum Era. Upshur originally opposed slavery in principle, confident that the 'slow operation of moral causes' would lead to abolition over time. When a Virginian slave named Nat Turner led a gang of slaves on a killing spree through Southampton County, however, butchering random white families in their sleep (especially targeting women and children) and engaging in barbaric rituals straight out of Africa, the fear that such uprisings would spread pushed Upshur to support strengthening the States' internal controul over their slave populations. At the same time, the emergence of the Northern abolitionist movement, marked by the publication of William L. Garrison's uncompromising, unapologetic newspaper, the *Liberator*, pushed Upshur to strengthen slavery from external attacks as well. 'Whether for good or evil the institution is fixed upon us,' protested Upshur. 'We cannot shake it off, nor permit it to be disturbed by a foreign power, without introducing a train of worse evils, the end of which no human can foresee.' Upshur's conflicted position on slavery mirrored that of the equally conflicted Founding Fathers. 'Why keep alive the question of slavery?' asked Charles Carroll of Carrollton, a slave-holding planter from Maryland and one of few living Founders at the time of the Missouri Crisis. 'It is admitted by all to be a great evil; let an effectual mode of getting rid of it be pointed out, or let the question sleep forever.' As time passed, Southerners like Upshur became increasingly convinced that there simply was no effectual mode of getting rid of slavery and that the question should indeed sleep forever.

Unlike most Southerners, who concurred that the 'Tariff of Abominations' was unconstitutional and oppressive, but demurred at the idea that a State could rightfully resist a duly enacted law, Upshur supported John C. Calhoun's 'Carolina Doctrine' of unilateral nullification – particularly when President Andrew Jackson, branding nullification 'treason,' threatened to invade South Carolina, hang her leaders, and collect the tax at bayonet-point. In *An Exposition of the Virginia Resolutions of 1798*, a series of essays published by the *Richmond Enquirer* in 1833, Upshur defended the constitutionality of Carolina-style nullification on the basis of James Madison and Thomas Jefferson's *Virginia and Kentucky Resolutions* and the 'Principles of '98.' 'They are propounded not in the spirit of a controversialist,' Upshur prefaced his essays, 'but with a deep conviction that they invoke the only principles upon which the rights of States can be maintained, and of course the only security against a consolidated and essentially monarchical government.'

To the former Federalist Upshur, the populism of the presidential election of 1840 between the Democrat Martin Van Buren and the Whig William Henry Harrison (the first election in American history in which personality took precedence to policy) was a revolting spectacle. 'To speak *ex cathedra*, the Pope damns Luther, and Luther damns the Pope; and yet neither is right except that he does damn the other,' Upshur remarked of the election. 'I think it must be obvious to anyone with half an eye, that the contest now is only between the ins and the outs.' In the end, Upshur was persuaded to campaign with the Whigs out of loyalty to John Tyler, Jr., the candidate for Vice President who was a fellow conservative Virginian.

When President Harrison died of pneumonia shortly after taking office, Upshur closely advised John Tyler during his controversial stand against Henry Clay's boasted 'American System.' Upshur was impressed with President Tyler's continual vetoes of bills for tariffs, internal improvements, and banks, and accepted the position of Secretary of the Navy when Tyler's Cabinet deserted in protest. Upshur developed a plan to modernise, reform, and expand the navy, but had to fight the Congress' 'starving out' of any policy coming from the Tyler Administration. 'How can these men look the *women* of the country in the face, when they are calculating the pence and farthings it will cost to defend them?' vented Upshur.

President Tyler's vetoes, however, came with a cost. Northern Whigs, bitter over the 'American System' slipping through their fingers due to Harrison's untimely death, began to believe that the 'free' North was, in fact, ruled by a Southern 'slave power.' In the next presidential election, Southern Democrats supported the pro-Texas Tennessean, James K. Polk, over the Northern Democrats' anti-Texas New Yorker, Martin Van Buren, splitting the Democratic Party between the North and the South. President Polk went on to sign tariff cuts over tariff hikes, veto internal-improvements bills, and reject a national bank in favour of separating banking from government altogether. At the same time, President Polk went to war with Mexico to defend territory in the Southwest but refused to risk war with Great Britain for territory in the Northwest. It was the total triumph of the Jeffersonian political economy and enormous expansion of Southern territory in the 1840s which drove Northern Whigs and Northern Democrats, left with no other viable issue, to unite against slavery in the Territories – a position intended to shift political power from the South to the North. This sectionalisation of American politics became alarmingly clear in 1846 when David Wilmot, a Pennsylvania Congressman and Democrat, introduced a proviso prohibiting slavery in the territory acquired from the Mexican War. Wilmot called this proviso 'the White Man's Proviso,' explaining that he was not motivated by 'squeamish sensitiveness upon the subject of slavery, nor morbid sympathy for the slave,' but rather 'to plead the cause and rights of white freemen.' This new 'Free Soil' Party eventually merged with the Whig Party to form the Republican Party, described by the Illinois politician and founding member Lyman Trumbull as 'the White Man's Party,' and by the

Massachusetts abolitionist Wendell Phillips as 'a party of the North, organized against the South.'

Appointed Secretary of State by President John Tyler, Upshur laid the groundwork for Texas statehood. Upshur masterfully reconciled the interests of the North and the South, impressing upon the latter that it was a matter of 'safety' (i.e. securing their borders against foreign powers) and the former that it was a matter of 'interest' (i.e. protecting their manufacturing industries against foreign competition). Indeed, there were elements of the British government that did have their eye on Texas, which would have meant more fugitive slaves and foreign manufactures crossing the border – anathema to the South and North, respectively. Having convinced the North and the South that 'the salvation of our Union' depended upon the acquisition of Texas, Upshur negotiated a treaty which was sure to be ratified by the Senate. Tragically, on 28 February 1844, while aboard the *USS Princeton* with President Tyler and other officials, a ship gun accidentally exploded, killing Upshur along with five others. With Upshur's death, the ratification of the Texas treaty which he had negotiated stalled, and when it was revived it was mishandled as a sectional/pro-South rather than a national/pro-Union measure. Upshur died just as his star was reaching its peak.

Upshur was a part of the generation of Virginians who experienced the decline and fall of their influence in the Union which their forefathers had done more than any other Americans to found. 'In Upshur, the philosophical judge,' claims his biographer, Claude H. Hall, 'may be found many of the attitudes, the prejudices, the passions, and the judgments necessary to understand Virginia in the 1830s and 1840s, a state no longer in its golden era, but not yet wrapped up in the nostalgia of the past.' The reason for Virginia's fate, however, was not that her sons were unworthy of their fathers, but that they could not have adapted to the changing times without betraying everything for which their fathers had fought. According to Hall, Upshur remained a 'sectional conservative in an era of dynamic national expansion,' defending his section's interests and protecting minorities from tyrannous majorities when the growing American republic was singing the praises of Unionism and democratisation. 'Their speeches were still brilliant, their writings as polished as before, their arguments as cogent, their principles as fervently held, but generally their faces were turned to the past,' explains Hall. 'The nation, by contrast, looked confidently to the future.'

II

In 1840, Upshur wrote A Brief Enquiry into the Nature and Character of Our Federal Government not as a standalone treatise, but as an exhaustive refutation of Justice Joseph Story's own *Commentaries on the Constitution of the United States*. Upshur's Enquiry was originally intended for limited circulation, but it went public after he joined the Tyler Administration. The finest Southern constitutional treatise in some time, the *Enquiry* was adopted by the University of Virginia's Nathaniel Beverly Tucker and the College of William and Mary's Henry St. George Tucker (both the sons of the Virginian jurist, St. George Tucker) as a constitutional text. During the Republican regime of Abraham Lincoln, anti-war Northern Democrats, hoping to convince their countrymen that secession was indeed a constitutional right, reprinted the Enquiry in Philadelphia. According to biographer Claude H. Hall, 'Along with John C. Calhoun's Discourse on the Constitution and Government of the United States, it is certainly the most representative work of the particularistic school which attempted to revitalize the ideas of Thomas Jefferson, Spencer Roane, and John Taylor of Caroline, and to refute the Unionist concepts of Chief Justice Marshall, Justice Joseph Story, and Chancellor James Kent.' Thomas E. Woods, senior fellow at the Mises Institute and author of *Nullification: How to Resist Federal Tyranny in the 21ˢᵗ Century*, calls Upshur's *Enquiry* 'one of the finest and most systematic defenses of the Virginian states' rights school of constitutional interpretation ever written.' According to Donald Livingston, Chairman of

209

the Abbeville Institute, the conflict between Story and Upshur was about more than just the Constitution, boiling down to a conflict between the 'Hobbesian unitary state' and the 'Aristotelian polycentric order' – the former centralised and coercive ('Leviathan'), the latter decentralised and consensual (the city-states of Classical Greece and the kingdoms of Christendom).

In the preface to the *Enquiry*, Upshur conceded that while Story's *Commentaries* were 'a valuable compendium of historical facts' which also contained some 'just views' of the Constitution,' he was interested in 'its political principles alone,' which he found misleading, fallacious, and even downright deceptive. 'My sole purpose,' began Upshur, 'has been to enquire into the correctness of those principles, so far as they relate to the true notion and character of our federal government.' Considering the nationalism and democratisation of the Jacksonian Era, however, Upshur doubted that his reassertion of traditional constitutionalism would be well-received. 'I know that the actual practice of the federal government for many years past, and the strong tendencies of public opinion in favour of federal power, forbid me to hope for a favourable reception, except from the very few who still cherish the principles which I have endeavored to reestablish.' Upshur admitted that to most, the original intentions of the Founding Fathers, though 'not wholly forgotten,' were 'no longer respected,' but acknowledged that there were still some with a 'sincere desire for truth.' Upshur disavowed that the ideas of the *Enquiry* were anything new, maintaining that he was simply restating and analysing historical facts. 'I do not claim the merit of originality,' clarified Upshur. 'My conclusions are drawn from the authentic information of history, and from a train of reasoning, which will occur to every mind, on the facts which history discloses.' Upshur's goal was to restore what was once widely understood but had since been forgotten – 'the great principles upon which political poles in our country were once divided,' or Tory versus Whig.

Upshur began the *Enquiry* with a respectful nod to the *Federalist*, one of the first commentaries on the Constitution and certainly the most popular. Upshur noted that the authors of the *Federalist* (James Madison, Alexander Hamilton, and John Jay) were all influential participants in the actual creation of the Constitution. Despite the obvious strengths of these wise, experienced statesmen, Upshur believed that their obvious biases also weakened their authority as commentators. Indeed, while the *Federalist* was 'a very full and philosophical analysis of the subject,' it remained 'a mere argument in support of a favourite measure.' Plus, added Upshur, everything that Madison, Hamilton, and Jay wrote about the Constitution was conjectural; they had an idea about how their new government should work in theory, but no idea how their new government would work in practice. 'Much has been developed in the actual practice of government, which no politician of that day could have seen or imagined,' explained Upshur. 'New questions have arisen, not then anticipated, and difficulties and embarrassments wholly unforeseen have sprung from new events in the relation of the states to one another, and to the general government.' For example, Madison and Hamilton had sworn in the *Federalist* that the States were sovereign and denied that the federal government could ever coerce the States, yet Upshur had seen President Andrew Jackson deny that the States were sovereign and threaten to coerce South Carolina. While the Founding Fathers understood 'the great principles of civil and political liberty' better than Upshur's generation, Upshur's generation better understood the 'practical operation' of the Constitution, particularly key provisions (such as the Preamble and the Necessary and Proper Clause) which had been considered innocuous at the time but proven important later. Due to these problems with contemporaneous commentaries on the Constitution, Upshur recognised the need for modern commentaries and acknowledged why Story's work was so celebrated.

Story's *Commentaries* was divided into three sections. The first covered the Colonial Era, the second the American Revolution and the Articles of

Confederation, and the third the formation and adoption of the Constitution. Upshur approved of this 'natural order of investigation' and 'judicious' structure, agreeing with Story that interpreting the Constitution required going back in time. 'In order for a correct understanding of the Constitution,' argued Upshur, 'it is absolutely necessary to understand the situation of the States before it was adopted.'

According to Upshur, the history of the American Colonies, particularly their settlement and 'the charters from which they derived their rights and powers as separate governments,' was 'the true starting point in the investigation of those vital questions of constitutional law which have so long divided political parties in the United States.' Since the political status of the States was ultimately derived from the political status of the Colonies, whether the Colonies were *unum* or *pluribus* ultimately determined whether the States were *unum* or *pluribus* – a question with major implications concerning the correct construction of the Constitution and the rights of the States. 'Many of the powers which have been claimed for the federal government by the political party to which he belongs,' Upshur commented on Story and the Tories, 'depend upon a denial of that separate existence, and separate sovereignty and independence which the opposing party has uniformly claimed for the States.' Story grasped the importance of this point, claimed Upshur, which was why he strenuously denied that the Colonies were ever *pluribus*. Indeed, Story's central theme – his 'favourite object...to impress upon the mind of the reader' – was that Americans had always been 'one people.' Story argued that since the American colonists were all 'fellow subjects' of the Crown, they were therefore one people. After detailing all of the myriad ways in which the colonists were indeed fellow subjects (e.g. the right to travel and trade between Colonies) Story quoted Chief Justice John Jay:

> All the people of this country were then subjects of the king of
> Great Britain, and owed allegiance to him, and all of the civil

authority then existing or exercised here flowed from the head of the British Empire. They were in a sense fellow subjects, and in a variety of respects one people. When the revolution commenced, the patriots did not assert that only the same affinity and social connexion subsisted between the people of the Colonies, which subsisted between the people of Gaul, Britain, and Spain, while Roman provinces, to wit, only that affinity and social connexion which results from the mere circumstance of being governed by the same prince.

Upshur conceded that the American colonists were indeed fellow subjects, but denied that this proved Story's point that the Colonies were one people. 'Every one of them,' Upshur remarked of all the facts which Story had adduced as proof, 'is the result of the relation between the Colonies and the mother country, and not the result of the relation between the Colonies themselves.' The Colonies' common relation to Great Britain did amount to a common relation amongst themselves, admitted Upshur. 'They do, indeed, prove a unity between all the Colonies and the mother country, and show that these, taken altogether, are, in the strictest sense of the terms, "one people,"' argued Upshur, 'but I am at a loss to perceive how they prove, that two or more parts or subdivisions of the same empire necessarily constitute "one people."' By that logic, reasoned Upshur, *reducto ad absurdum*, then any combination of parts of the British Empire were also one people. 'If so,' he quipped, 'the people of Jamaica, the British East Indian possessions, and the Canadas are, for the very same reason, "one people" to this day.' Clearly, Story's logic was flawed. Lastly, contrary to Jay's contrast between the American Colonies and the Roman provinces, Upshur pointed out that if a 'common allegiance' to a 'common sovereign' were enough to make different countries 'one people,' as he had argued with respect to the Colonies due to their common relation to Great Britain, then the old Roman provinces of Gaul, Britain, and Spain were indeed all one people, too, due to their common relation to Rome. In short, the fact that the Colonies were fellow subjects did not mean that they were necessarily one people.

Upshur stressed that this question was not a trivial technicality, but the vital foundation of any interpretation of the Constitution and understanding of the Union. 'The great effort of the author, throughout his entire work,' Upshur noted of Story, 'is to establish the doctrine that the Constitution of the United States is a government of "the people of the United States," as contradistinguished from the people of the several States; or, in other words, that it is a consolidated, and not a federative system.' According to Upshur, all of the powers which Story wanted for the federal government depended upon proving those points. Therefore, 'establishing a one-ness' among the Colonies was a 'necessity' to Story, and vice versa to Upshur.

According to Upshur, a 'people' was defined as 'a political corporation, the members of which owe a common allegiance to a common sovereignty, and do not owe any allegiance which is not common.' The Colonies, however, did not owe allegiance to the Crown in common; each Colony owed allegiance separately. There was never any common legislature, treasury, military, or judiciary among the Colonies; each Colony governed herself separately. The Colonies did not share a common settlement; each Colony was established at a separate time and place and in a separate manner. The Colonies had not been chartered in common; each Colony had a separate charter, which was occasionally amended without affecting the charters of others. 'Thus,' Upshur concluded, 'they were separate and distinct in their creation; separate and distinct in the forms of their government; separate and distinct in the changes and modifications of their governments, which were made from time to time; separate and distinct in political functions, in political rights, and in political duties.' If the Colonies were separate and distinct, then they were still separate and distinct when they declared independence from Great Britain and became States.

Upshur used two examples to illustrate the problem with Story's concept of the Colonies as one people. The Colony of Virginia, he began, was the first English colony in North America, with clearly demarcated borders. Within those borders, the people of Virginia, though subjects of the Crown, had a government of their own. Those living within those borders comprised the one people of Virginia. The next English colony to be established, Plymouth (now known as Massachusetts), likewise had clearly demarcated borders, a government of her own, and was comprised of one people. 'When the colony of Plymouth was subsequently settled, were the people of that colony "one" with the people of Virginia?' asked Upshur. 'When, long afterwards, the proprietary government of Pennsylvania was established, were the followers of William Penn "one" with the people of Plymouth and Virginia?' Each Colony had separate borders, a separate government, and a separate people. What if, continued Upshur, one of the Colonies had refused to sign the Declaration of Independence? Would the other Colonies have forced her to unite with them, or would she have been left alone? The right to coerce a Colony, as a rebellious minority in a mass of one people, was never claimed or contemplated, answered Upshur. Such a Colony would have been viewed as an enemy to be fought, but not a traitor to be coerced. 'To what purpose, then, were the people of the Colonies "one people," if, in a case so important to the common welfare, there was no right in all the people together, to coerce the members of their own community to the performance of a common duty?'

In the second section of Story's *Commentaries*, covering the American Revolution and the Articles of Confederation, Upshur observed the same Tory revisionism. 'The desire to make "the people of the United States" one consolidated nation is so strong and predominant,' Upshur claimed, 'that it breaks forth, often uncalled for, in every part of his work.'

According to Story, the Declaration of Independence sealed the Colonies as a 'nation,' and the revolutionary government was a 'national government' of the American people rather than of the Colonies. Upshur objected, claiming that Story had 'ventured to express decisive and important opinions, without due warrant.' The Continental Congresses held by the Colonies prior to the American Revolution (conventions which Tories like Abraham Lincoln later cited as specious proof that the Union predated the Constitution) were not governments, explained Upshur: they issued 'resolutions,' not 'laws,' and were not even attended by all of the Colonies. 'It recommended to its constituents whatever it believed to be to their advantage,' explained Upshur, 'but it commanded nothing.' The Continental Congress operated in this fashion until it declared the independence of the represented Colonies, after which it assumed the position of a 'de facto' rather than 'de jure' government. Far from a national government consolidating power in the name of the one people, the delegates – without any common constitution regulating their actions – referred back to their Colonies to determine the extent of their authority as well as for instructions on what to do. All of the acts of the revolutionary government referred to the Colonies, not one American people. Indeed, without the consent and cooperation of the Colonies, the revolutionary government was powerless to enforce its acts. The acts of the revolutionary government were adopted by the Colonies, not by the 'numerical majority' of a 'mass' of one American people. As an example of the fact that the Colonies remained sovereign, Upshur mentioned that the revolutionary government defined treason as a crime against an individual Colony, not against one American people. 'The course of the revolutionary government,' concluded Upshur, 'attests the fact, that however the people may have occasionally acted, in pressing emergencies, without the intervention of the authorities of their respective colonial governments, they never lost sight of the fact that they were citizens of separate Colonies, and never, even impliedly, surrendered that character or acknowledged a different allegiance.'

Upshur was just as adamant against Story's claim that the Declaration of Independence fused the Colonies into one. 'It was not an act done by the State governments, then organised, nor by persons chosen by them,' Upshur quoted Story. 'It was emphatically the act of the whole people of the United Colonies.' To Story, the Declaration was 'the united act of all' and 'the achievement of the whole, for the benefit of the whole.' Upshur countered that the Declaration was not a collective act, but rather 'the joint expression of their separate wills.' According to Upshur, 'We should see, in that act, nothing more than the union of several independent sovereignties, for the purpose of effecting a common object, which each felt itself too weak to effect, alone.' If Spain, Naples, and Holland, Upshur asked rhetorically, while they were subjects to the French Crown, had jointly stated their grievances with France, renounced their allegiance to France, and declared themselves 'free and independent States,' as the Colonies had done with Great Britain, would they therefore become one people? 'The case here supposed is precisely that of the American Colonies,' argued Upshur. 'The fact that they united in the Declaration of Independence does not make them "one people" any more than a similar declaration would have made Spain, Naples, and Holland one people.'

After making this philosophical point, Upshur delved into the actual history of the Declaration of Independence. It was the Colonies that convened the Continental Congress which adopted the Declaration, 'in their separate and distinct capacity, each acting for itself, and not conjointly with any other.' The delegates were not 'joint representatives of any one people,' but rather 'representatives of separate and distinct Colonies.' The Colonies, not one American people, voted on the Declaration, each delegate acting under instructions from his respective sovereign. One Colony, New York, initially abstained from the vote! If all this were not clear enough, Upshur claimed that the language of the Declaration itself settled the issue: 'The instrument itself is entitled "the unanimous declaration of the thirteen United States of America;" of States, separate and distinct bodies politic, and not of "one people" or nation, composed of all of them together; "united," as independent States may be by compact or agreement, and not amalgamated, as they would be, if they formed one nation or body politic.'

As Thomas Jefferson, the author of the Declaration of Independence, remarked of his own State of Virginia during the American Revolution, 'We are but one of thirteen nations, who have agreed to act and speak together.'

Upshur noted that Story dismissed as insignificant the fact that many of the Colonies had formed independent governments prior to the Declaration of Independence and that these governments were exercising the powers of sovereign nations. According to Story, since these governments were formed under the recommendation of the Continental Congress, they did not establish the sovereignty of the Colonies. Upshur replied that it did not matter whose idea it was to establish the governments; all that mattered was who established them. 'With whatever motive the act was performed,' argued Upshur, 'it was one of supreme and sovereign power, and such as could not have been performed except by a sovereign people.'

Upshur believed that two documents, the Treaty of Paris (the peace treaty between Great Britain and the United States) and the Articles of Confederation (the first common constitution among the States) were significant in the question of whether the Colonies were one people or separate and distinct. In the Treaty of Paris, just as each individual Colony had declared herself a sovereign State in the Declaration of Independence, so the Crown recognised each individual State by name, from Georgia to New Hampshire, as 'free, sovereign, and independent.' If the United States truly formed one people, argued Upshur, then the Treaty would have recognised only a single sovereignty, rather than recognising several sovereignties. In the Articles of Confederation, it was clearly spelled out that 'each State retains its sovereignty, freedom, and independence, and every power, jurisdiction, and right, which is not, by this confederation, expressly delegated to the United States, in Congress assembled.' To Upshur, this clause 'left no room for doubt on the subject.' Upshur observed that while powers, jurisdictions, and rights were divisible, sovereignty, freedom, and independence were indivisible; the States could delegate authority, but they could not delegate their sovereignty. Upshur added that as with the

218

Declaration, the States, 'each acting separately for itself,' ratified the Articles, not one American people. Lastly, Upshur reasoned that in order for something to be retained, as the Articles stipulated the States retained their sovereignty, then it must first be possessed. Therefore, the States had always been sovereign; they could not have retained their sovereignty otherwise.

Concluding his critique of Story's second section, Upshur denied that the Colonies had ever formed 'one people,' before or after the Declaration of Independence, but rather 'a mere league of confederation between sovereign and independent States' – or, as Thomas Jefferson put it, 'united nations.'

In Story's third and final section, covering the framing and ratifying of the Constitution, Upshur confirmed the same contaminating biases of the previous two. 'Having informed us that as Colonies we were "for many purposes one people," and that the Declaration of Independence made us "a nation de facto,"' Upshur scoffed at Story, 'he now assumes the broad ground that this one people or nation de facto, formed the Constitution under which we live.' Upshur also mentioned that Story's Commentaries relied heavily on Supreme-Court rulings, especially his own. Upshur allowed the latter ('we could not suppose that one, whose opinions are not lightly adopted, would advance, as a commentator, a principle which he rejected as a judge'), though he opposed deferring to the Supreme Court in all cases. 'In most cases, too, no higher authority in the interpretation of the Constitution is known in our systems, and none better could be desired,' admitted Upshur. 'It is only in questions of political power, involving the rights of the States in reference to the federal government, that any class of politicians are disposed to deny the authority of the judgments of the Supreme Court.' According to Upshur, the Supreme Court simply did not have jurisdiction over the States.

Story was impressed with the language of the Preamble ('We, the People of the United States, do ordain and establish this Constitution for the United States of America...'), which he believed proved that the Constitution was ratified by one American people rather than the States – a possibility which the Anti-Federalists had feared and foretold. Upshur explained, however, that while the preambles of a statute may be used in interpreting its 'true object and intention,' they have no 'law-making power' of their own. As a judge, remarked Upshur, Story surely understood this. The question should not be how to construe the Preamble (Story was making something out of nothing, as Upshur would show), but how the Constitution was actually adopted, a question which Upshur was confident that history plainly answered.

The Preamble did not always read, 'We, the People,' but originally read, 'We, the People of the States,' each of which were then enumerated, from Georgia to New Hampshire. Unlike the rest of the Constitution, which was rigorously debated and diligently amended, this version of the Preamble was adopted unanimously. Later, the Committee of Style (unfortunately comprised of the Constitutional Convention's top Tories), tasked with editing the wording of the draft but not amending its meaning, shortened the Preamble to its current form without any debate. 'It is manifest that this committee had no power to change the meaning of anything which had been adopted, but were authorised merely to "revise the style," and arrange the matter in a proper order,' argued Upshur. Furthermore, continued Upshur, there was a good reason for the change in the wording from 'We, the People of the States' to 'We, the People.' The Constitution required the ratification of nine States to be enacted into law – only 'between' those States which had ratified, of course. At the time, however, it was unknown whether nine States would ratify the Constitution, and would have been presumptuous to name States as parties to a compact to which they had not consented. Indeed, Rhode Island did not even send a delegate to the Constitutional Convention of 1787 and would not ratify the Constitution until 1790, yet she was named in the original Preamble! 'Hence it became necessary to adopt a form of expression which would apply to those who should ratify the Constitution, and not to those who should refuse to do so,' explained Upshur. 'This construction corresponds with the historical fact, and reconciles the language employed with the circumstances of the case.' Upshur was astounded at how much Story's interpretation of the Constitution was based on this piece of pure pettifoggery. In no way, shape, or form did the Preamble mean that one American people, as opposed to the States, ratified the Constitution.

As a Virginia Assemblyman asked in 1798, during the debate over James Madison's Virginia Resolutions, 'Should the words "we the people," then change the nature of the compact, contrary to the historical facts of the day?'

After disposing of Story's construction of the Preamble, Upshur took on Story's theory that one American people, not the States, ratified the Constitution. First, according to Upshur, Story himself provided ample documentation in his Commentaries that the Constitutional Convention itself was convened by the States, its delegates appointed by the States, and its proceedings confirmed by the States. 'We may well ask, therefore,' remarked Upshur, 'from what unknown source our author derives the idea, that the Constitution was formed by "the people of the United States," since the history of the transaction, even as he himself has detailed it, proves that "the people of the United States" did not appoint delegates to the Convention, were not represented in the body, and did not adopt and confirm its act as their own.' Furthermore, Upshur insisted that despite the rising Tory rhetoric of his day and age, 'there were no such people as "the people of the United States."' Under the Articles of Confederation, the States expressly retained their sovereignty – 'a league between independent sovereignties, and not one nation composed of them all together.' Congress was 'the representative of the States,' not one American people. Significantly, citizenship was by State; there were no American citizens, only State citizens. Even the provision in place for alterations to the Articles required the consent of each State, not the will of one American people. More fundamentally, however, was the fact that only the States had the power to change their form of government. 'What authority was there, superior to the States, which could undo their work?' asked Upshur. 'What power was there, other than that of the States themselves, which was authorised to declare that their solemn league and agreement should be abrogated?' For any other power to have done so, asserted Upshur, would have been illegitimate – 'an act of usurpation and violence.' Only the States could have rightfully replaced the Articles with the Constitution.

Upshur made the essential point that it was not the delegates in Philadelphia who enacted the Constitution into law and gave it its true meaning, but the delegates of the State conventions. 'It is not the mere framing of a constitution which gives it authority as such,' noted Upshur. 'It becomes obligatory only by its adoption and ratification; and surely that act, I speak of free and voluntary government, makes it the constitution of those only who do adopt it.' Upshur emphasised that it was the States which adopted and ratified the Constitution. Each State ratified the Constitution at different times and on different terms. 'This was certainly State action,' insisted Upshur, 'in as distinct a form as can be imagined.' That only nine States needed to ratify the Constitution in order for it to be enacted into law proved that Americans were 'separate and distinct political communities.' If they were an 'aggregate mass,' then ratification would have been a national referendum rather than a series of separate State conventions and would have been imposed on States that did not ratify. To illustrate this point, Upshur demonstrated that if Massachusetts, New York, Pennsylvania, and Virginia (four States with a majority of the American population) had refused to ratify, but the other nine States had ratified, then the Constitution would still have been enacted into law for the latter States, despite them comprising a minority of the American population. In other words, a minority of the so-called one American people could have enacted the Constitution into law. 'This single example shows, conclusively,' boasted Upshur, 'that the people of the United States, as contradistinguished from the people of the several States, had nothing to do, and could not have had anything to do with the matter.'

'I do not perceive with what propriety it can be said that the "people of the United States" formed the Constitution,' summarised Upshur, 'since they neither appointed the Convention, nor ratified their act, nor otherwise adopted it as obligatory upon them.' According to Upshur, the history that he had brought to light and logic that he had applied 'should silence forever, all those arguments in favour of consolidation, which are founded on the preamble to that instrument.' Unfortunately, the exact opposite has happened – truth and reason are silenced and Story's spurious notion of 'one nation, under God, indivisible, with liberty and justice for all' is now recited in churches and classrooms across the United States.

Upshur quoted Story as claiming that the Constitution was 'not a contract imposing mutual obligations, and contemplating the permanent subsistence of parties having an independent right to construe, controul, and judge of its obligations.' Upshur frankly admitted that he did not think that this statement made any sense. Regardless of whether the Constitution was ratified by 'the people of the United States' or 'the States as such,' it was clear that it was indeed a 'contract' between 'parties.' Upshur also clarified that none of the parties to the Constitution ever mentioned that they had power over the 'obligations' of the federal government. 'We all admit that the power and authority of the federal government, within its constitutional sphere, are superior to those of the States, in some instances, and co-ordinate in others, and that every citizen is under an absolute obligation to render them respect and obedience,' conceded Upshur. 'We all admit it to be true, as a general proposition, that no citizen nor State has an independent right to "construe," and still less to "controul," the constitutional obligations of that government.' All that had been asserted was that the States could construe, controul, and judge their own rights against the federal government. 'All that has ever been contended for,' explained Upshur, 'is, that a State has a right to judge of its own obligations, and, consequently, to judge those of the federal government, so far as they relate to such State itself, and no farther.' According to Upshur, if the federal government 'transcends' its constitutional authority, then it would be outside of its 'obligations,' and thus the States would be within their rights to resist such encroachment. The problem, however, was the question of who had the responsibility of determining whether the federal government was within or outside of its sphere: 'Who is the common umpire?'

In Upshur's day and age, a compact was understood as an agreement of mutual obligations between independent parties. If the Constitution were a compact, then it was a 'confederation,' but if not, then it was a 'consolidated government.' Story denied that the Constitution was a compact on the grounds that the Constitution never explicitly identified itself as a compact. Upshur disputed Story's logic, arguing that 'a deed, or other instrument, receives its distinctive character, not from the name which the parties may choose to give to it, but from its legal effect and operation.' In other words, the original intentions of the parties were what mattered, not how their language could be later construed. Upshur added, however, that Story's own Massachusetts referred to the Constitution as a compact in her act of ratification – 'an explicit and solemn compact,' in fact.

Story claimed that the Supremacy Clause ('This Constitution, and the laws of the United States, which shall be made in pursuance thereof, and all treaties made, or which shall be made, shall be the supreme law of the land') proved that the Constitution was not a compact, as 'the people of any State cannot, by any form of its own constitution or laws, or any other proceedings, repeal, or abrogate, or suspend it.' Upshur countered that there was nothing irreconcilable between a supreme constitution and a compact. Nullification and secession (two essential rights of parties to a compact) did not affect the Constitution itself or violate the Supremacy Clause. 'The Nullifier contends only for the right of a State to prevent the Constitution from being violated by the general government, and not for the right to repeal, abrogate, or suspend it,' avowed Upshur, himself an ardent nullifier. 'The Seceder asserts only that a State is competent to withdraw from the Union whenever it pleases; but that does not assert that in so doing it can repeal, abrogate, or suspend the Constitution as to the other States.' Besides, noted Upshur, all the Supremacy Clause meant was that the Constitution was '"supreme" within its prescribed sphere of action,' not supreme over the States themselves 'in all cases whatsoever,' as the Parliament had asserted against the Colonies.

Story charged that 'the cardinal conclusion for which this doctrine of a compact has been with so much ingenuity and ability, forced into the language of the Constitution (for the latter nowhere alludes to it) is avowedly to establish that, in construing the Constitution, there is no common umpire; but that, each State, nay, each department of the government of each State, is the supreme judge for itself, of the powers, and rights, and duties arising under that instrument.' Begging Story's pardon, Upshur expressed 'unfeigned astonishment' at such a 'careless' statement from a Supreme-Court Justice in a scholarly study. Upshur stopped short of accusing Story of deliberately distorting the compact theory of the Union, charitably ascribing it to mere ignorance. Indignant over being grossly 'misunderstood' and 'misrepresented,' Upshur delivered a mini-manifesto of the 'State rights school of politics':

> They believe that those doctrines contain the only principle truly conservative of our Constitution; that without them there is no effective check on the federal government, and, of course, that that government can increase its own powers to an indefinite extent; that this must happen in the natural course of events, and that ultimately the whole character of the government will be so changed that even its forms will be rejected as cumbrous and useless, under the monarchy, in substance, into which we shall have insensibly glided. It is, therefore, because they are lovers of the Constitution and of the Union, that they contend strenuously for the rights of the States. They are no lovers of anarchy nor of revolution. Their principles will cease to be dear to them, whenever they shall cease to subserve the purposes of good order, and of regular and established government. It is their object to preserve

the institutions of the country as they are, sincerely believing that nothing more than this is necessary to secure to the people all the blessings which can be expected from any government whatever. They would consider themselves but little entitled to respect as a political party, if they maintained the loose, disjointed, and worse than puerile notions, which the author has thought it not unbecoming to impute to them.

The compact theory of the Union, explained Upshur, was not derived from the 'express terms of the Constitution,' but was rather 'an incident of [the States'] sovereignty, which the Constitution has not taken away.' Therefore, it was misleading for Story to accuse the compact theory of being 'forced' into the Constitution, as no one had ever claimed that it was in the Constitution in the first place.

Concerning the question of the 'essential character' of the Constitution, Upshur concluded that 'every fair and legitimate inference' pointed to that of a compact. After all, the Constitution 'was made by sovereign States, and...that is the only way in which sovereign States treat with one another.' Since 'sovereignty is the very last thing which a nation is willing to surrender,' constructions of the Constitution should always err on the side of State sovereignty rather than national supremacy. 'In all cases, therefore, where the language and spirit of the Constitution are doubtful, and even in favour of consolidation,' asserted Upshur, 'we should still incline against it, and in favour of the rights of the States, unless no other construction can be admitted.'

As Thomas Jefferson informed the Massachusetts framer Elbridge Gerry, 'I am for preserving to the States the powers not yielded by them to the Union, and to the legislature of the Union its constitutional share in the division of powers; and I am not for transferring all the powers of the States to the general government, and all those of that government to the executive branch.'

After answering the 'preliminary question' of whether the Constitution was a compact (and thus whether it formed a 'federative' or 'consolidated' government), Upshur analysed the basic structure of each branch of the federal government.

The federal legislature was comprised of two houses, the Senate and the House of Representatives. In the Senate, each State had two Senators, chosen by their State legislature (this was before the misguided Seventeenth Amendment, which severed Senators from allegiance to their States with direct elections). The Senate, therefore, with the States equally represented regardless of population (preserving their 'perfect equality as sovereign States') was 'strictly federative.' In the House of Representatives, each State's number of Representatives was proportional to her population. The States, according to their own laws, elected Representatives. Upshur added that one American people would have national elections rather than State elections and uniform voter qualifications rather than separate qualifications. 'If the House of Representatives were national, in any practical sense of the term,' argued Upshur, 'the "nation" would have authority to provide for the appointment of its members, to prescribe the qualifications of votes, and to enforce the performance of that duty.'

To the argument that the House was a national rather than federal body because the States were proportionally rather than equally represented, Upshur replied that proportional representation was not necessarily incompatible with confederation – the States General of the United Provinces [the Dutch Republic], for instance. 'There is no reason, apparent to me,' objected Upshur, 'why a league may not be formed among independent sovereignties, giving to each an influence in the management of their common concerns, proportioned to its strength, its wealth, or the interest which it has at stake.' Besides, Upshur also noted, the States were still equally represented in the Senate. Even if the House were national, continued Upshur, it still would not matter. The legislature, comprised of the Senate and the House, would still be federal due to the undeniably federal

Senate. A legislature can have national features but still be federal overall, but it cannot have federal features and still be national overall. 'The question is whether or not the States have preserved their distinct, sovereign characters in this feature of the Constitution,' explained Upshur. 'If they have done so, in any part of it, the whole must be considered federative.' The *'unity'* implied of a nation was 'absolutely inconsistent' with a confederation, while *'joint action'* was permissible between 'the members of a confederation…exerting their several powers.'

The President and Vice President were chosen by electors, delegates chosen by their own States. The elections for the State electors were held separately by each State. A State's number of electors was the sum of its Representatives and Senators – a combination of proportionality and equality. The States, therefore, controulled the process of electing the federal executive from start to finish As Upshur said, 'There is not the least trace of national agency, in any part of this proceeding.'

Upshur used a hypothetical example to expose the shortcomings of Story's theory of one American people. If one American people elected the President, rather than the States, then all a candidate should need to win would be a popular majority. Presidential elections, however, were decided by the votes of the State electors; the popular majority was, essentially, irrelevant. Indeed, a candidate could lose the popular vote and still win the presidency – a phenomenon which has happened on several occasions in American history. 'If the president could be chosen by the "people of the United States" in the aggregate, instead of by the States,' Upshur pointed out, 'then it is difficult to imagine a case in which a majority of those people, concurring in the same vote, could be overbalanced by a minority.' Since the States elected the President, not one American people, the United States had to be a confederation, not a nation.

The protocol in the event that no candidate received a majority of the State electors removed 'all doubt upon this point,' claimed Upshur. The House settled the election, all of the Representatives voting as single States.

'Why, then,' asked Upshur, 'should this federative principle be preserved, in the election of the president in the House of Representatives if it was designed to abandon it, in the election of the same office by the electoral colleges?' Upshur answered that Tories like Story had 'no good reason' to explain this discrepancy in their theory.

Although he was a judge, Upshur did not spend much time on the structure of the federal judiciary. Since judges were nominated by the President and approved by the Senate (a federal officer and a federal body) the judiciary was 'manifestly federative.'

After his overview of the federal structure of all three branches of government, Upshur argued that the amendment process was federal, too. Proposing an amendment required either two-thirds of both houses of the federal legislature or two-thirds of the State legislatures. The fact that the same proportion was required from the federal legislature and the States indicated to Upshur that the two were 'the same power.' Whether through 'separate action' or a 'common federative agent,' it was 'the power of the States' which amended the Constitution.

Ratification of an amendment required three quarters of the States. Since the power to alter or amend a government was the same as the power to create a government, Upshur believed that this proved that the States were the sovereign parties to the Constitution, not one American people. 'The idea of separate and independent political corporations could not be more distinctly conveyed,' claimed Upshur. Indeed, it was contradictory that 'the people of the United States,' whom Story alleged ratified the Constitution, could not alter or amend the government of their own creation. If the United States were truly one American people as opposed to a confederation of States, then an amendment to the Constitution should require three-quarters of the total population rather than three-quarters of the States. As with each branch of the government, the amendment process was fully federal.

Upshur found Story's answer to the question, 'Who is the final judge or interpreter in constitutional controversies?' incomplete and weak. According to Upshur, Story claimed that because the role of the judiciary was to interpret the law, the federal judiciary must interpret federal law, i.e. the Constitution. Therefore, the Supreme Court was the final judge over the Constitution.

Upshur recognised that the Supreme Court was the final judge within its jurisdiction. 'Whatever comes within the legitimate cognizance of that tribunal, it has a right to decide, whether it is a question of the law, or of the Constitution,' admitted Upshur. No one denied this, held Upshur, despite Story's misrepresentations. The issue, however, was the extent of that 'legitimate cognizance,' or what 'constitutional controversies' the federal judiciary had the right to judge. Article III of the Constitution defined the jurisdiction of the federal judiciary as 'all cases in law and equity, arising under the Constitution, the laws of the United States, and treaties made, or which shall be made, under their authority,' as well as cases of foreign relations, cases between State governments or the citizens of separate States, and cases to which the United States were a party. The Eleventh Amendment ensured that 'the judicial power of the United States shall not be construed to extend to any suit in law or equity, commenced or prosecuted against one of the United States, by citizens of another State, or by citizens or subjects of a foreign State.' Contrary to Story, Upshur believed that the powers of the federal judiciary were the most strictly limited of all. 'There is no part of the Constitution in which the framers of it have displayed a more jealous care of the rights of the States,' held Upshur, 'than in the limitations of the judicial power.' Federal jurisdiction was limited to what was 'absolutely necessary to carry into effect the general design, and accomplish the general object of the States, as independent, confederated States.' While the federal judiciary was indeed the final judge in cases within its jurisdiction, Upshur maintained that it was not the final judge of the limits of its jurisdiction: 'The right to decide a case arising *under* the

Constitution does not necessarily imply the right to determine *in the last resort* what that Constitution is.'

Upshur recognised that the term 'all cases arising under the Constitution, and the laws made in pursuance thereof' could be twisted to encompass virtually all cases, rather than only those concerning things enumerated in the Constitution, but doubted that such a 'latitudinous' construction would be taken seriously. Today, however, there is nothing free from the scrutiny of the Supreme Court; not even State licence plates are safe from 'Wise Latinas' and 'Notorious R.B.G.s.'

Upshur raised the possibility that the Supreme Court 'may assume jurisdiction over subjects and between parties, not allowed by the Constitution.' Upshur realised that this posed a serious problem, as the federal judiciary could essentially judge the extent of its own authority, usurping power unchecked and uncontroulled. 'Who, then, is to decide this point?' asked Upshur. 'Shall the Supreme Court decide it for itself, against the world?' Fortunately, answered Upshur, the Constitution provided a solution.

According to the Tenth Amendment, 'The powers not delegated to the United States by the Constitution, nor prohibited by it to the States, are reserved to the States respectively, or to the people.' The States kept whatever powers they did not delegate to the federal government and enumerate in the Constitution. Anticipating Abraham Lincoln's red herrings about collective, consensual secession – that is, the specious claim that secession was only legitimate with the collective consent of the Union – Upshur stressed that the undelegated, unenumerated powers were reserved 'to the States *respectively*,' as opposed to the States collectively. Thus, the powers reserved by the States were 'independent' of one another and could be exercised without 'reference or responsibility' to each other. Such unilateral power, as the States reserved under the Tenth Amendment, was the hallmark of sovereignty. To Upshur, the Tenth Amendment was proof that the States 'acted as independent and sovereign States' in ratifying the

Constitution and that the Constitution was an 'agreement between sovereign States.' A sovereign, explained Upshur, has the right 'to be alone the judge of its own compacts and agreements.' As sovereign parties to the Constitution, therefore, each State had the right to interpret the Constitution for herself. If the federal judiciary were the 'sole judges of the extent of their own powers,' then their powers would be 'universal,' and the Constitution 'idle and useless.'

The federal government, after all, was simply the 'creature' of the States – not a party to the Constitution, but its product. The federal government was a 'mere agent' of its principals, the States, to which the limited powers for particular objects with which it was entrusted were enumerated in the Constitution. Upshur allowed that the federal government would naturally try to define its power for itself, but stipulated that this probing must be done 'in subordination to the authority by whom his powers were conferred.' For the federal government to 'judge the extent of its own powers, without reference to its constituent' would grant unlimited power to the former, 'notwithstanding the plainest and most express terms' of the Constitution. If the federal government were the ultimate authority over itself, then the Constitution would be 'the idlest thing imaginable,' and there would be 'no barrier against the usurpations of the government' and 'no security for the rights and liberties of the people.' Upshur argued that given such a 'pernicious' outcome for a 'free and equal government,' it should be self-evident to everyone that Story was wrong, *reductio ab absurdum*.

According to Upshur, in questions of 'political power' between the States and the federal government, the Constitution granted no jurisdiction to the federal judiciary – no 'common umpire' whatsoever. Accordingly, each State, 'by virtue of that inherent, sovereign power and authority, which, as to this matter, it has never surrendered,' has the right and duty to judge for herself. Contrary to Story, who argued that the rulings of the Supreme Court were 'binding' upon the States, Upshur countered that such rulings were binding only upon the parties to a particular case and that the federal judiciary had no jurisdiction over the States. 'This agreement they made in their character of sovereign States, not with the federal government, but with one another,' Upshur said of the Constitution. 'As sovereign States they alone are to determine the nature and extent of that agreement, and, of course, they alone are to determine whether they have given the federal courts authority to bind them in any given case.'

Such 'technical rules,' however, did not get to the heart of the matter for Upshur. The States were 'sovereign nations,' and sovereign nations did not petition for their rights from judges, particularly 'tribunals of that power against which their own power is asserted.' Since the States had demonstrated 'the most jealous care of their separate sovereignty and independence' throughout the Constitution, it made no sense for them to grant unlimited powers of interpretation to the Supreme Court.

Having answered the question of the common umpire in questions of power between the States and the federal government, Upshur turned to how Story interpreted the Constitution. According to Story, the Constitution was formed by the 'people of the United States,' and thus was no different from any of the State constitutions, formed by the people of each State. Since State constitutions were interpreted liberally, the United States' Constitution should also be interpreted liberally. Upshur, of course, disagreed. 'There is no such analogy between them, as will presently be shown, as to require that they should be construed by the same rules,' avowed Upshur. *'The Constitution of the United States is to be considered as a compact or confederation between free, independent and sovereign States, and is to be construed as such, in all cases where its language is doubtful.'* To Upshur, this meant that the Constitution should be construed *'strictly'* – taking the words of the parties to the compact as 'the true exponents of their meaning.' Elaborating on the meaning of strict constructionism, Upshur turned Story's own arguments against him. Story said that since the Constitution was a 'grant' of power from the 'people of the United States' (the 'grantor') to the federal government (the 'grantee'), the Constitution should be interpreted liberally 'for the benefit of the grantor' – presuming in favour of consolidation. Conceding Story's logic for the sake of argument, Upshur challenged Story's premises, claiming that the States, giving and receiving power amongst themselves for their common benefit, were both the grantor and grantee. If the States were the grantor, however, and the grantor was entitled the most favourable construction, then the Constitution should be interpreted strictly – presuming in favour of the States. Strict construction, however, did not mean clinging to the letter of the law, but upholding its spirit, 'the *intention* of the framers of the Constitution.'

As Thomas Jefferson explained to Elbridge Gerry, the Constitution should be interpreted 'according to the true sense in which it was adopted by the States [and] that in which it was advocated by its friends.'

Story's comparison of the Federal Constitution to the State constitutions was incorrect on a number of counts, claimed Upshur, chief among them the differing purposes of a federal and social compact. State constitutions, or social compacts, were the 'primary social relation' of the people of the States. The State constitutions governed the whole domestic life of their people and were responsible for protecting 'the great rights of life, liberty, and property.' The Constitution, by contrast, was a federal compact formed for the 'common purposes of all the States,' namely, foreign relations. 'Take away the federal government altogether, and still we are free, our rights are still protected, our business still regulated, and we still enjoy all the other advantages and blessings of established and well-organised government,' observed Upshur. 'But if you take away the State governments, what have you left? A federal government which can neither regulate your industry, secure your property, nor protect your person!' Given that the States were essential while the federal government was expendable (combined with the susceptibility of the federal government 'to encroach on the rights and powers of the States' and form 'combinations by which a majority of the states may oppress the minority'), it was safest to construe the Constitution as strictly as possible, in order that the mass of undelegated, unenumerated powers remained with the States while the delegated, enumerated few went to the federal government. Strict construction of the Constitution, held Upshur, was necessary to maintain a 'just balance' between the States and the federal government.

The Tenth Amendment, reminded Upshur, also affirmed that the Constitution should be 'strictly' rather than 'liberally' construed. The corresponding provision in the Articles of Confederation held that all powers not delegated to Congress were *expressly* reserved, yet the Tenth Amendment omitted this term. From this omission, Story surmised that the Constitution was supposed to be loosely rather than strictly constructed. As with the Preamble, however, Upshur set Story's sophistry straight. According to Upshur, the Necessary and Proper Clause permitted the federal government to exercise some 'incidental powers' which were not enumerated in the Constitution yet were clearly intended by the framers and ratifiers. 'For example, the power to provide a navy is not, *in itself*, the power to build a dry dock,' explained Upshur, 'but, as dry docks are necessary and proper means for providing a navy, Congress shall have the power to authorise the construction of them.' If the term 'expressly' had been included in the Tenth Amendment, however, then this fair inference could have been disputed. While the omission was intended to free Congress 'to provide the necessary and proper means of executing the granted powers,' the Tenth Amendment 'denied to the federal government every power which was *not* granted.' Only a conservative construction of the Constitution could reconcile the reserved powers of the Tenth Amendment with the incidental powers of the Necessary and Proper Clause.

Upshur knew, however, that Tories like Story had abused the Necessary and Proper Clause to justify the usurpation of powers reserved to the States. As Story put it, the federal government could claim 'all the means requisite, and fairly applicable to the attainment of the end of such power, unless they are excepted in the Constitution.' This violated 'the letter and spirit' of the Constitution, charged Upshur. The federal government possessed no power except those which the States had delegated. 'The author's idea is, that everything is granted which is not excepted,' reiterated Upshur. 'Whereas the language of the Tenth Amendment is express, that everything is excepted which is not granted.' If all power but that which was excepted was open to Congress, warned Upshur, then the 'discretion' of politicians rather than the 'limitations of the Constitution' would prevail, overthrowing the rule of law for the rule of men.

As Thomas Jefferson warned, in a choice between evils, 'living under a government of discretion' was 'the only one greater than separation.'

To Upshur, the correct interpretation of the Necessary and Proper Clause simply took its words at face value. 'Incidental powers' should be truly necessary means for the execution of an enumerated power, not ends in themselves masquerading as means. 'Congress have no right to use for the accomplishment of one purpose, means ostensibly provided for another,' explained Upshur. 'To do so would be a positive fraud, and a manifest usurpation.' Means should also be proper, which meant 'consistent with the spirit of liberty and equality,' respectful of the 'distinct sovereignty of the States,' and within the 'limited and specifically enumerated' powers of the Constitution. To prevent the consolidation of power (which Upshur noted was already getting out of controul), the Necessary and Proper Clause had to be correctly interpreted and enforced.

Upshur was concerned that the people, seduced by the outward strength of a large, national government were sacrificing their 'free and happy' government for a 'splendid and shiny' one. The Founding Fathers, avowed Upshur, knew that with governments as with men, pride came before the fall. 'Those nations who have gone in search of grandeur, power, and splendor, have also fallen a sacrifice and been the victims of their own folly,' Upshur quoted from Patrick Henry's prescient warnings at Virginia's Ratification Convention. 'While they have acquired those visionary blessings, they lost their freedom.' Upshur suspected that behind the Tories' professions of the 'public good' lurked 'private interests.' Indeed, those who supported consolidated rather than confederated government were those with the most to gain – whether by protecting their industries from competition with high tariffs or plundering the Treasury through internal improvements. 'Here, that love of splendor and display, which deludes so large a portion of mankind,' sighed Upshur, 'unites with that self-interest by which all mankind are swayed, in aggrandising the federal government, and adding to its powers.'

After completing the 'political' section of his *Enquiry*, Upshur moved to 'a few topics, yet remaining, of great public concern,' namely the Constitution's Three-Fifths Clause. Story considered the Three-Fifths Clause, which counted three-fifths of the slave population for representation of the States in the House of Representatives as 'unjust in principle and decidedly injurious to the people of the non-slaveholding States.' Furthermore, Story considered the clause which counted three-fifths of the slaves for the apportionment of direct taxes as 'more specious than solid.' For while direct taxes were 'occasional and rare,' with most federal revenue collected by indirect taxes, representation was 'constant and uniform.' In Story's opinion, the Southern States were aggrandised in representation and exempted in taxation. Upshur found Story's analysis of the Three-Fifths Clause 'a very imperfect, and...not a very candid view of a grave and important subject.' It was beneath the author of a supposedly scholarly constitutional commentary to complain that a particular clause 'is unjust to his own peculiar part of the country.' In fact, throughout the *Enquiry*, Upshur avoided special pleading for his own peculiar part of the country. The Three-Fifths Clause, explained Upshur, 'rests on no particular principle, but is a mere compromise between conflicting interests and powers.' While the South had always tried to 'avoid' rather than 'agitate' the conflict, the North had always 'complained' of the Three-Fifths Clause as a 'grievance.'

Indeed, beginning with the victory of President Thomas Jefferson and the Democratic-Republican Party in 1800, Northerners had complained of 'Negro Presidents' and 'Negro Congressmen,' and tried to thwart the acquisition of new Southern territory and the admission of new Southern States, as well as secede from the Union. 'I will not yet despair,' Timothy Pickering (a Revolutionary-War veteran, military chief of staff and civil official to George Washington, Massachusetts Congressman, and 'Federalist Ultra') had announced in 1803. 'I will rather anticipate a new confederacy, exempt from the corrupt and corrupting influence and oppression of the aristocratic democrats of the South.' According to Pickering, 'There will be a separation...The white and black population will mark the boundary.'

Story thought that the Constitution should have apportioned taxation by property rather than by representation, but Upshur pointed out that taxation by representation was derived from 'the great principle upon which the Revolution itself was based' and 'results from the federative character of our government.' Story, charged Upshur, 'seems to have forgotten this connexion between representation and taxation' and 'looks only at the sources whence the Union may draw wealth from the South.' Apportioning taxes any other way than by representation 'might subject the weaker States to intolerable oppression,' in which 'a combination among a few of the strongest States might, with a little management, throw the whole burden of taxation upon the others, by selecting only such subjects of taxation as they themselves did not possess.' Slaves were one such form of property which could be singled out for taxation, warned Upshur, who claimed that the Southern States would never have ratified the Constitution under such conditions. 'This provision of the Constitution, therefore,' held Upshur, 'resulted necessarily from the very nature of the Union; it is an appropriate and necessary feature in every confederacy between sovereign States.' In fact, Upshur regarded the Three-Fifths Clause as 'a concession made by the South.'

Upshur explained that although taxes were levied on property, there was no way for the federal government to measure the total value of property of a State without becoming burdensome and bothersome. Population was thus the 'best measure' of the property of a State, as 'the greater the number of people, the greater is the amount of productive industry.' Therefore, whether the people in question were freemen or slaves was irrelevant; for the purposes of representation and taxation, all that mattered was whether they were engaged in productive industry. 'So far, then, from limiting representation to three-fifths of the slaves,' countered Upshur, 'they ought *all* to be represented, for all contribute to the aggregate of the productive industry of the country.'

Avowing that 'we shall be governed by our interests, and ought to be,' Samuel Chase, a Maryland delegate to the Continental Congress, objected to taxing slave property without counting the slave population towards representation. 'If negroes are taken into the computation of numbers to ascertain wealth, they ought to be, in settling representation,' argued Chase. 'If I am satisfied in the rule of levying and appropriating money, I am willing the small Colonies should have a vote.'

Upshur recognised the objection 'that slaves are property, and, for that reason, are not more entitled to representation than any other species of property,' replying that slaves were 'also *people*, and upon analogous principles, are entitled to representation as people.' According to Upshur, 'It is enough that a State possesses a certain number of *people*, of living, rational beings.' In fact, it was the Northern delegates at the Constitutional Convention who argued that slaves should be counted only as property and the Southern delegates who argued that slaves should be counted as people. 'Why then should the blacks, who were property in the South, be in the rule of representation more than the cattle and horses of the North?' asked Massachusetts delegate Elbridge Gerry. When Upshur wrote his *Enquiry*, not all white men could even vote or hold office in Virginia, so his belief that Southern Congressmen would represent the interests of black slaves (just as they represented the interests of disfranchised whites) was not as self-serving as it may sound. As Italian historian Raimondo Luraghi puts it, the Old South was indeed an 'oligarchy,' not a 'democracy,' but it was an oligarchy 'governed by a very intelligent, mild, shrewd, benevolent, and

239

tolerant paternalistic class' – 'one of the most remarkable political classes in history,' which 'succeeded in understanding and interpreting the interests of the most dependent classes, even, in part, of black slaves.'

Indeed, it was future Confederate President Jefferson Davis who, as a Mississippi Senator, expressed his 'surprise and horror' at how Northern Senators treated the 'extinction' of the slave population as 'a matter of public policy or of speculative philosophy,' as well as his 'sympathy and indignation' on behalf of the slaves, for whom he felt 'kindness and protection.' Shocked and appalled, Davis announced, 'If I believed slavery to be the moral, social, and political evil which it is described; if I believed the advantage of rendering our population homogeneous to be as great as it is asserted, not then – no, nor if both were ten times greater – would I be reconciled to such a policy for such a purpose.'

If Story framed the Constitution, then slaves would have been excluded from representation and direct taxation would have been apportioned according to property. Upshur objected that such a system would require 'a host of officers, whose compensations would consume a large proportion of the tax, while, from the very nature of their duties, they would be forced into minute examinations, inconsistent with the freedom of our institutions, harassing and vexatious in their details, and leading inevitably to popular resistance and tumult' (here, Upshur perfectly anticipates the infernal Internal Revenue Service). In addition, Upshur stressed that under Story's Constitution 'the South would be, indeed, little better than the lamb in the embrace of the wolf.' With the slaves not counted as people, 'they would have no right to be heard in their own defence, through their representatives in the federal councils.' Meanwhile, the 'whole numbers' of the Northern people would be represented, and Southern property would be singled out for taxation. 'The rule, then, which considers slaves only as property to be taxed, and not as people to be represented,' summarised Upshur, 'is little else than a rule imposing on the Southern States almost the entire burthens of the government, and allowing to them only the shadow of influence in the measures of that government.'

Story's opinion exasperated Upshur. 'The truth is, the slave-holding States have always contributed more than their just proportion to the wealth and strength of the country, and not *less* than their just proportion to its intelligence and public virtue.' Upshur was no doubt thinking of the Southerner who wrote the Declaration of Independence, the Southerner who commanded the American Revolution and the Southerners who won some of its greatest victories, the Southerners who framed the Constitution, the Southerners who remained loyal during the War of 1812, the Southerners who tamed the wild frontier, as well as the Southern economy that supplied the bulk of American exports and financed the federal government. The Three-Fifths Clause was a compromise made by the South for the North, not by the North for the South, insisted Upshur. While the South was not bitter over the sacrifice she had made for the sake of the Union, she was bitter 'that grave authors, in elaborate works designed to form the opinions of rising generations, should so treat the subject as to create an impression that the Southern States are enjoying advantages under our Constitution, to which they are not fairly entitled, and which they owe only to the liberality of other States; for the South feels that these supposed advantages are, in fact, *sacrifices*, which she has made only to a spirit of conciliation and harmony, and which neither justice nor sound principle would ever have exacted from her.'

Upshur conceded that Story's *Commentaries* was an impressive display of scholarship, but concluded that Story's unabashed advocacy of his political agenda had driven him to bend logic and stretch the truth. Upshur feared that Story's 'false views,' 'forced constructions,' and 'strange misapprehensions of history' were 'mischievous' and 'dangerous.' Especially at risk under Story's *'beau ideal'* government was the minority – in particular, the Southern States. According to Story, the one American people were sovereign and answered to no one. In the States, this was fine, as the separate and distinct people of each shared common 'character, interests, and pursuits.' Across the entire United States, however, where character, interests, and pursuits were different and divided along sectional lines, 'a fair opportunity is afforded for the exercise of an oppressive tyranny, by the majority over the minority.' Federal courts could not be trusted for 'redress,' as they were a branch of the very government whose acts would be challenged in court. The 'virtue and intelligence' of the people was not reliable, either, as the people (and especially their politicians) were not always virtuous or intelligent. 'Of what people?' asked Upshur. 'Of that very majority who have committed the injustice complained of, and who, according to the author's theory, are the sole judges whether they have power to do it or not, and whether it be injustice or not,' he answered. If the purpose of the government was 'to protect the weak, to restrain the violent, to punish the vicious, and to compel all to the performance of the duty which man owes to man in a social state,' Story's framework, by consolidating all power in the majority, failed spectacularly. Upshur bitterly noted that such an 'unbalanced, unchecked' government would eventually become a 'victim to its own excesses.'

Upshur did not trust in the checks and balances between federal branches of government in which Story had such faith (a clockwork), preferring, in the old-fashioned Southern political tradition, the separation of powers (counterweights). Checks and balances, insisted Upshur, were 'illusory,' as one department would inevitably dominate the others and consolidate all powers in itself. What was needed were 'many and severe restraints' and a 'salutary countervailing interest' on the entire federal government, not just between its branches. According to Upshur, this was the rightful role of the States – 'the true balance-wheel, the only effectual check upon federal encroachments.' The people of the States, already organised with governments of their own and naturally united in interests, would be more effective guardians of their rights and liberties than the disorganised and divided one American people. Indeed, the States had the greatest reason and ability to regulate the federal government – 'to give it power enough, and to prevent it from assuming too much.' If the federal government ever did usurp the rights of the States, then the States were free to 'interpose,' judging the constitutionality of federal legislation for themselves and, if necessary, blocking its enforcement within their jurisdiction.

Upshur was confident that a confederated Union of strong, free States would be peaceful, prosperous, and perpetual. For small-f federalism and small-r republicanism to flourish, however, love of as well as loyalty to the States must be cultivated. The people should look to their States as truly sovereign and not mere 'municipal corporations' of the federal government. 'They ought to know that they can look nowhere else with perfect assurance of safety and protection,' urged Upshur. 'Let them then maintain those governments, not only in their rights, but in their dignity and influence.' To the objection that the States would abuse the power of interposition, Upshur retorted that the real danger was not disunion among the States, but submission of the States to a 'gigantic' federal government. For freedom's sake, the States must be restored to their 'proper position' as the 'palladium' of the people. 'Then alone will their voice be heard with respect at Washington; then alone will their interposition avail to protect their own people against the usurpations of the great central power,' avowed Upshur. 'It is vain to hope that the federative principle of our government can be preserved, or that anything can prevent it from running into the absolutism of consolidation, if we suffer the rights of the States to be filched away, and their dignity and influence be lost, through our carelessness or neglect.'

III

Long after the publication of the Story's *Commentaries* and Upshur's *Enquiry*, and long after the judges were dead, their two opposing philosophies stood in stark contrast in the inaugural addresses of two opposing American presidents.

'Our present condition, achieved in a manner unprecedented in the history of nations,' declared Confederate President Jefferson Davis from Montgomery, 'illustrates the American idea that governments must rest upon the consent of the governed, and that it is the right of the people to alter or abolish governments whenever they become destructive of the ends for which they were established.' Channeling Upshur, Davis described the Union as a 'compact,' the States as 'sovereign,' the federal government as an 'agent,' and the Constitution as a document which was to be 'strictly construed.' According to Davis, the recently ratified Confederate Constitution, which explicitly named the States as sovereign and eliminated clauses which had been abused by liberal constructionism, preserved the 'true meaning' of the old Constitution and the 'well-known intent' of the Founding Fathers. 'We have changed the constituent parts, but not the system of our government,' explained Davis. 'The Constitution formed by our fathers is that of these Confederate States.' The Confederacy's 'true policy' was 'peace and commerce,' avowed Davis, but if Northern 'lust of dominion' threatened her independence, then she would resort to 'any measures of defence which honour and security may require.'

U.S. President Abraham Lincoln, however, disagreed. 'A disruption of the Federal Union, heretofore only menaced, is now formidably attempted,' announced Lincoln from Washington, D.C. 'I hold that in contemplation of universal law and of the Constitution, the Union of these States is perpetual.' Channeling Story, Lincoln averred that 'the Union is much older than the Constitution,' described the Union as a 'national government' rather than 'an association of States,' suggested that whatever the Constitution did not 'expressly say' was open to interpretation, insisted that the minority was obligated to 'acquiesce' to the 'sovereign' majority, and branded secession as 'anarchy.' Lincoln reiterated his longstanding disavowal that he had any right or intention to abolish slavery, pledged to enforce the Fugitive Slave

Act, and endorsed a constitutional amendment permanently sealing slavery in the South (the first of several offers to trade reunion for slavery, all of which the Confederacy rejected). If any States resisted his authority, however, then Lincoln threatened to retaliate with 'invasion,' 'bloodshed,' and 'civil war.'

In the end, what Upshur and Story could not settle with ink, Davis and Lincoln would settle with blood.

V. John Caldwell Calhoun & *Disquisition on Government* and *Discourse on the Constitution and Government of the United States*

'Union among ourselves is not only necessary for our safety, but for the preservation of the common liberties and institutions of the whole confederacy. We constitute the balance wheel of our complex and beautiful political system. We are, and must continue to be, in a permanent minority in the Union. Our geographical position, our industry, pursuits, and institutions, are all peculiar. Our safety and prosperity depend on maintaining, in their full vigour, the restrictions imposed on the powers granted by the Constitution. So long as these are so maintained, and the powers confined to the objects intended by that sacred compact, we will be safe and prosperous, but no longer. There is no fear, but the stronger portions of the Union will maintain the powers in their full vigour. The limitations are of far less comparative value to them. They can protect themselves without them; and, in fact, so far from a benefit, they are but too apt to regard them as unnecessary restraints on their power. If we do not take care of them, none will, and the government will practicably become one of unlimited powers.'
– John Caldwell Calhoun, 1840

TODAY, IT IS CONSIDERED a fact that the constitutional doctrine of States' rights was nothing more than a flimsy veneer for the foundational issue of slavery. Harry V. Jaffa, a prominent neo-conservative from the Claremont

247

Institute who engaged in written and oral debates over the legacy of Abraham Lincoln with the paleo-conservative M.E. Bradford and libertarian Thomas J. DiLorenzo, argues that States' rights were a proto-'Nazi' ideology invented by John C. Calhoun for the preservation of slavery. According to Jaffa, there was a fundamental 'opposition' between 'Calhoun's doctrine of state rights' and 'the doctrine of human rights encompassed by the Declaration.' Of course, the Declaration of Independence was never meant to be a doctrine of human rights, but no matter. Manisha Sinha, a professor of Afro-American Studies from the University of Connecticut, claims that States' rights were, in fact, a 'counter-revolution of slavery' against the American Revolution, concocted and propagated by wealthy planters like Calhoun. 'For him, states' rights theory was not a vindication of local democracy,' Sinha declares, 'but a safeguard for the distinct interests of the Southern slave-holding minority.' Of course, States' rights predated, outlasted, and in some cases even clashed with slavery, but no matter. According to Jaffa and Sinha, the Southern political tradition was un- or even anti-American, but to Calhoun, it was 'historically as certain as our Revolution itself.'

This essay series aims to set the story straight. The truth is that the great political treatises of the Old South prove that the doctrine of States' rights was never a mere pretence for slavery, but reflected a deep passion for self-government rooted in Southern culture as well as an earnest understanding of the Constitution rooted in Southern history. According to the scholarly, gentlemanly M.E. Bradford, States' rights were part of a Southern political tradition – a 'patrimony' and 'birthright' – dating from the foundation of the Colonies through the independence of the States and to the creation of the Constitution. At the crowning of the Confederate capital in Richmond, President Jefferson Davis honoured this heritage. 'The cause in which we are now engaged is the cause of the advocacy of the rights to which we were born, those for which our fathers of the Revolution bled – the richest inheritance that ever fell to man, and which it is our sacred duty to transmit untarnished to our children,' announced Davis. 'Upon us is devolved the high and holy responsibility of preserving the constitutional liberty of a free government.'

John C. Calhoun and his books, *Disquisition on Government* and *Discourse on the Constitution and Government of the United States*, published posthumously in 1851, are the subjects of this chapter.

I

John C. Calhoun was born on 18 March 1782 in Abbeville, South Carolina. Calhoun's father, Patrick, was a tough Scotch-Irish frontiersman who fought Cherokee and Tory marauders in the backcountry. Patrick was also a prominent local citizen who opposed the ratification of the Constitution because it allowed other States to tax South Carolina (in his view, a prime example of 'taxation without representation') and prohibited religious tests for federal offices. Patrick served as the Upcountry's first representative in South Carolina's General Assembly, walking all the way to Charleston from Abbeville on his own. According to Calhoun, it was his father who introduced him to the idea that the best government was that which 'allowed the largest amount of individual liberty compatible with social order and tranquility.' Calhoun grew up working in the fields and hunting in the woods, and after the death of his father took care of his mother and younger brother by himself. Although Calhoun's only education had been the tutelage of his brother-in-law, a Presbyterian minister who took promising young South Carolinians under his wing, his family realised his intelligence and insisted that he attend college. Thus, in 1800, the young Scotch-Irishman from the Carolinian backcountry traveled to Yale College (now Yale University) in the puritanical Yankee stronghold of Connecticut. There, he excelled in his studies, attaining admission to Phi Beta Kappa and rising to the rank of valedictorian. Calhoun so impressed his peers and his faculty with his powerful and passionate mind that many of them, including the arch-

Federalist college president Timothy Dwight, were sure that he was destined for the presidency. Calhoun briefly read law in Charleston, but he was disgusted with frivolous city life (though he ultimately married into Charleston society) and returned to his humble hometown of Abbeville. Later in his life, he established a plantation, 'Fort Hill,' in the nearby district of Pendleton, where, when he was home, he spent sunup to sundown in the field with about 60 slaves.

Legend has it that on his way home from New England, the young Calhoun stopped at Monticello to visit with Thomas Jefferson. During this midnight visit the two supposedly made a deep impression on one another before parting ways, never to meet again. Even if the story is mythical (which it very well may be) myths reveal symbolic if not literal truths about a time, a place, and a people. This myth, in particular, reveals that Southerners did indeed see in Calhoun the spiritual successor to Jefferson. Even if not literally true, there is at least a poetic truth in this passing of the torch from the sage to the student.

On the force of a speech he gave in Abbeville condemning the British attack on the *USS Chesapeake*, Calhoun was elected to represent his district in South Carolina's General Assembly in 1808. There, Calhoun witnessed a historic compromise between the Lowcountry and the Upcountry concerning legislative representation, sparking his interest in what would become his major contribution to political philosophy: rule by consensus over rule by majority. Soon after, in 1811, Calhoun was elected to represent South Carolina in the House of Representatives. In his first major speech on the floor of the Congress, Calhoun boldly challenged John Randolph of Roanoke, the spellbinding orator and fearsome debater who vehemently opposed the War of 1812 and had criticised a pro-war report issued by Calhoun. Randolph had objected that the United States was not prepared for a war with Great Britain. 'If our country is unprepared, let us remedy the evil as soon as possible,' retorted Calhoun. Randolph had objected that a war with Great Britain would be expensive. 'Sir,' retorted Calhoun, 'I am not versed in this calculating policy; and will not, therefore, pretend to estimate in dollars and cents the value of national independence.' Randolph had objected that war with Great Britain would be dangerous. 'If he desires to repress the gallant ardour of our countrymen by such topics,' retorted Calhoun, 'let me inform him, that true courage regards only the cause, that it is just and necessary; and that it condemns the sufferings and dangers of war.' Randolph had objected that the Constitution was not built for war. 'The Constitution, then, it seems, has failed in an essential object, "to provide for the common defence,"' retorted Calhoun. If Randolph opposed war, Calhoun continued, then 'let his eloquence be addressed' to the warmongering British ministry. 'Tell them if they persist in such daring insult and injury to a neutral nation, that, however inclined to peace, it will be bound in honour and safety to resist.' After this impressive debut, one of America's leading Jeffersonian newspapers, the *Richmond Enquirer*, described Calhoun as 'a master spirit who stamps his name upon the age in which he lives.' For his militancy in bringing on and waging the war, Randolph himself dubbed Calhoun a 'war hawk,' a term which came to include the new representatives from the backcountry demanding 'submission or war.' To Calhoun and the War Hawks, the War of 1812 was nothing less than a Second American Revolution. 'The Americans of the present day will prove to the enemy and the world,' declared Calhoun, 'that we have not only inherited that liberty which our fathers gave us, but also the will and power to maintain it.'

After the war, Calhoun championed strengthening American national defence with a system of federally financed roads and canals as well as federally protected industries. Calhoun hoped that building up domestic industries would 'bind together our widely spread republic' and that 'connecting the interests of the varied sections of this great country' with a transportation infrastructure would expedite the movement of goods in peacetime and armies in wartime. Thomas Jefferson himself – as much an enemy of taxes, spending, and debt as any man – supported such a policy for the very same reasons. Calhoun intended protectionism and internal improvements to be temporary measures of war reconstruction, however, not the permanent policy which its beneficiaries would soon dub 'the American System.' Nevertheless, Randolph of Roanoke, opposed to the consolidation of money and power in the federal government, challenged Calhoun. 'I have long believed there was a tendency in the administration of this government, in the system itself indeed, to consolidation, and the remarks made by the honourable gentleman from South Carolina have not tended to allay any fears I have entertained from that quarter,' charged Randolph. In a rare appeal rather than denunciation, Randolph asked Calhoun 'whether the honourable gentleman's principles (which he had demonstrated with an ability honourable to the State he represented, to the House, and to himself) did not go to the destruction of the State governments.' Randolph, perhaps sensing potential in his apparent adversary, planted seeds which Northern arrogance and aggression would soon cultivate into a severe, sincere change of mind in Calhoun.

Appointed Secretary of War by President James Monroe in 1817, Calhoun reinvigorated what had become a defunct position, designing a brilliant network of roads and canals (facilitating transportation and communication), humanising Indian policy (upholding the traditional policy of acculturation and aid), contributing to the formation of the 'Monroe Doctrine' (declaring the Western Hemisphere to be the United States' sphere of influence and forswearing any intervention in European affairs), and building up the stature of West Point (admitting students such as Robert E. Lee, Jefferson Davis, and Joseph E. Johnston). Calhoun's friends objected that he was too philosophical for the position and that it would stall his career in the prime of his life, but Calhoun believed that he had a duty to serve wherever needed and was enticed by the challenge.

Calhoun campaigned for the presidency in the seven-way race of 1824, but bowed out once it was clear that General Andrew Jackson, the hero of the Battle of New Orleans, would receive the nomination. When there was a four-way stalemate, the election passed to the House of Representatives, where the State delegations would resolve the matter. The appearance of a backroom deal between the candidates Henry Clay and John Quincy Adams (in which Clay, as Speaker of the House, delivered the election to Adams in exchange for his appointment as Secretary of State, despite Jackson's plurality) troubled Calhoun. According to Calhoun, power 'improperly acquired' would be 'improperly used.' Meanwhile, Calhoun had been elected Vice President in his own right, and cast tie-breaking votes against tariff and internal-improvement bills which he realised were padding the profits of Northern industry and pilfering the pockets of Southern agriculture under the pretence of protection for the American economy. 'This is the point of the greatest danger,' warned Calhoun, 'and, if not guarded with the greatest vigilance, combinations will be formed on separate and opposing interests, which will end in despotism, as complete as that of a single and irresponsible ruler.' When Calhoun did not restrain his old nemesis, Randolph of Roanoke, from viciously denouncing the 'corrupt bargain' of Adams and Clay in the Senate (whom he branded 'the Puritan' and 'the Blackleg,' respectively), Adams, writing under the pseudonym 'Patrick Henry,' publicly accused Calhoun of dereliction of duty. Calhoun, replying as 'Onslow' (after Sir Arthur Onslow, a Speaker of the House of Commons who had influenced Thomas Jefferson's *Manual of Parliamentary Practice*), countered that it would be tyrannical for the executive branch to suppress freedom of debate in the legislature. In the last year of Adams' presidency, he signed into law what was then the heaviest protectionist tariff in American history, the 'Tariff of Abominations.' Calhoun regarded the Tariff of Abominations, which subjected America's vast agricultural, commercial, and maritime interests to a single, narrow industrial interest as 'worse than folly,' and, in fact, 'madness itself.'

In 1828, Calhoun was again elected Vice President, this time beneath President Andrew Jackson, the head of the newfound Democratic Party. Calhoun had high hopes for Jackson, whom he believed would inaugurate another Jeffersonian-style reform of the federal government – particularly by reducing the record-high tariff rates to equitable levels. Unfortunately, Jackson was a disappointment, continuing to preside over the consolidation of national power and formation of sectional factions which had been troubling Calhoun for some time. 'Never has a man been worse advised; and never has one lost such an opportunity to do good,' admitted Calhoun. 'My ardent hope was, when he was elected, that his great popularity would have been used to restore the Constitution, and to avert the calamity, that seems impending over our country.' Indeed, the challenge of forming a common government between differing peoples and preventing a struggle for power between those peoples was now painfully clear to Calhoun. 'It is this very circumstance,' worried Calhoun, 'that the same enactment should operate on the different sections of the country from their different condition in a mode so opposite as to be considered a blessing in one section and a curse in another, that has filled me with apprehension for some years past.' In addition, Calhoun and Jackson's Scotch-Irish blood and backcountry upbringing (in fact, they even looked alike) made them especially headstrong and sensitive to points of honour. As a result, personal disputes between the two men further strained their relationship and ruined what was once a mutual respect. A commemoration of Thomas Jefferson's birthday provided a tableau of the growing tension not merely between Calhoun and Jackson, but between the Union and the States as well. 'Our Federal Union: It must be preserved!' toasted Jackson, staring down Calhoun. 'The Union,' Calhoun toasted in reply, staring back, 'next to our Liberty, the most dear!'

South Carolina was smoldering with hatred of the Tariff of Abominations and fear of Southern enslavement to the North. Congressman George McDuffie was spreading his 'Forty Bale Theory,' which held that for every one-hundred bales of cotton that South Carolinians raised, forty were paid to the North in taxes. Thomas Cooper, President of South Carolina College (now the University of South Carolina) was urging South Carolinians 'to calculate the value of the Union...by which the South has always been the loser and the North always the gainer.' Robert J. Turnbull, writing under the pseudonym *Brutus*, warned in his pamphlet, *The Crisis*, 'The GREAT SOUTHERN GOOSE will yet bear more plucking.' Indeed, South Carolinians had counted the votes in the Congress and realised that even if the South were united, she still could not stop the North from taxing the South and spending on herself. Amid this tense atmosphere, Calhoun authored the *Exposition and Protest*, a report to South Carolina's General Assembly declaring the Tariff of Abominations 'unconstitutional, unequal, oppressive, and calculated to corrupt the public virtue and destroy the liberty of the country.' Calhoun claimed that the 'protection' and 'appropriation' powers of the so-called American System (i.e. tariffs and internal improvements, respectively) suppressed Southern agriculture and subsidised Northern industry, thus benefiting the North by burdening the South. 'We are the serfs of the system, out of whose labour is raised, not only the money paid into the Treasury, but the funds out of which are drawn the rich rewards of the manufacturer and his associates in interest,' exclaimed Calhoun. 'Their object in the tariff is to keep down foreign competition, in order to obtain a monopoly of the domestic market...to compel us to purchase at a higher price, both what we obtain from them and from others, without receiving a correspondent increase in the price of what we sell.' As sovereign parties to the Constitution, reasoned Calhoun, the States had the right to resist any federal encroachment upon their reserved powers. This 'veto,' averred Calhoun, was 'the remedy which the Constitution has provided to prevent the encroachments of the general government on the reserved rights of the States...by which the distribution of power, between the general and State governments, may be preserved forever inviolable.' Once a State nullified a law, continued Calhoun, the States should call a constitutional convention – the 'creating and preserving power of the system' – to amend or not amend the Constitution accordingly. 'If, on an appeal to this purpose, the decision be favourable to the general government, a disputed power will be converted into an expressly granted power,' reasoned Calhoun, 'but, on the other hand, if it be adverse, the refusal to grant will be tantamount to an inhibition of its exercise; and thus, in either case, the controversy will be determined.' According to Calhoun, carrying out James Madison and Thomas Jefferson's 'rightful remedy' from the *Virginia and Kentucky Resolutions* was 'a sacred duty to the Union, to the cause of liberty over the world,' and South Carolinians would be 'unworthy of the name of freemen, of Americans – of Carolinians, if danger, however great, could cause them to shrink from the maintenance of their constitutional rights.' South Carolina's General Assembly adopted the *Exposition and Protest*, but opted to wait and see what their Southern Democratic President would do first before taking any further action.

Although the tariff was an issue of vital importance, Calhoun realised that the threat facing the South was about more than just economic interest, but political, cultural, and social/racial existence as well. 'The question is no longer one of free trade,' declared Calhoun, 'but of liberty and despotism.' According to Calhoun, Southern civilisation could not survive under a 'consolidated government of unlimited power' controulled by an 'unchecked majority' of Northerners. 'Under its baneful influence,' he warned of such a sectional regime, 'the noble, high-minded, chivalric spirit of the South would be beat down in low and base subserviency.' Calhoun expanded on the argument of the *Exposition and Protest* in the *Fort Hill Address* and a letter to South Carolina's Governor, James Hamilton, both of which were widely published under his name. 'The ground we have taken,' summarised Calhoun, 'is that the tariff is unconstitutional, and must be repealed, that the rights of the South have been destroyed, and must be restored, and that the Union is in danger, and must be saved.'

South Carolina's hopes were dashed when in 1832 federal tariff rates on key articles of import actually rose instead of fell. Angry and afraid, South Carolina called a convention and nullified the tariffs of 1828 and 1832, declaring them unconstitutional within her jurisdiction, refusing to comply with their collection, and swearing to secede from the Union if coercion were attempted against her. This development forced Calhoun to choose between his presidential ambition and the cause of his State – a promising, powerful career or his principles and his people. Ultimately, Calhoun resigned the vice presidency and returned to take his stand in South Carolina. 'Had my love of the Union and the Constitution been less, or ambition greater,' reflected Calhoun, 'I certainly would not have ventured the step.' Promptly elected to the Senate to represent his State in the crisis, Calhoun was shocked and appalled when President Jackson called for an invasion of South Carolina to enforce the tariff and defeat nullification. 'Does any man in his senses believe that this beautiful structure – this harmonious aggregate of States, produced by the joint consent of all – can be preserved by force?' asked Calhoun. 'No, no. Force may, indeed, hold the parts together, but such union would be the bond between master and slave – a union of exaction on one side and unqualified *obedience* on the other.' When Massachusetts Senator Daniel Webster supported Jackson's proposed Force Bill, arguing that nullification was chaotic and that coercion would restore peace, Calhoun could scarcely contain himself. 'Yes, the peace of despotism: that peace which is enforced by the bayonet and the sword; the peace of death, where all the vital functions of liberty have ceased,' charged Calhoun. 'It is this peace which the doctrine of State sovereignty may disturb by that conflict, which in every free State, if properly organised, necessarily exists between liberty and power.' Faced with civil war, Calhoun reluctantly endorsed the Compromise of 1833, brokered by Kentucky Senator Henry Clay, which exchanged the repeal of nullification for annual reductions in the tariff over the next decade. Calhoun helped the proud South Carolinians see nullification as a victory: after all, a single, small State's stand had forced a compromise in federal policy! For the rest of his life, Calhoun not only served as the political leader of South Carolina – 'our gallant little State,' he boasted – but also a spokesman for the South in the 'Great Triumvirate' alongside the Whigs Clay and Webster, all of whom were American Ciceros united in opposition to Jackson, an American Caesar.

In 1816, Calhoun had contributed to the creation of the Second Bank of the United States, improving on the Madison Administration's charter by requiring higher specie reserves and prohibiting the suspension of specie payments and loans to the federal government. 'Instead of a mere paper machine,' held Calhoun, his new national bank would be 'an ally instead of an opponent in restoring the currency to a sound condition.' By 1834, however, Calhoun had turned against the bank he had built, confessing that it had not operated according to plan. Calhoun was equally against President Jackson's 'bank war,' however. It was illegal, inflationary, and corrupt, objected Calhoun, for Jackson to withdraw federal funds from the national bank and deposit them in a spoils system of State-chartered 'pet banks.' The issue was not, insisted Calhoun, 'a bank or no bank,' as Jackson framed it, but rather the 'union of the banking system with the executive.' After the disappointing outcome of his national bank, Calhoun's ideal banking system became a total 'divorce' between banks and the government – the combination of which had created a 'great overruling money power.' According to Calhoun, 'It is to this mischievous and unholy alliance that may be traced most of the disasters that have befallen us, and the great political degeneracy of the country.' At the same time, Calhoun noted that federal acceptance of private banknotes as currency had granted banks the power to inflate the money supply at will, which led to ruinous financial panics and debased the currency. Indeed, along with John Taylor of Caroline, Calhoun was one of the few statesmen in Antebellum America who grasped the fraudulence of fractional-reserve banking (i.e. not only holding a fraction of deposits as reserves and loaning out the rest, but also printing more in paper banknotes than they even held in reserves) as well as the political and economic problems it caused. 'Place the money power in the hands of a single individual, or a combination of individuals, and, by expanding or contracting the currency, they may raise or sink prices at pleasure; and may command the whole property and industry of the country,' explained Calhoun. 'Never was an engine invented better calculated to place the destiny of the many in the hands of the few, or less favourable to that equality and independence which be at the bottom of all free institutions.' In 1837,

Calhoun nobly suppressed his disdain for President Martin Van Buren (who had shamelessly fanned the flames between Jackson and Calhoun for his own political advancement) and supported his 'Independent Treasury System,' which separated the federal treasury from the banking system. In order to prevent inflation and strengthen the currency, Calhoun added an amendment prohibiting federal acceptance of bank paper, thus placing the government on a sounder specie standard. The Independent Treasury lasted without any financial crises until the erection of the National Banking System (the prototype of the current Federal Reserve System) during the so-called 'Civil War,' after which commenced an endless cycle of booms and busts.

Disturbed by the malicious motives and militant methods of the emerging abolitionist movement and the role which they played it stoking conflict between the North and the South, by 1837 Calhoun felt duty-bound 'to speak freely upon the subject where the honour and interests of those I represent are involved.' At the time, the Senate was flooded with abolitionist petitions denouncing slavery and slave-holders in vicious and vile terms. According to Calhoun, however, Southerners had nothing of which to be ashamed. 'I hold that in the present state of civilisation, where two races of different origin, and distinguished by colour, and other physical differences, as well as intellectual, are brought together,' argued Calhoun, 'the relation now existing between the two, is, instead of an evil, a good – a positive good.' Indeed, continued Calhoun, 'under the fostering care of our institutions, reviled as they have been,' the 'low, degraded, and savage condition' of the blacks had risen to 'a condition so civilised and so improved, not only physically but morally and intellectually.' This was no different from what Thomas Jefferson meant when he wrote in *Notes on the State of Virginia* that 'the improvement of the blacks in body and mind, in the first instance of their mixture with the whites, has been observed by everyone, and proves that their inferiority is not the effect merely of their condition of life,' as well as that 'this unfortunate difference of colour, and perhaps of faculty, is a powerful obstacle to the emancipation of these people.' At the same time, held Calhoun, slavery had not 'degenerated' Southern whites, either. 'I appeal to all sides whether the South is not equal in virtue, intelligence, patriotism, courage, disinterestedness [i.e. political integrity], and all the high qualities which adorn our nature,' challenged Calhoun. 'I ask whether we have not contributed our full share of talents and political wisdom in forming and sustaining this political fabric; and whether we have not constantly inclined most strongly to the side of liberty, and been the first to see and resist the encroachments of power.' When contrasted with the 'conflict between labour and capital' in the North and the degraded living conditions of the industrial proletariat in Northern cities, Calhoun further challenged, Southerners had no reason to apologise for their calm, comfortable feudal way of life. 'The condition of society in the South exempts us from the disorders and dangers resulting from this conflict,' claimed Calhoun, 'and which explains why it is that the political condition of the slave-holding States has been so much more stable and quiet than those of the North.' Calhoun was not launching a so-called counter-revolution of slavery, but merely reaffirming the American social/racial consensus (that whites and blacks could not coexist freely and equally), correcting vicious slanders against his home (that slavery was malevolent rather than benevolent), and trying to counter forces which he feared would lead to disunion (a burning hatred and fear between the sections). 'However sound the great body of the non-slaveholding States are at present, in the course of a few years they will be succeeded by those who will have been taught to hate the people and institutions of nearly one half of the Union, with a hatred more deadly than one hostile nation ever entertained toward another,' warned Calhoun. 'It is easy to see the end. By the necessary course of events, if left to themselves, we must become, finally, two peoples.'

After the tragic explosion on the USS *Princeton* in 1844, President John Tyler, Jr., selected Calhoun to replace Abel P. Upshur as Secretary of State. In his brief term, Calhoun helped finalise Upshur's work towards Texas statehood, forcing the controversial issue into the presidential election, which resulted in the election of pro-Texas Democrat James K. Polk. Back in the Senate, Calhoun counseled 'wise and masterly inactivity' in boundary disputes with Great Britain and Mexico, trusting that the natural course of continental migration would deliver the disputed territories to the United States without any sacrifice in blood or treasure. 'Time is acting for us,' observed Calhoun. 'If we shall have the wisdom to trust its operation, it will assert and maintain our right with resistless force, without costing a cent of money or a drop of blood.' When President Polk escalated the conflict with Mexico, however, sending American troops to the Rio Grande River (which inevitably led to the outbreak of hostilities), Calhoun stood alone among Southerners against what he considered an 'odious' war. According to Calhoun, a 'war of conquest' would corrupt the executive branch with power and patronage, burden the people with debt and taxes, yield the 'forbidden fruit' of new territory which the North and the South would struggle to controul, and transform the American republic into an American empire. Calhoun, deeply disturbed by any precedent that empowered the President to start a war unilaterally, refused to vote for the Congress' 'lying' war resolution, but once the war was underway Calhoun tried to minimise the damage by supporting a strategy of holding a 'defensive line' along the Rio Grande instead of going on the offensive in Mexico. When the President and the Congress considered conquering all of Mexico, Calhoun argued that it was a 'sad delusion' to believe that 'it is the mission of our country to spread civil and religious liberty all over the world, even by force if necessary,' as well as a 'great mistake' to believe that 'free popular governments may be made under the authority and protection of a conqueror.' According to Calhoun, 'None but people advanced to a very high state of moral and intellectual improvement are capable, in a civilised state, of maintaining free government.' Calhoun's oft-quoted remark, 'It is harder to preserve than to obtain liberty,' was made in protest of the Mexican War. 'Our people have undergone a great change,' lamented Calhoun. 'Their inclination is for conquest and empire, regardless of their institutions and liberty; or, rather, they think they hold their liberty by a divine tenure, which no imprudence on their part can defeat...We act, as if good institutions and liberty belong to us of right, and that neither neglect nor folly can deprive us of their blessing.'

In the last major speech of his life, Calhoun denounced the Compromise of 1850 (a series of measures which Henry Clay had cobbled together to resolve the controversy surrounding the territory conquered from Mexico) for treating the symptoms of the sectional conflict rather than curing the disease. Too weak to speak, Calhoun intensely studied the reaction of the Senate as a colleague read his speech for him. The 'primary cause' of the conflict between the North and South, claimed Calhoun, was 'the fact that the equilibrium between the two sections in the government, as it stood when the Constitution was ratified, and the government put in action, has been destroyed.' Calhoun cited census data to prove that 'the weight of the two sections' leaned heavily to the North, arguing that the inequality was the product of three unconstitutional federal policies. 'The first is, that series of acts by which the South has been excluded from the common territory belonging to all the States as members of the Federal Union – which have had the effect of extending vastly the portion allotted to the Northern section, and restricting within narrow limits the portion left to the South,' Calhoun began. 'The next consists in adopting a system of revenue and disbursements, by which an undue proportion of the burden of taxation has been imposed upon the South, and undue proportion of its proceeds appropriated to the North,' Calhoun continued. 'The last is a system of political measures, by which the original character of the government has been radically changed,' concluded Calhoun, 'by concentrating all the power of the system in itself.' If the Compromise of 1850 were adopted, charged Calhoun, then the North would have shown that her 'real objects' were 'power and 'aggrandisement,' and the South would be 'infatuated not to act accordingly.' It was a foreboding final note.

Calhoun died on 31 March 1850. His fellow triumvirs, Henry Clay and Daniel Webster, eulogised him in the Senate. Clay praised Calhoun's 'elevated genius of the highest order,' recalled the 'charm and captivating influence of his colloquial powers,' and urged his colleagues to follow his example. 'I trust we shall all be instructed by the eminent virtues and merits of his exalted character, and be taught by his bright example to fulfill our great public duties by the lights of our own judgment and the dictate of our own consciences, as he did.' Webster praised Calhoun for 'his genius and character, his honour and integrity, his amiable deportment in private life, and the purity of his exalted patriotism.' In a time when Americans revered the Romans as exemplars of republican statesman, Webster paid Calhoun the ultimate compliment: 'We saw before us a Senator of Rome, when Rome survived.' In Calhoun's South Carolina, the eulogies were more partisan. 'We cannot but hate the tyranny that hurried him to his grave, and love the liberty for which he lived, and wasted, and died,' Robert B. Rhett, one of Calhoun's lieutenants, told South Carolina's General Assembly. 'Cherishing his memory, we dare not be slaves.'

Just over a century after his death, the Senate – led by the Yankee John F. Kennedy – honoured Calhoun as one of the five greatest Senators in American history, along with his fellow triumvirs Henry Clay and Daniel Webster. Kennedy also featured Calhoun in his famous book, *Profiles in Courage*. 'When I was selected as chairman of a committee to pick five outstanding Senators in the history of this country, John C. Calhoun's name led all the rest...and when I wrote a book about courageous Senators, I mentioned John C. Calhoun,' presidential candidate Kennedy told Governor Fritz Hollings, Senator Olin Johnston, and a cheering crowd in Columbia. 'What makes Calhoun so important as the major key to the understanding of American politics is not just that he saw the importance in American political life of sectional and interest pluralism; other major analysts of our government, [Alexis] de Tocqueville for instance, or [James] Bryce or [Woodrow] Wilson, saw that, too,' comments the 'social ecologist' Peter F.

Drucker. 'But Calhoun, perhaps alone, saw in it more than a rule of expediency...He saw in it a basic principle of free government.'

Although Calhoun's career is typically traced as a tragic descent from American unionism to Southern sectionalism, he was always devoted to preserving the American republic as it was founded. 'I am a conservative in its broadest and fullest sense,' averred Calhoun, 'and such shall I ever remain, unless, indeed, the government shall become so corrupt and disordered, that nothing short of revolution can reform it.' First, during the War of 1812 and the Era of Good Feelings, Calhoun believed that his duty was to defend the republic from the external threat of foreign powers by building national unity and securing commercial independence. 'I belong to no particular section or interest,' declared Calhoun. 'It has been my pride to be above all sectional or party feelings and to be devoted to the great interests of the country.' Later, beginning with the Age of Jackson and continuing to the Crisis of the Union, Calhoun believed that his duty was to defend the republic from the internal threats of consolidation and disunion by upholding the rights of the States and maintaining a balance of power between the sections. 'My aim is fixed,' pledged Calhoun. 'It is no less than to turn back the government to where it commenced its operations in 1789...to take a fresh start, a new departure, on the State-Rights Republican tack, as was intended by the framers of the Constitution.' It was the challenges that Calhoun faced which changed, not his principles.

Calhoun's career is also commonly mischaracterised as a relentless quest for the presidency. Although Calhoun desired the presidency as a young man, he knew that his personal dispute with Andrew Jackson and principled stand in the Tariff Crisis ended his promising prospects. Calhoun kept his name in future presidential elections in order to give his ideas and the South a national voice, but he recognised that he was no longer a serious contender – a fact of which he often reminded enthusiastic admirers and suspicious detractors. 'I did not suit the times, nor the times me, and I would not accept the presidency, unless my services were demanded by the country to reform the government from top to bottom,' admitted Calhoun. 'So far from overestimating, I have no doubt, that the very services, which ought to recommend me to the country, and the qualities, which ought to give confidence, constitute insuperable objections to my election.' Just as Ron Paul's 2008 and 2012 presidential campaigns exposed Americans to liberty, peace, and sound money, Calhoun's exposed Americans to 'Free Trade; Low Duties; No Debt; Separation from Banks; Economy, Retrenchment; and Strict Adherence to the Constitution.' The best way to characterise Calhoun's career is not as a foiled presidential aspirant, but as that of a statesman, rising above the temporising and dissembling politician in order to discern and perhaps direct the underlying forces determining the fate of his people. While Democrat and Whig politicians thought only of the next election, Calhoun thought of the next generation. 'Far higher motives impel me, a sense of duty – to do our best for our country, and leave the rest to Providence,' Calhoun confided to his daughter, Anna, who wondered what motivated him to fight what seemed a lost cause. 'I hold the duties of life to be greater than life itself, and that in performing them manfully, even against hope, our labour is not lost, but will be productive of good in after times.'

Far from a 'disunionist,' Calhoun did as much as anyone to preserve the Union in a time of tremendous social and economic change as well as political and sectional conflict. Indeed, the charge 'disunionist' incensed the statesman Calhoun like nothing else. For example, in 1843, Calhoun quelled the Bluffton Movement, a truly disunionist revolution among his own followers in South Carolina reacting against the 'Black Tariff' and Northern opposition to Texas statehood. In 1842, he opposed a reduction in federal tariffs which he believed violated the Compromise of 1833, and in 1846, he supported a comprehensive programme of internal improvements to develop the economy of the Mississippi Valley – both positions which put the interests of the Union above those of South Carolina. Unlike many of his peers, who worshipped the Union with eloquent but empty rhetoric,

Calhoun searched for actual solutions to the sectional conflict. 'The Union cannot be saved by eulogies on the Union, however splendid or numerous,' exclaimed Calhoun. 'The cry of "Union, Union, the glorious Union!" can no more prevent disunion than the cry of "Health, health, glorious health!" on the part of the physician, can save a patient lying dangerously ill.'

The signature description of Calhoun is as 'a cast-iron man, who looks as if he had never been born and never could be extinguished.' Photographs of a skeletal Calhoun are shown to reinforce this grim image. Yet those insults came from a stuffy Englishwoman who only met him once, and those skeletal photographs were taken at the end of his life during his final illness. The truth is that Calhoun was a charming and handsome man and loved by those who knew him. He was patient with a difficult wife, Floride, standing by her side and breaking with Andrew Jackson over an affair of honour. He was affectionate to and supportive of his children, especially his eldest daughter and kindred spirit, Anna. When Varina Davis, the wife of Mississippi Senator and future Confederate President Jefferson Davis, met Calhoun for the first time, she braced herself for the 'stern zealot' of legend. Instead, to the envy of other ladies at the ball, the two spent the evening in conversation and became lifelong friends.

II

In the final years of his life, Calhoun wrote two complementary political treatises, *A Disquisition on Government* and *A Discourse on the Constitution and Government of the United States*. The *Disquisition* is an original and outstanding work of political theory – 'the elementary principles of the science of government,' as Calhoun put it – comparable to the works of John Locke and the Baron de Montesquieu. Lord Acton, the great English classical liberal, described the *Disquisition* as 'the very perfection of political truth' and 'extremely applicable to the politics of the present day.' John Stuart Mill, another leading English classical liberal, described the *Disquisition* as a 'work of great ability,' specifically admiring Calhoun's 'extension of the practice of cooperation through which the weak, by uniting, can meet on equal terms with the strong.' The *Disquisition*, however, was a 'preliminary' to the *Discourse*, a work of political history drawing heavily from Founding-era documents – the records of the Constitutional Convention and the ratification debates, the *Virginia and Kentucky Resolutions*, and the *Report on the Virginia Resolutions* – to demonstrate that the American republic was the embodiment of the principles of the *Disquisition*. The *Discourse*, hoped Calhoun, would have the scope of the *Federalist*, the truth of the *Virginia and Kentucky Resolutions*, and better organisation than South Carolina's various nullification documents. Together, the *Disquisition* and *Discourse* form the pinnacle of Southern political philosophy and constitutional doctrine.

Calhoun began his *Disquisition* with a question: 'What is that constitution or law of our nature, without which government would not exist, and with which its existence is necessary?' In other words, why was government necessary? Calhoun's answer was premised on two 'incontestable' facts. The first was that man was a social creature. 'His inclinations and wants, physical and moral, irresistibly impel him to associate with his own kind; and he has, accordingly, never been found, in any age or country, in any state other than the social.' The second was that man's social state required a government. 'In no age or country has any society or community ever been found, whether enlightened or savage, without government of some description.' Calhoun asserted that these premises – man's need for society and a society's need for government – were 'unquestionable phenomena of our nature.'

Calhoun next asked why government was necessary for society when man was naturally a social creature. Man's 'direct or individual affections' were stronger than his 'sympathetic or social feelings,' he answered. There were, of course, 'extraordinary' exceptions, such as the selfless love of a mother for her child, but these were merely exceptions that proved the rule. Calhoun believed that the preference for oneself over others was a law 'of all animated existence,' not just human nature. 'It would, indeed, seem to be essentially connected with the great law of self-preservation which pervades all that feels, from man down to the lowest and most insignificant reptile or insect,' Calhoun observed. However civilised man became, held Calhoun, he would never outgrow this basic instinct. 'His social feelings may, indeed, in a state of safety and abundance, combined with high intellectual and moral culture, acquire great expansion and feeling; but not as great as to overpower this all-pervading and essential law of animated existence.'

Because man was fundamentally self-interested rather than selfless, he valued his own wellbeing over the wellbeing of others and was willing to sacrifice that of others for the sake of his own. To prevent this anarchic state of nature – the violent 'passions' of which were destructive of the social state for which man was intended – a 'controulling power' of government, to protect and perfect society, was necessary. Therefore, Calhoun concluded that government came from man's duality: his social nature the 'remote' cause, his individual nature the 'proximate' cause.

Between the government and society, however, society was 'greater.' Society, or the 'social state,' was man's natural condition; government, or the 'political state,' was an artificial institution. 'It is the first in the order of things, and in the dignity of its object,' explained Calhoun. 'That of society being primary – to preserve and perfect our race; and that of government secondary and subordinate, to preserve and protect society.'

Although government was entrusted with power for the protection of society, Calhoun pointed out that history proved that government would abuse its power and oppress society. A government, after all, was nothing more than an organisation of men, all of whom had the same self-interested nature which necessitated government in the first place. 'Hence, the powers vested in them to prevent injustice and oppression on the part of others, will, if left unguarded, be by them converted into instruments to oppress the rest of the community.' A 'constitution,' according to Calhoun, had the same role vis-à-vis the government as the government had vis-à-vis society: its protection and perfection. 'Having its origin in the same principle of our nature, *constitution* stands to *government*, as *government* stands to *society*; and as the end for which society is ordained, would be defeated without government, so that for which government is ordained would, in a great measure, be defeated without constitution.' The ideal constitution, therefore, was one that would 'completely counteract the tendency of government to oppression and abuse, and hold it strictly to the great ends for which it is ordained.'

To prevent the abuse of power and oppression, Calhoun argued that extremes should be avoided. On the one extreme, creating a higher power over the government ignored the fundamental problem of trusting man with absolute power. 'This would be but to change the seat of authority, and to make this higher power, in reality, the government; with the same tendency, on the part of those who might controul its powers, to pervert them into instruments of aggrandisement.' On the other extreme, weakening the government so that it was 'too feeble to be made an instrument of abuse' would leave it unable to protect and preserve society. The former extreme made government dangerous; the latter extreme, useless.

Calhoun concluded that the only way to prevent the abuse of power and oppression of society was 'to furnish the ruled with the means of resisting successfully this tendency on the part of the rulers.' As Calhoun put it, 'Power can only be resisted by power,' echoing James Madison's phrase from the *Federalist* that 'ambition must be made to counteract ambition.' With 'the means of making peaceable and effective resistance,' abuse and oppression would be thwarted. This form of civil resistance was 'the responsibility of the rulers to the ruled, through the right of suffrage,' which Calhoun considered 'the indispensable and primary principle in the foundation of a constitutional government.' According to Calhoun, 'Where this right is properly guarded, and the people sufficiently enlightened to understand their own rights and the interests of the community, and duly to appreciate the motives and conduct of those appointed to make and execute the laws, it is all-sufficient to give to those who elect, effective controul over those they have elected.'

Suffrage, however, was not the final solution to the problem, insisted Calhoun. All that suffrage could accomplish was allowing the ruled to choose their own rulers, thus establishing the 'sovereignty' of society over the government and converting 'irresponsible rulers' into 'true and faithful representatives.' This was a vital first step, conceded Calhoun, but while suffrage may turn rulers into representatives, it did not prevent man, with his self-interested nature, from electing representatives who would advance his own interests over those of others. 'It only changes the seat of authority,' explained Calhoun, 'without counteracting, in the least, the tendency of the government to oppression and abuse of its powers.'

If the interests (which Calhoun did not mean as a Marxist-Leninist class consciousness, but as a Jeffersonian 'pursuit of happiness') of every part of society were identical, then suffrage alone would be a sufficient constitution, for the law would affect all equally. Society, however, was comprised of many different interests, meaning that the law would not affect all equally and that there was the possibility that one part of society could abuse its power and oppress another part. 'Nothing is more difficult than to equalise the action of the government, in reference to the various and diversified interests of the community,' observed Calhoun, 'and nothing more easy than to pervert its powers into instruments to aggrandise and enrich one or more interests by oppressing and impoverishing the others.' Calhoun noted that this problem increased with scale: the larger and more diverse the society, the harder it was for the government to 'equalise' the law and the easier it was for a majority of society to enrich itself at the expence of a minority.

As James Madison observed in the *Federalist*, differing interests, opinions, and allegiances 'have, in turn, divided mankind into parties, inflamed them mutual animosity, and rendered them much more disposed to vex and oppress each other than to cooperate for their common good.' Suffrage alone, therefore, was no safeguard against the self-interested nature of man.

To paint a picture of this oppression of the smaller part of society by the larger part, Calhoun drew on his own experience with 'unequal fiscal action of the government.' Taxation and expenditure were two of the basic functions of the government, but while they were 'correlatives' they were not 'equal.' The money taxed from society was not expended equally among society (indeed, it could not be, for if it were, then fiscal policy would be 'nugatory and absurd'), but rather was redistributed from one part of society to another. In other words, even if the burden of taxation were equal among each of the parts of society, the benefits of expenditures would still be unequal. 'Such being the case, it must necessarily follow,' deduced Calhoun, 'that one portion of the community must pay in taxes more than it receives back in disbursements; while another receives in disbursements more than it pays in taxes.' Thus, to one part of society, taxes represented 'burthens,' while to another, taxes represented 'bounties' – two classes which Calhoun termed 'tax-payers' and 'tax-consumers,' respectively. Calhoun freely conceded that this disparity between taxes and expenditures, however unfortunate, was 'unavoidable,' and not necessarily oppressive. The risk, to Calhoun, was in the abuse of the taxing and spending power, not in the power itself. 'This, indeed,' cautioned Calhoun, 'may be carried to such an extent, that one class or portion of the community may be elevated to wealth and power, and the other depressed to abject poverty and dependence, simply by the fiscal action of the government.' Due to man's self-interested nature, however, Calhoun was certain that this power would be perverted. 'That it *will* be so used, unless prevented, is, from the constitution of man, just as certain as that it *can* be so used,' Calhoun concluded. To Calhoun, this illustration was all too real, as his South Carolina was indeed a tax-paying minority to a Northern tax-consuming majority.

'The apportionment of taxes on the various dispositions of property is an act which seems to require the most exact impartiality; yet there is, perhaps, no legislative act in which greater opportunity and temptation are given to a predominant party to trample on the rules of justice,' noted James Madison in the *Federalist*. 'Every shilling which they overburden the inferior number is a shilling saved to their own pockets.'

Since suffrage was not sufficient to prevent the tyranny of a tax-consuming majority over the tax-paying minority (in fact, suffrage actually enabled such abuse and oppression), Calhoun concluded that suffrage alone was not a just constitution. Another provision, one which would keep the majority from enriching itself at the expence of the minority, was therefore necessary. This meant obtaining the consent of each part of society (especially that of the interests 'unequally and injuriously affected') before proceeding with any course of action. Each part of society would have 'either a concurrent voice in the making and executing of laws, or a veto on their execution.' According to Calhoun, 'It is only by such an organism, that the assent of each can be made necessary to put the government in motion, or the power made effectual to arrest its action, when put in motion; and it is only by the one or the other that the different interests, orders, classes, or portions, into which the community may be divided, can be protected, and all conflict and struggle between them prevented – by rendering it impossible to put or keep it in action, without the concurrent consent of all.' Thus, Calhoun proposed rule by consensus rather than rule by majority.

According to Calhoun, the right of suffrage combined with the principle of a 'concurrent majority' formed the twin pillars of a just constitution. 'Suffrage, by rendering those who make and execute the laws responsible to those on whom they operate, prevents the rulers from oppressing the ruled,' explained Calhoun. A concurrent majority, 'by making it impossible for any one interest or combination of interests, or class, or order, or portion of the community, to obtain exclusive controul, prevents any one of them from oppressing the other.' In other words, while suffrage prevented tyranny over all, concurrence prevented tyranny of the majority over the minority.

'It is of great importance in a republic,' advised James Madison in the *Federalist*, 'not only to guard the society against the oppression of its rulers, but to guard one part of the society against the injustice of the other part.'

A common criticism of Calhoun's idea of a concurrent majority then and now is that it is anti-democratic because it allows a minority to overrule the will of the majority. Indeed, the Tenth Amendment Center, a public-policy institute dedicated to the constitutional doctrine of States' rights, dismisses Calhoun's theory as 'absurd' and 'idiotic,' claiming that Calhoun was a 'slaver from South Carolina' who 'dreamed up' the idea to 'allow one geographical area to hold the rest of the country hostage' in order to 'protect and advance human bondage.' Calhoun did not see it that way, however. Rather than undermine the democratic process, the role of concurrence was to 'aid and protect it.' The role of suffrage, explained Calhoun, was to 'collect the sense of the greater number; that is, of the stronger interests, or combination of interests.' The sense of the majority, however, was not necessarily the sense of the whole of society. Concurrence, therefore, did not make minorities rulers over majorities, but ensured that all of society was united behind the government's course of action. According to Calhoun, there were two different conceptions of a majority. One, 'the numerical, or absolute majority,' regarded the will of the greater number as the will of society. Calhoun's majority, however, the 'concurrent, or constitutional majority,' regarded the sense of all of society's separate and opposing interests as the will of society – 'the united sense of all.' To Calhoun, democracy must mean more than just two wolves and a sheep voting on what to eat for dinner – majority rule must mean more than just monopoly rule.

Calhoun boldly challenged the two dominant strains of the American political tradition: the liberalism of Thomas Jefferson, who believed that 'governments are more or less republican, as they have more or less of the element of popular election and controul in their composition,' and the conservatism of John Adams, who believed that 'the very definition of a republic, is "an empire of laws, and not of men."' Both were correct in their basic premises, recognised Calhoun, but had strayed in their logic and come to wrong conclusions. Feeling the immense responsibility of maintaining what the Founding Fathers had achieved, Calhoun eschewed mere ancestor worship and undertook the intimidating but important task of critically reexamining their philosophy in order to uphold its essential elements and amend its errors and excesses.

Against the liberals, Calhoun denied that the absolute majority was a just basis for constitutional government. 'If the numerical majority were really the people; and if, to take its sense truly, were to take the sense of the people truly, a government so constituted would be a true and perfect model of popular constitutional government,' reasoned Calhoun. 'But, as such is not the case – as the numerical majority, instead of being the people, is only a portion of them – such a government, instead of being a true and perfect model of the people's government, that is, a people self-governed, is but the government of a part, over a part – the major over the minor portion.' Conflating the absolute majority with the will of society, avowed Calhoun, was 'false and fatal' to 'preserving and perpetuating' a constitution, and thus to protecting and perfecting society.

Against the conservatives, Calhoun denied that paper constitutions – with all their carefully written checks and balances – could limit the government. 'A written constitution certainly has many and considerable advantages,' acknowledged Calhoun, 'but it is a great mistake to suppose, that the mere insertion of provisions to restrict and limit the powers of the government, without investing those for whose protection they are inserted with the means of enforcing their observance, will be sufficient to prevent the major and dominant party from abusing its powers.' In other words, a paper constitution could not enforce itself and governments would not limit themselves; the people must have the power to do both themselves. If the people could not uphold their constitution themselves, then the constitution would become a battleground of competing constructions: the majority party adopting a loose construction so as to maximise its power and the

274

minority party adopting a strict construction for its own protection. In a clash of 'construction against construction,' the minority would have no recourse save for 'an appeal to reason, truth, justice, or the obligations imposed by the constitution,' and although it may make an inspiring stand against 'the march of encroachment,' it would ultimately be 'overpowered' by the majority and branded 'mere abstractionists.' As Calhoun bitterly remarked, if reason, truth, and justice were enough to persuade men to do right, then government would not be necessary in the first place. Once the minority was defeated, the 'subversion of the constitution' would be complete and the government would be 'converted into one of unlimited powers.' Calhoun might have known that he had written the epitaph of the American federal republic.

After addressing the flaws of 'liberalism' and 'conservatism' (at least as those terms were once understood), Calhoun elaborated on his idea of the concurrent majority. The essence of the concurrent majority, he explained, was for each part of society to have a 'negative' on the others. 'It is this mutual negative among its various conflict interests,' explained Calhoun, 'which invests each with the power of protecting itself, and places the rights and safety of each, where they can only be securely placed, under its own guardianship.' Without this negative, there would be no legal mechanism for the enforcement of a constitution, and thus no constitution at all. According to Calhoun, the negative, by whatever name it was called ('veto, interposition, nullification, check, or balance of power'), was the cornerstone of a constitution. On the other hand, the 'positive' power (the power of the government to act) was the cornerstone of the government. 'The one is the power of acting; and the other the power of preventing or arresting action,' noted Calhoun. 'The two, combined, make constitutional governments.' Therefore, a government of the absolute majority, lacking the crucial negative power, was not a true constitutional government at all. Indeed, a democracy of 'one power' – in which the absolute majority had 'sole controul' of the government – could be just as tyrannous as any 'monarchical or aristocratical' government. A constitutional government, by contrast, did not permit one power to possess sole controul, but governed with the consent of every part of society. According to Calhoun, the difference between governments was not whether they were 'of the few, or the many,' but whether they were 'constitutional' or 'absolute.'

A constitutional and absolute government could be distinguished by their philosophical bases – 'the principle by which they are upheld and preserved.' In a constitutional government, this 'conservative principle' was 'compromise,' but in an absolute government, it was 'force.' No doubt Calhoun had in mind President Andrew Jackson's threat to invade the single State of South Carolina and have him hanged, as well as the gathering storm that would break in President Abraham Lincoln's war against the eleven Confederate States of South Carolina, Mississippi, Florida, Alabama, Georgia, Louisiana, Texas, Virginia, Arkansas, North Carolina, and Tennessee, as well as the Border States of Missouri, Kentucky, Maryland, and Delaware.

Under an absolute government, there was no legal recourse against abuse of power and oppression, leaving the people no choice but to 'acquiesce in oppression' or 'resort to force to put down the government.' Afraid of such popular resistance, an absolute government naturally prepared to counter force with force – 'and hence, of necessity, force becomes the conservative principle of all such governments.' Under a constitutional government, however, where each part of society had a negative power to protect itself against the other parts, all of the parts must cooperate to promote the interests of all rather than the interests of one over another. 'It is by means of such authorised and effectual resistance, that oppression is prevented, and the necessity of resorting to force superseded, in governments of the concurrent majority,' Calhoun asserted of the negative power, 'and, hence, compromise instead of force, becomes their conservative principle.'

Like the Founding Fathers and unlike his partisan generation, Calhoun despised political parties, believing that they corrupted republican virtue and destroyed constitutional government. He surely shared James Madison's warning against 'factions' in the *Federalist*: 'By faction, I understand a number of citizens, whether amounting to a majority or a minority of the whole, who are united and actuated by some common impulse of passion, or an interest, adverse to the rights of other citizens, or to the permanent and aggregate interests of the community.' According to Calhoun, party strife would eventually degenerate into civil war. 'The conflict between the two parties must be transferred, sooner or later,' predicted Calhoun, 'from an appeal to the ballot-box to an appeal to force.' In order to maintain unity in the partisan struggle for power, parties would come under the controul of a few unscrupulous Van Buren-type leaders, dispensing 'rewards' to their followers and 'discipline' on members who disobey the party line. If parties were in the hands of a few men, reasoned Calhoun, and an absolute government was in the hands of the majority party, then the government would be, in effect, in the hands of those party leaders. The two parties, fixated on power, would become more preoccupied with simply holding office than serving society, and thus adopt increasingly dishonourable tactics to stay in power. 'Principles and policy would lose all influence in the elections,' warned Calhoun, 'and cunning, falsehood, deception, slander, fraud, and gross appeals to the appetites of the lowest and most worthless portions of the community, would take the place of sound reason and wise debate.' The government would lurch back and forth between two parties which stood for nothing until 'confusion, corruption, disorder, and anarchy, would lead to an appeal to force – to be fulfilled by a revolution in the form of government' – probably a 'military power.' Parties also divided society against itself, replacing sympathy and loyalty with antipathy and rivalry. 'In such governments, devotion to party becomes stronger than devotion to country,' observed Calhoun, 'the promotion of the interests of one party more important than the promotion of the common good of the whole.' As a result, society's sense of 'moral obligations' to all of its parts would dissolve. 'That which corrupts and debases the community politically,' held Calhoun, 'must also corrupt and debase it morally.'

Calhoun was thinking of the Whigs and Democrats of his own time, but he also painted a perfect picture of today's farcical contest between the Republicans and Democrats, neither of whom believe in anything except getting elected, and both of whom are constantly at daggers drawn over the most trivial of issues.

A concurrent majority avoided all of the pitfalls of party politics, claimed Calhoun, by uniting instead of dividing society. Since each part of society had a 'power of self-protection,' the whole point of party politics – to gain controul of the government for the advancement of its own interests – was void. Instead of struggling to advance one interest over another, the only way to advance the interest of one would be to advance the interest of all. 'Instead of faction, strife, and struggle for party ascendancy,' imagined Calhoun, 'there would be patriotism, nationality, harmony, and a struggle only for supremacy in promoting the common good of the whole.'

According to Calhoun, the role of government was to 'protect' and 'perfect' society. While the protection of society required security, the perfection of society required liberty. 'Liberty leaves each free to pursue the course he may deem best to promote his interest and happiness, as far as it may be compatible with the primary end for which government is ordained,' explained Calhoun, 'while security gives assurance to each, that he shall not be deprived of the fruits of his exertion to better his condition.' Extremes on both sides must be avoided, cautioned Calhoun: weakening the government beyond its legitimate sphere in the name of liberty would threaten the protection of society, but strengthening the government beyond its legitimate sphere in the name of security would threaten the perfection of society. Thus, the government must balance liberty and security in their 'proper spheres.'

Calhoun warned against two 'great and dangerous errors' relating to liberty. The first error was that 'all people are equally entitled to liberty.' Clearly inspired by the wisdom of the primordial 'conservative' Edmund Burke, who understood that 'society is a partnership not only between those who are living, but between those who are living, those who are dead, and those who are to be born,' as well as that 'abstract liberty, like other mere abstractions, is not to be found,' Calhoun believed that liberty, strictly speaking, was not a right, but rather a privilege. 'It is a reward to be earned, not a blessing to be gratuitously lavished on all alike,' explained Calhoun. 'A reward reserved for the intelligent, the patriotic, the virtuous, and deserving; and not a boon to be bestowed on a people too ignorant, degraded, or vicious, to be capable of either appreciating or enjoying it.' Liberty was the crowning achievement of civilisation, held Calhoun, signifying 'the development of our faculties, moral and intellectual.' Liberty was not an abstract endowment to which all men were entitled, but a patrimony of particular peoples – Greeks, Romans, Englishmen, Americans, and so on – to which each generation of must prove itself the rightful heir and pass on to posterity. Calhoun elaborated that while liberty was 'among the greatest of blessings' to the civilised, it could be among the greatest of curses to the uncivilised, resulting in 'lawless and despotic rule.'

While Calhoun did not mean that some cultures and societies would never be worthy of liberty, he warned that interfering with 'the progress of a people rising from a lower to higher point in the scale of liberty' would either 'retard' or 'defeat' such progress altogether – much like how the neo-conservative and neo-liberal hubris of 'invading the world and inviting the world' has caused a worldwide clash of civilisations both at home and abroad.

The second error was that 'liberty and equality are so intricately united, that liberty cannot be perfect without perfect equality.' As with the concept of a majority, Calhoun pointed out that there were two different conceptions of equality – in this case, legal and material equality – and that it was necessary to distinguish between them. Legal equality of all citizens was indeed imperative to liberty, but material equality was, in fact, inimical to liberty. Since all men differed in abilities and circumstances, argued Calhoun, there will always be material inequality between them. The 'mainspring' of progress, however, was 'the desire of individuals to better their condition.' A Procustean programme of material equality, however, whether intended to make the rich poorer or the poor richer, would foster complacency and stifle progress. 'To force the front rank back to the rear, or to attempt to push forward the rear into line with the front, by the interposition of the government,' summarised Calhoun, 'would put an end to the impulse, and effectually arrest the march of progress.'

For viewing politics in terms of class conflict – that is, between tax-payers and tax-consumers – Calhoun has been branded 'the Marx of the Master Class,' yet his refutation of material inequality was as succinct of a refutation of Marxism as Ludwig von Mises or Friedrich A. Hayek ever conceived.

Calhoun controversially concluded that it was 'unfounded and false' that 'all men are born free and equal.' Nothing could be further from the truth, insisted Calhoun. Men were not born free; liberty was a privilege to be earned and a patrimony to be protected (as the English had done over time in developing constitutional government). Men were not born equal; they were unequal in circumstances, character, and configuration (consider the link between heredity and intelligence) and must work to improve their own condition as individuals as well as the collective condition of their people. Here, Calhoun is easily mischaracterised as merely rationalising the supremacy of the white race over the black race and thus defending slavery. Indeed, the controversy over slavery had become a crisis which deeply troubled Calhoun, but his opinion was similar to that of John Taylor of Caroline's: regardless of the Northern and the Southern disagreement on slavery, since neither side was willing to tolerate equality for freedmen, and emancipation without equality would risk a race war, then maintaining slavery (while continually reforming it to be as paternalistic as possible) was, at the time, their only choice. In that sense, then, Calhoun was a "white supremacist," but then so were Calhoun's rivals, Daniel Webster and Henry Clay, not to mention Abraham Lincoln. Nevertheless, Calhoun's overarching concern in the *Disquisition* was not the supremacy of white over black, but the rise of a levelling, consolidating egalitarianism which threatened to subvert traditional American republicanism. Or, to employ Calhoun's favoured terms, he was most concerned with the rise of 'absolutism' over 'concurrence.'

Calhoun's theory of liberty and equality is typically held up in contrast to the egalitarian idealism that inspired the Founding Fathers. This egalitarianism, however, is mostly modern sentimentalism and the projection of present values onto the past. For example, George Washington, the quintessential Founder who commanded the American Revolution, presided over the Constitutional Convention, and inaugurated the presidency also distrusted democracy, quelled insurrection, speculated in land, and held hundreds of slaves. Indeed, Washington wondered if 'mankind when left to themselves are unfit for their own government,' warned about the 'poison' of the 'principles' of the French Revolution, and worried that abolitionism 'induced more evils than it could cure.' Furthermore, the American secession from the British Empire was not a radical revolution in the name of equality and democracy, but a conservative counter-revolution to protect the Colonies' traditional rights and liberties from an absolutist revolution in the British government, all of which is amply detailed in the Declaration of Independence (for those who read past the first few sentences). 'I did not consider it as any part of my charge to invent new ideas altogether and to offer no sentiment which had never been expressed before,' Thomas Jefferson informed James Madison of the inspiration for the Declaration, and to Richard Henry Lee Jefferson explained that the Declaration was simply 'an expression of the American mind...whether expressed in conversation, in letters, printed essays, or the elementary books of public right, as Aristotle, Cicero, Locke, Sidney, etc.'

Last, but not least, the Constitution was framed and ratified to protect and perfect the separate States and their shared Union, not to revolutionise them – for 'requisitions of men and money,' not 'human rights,' quipped the Virginian framer and ratifier Edmund Randolph. 'Americans had not struggled through the Revolution to cut themselves off from their inherited cultural identity as a distinctive offshoot of English history, nor had they come to Philadelphia to drive such a wedge between their present and their past,' explains the courtly paleo-conservative, M.E. Bradford. 'Their task, rather, was one of preservation and of such innovations as were necessary if a known and cherished world was to be handed on intact to their posterity.'

It was a concurrent majority, claimed Calhoun, which maximised the twin responsibilities of the government – liberty and security. Because a concurrent majority prevented the government from 'passing beyond its proper limits' and limited it to 'the protection of society,' all else was left 'open and free,' thus securing liberty. A constitutional government, explained Calhoun, 'by giving to each portion of the community which may be unequally affected by its action, a negative on the others, prevents all partial or local legislation, and restricts its action to such measures as are designed for the protection and the good of the whole.' This negative, he continued, 'secures, at the same time, the rights and liberty of the people, regarded individually; as each portion consists of those who, whatever may be the diversity of interests among themselves, have the same interest in reference to the action of the government.' Furthermore, concurrence did not merely protect liberty, but did so civilly and peaceably. 'It is only through an organism which vests each with a negative, in some form or another,' explained Calhoun, 'that those who have like interests in preventing the government from passing beyond its proper sphere, and encroaching on the rights and liberties of individuals, can cooperate peaceably and effectively in resisting the encroachments of power, and thereby reserve their rights and liberty.' Individual resistance, argued Calhoun, was too disorganised and weak against an organised and powerful government. Even if enough force were marshaled to overthrow an oppressive government, added Calhoun, that same force could be used to establish a government just as bad or even worse, as had happened in France. Indeed, like many Americans, Calhoun was deeply disturbed by the French Revolution, in which the people overthrew the corrupt, absolutist *Ancien Regime*, only to replace it with the bloody collectivism of the Reign of Terror and the bloodier imperialism of Napoleon Bonaparte. Only through well-established local institutions and a well-functioning rule of law, as were destroyed by the French Revolution but preserved in the American Revolution, could the people effectively retain or reclaim their liberty. As David Ramsay (the South-Carolinian Revolutionary-War veteran, medical doctor, and gentleman-amateur historian) described the aftermath of American independence, 'The people felt an uninterrupted continuation of the blessings of law and government under old names, though derived from new sovereignty, and were scarcely sensible of any change in their political constitution.'

In addition to protecting liberty, continued Calhoun, a concurrent majority also promoted security, without which there could be no liberty. Since such a concurrent majority protected liberty, reasoned Calhoun, and liberty enabled progress, it followed that a concurrent majority would also promote progress. The 'inventions and improvements' from progress – Calhoun cited gunpowder and the steam engine as examples – had made societies more powerful, and therefore safer. Thus, the freest societies were also the safest societies. Liberty, continued Calhoun, was also morally uplifting, promoting virtues which made society stronger, such as industry and duty. 'All these causes combined,' observed Calhoun, 'give to a community its maximum of power.' The Harvard-, Stanford-, and Oxford-affiliated scholar Niall Ferguson argues that values and qualities such as these (liberty, progress, power, and safety) explain the strength of Western Civilisation and how it came to rule the world, as well as why European colonialism (the extraction of untapped resources in exchange for the establishment of infrastructure, technology, institutions, and trade which catapulted the local standard of living) was generally more benevolent than malevolent.

Calhoun noted three 'plausible' objections to the concurrent majority and dispatched of them in detail. The first objection was that freedom of the press would positively influence public opinion so as to prevent oppression and the abuse of power, thereby defeating the vices of an absolute majority and rendering such a complicated constitution obsolete – 'that the defects inherent in the government of the numerical majority may be remedied by a free press, as the organ of public opinion.' Calhoun recognised that a free press was a 'new and important political element' responsible for 'great and beneficial' improvements in society, but held that it was, at best, a complement to rather than a substitute for a concurrent majority. The press may keep the people informed and make society safer and freer, admitted Calhoun, but it could not change the self-interested nature of man. So long as man's individual feelings prevailed over his social feelings, a government was necessary to protect and perfect society, and so long as a government was necessary, a concurrent majority was necessary to prevent the abuse of power and oppression. Furthermore, the press could be used for evil as well as good. According to Calhoun, 'what is called public opinion' was not always 'the united opinion of the whole community,' but rather 'the opinion or voice of the strongest interest, or combination of interests; and, not infrequently, of a small, but energetic and active portion of the whole.' Rather than an 'organ of the whole,' the press was often an organ of parties, used not for enlightening public opinion, but for 'controulling public opinion, and of so moulding it, as to promote their peculiar interests, and to aid in carrying on the warfare of party.' If anything, concluded Calhoun, the potential vicious influence of a free press upon public opinion underscored the necessity of a concurrent majority. Today, when the news networks all spin the same story so much that their separate accounts are practically unrecognisable, the press' status as a party lapdog rather than a public watchdog is painfully evident.

The second objection was that a concurrent majority was too complicated of a constitution. Calhoun conceded that an absolute majority was indeed simpler than a concurrent majority, but noted that if simplicity were the standard, then absolute monarchy – 'the most simple of all' – would be the ideal form of government. To Calhoun, however, a constitution was not theoretical, but organic, growing from the historical experience of a people rather than an ideology developed in the abstract. The framing of a constitution was not the remaking of a society in the name of reason, but the preserving of a society in the name of tradition – a conservation rather than a revolution. 'A constitution, to succeed,' explained Calhoun, 'must spring from the bosom of the community, and be adapted to the intelligence and character of the people, and all the multifarious relations, internal and external, which distinguish one people from another.' Thus, necessity, not simplicity, was the point: constitutions were 'products of circumstances.' A complicated constitution grown from the historical experience of a people – that is, one which balanced all of the parts of society and governed with consensus – was superior to a theoretically simpler and sounder constitution which empowered the majority to tyrannise the minority. That was what John Dickinson meant at the Constitutional Convention when he told the framers that 'experience' rather than 'reason' had produced the 'singular and admirable mechanism of the English Constitution,' which had served as the model for the American. That was what Charles Carroll of Carrollton, also referring to the English Constitution (not 'the work of a day,' but rather 'the lapse of ages') as the model for the American, meant at the Maryland Convention when he told the ratifiers, 'In matters of government, experience is a better guide than theory.'

Instead of reading fourteen Abraham Lincoln biographies for inspiration and consulting with Princeton historian James M. McPherson on how to reconstruct the Middle East as democracy (using the 'reconstruction' of the conquered Confederate States as a model), President George W. Bush might have profited immensely from Calhoun's insight that the best constitutions were those adapted to their people. Indeed, neo-conservatives and neo-liberals would do well to rethink their belief that the United States is a 'proposition nation,' with a purely ideological identity, rather than a traditional 'blood-and-soil' nation, based on people and place, with Calhoun's wisdom in mind.

The third objection was that a concurrent majority was 'impracticable' – that all of the parts of society would never be able to agree on anything. Calhoun held that the 'necessity' of maintaining the government would force opposing interests into settling on compromises. 'When something *must* be done, and when it can be done only by the united consent of all, the necessity of the case will force to a compromise,' claimed Calhoun. 'On all questions of acting, necessity, where it exists, is the overruling motive.' As an example of necessity forcing compromise, Calhoun cited the trial by jury: twelve jurors, with nothing more than a 'disposition to harmonise,' coming to a unanimous verdict. According to Calhoun, the same incentive that made jury trials so effective would also make a concurrent majority effective. In fact, Calhoun believed that because of the patriotic virtues that a fair, balanced constitution fostered among the people, all the parts of society would cooperate in sacrificing their own interests for the greater good. 'Impelled by the imperious necessity of preventing the suspension of the action of government, with the fatal consequences to which it would lead, and by the strong additional impulse derived from an ardent love of country,' imagined Calhoun, 'each portion would regard the sacrifice it might have to make by yielding its peculiar interest to secure the common interest and safety of all, including its own, as nothing compared to the evils that would be inflicted on all, including its own, by pertinaciously adhering to a different line of action.' For those who still doubted the practicality of a concurrent majority, Calhoun cited Poland, the Iroquois Confederacy, Great Britain, and the Roman Republic as models for constitutional governments of rule by consensus rather than rule by majority.

After concluding the *Disquisition*, Calhoun then applied his political theory to the American federal republic in the *Discourse*, opening with a brief summary of the structure of government:

> Ours is a system of governments, compounded of the separate governments of the several States composing the Union, and of one common government of all its members, called the government of the United States. The former preceded the latter, which was created by their agency. Each was framed by written constitutions; those of the several States by the people of each, acting separately and in their sovereign character; and that of the United States, by the same, acting in the same character but jointly instead of separately. All were formed on the same model. They all divide the powers of government into legislative, executive, and judicial; and are founded on the great principle of the responsibility of the rulers to the ruled. The entire powers of government are divided between the two; those of a more general character being specifically delegated to the United States; and all others not delegated, being reserved to the several States in their separate character. Each, within its appropriate sphere, possesses all the attributes, and performs all the functions of government. Neither is perfect without the other. The two, combined, form one entire and perfect government.

According to Calhoun, the United States were a 'democratic, federal republic.' In the first section of the *Discourse*, Calhoun undertook to explain the meaning of each of these three terms.

The American republic was democratic, claimed Calhoun, for 'classes, orders, and all artificial distinctions' were prohibited. Moreover, its 'fundamental principle' and 'great cardinal maxim' was that the people were 'the source of all power,' that governments were 'created by them, and for them,' that powers were 'delegated' rather than 'surrendered,' and that delegated powers were 'held in trust.' According to Calhoun, 'The whole system is, indeed, democratic throughout.'

The American republic was federal rather than national, continued Calhoun, because it was 'the government of States united in political union, in contradistinction to a government of individuals socially united...the government of a community of States, and not the government of a single State or nation.' Calhoun would spend some time on this particular point.

In distinguishing between a federal and national government, Calhoun was not splitting hairs or dancing on the head of a pin. 'Of all the questions which can arise under our system of government, this is by far the most important,' avowed Calhoun. 'It involves many others of great magnitude.' If the American republic were federal, for example, then the States would 'stand as equals and coordinates in their respective spheres,' the citizens would be 'politically connected through their respective States,' and the allegiance of the citizen would be 'due to his respective State.' If the American republic were national, however, then the States would 'stand...in the relation of inferior and subordinate, to superior and paramount,' the citizens would be 'fused...into one general mass...united *socially* and not *politically*,' the allegiance of the citizen would be owed to 'the nation...what is called the American people' – all of which would have amounted to 'a revolution much more radical, indeed, than that which followed the Declaration of Independence.' Thus, the answer to the question was indeed momentous.

To prove that the American republic was federal, Calhoun referred back to the Constitutional Convention itself. When George Washington, as President of the Convention, submitted the new Constitution to the Confederation Congress, he described it as 'the general government of the Union' and 'the federal government of these States.' Thus, the Constitution, if adopted, would form a government of the States in a political union. Washington's words were full of meaning, insisted Calhoun, and not used without 'due consideration, and an accurate and full knowledge of their true import.' At the beginning of the proceedings, the party behind the Convention (the Federalists) proposed a plan for a new constitution which they described as 'national.' By the end, after fierce debate, the Convention revolted against the Federalists, and the national plan was replaced with a plan for 'the United States' – the term 'national' was omitted altogether. Calhoun argued that the name 'United States' clearly meant 'the States united in a federal union,' as Washington had informed the Congress.

Indeed, explained Calhoun, 'United States' could not have meant anything else, for it was 'an old and familiar phrase, having a well-defined meaning.' It was the 'baptismal name of these States,' first used in the Declaration of Independence, which proclaimed the former Colonies to be 'free and independent States,' with the 'full power to levy war, conclude peace, contract alliances, and to do all the other acts and things which independent States may of right do.' Thus, 'United States' was first used by the Continental Congress to declare that the States were sovereign – just as sovereign as their mother country or any other nation. The name was next used in the first American constitution, the Articles of Confederation, which declared, 'Each State retains its sovereignty, freedom, and independence; and every power, jurisdiction, and right, which is not, by this confederation, expressly delegated to the United States in Congress assembled.' Thus, the sovereignty of the States first claimed in the Declaration was explicitly retained under the Articles. 'The retention of the same style, throughout every stage of their existence, affords strong, if not conclusive evidence that the political relation between these States, under their present constitution and government, is substantially the same as under the confederacy and revolutionary government; and what that relation was we are not left to doubt; as they declared expressly to be "free, independent, and sovereign States,"' argued Calhoun. 'They, then, are now united, and have been, throughout, simply as confederated States.' The changes in the Confederation through the Constitution were 'not in the foundation' (in which case, a new name other than 'United States' would have been appropriate), but merely 'in the superstructure of the system.' In his letter to the Confederation Congress on behalf of the Constitutional Convention, George Washington described the Constitution as but a *different organisation* of government, not a revolution in their principles of government. 'We thus have the authority of the Convention itself, for asserting that the expression, "United States," has essentially the same meaning, when applied to the present constitution and government, as it had previously,' concluded Calhoun, 'and, of course, that the States have retained their separate existence, as independent and sovereign communities, in all forms of political existence, through which they have passed.'

Despite this 'conclusive' evidence that the American republic was indeed federal rather than national, Calhoun admitted that the latter opinion was nevertheless a popular misconception. 'The question involved is one of the first magnitude, and deserves to be investigated thoroughly in all it aspects,' explained Calhoun. 'With this impression, I deem it proper – clear and conclusive as I regard the reasons assigned to prove its federal character – to confirm them by historical references; and to repel the arguments adduced to prove it to be a national government.'

According to Calhoun, the States had framed and ratified the Constitution. 'That the delegates who constituted the Convention which framed the Constitution, were appointed by the several States, each on its own authority; that they united in the Convention by States; and that they voted in the Convention by States; and that they were counted by States, are recorded and unquestionable facts,' stressed Calhoun. 'So, also, the facts that the Constitution, when framed, was submitted to the people of the several States, for their respective ratification; that it was ratified by them, each for itself; and that it was binding on each, only in consequence of being so ratified by it.' Indeed, it was the ratification of the Constitution by the States (nine were needed for it to take effect between them) which enacted the Constitution into law. If the United States were truly national rather than federal, then the States must have divested themselves of their sovereignty in their acts of ratification. 'Whether, then, the government is federal or national, is reduced to a single question,' reasoned Calhoun. 'Whether the act of ratification, of itself, or the Constitution, by some one or all of its provisions, did, or did not, divest the several States of their character of separate, independent, and sovereign communities, and merge them all in one great community or nation, called the American people?'

Calhoun claimed that such a 'radical revolution' in the relations of the States would require overwhelming evidence – the burden of proof is on the positive claim, after all – but noted that there was little to none of such evidence, and that most of what was adduced was nothing more than pettifoggery and sophistry. There was, however, ample evidence that the American republic remained federal under the Constitution. In their 'colonial condition,' the States were 'distinct communities, each with her separate charter and government, and in no way connected with each other, except as dependent members of a common empire.' Their first union was as the 'United Colonies,' pledged against the usurpation of their chartered and constitutional rights as loyal British subjects. They remained the United Colonies – 'always, in joint councils, voting and acting as separate and distinct communities; and not in the aggregate, as composing one community or nation' – until they 'passed from their dependent colonial condition, into that of free and sovereign States.' The vote to declare independence was made by the delegations from each Colony in the Continental Congress, each of which voted on her own behalf. The vote was announced as 'unanimous,' not because every delegate voted aye, but because the majority of each delegation did – 'showing clearly, that the body itself, regarded it as the united act of the several Colonies, and not the act of the whole as one community.' Having declared themselves 'free and independent States,' the Continental Congress then formed the Articles of Confederation, which were ratified by the States in their sovereign capacities. Soon after the American Revolution, the States adopted the Constitution for the purpose of amending some of the supposed shortcomings of the Articles. According to Calhoun, the Constitution 'received the assent of the States in all the possible modes in which it could be obtained: first, in their confederated character, through its only appropriate organ, the Congress; next, in their individual character, as separate States, through their respective State governments, to which the Congress referred it; and finally, in the high character of independent and sovereign communities, through a convention of the people, called in each State, by the authority of its government.'

Calhoun concluded his argument by asking and answering some questions of his own. By whom was the Constitution ordained and established? 'The people of the several States of the Union, acting as free, independent, and sovereign States.' For whom was the Constitution ordained and established? '*For* the people of the several States, by whom it was ordained and established.' For what was the Constitution ordained and established? 'The Constitution was ordained and established *by* the several States, as *distinct, sovereign communities*; and...it was ordained and established by them for *themselves* – for the common welfare and safety, as *distinct and sovereign communities*.' Over whom was the Constitution ordained and established? 'The several States of the Union...established it as a compact *between* them, and not as a constitution *over* them.' Calhoun was confident that the answers to his questions proved that the Constitution was federal – that is, between sovereign States.

In spite of all this evidence, noted Calhoun, many clung to the opening expression of the Preamble, 'We, the People of the United States,' as proof that the United States were a nation of one people rather than a federal union of sovereign States. This argument, Calhoun pointed out, not only took the terms 'people' and 'United States' out of context (the latter had historically been used to denote the States 'in their confederated character,' and the former had no plural form 'even when applied to many communities or states confederated in a common union'), but also overlooked the fact that the original draft of the Preamble individually enumerated each State, as in the Declaration and the Articles, but was revised for reasons of style and propriety – it was uncertain which States, if any, would ratify the Constitution, and thus considered presumptuous to name parties to an instrument to which they might not consent.

Calhoun also mentioned that some argued that the expression 'ordained and established' was incompatible with 'the idea of a compact' – which, in the period when the Constitution was framed and ratified, was understood as an agreement between equal parties. Instead of getting bogged down in such a frivolous argument (what Thomas Jefferson would have called a 'twistification'), Calhoun took the high ground and made the case for the 'compact theory.' First, according to Article VII, the Constitution was only binding 'between the States so ratifying the same,' rather than put to a national referendum to be binding upon all the States. That each State was free to ratify or reject the Constitution was characteristic of a compact rather than a nation. Second, the Preamble proclaimed that one of the purposes of the Constitution was 'to form a more perfect union,' and George Washington had informed the Confederation Congress that the Constitutional Convention's 'greatest interest' was 'the consolidation of our union.' Taken together, these two statements proved that the Constitution was intended to 'consolidate and perfect' the previous union (the Confederation, an unquestioned compact), not to 'destroy' it. Third, the actual 'body of the Constitution' was federal from start to finish. 'It everywhere recognises the existence of the States, and invites their aid to carry its powers into execution.' Both houses of Congress, noted Calhoun, were elected by the States: the Senate by State legislatures, the House of Representatives by the people of the States. The President and Vice President were chosen by State-appointed electors. Judges were appointed by the President and confirmed by the Senate – 'and, of course, as these are elected by the States, they are appointed through their agency.' The power of amending the Constitution, however, was the strongest proof of the compact theory of all. Under this power, a proposed constitutional amendment, whether originating from two-thirds of both houses of Congress or two-thirds of the State legislatures, required the consent of three-fourths of the States. 'It shows, conclusively,' declared Calhoun, 'that the people of the several States still retain that supreme ultimate power, called sovereignty – the power by which they ordained and established the Constitution; and which can rightfully create, modify, amend, or abolish it at its pleasure.' From its voluntary ratification, self-admitted conservative intentions, and federal structure, summarised Calhoun, the Constitution was indeed a compact.

Calhoun continued to refute some of the lesser claims of the more-perfect-unionist revisionists – claims he suspected they held not out of genuine conviction, but for the same reason a good lawyer argues a bad case as best he can. Calhoun made clear his disdain for 'the theory of the nationality of the government,' which he claimed was 'of recent origin' and 'founded on fiction.' In fact, Calhoun was present at the arguable birth of this more-perfect-unionist revisionism – the storied Senate debate between Daniel Webster of Massachusetts and Robert Y. Hayne of South Carolina, the latter of whom Calhoun (presiding over the Senate as Vice President) aided with sympathetic nods as well as scribbled notes.

Calhoun noted that it was sometimes conceded that the American republic was partly federal and partly national. 'They admit that the people of the several States form separate, independent, and sovereign communities – and that, to this extent, the Constitution is federal,' Calhoun explained. 'But beyond this, and to the extent of the delegated powers, regarding them as forming one people or nation, they maintain that the Constitution is national.' Calhoun considered this theory not just as 'unreasonable' as the theory that the Constitution was fully national, but 'absurd' altogether. Calhoun traced this particular error to the confusion arising from the description of powers that the States had 'delegated' to the American republic as having been 'granted' or even 'surrendered.' The latter expressions implied that the powers had been permanently sacrificed, but under the Constitution, all powers were 'trust powers,' meaning their delegation was conditional and revocable. 'It is not, therefore, surprising,' explained Calhoun, 'that they who do not bear in mind that all powers of government are, with us, trust powers, should conclude that the powers said to be granted and surrendered by the States, are absolutely transferred from them to the government of the United States, as it is sometimes alleged, or to the people as constituting one nation, and, thence, to infer that the government is national to the extent of the granted powers.'

According to Calhoun, the 'clear and decisive authority' of the Tenth Amendment ('The powers not delegated to the United States by the Constitution, nor prohibited by it to the States, are reserved to the States respectively, or to the people') reconciled whatever confusion could possibly exist between the expressions 'granted' and 'delegated,' both of which were used in the Constitution. A full appreciation of the Tenth Amendment, explained Calhoun, required an understanding of its history and a detailed analysis of its provisions. The Tenth Amendment, along with the rest of the Bill of Rights, was adapted from the recommendations of the States for the purpose of amending the Constitution's 'defects' and preventing 'misconceptions of its meaning.' According to Calhoun, 'Its principal object was to prevent the reserved from being drawn within the sphere of the granted powers, by the force of construction – a danger, which, at the time, excited great, and, as experience proved, just apprehension.' The Tenth Amendment, continued Calhoun, was carefully written, its every word full of meaning. By the expression, 'the powers not delegated to the United States,' it was implied that powers that were delegated were delegated in a compact – for 'United States' historically stood for the States' 'confederated character.' By the expression, 'are reserved to the States respectively, or to the people,' it was meant that the reservation applied to the States in their separate capacities, not collectively. The inclusion of 'or the people' did not mean that the States and the people were interchangeable terms for one nation of one people. Calhoun noted that there were 'two distinct classes' of reserved powers: 'those delegated by the people of the several States to their State governments' as well as 'those which they still retain, not having delegated them to either government.' It was the former powers to which the expression 'the States respectively' referred, and the latter powers to which the expression 'or to the people' referred. The Tenth Amendment, therefore, protected the rights reserved by the governments of the States as well as the rights reserved by the people of the States. By substituting the expression 'delegated' for 'granted,' the Tenth Amendment also clarified the terminology and reduced the possibility of misinterpretation. 'Both terms – "granted," used in the Constitution as it came from its framers, and "delegated," used in the amendments – evidently refer to the same class of powers,' explained Calhoun, 'and no reason can be assigned, why the amendment substituted "delegated" in the place of "granted," but to free it from its ambiguity, and to provide against misconstruction.'

The concept of delegated powers – powers held in trust rather than permanently surrendered – was the key to understanding the Constitution, claimed Calhoun. Thus regarded, it will be easy to perceive how the people of the several States could grant certain powers to joint, or, as its framers called it, a general government, in trust, to be exercised for their common benefit, without an absolute surrender of them – or without impairing their independence and sovereignty,' explained Calhoun. 'Regarding them in the opposite light, as powers absolutely surrendered and irrevocably transferred, inexplicable difficulties present themselves.' One such difficulty was the problem of 'divided sovereignty,' by which the States were 'partly sovereign and partly *not* sovereign – sovereign as to the reserved, and *not* sovereign as to the delegated powers.' Yet this notion of divided sovereignty (known then as *imperium en imperio*, Latin for 'sovereignty within sovereignty') misunderstood that it was the powers 'appertaining to sovereignty' which the States had delegated, not their sovereignty itself. Indeed, sovereignty could not be divided without being destroyed. 'Sovereignty is an entire thing,' avowed Calhoun. 'To divide, is, to destroy it.'

Since the Constitution was federal, it should follow that the government it formed was federal, yet Calhoun sighed that this was not the case. 'There are those, who admit the *Constitution* to be entirely federal, but insist that the *government* is partly federal, and partly national.' The source of this particular error, claimed Calhoun, was the *Federalist*, the collection of political pamphlets written by James Madison, Alexander Hamilton, and John Jay to advocate the ratification of the Constitution in New York. Calhoun argued that since the Constitution formed the government of the American republic, it was nonsensical for a federal constitution to form a partly federal and partly national government. It made as much sense for a constitution that was fully monarchical to form a government that was partly monarchical and partly democratic. If anything, continued Calhoun, it made even less sense than such an example, for federal and national governments were fundamentally opposed. A federal government, according to Calhoun, was 'one to which States are parties in their distinct, independent, and sovereign character,' but as the *Federalist* itself admitted, a national government 'is one in which all local authorities are subordinate to the supreme, and may be controulled, directed, and abolished by it at pleasure.' The irreconcilability between 'federal' and 'national' could not be clearer. 'How, then,' asked Calhoun, 'is it possible for institutions, admitted to be so utterly repugnant in their nature as to be directly destructive of each other, to be blended as to form a government partly federal and partly national?' The *Federalist* attempted to support its theory of a partly federal and partly national government by claiming that the intention of the Constitutional Convention was to form a national government. If it were true that the intention of the Convention was to form a national government, reasoned Calhoun, then the commissions of the State delegates would have given them such authority, yet the commissions simply instructed the delegates to amend the Articles of Confederation. In fact, the term 'national' was absent from all of the commissions. The *Federalist* also ignored the Congressional resolution recommending a convention 'for the *sole* and *express* purpose of revising the *Articles of Confederation*; and reporting to Congress and the several legislatures said *alterations* and *provisions therein* as shall render the *Federal Constitution* adequate to the exigencies of the government and the preservation of the Union.' Calhoun believed that the authors of the *Federalist* had been blinded by their prejudices, all having been members of the national party during the creation of the Constitution (with Madison and Hamilton no less than its leaders in the Convention). Although they accepted the federal constitution which prevailed over their national constitution, and made an honest effort in the *Federalist* to present the Constitution as it was framed rather than the Constitution as they wanted it, their analysis was often tainted by their personal preferences. Unfortunately, noted Calhoun, their honest mistake produced a terrible misconception 'which has contributed, more than all others combined, to cast a mist over our system of government, and to confound and lead astray the minds of the community as to a true conception of its real character.'

Having established to his satisfaction that the American republic was federal 'in contradistinction to a national government,' Calhoun next established that the American republic was federal 'in contradistinction to a confederacy.'

Although the American republic was originally a confederation, the Constitution had changed it into a federation. According to Calhoun, the difference between a confederation and federation was that the latter was a government while the former was not. A confederation was not a government, but 'an assembly of diplomats, convened to deliberate and determine how a league or treaty between their several sovereigns, for certain defined purposes, shall be carried into execution; leaving to the parties themselves, to furnish their quota of means, and to cooperate in carrying out what may have been determined on.' In other words, a confederation was a strictly deliberative body which could appeal to its constituents but could execute no power itself. This was how the Articles of Confederation functioned. The transition from a confederation to a federation – the creation of an actual government, capable of executing power itself – was the 'great and essential change' of the Constitution, all else consisting of mere details related to this change.

From this single change stemmed major consequences. First, the source of all political power changed. The Confederation was a compact between the State governments, but the new federation was a compact between the people of each State – for only the people had the 'sovereign power' to form a government. Second, the nature of the American republic changed: previously 'in league between the governments of the several States,' the American republic became a 'union,' ordained and established by the people of the States. This was what it meant 'to form a more perfect union,' Abraham Lincoln's sermons on the ineffable, indissoluble Union notwithstanding. Third, a strict enumeration of delegated powers was necessary 'in order to prevent collision between them and the powers reserved to the several States respectively.' Under the Confederation, there was no such vigilance against usurpation of power, for the Congress was not a government capable of exercising power on its own, but a mere council dependent upon on the States. Fourth, the relations between the State governments and the Congress (now between the people of the States and the United States) changed. Under the Confederation, the relations between the State governments and the Congress were that of 'superior to subordinate,' but under the new federation, the relations between the people of the States and the United States were that 'of equal and coordinates.' It was vital, however, to keep this shift from turning the relations between the States and the United States upside-down – 'to reduce the several States to subordinate and local divisions; and to convert their separate constitutions and governments into mere charters and subordinate corporations.' Fifth, the execution of powers changed. Under the Confederation, the Congress had no power of its own. Its diplomats could deliberate amongst themselves and appeal to their respective States to execute their decisions, but they could not execute their decisions themselves. The new federation, however, was a government capable of executing power on its own, without relying on the cooperation of the States.

Having established that the 'essential distinctions between a federal government and a confederacy,' and the changes involved in substituting a federation for a confederation, Calhoun next established that the American republic was a 'republic' – or 'constitutional democracy, in contradistinction to an absolute democracy.' Here, Calhoun began the comparison of the Constitution to what he had outlined in his *Disquisition on Government*.

The American republic was commonly mistaken as a government of majority rule – 'that numbers are its only element, and a numerical majority its only controulling power...that it is an absolute democracy.' On the contrary, the American republic was a government of consensus. 'It is, in all aspects in which it can be regarded, preeminently a government of the concurrent majority,' claimed Calhoun, 'with an organisation, more complex and refined, indeed, but far better calculated to express the sense of the whole (in the only mode by which this can be fully and truly done – to wit, by ascertaining the sense of all its parts), than any government ever formed, ancient or modern.'

To prove that the American republic was a concurrent majority rather than an absolute majority, Calhoun demonstrated that numbers played no part in the framing and ratifying of the Constitution. The Confederation Congress which called the Constitutional Convention derived its authority from the Articles of Confederation, which had been unanimously adopted by the States, not by a majority of the States or of the total population as one nation. The Congress voted as equal States, each receiving a single vote regardless of her size. A 'nay' vote from the seven smallest States (with a population of less than one-third of the total) would have blocked the call for a convention and thus aborted the Constitution. As in the Confederation Congress, the Constitutional Convention voted as equal States, each State delegation received a single vote, a majority of States was required to adopt any measure, and the seven smallest States (less than one-third of the total population) could have defeated the Constitution. Once approved, the Constitution was submitted to the Congress for adoption, where the seven smallest States (less than one-third of the total population) could have rejected the Constitution. Once approved by the Congress, the final and toughest test was the ratification of the States. Nine States had to ratify the Constitution in order for it to take effect between the ratifying States, meaning that the four smallest States (with one-eleventh of the total population) could have prevented the ratification of the Constitution. 'It thus appears,' calculated Calhoun, 'that the numerical majority of the population, had no agency whatever in the process of forming and adopting the Constitution; and that neither this, nor a majority of the States, constituted an element in its ratification or adoption.'

The amendment process was an even more 'striking' example that the American republic was a concurrent majority rather than an absolute majority. Since an amendment required three-fourths of the States to ratify, it would take twenty-three States to ratify an amendment and only eight to reject one (there were thirty at the time of Calhoun's writing). The eight smallest States had a population of one-nineteenth of the total, meaning that one-nineteenth of the population could block an amendment. At the same time, twenty-three of the smallest States (forty-five percent of the total population) could amend the Constitution over the seven largest States, despite having a minority of the population. 'So that a numerical minority of the population can amend the Constitution, against a decided numerical majority,' observed Calhoun. 'When, at the same time, one-nineteenth of the population can prevent the other eighteen-nineteenths from amending it.'

These calculations proved not only that the absolute majority was powerless in the American republic and that it was the concurrent majority that governed, but also that the American republic was federal. 'The States, throughout, in forming, ratifying, and amending the Constitution, act as equals, without reference to population,' explained Calhoun. Indeed, it was the federal nature of the American republic– the equality of the States in spite of their size – that formed the cornerstone of their concurrent majority.

The States were represented in the American republic in two different capacities, explained Calhoun: their 'corporate character' and 'federal numbers.' Corporate character signified the States' status as equal sovereigns in a republic, while federal numbers signified their 'representative population' in a democracy. In the Congress, the two legislative houses were organised on the basis of these two capacities. In the Senate, where each State elected two Senators regardless of her population, the States were represented in their corporate character. In the House, where each State elected Representatives according to her population, the States were represented by their federal numbers. Both the Senate and the House required a majority of their members to adopt an act and could veto the acts of the other, meaning that no legislation could be adopted without the 'concurring assent' of the States in their corporate character and representative population. Since the executive was not composed of 'separate organs,' but rather the 'single functionary' of the President, 'concurrent action' was impossible. To compensate, the corporate character and representative population of the States were both factors in presidential elections. The representative population of each State determined her number of electors to vote for the President. If the election were a stalemate, however (no candidate receiving the minimum number of electoral votes), then the House, voting by States in their corporate character, chose the President. In the judiciary, the President (the election of whom was determined by the representative population and corporate character of the States) nominated judges, and the Senate (representing the States in their corporate character) confirmed or rejected them. 'It thus appears, on a view of the whole,' concluded Calhoun, 'that it was the object of the framers of the Constitution, in organising the government, to give the two elements, of which it is composed, separate, but concurrent action; and consequently, a veto on each other.'

Because the American republic represented its creators – that is, the States – in their 'twofold aspect,' it was thus more democratic rather than less. 'Indeed, the necessary effect of the concurrent majority is, to make the government more popular,' argued Calhoun. 'That is, to require more wills to put it in action, than if any one of the majorities of which it is composed, were its sole element.' Calhoun provided more calculations to prove his claim. If the States comprised the Congress in the capacity of their representative population alone, then the six largest States (with a population of fifty-one percent of the total) could overrule the other twenty-four States (forty-nine percent of the population). If the States comprised the Congress in the capacity of their corporate character alone, then the sixteen smallest States (with a population of twenty-one percent of the total) could overrule the other fourteen States (seventy-nine percent of the population). Since the House and the Senate possessed a 'negative' on each other's acts, however, it was necessary that 'a majority of each should concur to pass a bill before it becomes an act.' The minimum concurrent majority was the six largest States in the House and the six largest and ten smallest in the Senate, which amounted to fifty-nine percent of the total population – as opposed to the aforementioned alternatives of fifty-one percent and twenty-one percent. Thus, concluded Calhoun, the concurrent majority was actually more democratic than an absolute majority. 'From what has been stated,' deduced Calhoun, 'the conclusion follows, irresistibly, that the Constitution and government, regarding the latter apart from the former, rest, throughout, on the principle of a concurrent majority; and that it is, of course, a republic – a constitutional democracy in contradistinction to an absolute democracy.'

Having finally finished with his opening statement 'that the government of the United States is a democratic federal republic,' Calhoun noted that the federal government was only one part in the complex American system of government – or, to be precise, system of governments. Beyond the federal government, which was the 'representative and organ of the States,' were the

States themselves, each of which had a 'separate government' which was her 'exclusive representative and organ, as to all the other reserved powers of government.' Therefore, a complete understanding of the American federal republic must encompass 'the nature and character of the relation between the two – the government of the United States and the separate State governments.'

To begin this new inquiry, Calhoun endeavored 'to trace briefly downwards, from the beginning, the causes and circumstances which led to the formation, in all its parts, of our present, peculiar, complicated, and remarkable system of governments.' The American States, began Calhoun, originated as British Colonies, established by charters which recognised the sovereignty of the Crown (or 'the general power of supervision to the parent country'), but reserved the right of self-government (or 'popular representation in their respective governments') to the colonists as British subjects. While there was no political connection between the Colonies themselves, they did, as 'British-Americans,' share a common culture and commerce – and eventually, a common enemy. Even in this 'embryo stage of our political existence,' claimed Calhoun, the elements of the American federal republic were already in place.

'The Revolution, as it is called,' continued Calhoun, 'produced no other changes than those which were necessarily caused by the Declaration of Independence.' According to Calhoun, there were two such changes. The first change was 'to cut the cord which had bound the Colonies to the parent country – to extinguish all the authority of the latter, and, by consequence, to convert them into thirteen independent and sovereign States.' Just as the Colonies were 'wholly independent' of each other, so the States were 'distinct and separate communities...only united to the extent necessary to defend their independence.' The second change was 'to transfer the sovereignty which had, heretofore, resided in the British Crown, not to the *governments* of, but to the *people* composing the *several* States.' The people of each State ('the seat of sovereignty') replaced the now-powerless royal authorities with their own governments. Because the people were not 'a mere mass of individuals, without any organic arrangements to express their sovereign will, or carry it into effect,' but 'organised communities, in the full possession and constant exercise of the right of suffrage, under their colonial governments,' the governmental transition from dependence to independence was orderly and peaceable – the preexisting colonial governments simply assumed the powers of independent governments. If the Founding Fathers had remade their established communities into a single nation, rather than maintained their identities as separate, distinct entities, then Calhoun believed that the American Revolution would have been 'rather a curse than a blessing' (as was soon after proven in the French Revolution, which abolished the kingdom's historic provinces and consolidated power in Paris). Thus, the legacy of the American Revolution was not egalitarianism or more-perfect-unionism, but the independence and sovereignty of the people of the States. To Calhoun, the American Revolution was not the birth of a new nation founded on the proposition that all men were created equal, or the herald of a millenarian mission to spread democracy and capitalism around the world, but a conservative counter-revolution to protect, as George Washington put it, 'the liberty which we have derived from our ancestors.'

The States having separated from the sovereign Crown, sovereignty reverted to the people, where it was divided between 'constitution-making powers' and 'law-making powers.' Constitution-making power, which belonged to the people of the States, was the power to create and limit a government. Law-making power, which was entrusted to the representatives of the people, was the power to enact and execute laws. 'The one, emanating from the people, as forming a *sovereign community*, creates the government,' described Calhoun. 'The other, as a representative appointed to execute its powers, enacts laws to regulate and controul the conduct of the people.' Calhoun considered this division of power as 'essential' to the formation of the American system of governments as the

States themselves. 'Between them, it was our good fortune never to have been left, for a moment, in doubt, as to where the sovereign authority was to be found; or how, and by whom it should be exercised,' claimed Calhoun. 'And, hence, the facility, the promptitude, and safety, with which we passed from one state to the other.'

After a few years of war, the States (unofficially united by a revolutionary government) formed the Articles of Confederation, 'and made more perfect the union which had been informally constituted, in consequence of the exigencies growing out of the contest with a powerful enemy.' The Articles, however, were deficient in several important respects, and although there was a consensus that something must be done, there was conflict over what should or could be done. The two extreme solutions, the dissolution or consolidation of the Union, were anathema. As neighboring societies from the same mother country, the States had much in common culturally, but it was 'the common dangers to which they had been exposed, and the common glory they had acquired, in passing successfully through the War of the Revolution' that convinced them that they were safest and freest if united. At the same time, the people remained primarily loyal to their States and were watchful of 'the danger to their liberty and property, to be apprehended from a surrender of their sovereignty and existence, as separate and independent States, and a consolidation of the whole into one nation.' Thus, while the States bonded during the American Revolution, they remained cautious of their independence and suspicious of others. 'They regarded dissolution and consolidation as equally dangerous,' explained Calhoun, 'and were, therefore, equally opposed to both.'

As Patrick Henry declared at Virginia's Ratification Convention, 'The first thing I have at heart is American liberty; the second thing is American union.'

The Constitutional Convention was organised according to the two distinguishing features of the American system of governments, the division of the country into States and the division of power into constitution-making and law-making. Regarding the division into States, the Convention was comprised of State delegates, voted by State, and required a majority of the States to adopt the Constitution. Most importantly, if the Confederation Congress adopted the Constitution, then each State was free to ratify or reject it on her own. Therefore, a concurrent majority of the States was a necessary precondition for the Constitution. As in a concurrent majority, the necessity of taking action resulted in compromise between the States rather than the absolutism of the majority imposing its will on the minority (as Calhoun predicted would have happened if the Convention had been comprised of 'the people at large' instead of the States). 'It was the prevalence of these impressions, that stamped their work with so much fairness, equity, and justice, as to receive, finally, the unanimous ratification of the States,' Calhoun remarked of the Constitution, 'and which has caused it to continue ever since, the object of the admiration and attachment of the reflecting and patriotic.' Regarding the constitution-making and law-making powers, a confederation was a compact between governments, not a government itself, but a federation was an actual government, and thus required 'the high creating power' (i.e. the constitution-making power) of the sovereign people of the States. The people made a constitution and government for the United States just as they had made constitutions and governments for their own States, delegating specific powers to the latter and reserving the rest (including the inalienable constitution-making power) to themselves. 'It is this division of the powers of the government into such as are delegated, specifically, to the common and joint government of all the States, to be exercised for the benefit and safety of each and all,' concluded Calhoun, 'and the reservation of all others to the States respectively, to be exercised through the separate government of each, which makes ours *a system of governments*, as has been stated.'

Calhoun explained that the federal government and State governments were each 'parts to the whole.' The delegated powers to the federal government and the reserved powers to the States constituted all political power, and thus formed 'one entire government,' or 'one great federal community.' Each was 'paramount and supreme within the sphere of their respective powers,' standing as 'equals and 'coordinate governments.' As Thomas Jefferson put it, the States and federal government were 'as independent, in fact, as different nations.' Calhoun believed that such a system of governments was so grand, original, and sophisticated that it must have been blessed by the Providence of God. 'Intelligent, experienced, and patriotic as they were,' Calhoun remarked of the Founding Fathers, 'they were but builders under its superintending direction.'

After establishing that there was indeed a line between the delegated powers of the federal government and the reserved powers of the States, Calhoun proceeded 'to trace the line which divides their respective powers.' In the delegation of powers, the 'leading principle' of the framers was to delegate only those powers which could only be or were best-exercised jointly and to reserve the powers which were best-exercised separately. 'The object was not to supersede the separate governments of the States,' explained Calhoun, 'but to establish a joint supplemental government; in order to do that, which either could not be done at all, or as safely and well done by them, as by a joint government of all.' In short, the delegated powers concerned foreign and interstate relations: at home, the States were *'many,'* but abroad, they were *'one.'*

'Our citizens have wisely formed themselves into one nation as to others and several States as among themselves,' explained Thomas Jefferson. 'To the united nation belong our external and mutual relations; to each State, severally, the care of our persons, our property, our reputation, and religious freedom.' Calhoun agreed with Jefferson, commenting that the motto of the United States, *E Pluribus Unum*, which was Latin for, 'From Many, One,' did indeed capture the essence of the American federal republic.

Aside from the 'treaty-making power' of the President (which was still subject to the confirmation of the Senate and the funding of the House), the powers delegated to the federal government were 'carefully enumerated and specified,' as these powers were 'supplemental' and 'comparatively few' relative to the reserved powers of the States. According to the Constitution, the Congress had the power to declare war; to maintain a military; to regulate foreign trade; to build post offices and post-roads; to establish law for immigration, bankruptcy, and intellectual property; to coin money; to fix a standard of weights and measures; and to levy taxes for the payment of debts, provision of the national defence, and promotion of the general welfare. In Calhoun's time, the Jeffersonian political economy had totally triumphed over the Hamiltonian: there were no inland federal taxes, relatively low tariffs, little to no internal improvements, no national debt, and the Post Office was the only federal agency with which the average citizen had any contact. Today, there is not a single, solitary aspect of American life that the elephantine-executive, leviathan-legislature, juggernaut-judiciary, and behemoth-bureaucracy in Washington, D.C. does not somehow controul.

The Constitution, in the fashion of a treaty between States – or, as Thomas Jefferson put it, 'united nations' – also restricted what the States could do to one another. The States could not levy taxes on each other's exports, give any preference by regulation or revenue to the ports of another, enter into separate compacts with each other or foreign nations, coin or print money, make payments in anything but specie, impair the obligation of contracts, maintain troops in peacetime, or wage war. The States were also obligated to give 'full faith and credit...to the public acts, records, and judicial proceedings of any other State,' extend the 'privileges and immunities of citizens of the several States' to their citizens, return fugitive slaves to their State, establish a republican form of government, and contribute to the national defence.

In addition to delegations of power to the Congress, the Constitution also included specific restrictions of the Congress' power. The Congress could not suspend *habeas corpus* except in times of rebellion or invasion, pass bills of attainder or *ex post facto* laws, levy direct taxes unless they were in proportion to the population of the States, draw on the Treasury for anything other than official appropriations, grant any titles of nobility, or accept gifts from foreign nations. Constitutional amendments also restricted the power of the Congress. According to the first ten amendments (better-known as the Bill of Rights), the Congress could not make any laws which restricted the freedom of religion, the freedom of speech, the freedom of the press, the right of petition, the right to bear arms, or the right to trial by jury. The Congress could also not quarter soldiers in homes, search or seize any persons or property without probable cause, hold anyone without indictment, set exorbitant bail and fines, or inflict 'cruel and unusual punishment' (this did not entail capital punishment, as the Fifth Amendment allowed for the 'deprivation' of 'life, liberty, or property' under due process of law). The Ninth Amendment provided against 'construing the Constitution as that the enumeration of certain powers should be made to disparage or deny those not enumerated,' while the Tenth Amendment provided that 'the powers not delegated to the United States, nor prohibited to the States, are reserved to the States respectively or to the people.' These restrictions, noted Calhoun, were 'intended to guard against improper constructions of the Constitution, or the abuse of the delegated powers by the government.'

The President and the Supreme Court had little power of their own. Instead, their powers were 'restricted, in a great measure, to the execution, each in its appropriate sphere, of the acts, and, of course, the powers vested in the legislative department.' In other words, the main role of the President and the Supreme Court was to carry out the powers delegated to the Congress. The President's main power was to serve as commander-in-chief of the military in the event that the Congress declared war. The President also had the power to make treaties, appoint public officials, and grant pardons, although the former two powers were subject to the approval of the

Senate. The President's greatest peacetime power was the veto, by which he could either accept or reject legislation from the Congress.

The Supreme Court (and whatever other 'inferior courts' the Congress created) had jurisdiction over all legal cases under the law, treaties, and Constitution of the United States, including cases between two or more States, the citizens of two or more States, or States and foreign nations. To Calhoun, the Supreme Court's jurisdiction over foreign and interstate relations represented the basic difference between the delegated and reserved powers: delegated powers appertained to the States 'in their relations with each other, or in their relations with the rest of the world,' while reserved powers appertained to 'interior and local concerns' of the States, whose 'knowledge of local interests and domestic institutions...must be much more accurate, and the responsibility of each to their respective people much more perfect.'

With the line drawn between delegated and reserved powers – external relations to the former, internal affairs to the latter – Calhoun next examined and assessed the safeguards provided for these divisions of power. 'The next question,' asked Calhoun, 'which offers itself for consideration is, what provisions does the Constitution of the United States, or the system itself, furnish to preserve this, and its other divisions of power? And whether they are sufficient for the purpose?' According to Calhoun, there were four divisions of power in the American republic: first and foremost, the division between sovereign States; second, the division between constitution-making and law-making power; third, the division between delegated and reserved power; and fourth the division of power among departments. 'These divisions constitute the elements of which the organism of the whole system is formed,' claimed Calhoun. 'On their preservation depend its duration and success, and the mighty interests involved in both.'

Working from the least to the greatest, Calhoun began with the division of power among departments. The issue was whether the Constitution provided the departments with the power to check usurpations of its authority by other departments – the 'power of self-protection.' Without each department having the power of self-protection, the strongest department would 'inevitably absorb and concentrate' the powers of the other departments into itself. The Congress, 'backed by its widely extended and appropriate powers, its security resulting from freedom of speech in debate, and its close connection and immediate intercourse with its constituents,' was fully able to protect itself against the other departments. The President, who served as commander-in-chief, controulled the power and patronage of the government (at least since the presidency of Andrew Jackson), and was possessed of a near-absolute veto, was also capable of protecting itself. The Supreme Court, with the power to 'annul or veto' federal laws which it ruled unconstitutional, did not just have the power of self-protection, but more 'weight and dignity' than any other judiciary in history.

Although the Constitution created an 'equilibrium of power' between the legislative, executive, and judicial departments, 'regarded as independent and irresponsible [i.e. not beholden to one another] bodies,' Calhoun cautioned that they were not, in fact, independent and irresponsible. The departments, after all, were representatives of the States in their corporate character and representative population, and if the balance of power were upset between those two majorities, then the balance of power would be upset between the departments as well. 'In order, then, to preserve the equilibrium between the departments, it is indispensable to preserve that between the two majorities which have the power to controul them, and to which they are all responsible, directly or indirectly,' reasoned Calhoun. 'For it is manifest that if this equilibrium, established by the Constitution, be so disturbed, as to give the ascendancy to either, it must disturb, or would be calculated to disturb, in turn, the equilibrium between the departments themselves.' Calhoun worried that the greatest danger of usurpation came from the President, particularly due to the manner in which he was elected. Although the President was first chosen in a popular election according to the representative population of the States (or, in the event of a stalemate, chosen in the House according to the corporate character to the States), the unofficial practice of party nominations, by diminishing the total number of presidential candidates, 'virtually superseded' the corporate character of the States. Because the representative population of the States in effect elected the President, the most populous sections – that is, the absolute majority – would thus controul the presidency. Given the 'great and pervading' power and patronage of the President, the absolute majority would eventually dominate the Congress and the Supreme Court as well.

Today, as Calhoun predicted, the President rules Washington, D.C., and by extension, the absolute majority which the American republic has become.

Calhoun then moved to the constitutional safeguards for the division between delegated and reserved powers. 'On the preservation of this peculiar and important division of power, depend the preservation of all the others, and the equilibrium of the entire system,' explained Calhoun. 'It cannot be disturbed, without, at the same time, disturbing the whole, with all its parts.' According to Calhoun, the Constitution protected the division between delegated and reserved powers three ways. The first safeguard was 'the enumeration and specification of the powers delegated to the United States, and the express reservation to the States of all powers not delegated.' The second safeguard was 'imposing such limitations on both governments, and on the States themselves, in their separate character, as were thought best to prevent the abuse of power, or the disturbance of the equilibrium between the two coordinate governments.' The third was that all elected and appointed officials were 'bound, by oath or affirmation, to support the Constitution of the United States.' Although these safeguards were 'proper and indispensable,' Calhoun added that from the framing and ratifying of the Constitution, they were generally recognised as 'insufficient' in and of themselves. 'No question connected with the formation and adoption of the Constitution of the United States,' remarked Calhoun, 'excited deeper solicitude, or caused more discussion, than this important partition of power.' The controversy over the division of delegated and reserved powers was so wide and deep that it created the first two political parties – *'Federal'* and *'Republican,'* the former of which worried that that the reserved powers would overpower the delegated (and hence feared *'dissolution'*) and the latter of which feared that the delegated powers would overpower the reserved (and hence feared *'consolidation'*). The Federalists and the [Democratic-] Republicans both expected that the federal government and the States would be 'antagonistic...ready to seize every opportunity to enlarge their own at the expence of the powers of the other,' and thus relied upon 'reciprocal action and reaction' between the two, not the paper safeguards of the Constitution alone, 'to be sufficient to preserve the equilibrium, and keep each in its respective sphere.'

'The people, to whom all authority belongs, have divided the powers of government into two distinct departments, the leading characters of which are *foreign* and *domestic*,' explained Thomas Jefferson. 'These they have made coordinate, checking and balancing each other like the three cardinal departments in the individual States; each equally supreme as to the powers delegated to itself, and neither authorised ultimately to decide what belongs to itself or to its coparcener in government.'

Time and experience, argued Calhoun, proved the Federalists and [Democratic-] Republicans both half-right and half-wrong, as should be expected even among the wisest and noblest men in such a bold political experiment. While they were right about the 'means' of maintaining the balance of delegated and reserved powers, they were wrong about the 'mode' of the danger. Specifically, they seriously underestimated the consequences of transitioning from a confederation into a federation – of replacing a powerless council with a powerful government. Controul of the Confederation (the council of which was incapable of exercising power without the multilateral cooperation of the States) was not worth fighting over, but controul of the federation (with delegated powers that its government could execute unilaterally) was indeed worth fighting over. Thus, rather than struggling to defend their reserved powers against the encroachment of the delegated powers, the States struggled for controul over the delegated powers. The conflict was not between the States and the federal government, but between the most-populous States and the least-populous States – the majority and the minority. These two parties, due mainly to the unequal effect of taxation and expenditures, were slowly but surely concentrating into the two main sections of the Union – the tax-consuming North and the tax-paying South. 'When they shall have become so entirely (which must inevitably be the case, if not prevented), when the stronger shall concentrate in itself both the majorities which form the elements of the government of the United States (and this, it must shortly do), every barrier, which the Constitution, and the organism of the government oppose to one overruling combination of interests, will have been broken down, and the government become as absolute, as would be that of the mere numerical majority,' warned Calhoun. 'Unless, indeed, the system itself, shall be found to furnish some means sufficiently powerful to resist this strong tendency, inherent in governments like ours, to absorb and consolidate all power in its own hands.'

According to Calhoun, there were no such means in the Constitution to prevent an absolute majority from consolidating all power under its controul. Calhoun reiterated that neither the right of suffrage nor the existence of a written constitution was a sufficient safeguard. Suffrage, after all, was the 'instrumentality' by which party combinations were formed. Written constitutions, furthermore, could not enforce their own limitations upon the government, but required adherence to a conservative construction of their powers – one which the majority party would inevitably reject in favour of a self-serving liberal construction. The veto power of the President and the Supreme Court's power of judicial review, although positive checks in many respects, were impotent against the threat of consolidation, since the party which controuled the two majorities of the

American republic would also controul those departments – 'and make them all, in the end, the instruments of encroaching on, and absorbing the reserved powers.' The press ranged from useless to dangerous, serving as more of a 'party organ and an instrument of party warfare,' than a party check. None of these powers could mount an 'effective resistance' to consolidation; they were all 'auxiliary means,' at best.

Since the delegated powers in the Constitution did not provide for the protection of the reserved powers from usurpation, such protection must come from another part of the American system of governments – the reserved powers themselves, whether the powers vested in the State governments or the powers retained by the people of the States. 'In one, then, or the other of these, or in both,' deduced Calhoun, 'the means of resisting the encroachments of the powers delegated to the United States, on those reserved to the States respectively, or to the people thereof, and thereby to preserve the equilibrium between them, must be found.' Indeed, remarked Calhoun, it was irrational to expect the federal government, vested with delegated powers, to protect the reserved powers of the States – in other words, 'to look for protection against danger, to the quarter from which it was apprehended, and from which only it could possibly come.' Calhoun reasoned that just as the physical realm was a product of action and reaction, so in the political realm each division of power must have a 'self-protecting power' in order to react against the actions of other divisions and keep them all within their proper spheres – something a 'single power' simply could not do. 'Hence the political axiom, that there can be no constitution, without a division of power, and no liberty without a constitution,' stated Calhoun. 'To this a kindred axiom may be added – that there can be no division of power, without a self-protecting power in each of the parts into which it may be divided...without a division of power there can be no organism; and without the power of self-protection...the stronger will absorb the weaker, and concentrate all power in itself.'

Calhoun's next task was to determine whether the reserved powers, if fully exercised, were capable of resisting the encroachment of the delegated powers. To Calhoun, the means of remonstrance, resolutions, and requests, although valuable in other situations, were worthless when it came to resisting the usurpations of the federal government. After all, it was a constitution, not appeals to truth, reason, and justice, which restrained the self-interested nature of man and prevented the abuse of power and oppression. According to Calhoun, the only cure for the disease of consolidation was a negative power on the part of the States. 'Nothing short of a negative, absolute or in effect, on the part of the government of a State,' avowed Calhoun, 'can possibly protect it against the encroachments of the government of the United States, whenever their powers come in conflict.'

Calhoun first proved that a negative power was rightful in the American federal republic. The United States and the States were both governments, Calhoun pointed out, and as governments they had the right to judge the extent of their powers and enforce their powers within their rightful spheres. At the same time, however, they were also coordinate governments with power divided between them. Thus, neither of them had the right to enforce their judgment as to the extent of their power upon each other – for that would have contradicted their equality, deprived them of the right to judge the extent of their own powers, upset the general division of power, and ended either in consolidation or dissolution. 'An assumption, therefore,' argued Calhoun, 'which would necessarily lead to the destruction of the whole system in the end, and the substitution of another, of an entirely different character, in its place, must be false.' Although neither the federal government nor the State governments had the 'exclusive right' to enforce their powers upon each other, each did indeed have the right to judge the extent of their own powers. When their judgments disagreed, the effect was a 'negative on the acts of each,' thus vesting both with the power of self-protection. 'Nothing short of this,' claimed Calhoun, 'can possibly preserve this important division of power, on which rests the equilibrium of the entire system.'

According to Calhoun, it was clear that the Constitutional Convention and the States' separate ratification conventions all contemplated 'reciprocal action and reaction, between the delegated and the reserved powers – between the government of the United States and the separate governments of the several States' as the way in which each would protect the delegated and reserved powers against usurpation. In the Convention, the national party sought to deprive the States of this negative power by vesting their proposed national government with the power to veto the acts of the States. Virginia delegate Edmund Randolph proposed, 'To grant power to negative all acts contrary, in the opinion of the national legislature, to the articles, or any treaty, subsisting under the power of the union; and to call forth the force of the union, against any member of the union, failing to fulfill its duties, under the articles thereof.' South-Carolina delegate Charles Pinckney proposed, 'The legislature of the United States shall have power to revise the laws that may be supposed to impinge the powers exclusively delegated, by this Constitution, to Congress; and to negative and annul such as do.' New-Jersey delegate William Paterson proposed, 'If any State, or body of men in any State, shall oppose, or prevent the carrying into execution, such acts, or treaties, the federal executive shall be authorised to call forth the forces of the confederated States, or so much thereof, as shall be necessary, to enforce or compel obedience to such acts, or the observance of such treaties.' New-York delegate Alexander Hamilton proposed, 'The better to prevent such laws from being passed, the Governor, or President of each State, shall be appointed by the general government; and shall have a negative upon the laws, about to be passed in the State of which he is Governor or President.' All of these proposals, however, were defeated. 'The fact that they were proposed and so urged, proves, conclusively, that it was believed, even by the most distinguished members of the national party, that the former [i.e. the federal government] had no right to enforce its measures against the latter [i.e. the States], where they disagreed as to the extent of their respective powers, without some express provision to that effect,' deduced Calhoun. 'While the refusal of the Convention to adopt any such provision, under such circumstances, proves, equally conclusively, that it was opposed to the delegation of such powers to the government, or any of its departments, legislative, executive, or judicial, in any form whatever.'

If there were any doubt that the States retained their negative power, Calhoun argued that Virginia's Ratification Convention and the Tenth Amendment 'furnish proofs in confirmation so strong, that the most skeptical will find it difficult to resist them.' Despite the defeat of the national party in the Constitutional Convention, there was still strong opposition to the ratification of the Constitution among the States, stemming from fears of the consolidation of power and suspicion of the national party likely to controul the new government. When Virginia, a 'great and leading State,' convened to debate the adoption of the Constitution, seven other States had already ratified. North Carolina and Rhode Island were not expected to ratify, and New York, another great but divided State, looked to Virginia for guidance. Thus, Virginia's decision would determine the fate of the Constitution and the destiny of the United States. As Patrick Henry observed upon the occasion, 'The example of Virginia is a powerful thing.'

With so much at stake, the Virginia debate was, in Calhoun's words, 'long and ardent.' The talents of the best and brightest of the Old Dominion were on full display, both sides arguing passionately and persuasively for and against the Constitution. Against the Constitution were eminent Virginians such as Patrick Henry, George Mason, James Monroe, and William Grayson. For the Constitution were equally worthy Virginians, such as James Madison, Edmund Randolph, Henry Lee III, and George Wythe. Although Virginia ultimately ratified the Constitution in a narrow vote, the opposition's dire prophesies that a liberal construction would result in the consolidation of power were so powerful that safeguards against such risks were included in her act of ratification:

> We, the delegates of the people of Virginia, do, in the name and in behalf of the people of Virginia, declare and make known, that the powers granted under the Constitution, being derived from the people of the United States, may be resumed by them, whensoever the same shall be perverted to their injury or oppression; and that every power not granted thereby, remains with them and at their will: that, therefore, no right, of any denomination, can be cancelled, abridged, restrained, or modified, by the Congress, by the Senate, or House of Representatives, acting in any capacity, by the President or any department, or officer of the United States, except in those instances in which power is given by the Constitution for those purposes.

Among many proposed constitutional amendments, Virginia's Ratification Convention proposed one in particular which would affirm its strict construction of the Constitution: 'That each State in the Union shall respectively retain every power, jurisdiction, and right, which is not, by the Constitution, delegated to the Congress of the United States, or to the departments of the federal government.' This proposition (echoed by New Hampshire, Massachusetts, Rhode Island, New York, North Carolina, and South Carolina) would ultimately be adapted into the Tenth Amendment.

'Language cannot be stronger,' remarked Calhoun. 'It guards the reserved powers against the government as a whole, and against all its departments and officers; and in every mode by which they might be impaired; showing, clearly, that the intention was to place the reserved powers beyond the possible interference and controul of the government of the United States.'

Nevertheless, noted Calhoun, there were still many who believed that the federal government had the right to enforce its judgment of the extent of its powers against the States. Yet, clauses to which they clung did not grant this power, and, in fact, placed further limitations upon the delegated powers of the federal government.

The Supremacy Clause ('This Constitution, and the laws of the United States, which shall be made in pursuance thereof, and all treaties made, or which shall be made, under the authority of the United States, shall be the supreme law of the land') was mistakenly cited as proof that federal law was supreme to State law. Calhoun did not deny that federal law was indeed supreme to State law (indeed, he admitted that even without the clause the former would still be supreme to the latter), but challenged what was meant by 'supreme' and 'law.' The supremacy of federal law was not absolute, he noted, but limited to the delegated powers. 'Beyond these,' argued Calhoun, 'the Constitution is as destitute of authority, and as powerless as a blank piece of paper; and the measures of the government mere acts of assumption.' Furthermore, Calhoun pointed out that the clause itself stated that only laws 'made in pursuance of the Constitution' were supreme. Thus, concluded Calhoun, federal and State laws were each supreme within their rightful spheres – a far cry from the claim that federal laws were categorically supreme over State laws.

Nevertheless, the gross misconstruction of the Supremacy Clause has proven extremely enduring, and has become the weapon of choice for absolutists in office and on the bench. 'We have a supremacy clause in our Constitution,' opines President Barack Obama. 'When federal law is in conflict with state law, federal law wins out.' Such facile statements make a mockery of the Constitution and expose the utter worthlessness of the profession of 'constitutional law.'

The Necessary and Proper Clause ('The Congress shall have power ... to make all laws which shall be necessary and proper for carrying into execution the foregoing powers') was often misinterpreted to provide that

321

the means for the execution of the Congress' delegated powers were entirely discretionary. Yet according to Calhoun, the scope of the Necessary and Proper Clause was also strictly limited. First, the means must be 'necessary,' meaning essential to the execution of a delegated power. Second, the means must be 'proper,' meaning that they could not encroach upon the reserved rights of the States. Third, whatever discretionary power did exist was vested solely in the Congress and no other department. 'Necessary' and 'proper,' therefore, were restrictions upon the exercise of delegated powers, not grants of implied powers.

Article III, Section 2 of the Constitution supposedly granted to the federal judiciary the right to enforce the judgment of the federal government as to the extent of its powers against a State. According to Calhoun, the *subject matter* of the clause merely made federal jurisdiction 'commensurate with the authority of the Constitution and the several departments of the government, as far as it related to cases arising under them, and no further.' Furthermore, the *parties litigant* enumerated in the clause 'contains no provision which extends the jurisdiction of the judicial power to questions involving such conflict between the two coordinate governments.' Governments, explained Calhoun, possessed sovereign immunity, meaning that they could not be made defendants in a case without their consent. Since States were indeed governments, then they too possessed sovereign immunity and thus could not be made defendants without their consent. As the Eleventh Amendment (ratified in accordance with Georgia's nullification of judicial overreach in *Chisholm v. Georgia*) clearly stated, 'The judicial power of the United States shall not be so construed, as to extend to any suit in law or equity, commenced or prosecuted against one of the United States, by citizens of another State, or by citizens or subjects of foreign States.' Thus, in order for the federal judiciary to make a State a defendant, the States had to give their consent, yet no such consent had ever been given. A related claim was that the Supreme Court had the right to rule on the constitutionality of all laws and thus the right to enforce the judgment of the federal government as to the extent of its powers against a State. Calhoun conceded that the Supreme Court did indeed have the right to rule on the law in any case which it heard, but denied that this duty was 'peculiar' to it and that its rulings were binding on anyone but the parties to the case. In the American federal republic, 'where power is not only divided, but where constitutions and laws emanate from different authorities,' the rulings of the Supreme Court were binding only upon the parties to the case and insofar as the court remained within its rightful sphere.

With no clauses left to which to cling, some simply asserted that because governments must have the right to enforce their judgment as to the extent of their powers, the federal government, by definition, must also have this right. This argument, explained Calhoun, overlooked 'the distinction, in this respect, between *single* governments, vested with all powers appertaining to government, and *coordinate* governments, in a system where the powers of government are divided between two or more, as is the case with us.' If it were true that the federal government, as a government, must have the right to enforce its judgment, then it was equally true that the State governments, as governments, must also have this right, yet this would lead to civil war and thus destroy the system altogether. Thus, while neither government had the right of enforcement over the other, both governments retained the right of judgement for themselves, resulting in a 'mutual negative' in the event of a disagreement. 'The effect of this is, to make each, as against the other, the guardian and protector of the powers allotted to it, and of which it is the organ and representative,' explained Calhoun. 'By no other device, could the separate governments of the several States, as the weaker of the two, prevent the government of the United States, as the stronger, from encroaching on that portion of the reserved powers allotted to them, and finally absorbing the whole.'

Calhoun recognised the fear that a negative power would go to extremes in preventing consolidation, enabling 'collision and conflict' which would climax in 'disunion.' Calhoun admitted that any constitution, by dividing power between the parts of society, created conflict, yet insisted that the good of a constitutional government outweighed its evils. 'The choice between constitutional and absolute governments, lies between the good and evil incident to each,' explained Calhoun. 'If the former be exposed to collision and conflict between its various parts, the latter is exposed to all the oppressions and abuses, ever incident to uncontroulled and irresponsible power, in all its forms.' Calhoun denied, however, that a negative power would lead to dissolution. In fact, by preventing the delegated and reserved powers from encroaching upon each other, the negative power prevented the conflicts which would lead to dissolution, and thus was actually a safeguard against both consolidation and dissolution.

Calhoun saved the strongest safeguard of the States' reserved powers for last: State interposition. According to Calhoun, the States were the 'earliest and highest division of power,' originating with the settlement of America into separate and distinct Colonies and maturing into sovereign States with the Declaration of Independence. 'In them severally – or to express it more precisely, in the people composing them, regarded as independent and sovereign communities, the ultimate power of the whole system resided, and from them the whole system emanated.' Since, in the American federal republic, sovereignty belonged to the people, it necessarily belonged to the people of the States, as there was no one American people, but rather the separate and distinct people of each State. Accordingly, it was the people of the States who declared their independence, formed their own State constitutions and governments, ratified the Constitution, and retained the power to alter or abolish any government which no longer protected their liberty or security.

Indeed, as the sovereign power that had brought the Constitution into being, the people of the States were above the Constitution – or as Calhoun put it, 'in the relation of superior to subordinate – the creator to the created.' The Constitution, therefore, could not restrict the 'sovereign rights' of the people of the States in any way. Although the people of the States were superior to the Constitution as creators over their creation, they were not superior to each other as parties to a compact. 'Of all compacts that can exist between independent and sovereign communities,' described Calhoun, 'it is the most intimate, solemn, and sacred, whether regarded in reference to the closeness of connection, the importance of the objects to be affected, or to the obligations imposed.' Therefore, the Constitution was 'binding between them as a *compact*, and not on, or over them, as a constitution.'

As James Madison put it, 'The compact in the case of the United States was duly formed...by the people of the several States in their highest sovereign authority,' and the meaning of that compact was 'not in the opinions or intentions of the body which planned and proposed the Constitution, but in the sense attached to it by the people in their respective State governments, where it received all the authority which it possesses.'

In their constitutional compact, the people of the States formed a common government to which they delegated limited powers best-executed jointly rather than separately, each obligated to uphold the compact within its rightful sphere. 'The people of the several States, in their sovereign capacity, agreed to unite themselves together, in the closest possible connection that could be formed, without merging their respective sovereignties into one common sovereignty – to establish one common government, for certain specific objects, which, regarding the mutual interest and security of each, and of all, they supposed could be more certainly, safely, and effectually promoted by it, than by their several separate governments,' explained Calhoun. 'Pledging their faith, in the most solemn manner possible, to support the compact thus formed, by respecting its provisions, obeying all acts of the government made in conformity with them, and preserving it, as far as in them lay, against all infractions.' The States' obligation as parties to the constitutional compact were only to uphold the compact within its rightful sphere – or in other words, in the exercise of its rightful powers. 'To this extent the restrictions go,' averred Calhoun, 'but no further.' Indeed, as to the extent of the States' obligations to the constitutional compact, each party, according to 'the nature of contracts' and 'universal practice,' retained the right to judge the extent of her own obligations. Since this power was neither delegated to the federal government nor prohibited to the people of the States, it remained a reserved power.

The right of a State to judge the extent of her obligations to the compact, however, necessarily included the right to judge whether a particular act of the federal government exceeded the obligations of the compact and the right to interpose her sovereignty against an unconstitutional act. 'The right to judge as to the extent of the obligation imposed, necessarily involves the right of pronouncing whether an act of the federal government, or any of its departments, be, or be not, in conformity to the provisions of the constitutional compact; and, if decided to be inconsistent, of pronouncing it to be unauthorised by the Constitution, and, therefore, null, void, and of no effect,' reasoned Calhoun. 'If the Constitution be a compact, and the several States, regarded in their sovereign character, be parties to it, all the rest follow as necessary consequences.' To Calhoun, these latter rights of pronouncing an act unconstitutional and unenforceable (State interposition) were the 'indispensable' corollaries of the right to judge the extent of her obligations as to the constitutional compact (the State negative). Without the ultimate right of State interposition, the rest of the States' reserved powers would be 'barren and useless abstractions.' That is, if a right cannot be enforced, then it does not truly exist.

In the *Federalist*, James Madison described in detail how the States could and should resist such federal encroachment upon their reserved powers:

> Should an unwarrantable measure of the federal government be unpopular in particular States, which would seldom fail to be the case, the means of opposition to it are powerful and at hand. The disquietude of the people; their repugnance and, perhaps, refusal to cooperate with the officers of the Union; the frowns of the

executive magistracy of the State; the embarrassments created by legislative devices, which would often be added on such occasions, would oppose, in any State, difficulties not to be despised; would form, in a large State, very serious impediments; and where the sentiments of several adjoining States happened to be in unison, would present obstructions which the federal government would hardly be willing to encounter.

Calhoun was careful to distinguish between the power of the State negative and the power of State interposition, as each had unique effects and should be used differently. The former was an act of a State government, the latter an act of the people of a State. While a State government (as a mere representative of its sovereign people) could not rightfully enforce its judgment as to the extent of its power against its coordinate, the federal government, the people of a State (as sovereign parties to the constitutional compact) could indeed enforce their judgment as to the extent of their power against their subordinate, the federal government. A State negative did not prevent the enforcement of an act which a State judged to be unconstitutional, but only publicly protested the act. State interposition, however, did prevent the enforcement of a federal act which the State judged to be unconstitutional. State interposition, therefore, was a 'high and delicate' right not to be invoked lightly, but only as a 'last resort' in the face of egregious and urgent threats to liberty and security. 'Even when, in the opinion of the people of a State, such a case has occurred – that nothing, short of the interposition of her authority, can arrest the danger and preserve the Constitution, they ought to interpose in good faith,' cautioned Calhoun. 'Not to weaken or destroy the Union, but to uphold and preserve it, by causing the instrument on which it rests, to be observed and respected.'

Despite their differences, the State negative and State interposition were alike in that Calhoun expected either of them, if and when invoked, to appeal to the sovereign parties to the Constitution for a resolution of the dispute through their power of amendment. According to Calhoun, the amendment power was a 'modification' of the sovereignty by which the people of the States formed their separate State governments and their common federal government. 'Thus the power which, in its simple and absolute form, was the creator, becomes, in its modified form, the preserver of the system,' explained Calhoun. In the Constitutional Convention, the number of States required for a constitutional amendment was debated, with the national party in favour of an absolute majority and the opposition in favour of unanimity. The Convention rejected both extremes, settling on three-fourths of the States as a balance between the flexibility which constitutions sometimes required as well as the stability which they were required to provide. 'While three-fourths furnish a safe proportion against making changes in the Constitution, under the colour of amendments, by the dominant portion of the Union, with a view to oppress the weaker for its aggrandisement,' explained Calhoun, 'the proportion is equally safe, in view of the opposite danger; as it furnishes a sufficient protection against the combination of a few States to prevent the rest from making such amendments as may be necessary to preserve and perfect it.'

In the event that a State ever negatived an unconstitutional federal act, or the people of a State interposed their sovereignty against an unconstitutional federal act, the people of the States, assembled together in a 1787-style convention, could resolve the dispute by upholding or overruling the protesting State and, if necessary, amending the Constitution accordingly. 'It is, when properly understood, the *vis medicatrix* of the system – its great repairing and healing power – intended to remedy its disorders, in whatever cause or causes originating; whether in the original errors or defects of the Constitution itself, or the operation of time and change of circumstances, or in conflicts between its parts, including those between the coordinate governments,' explained Calhoun. 'In this character, it can amend the Constitution, by modifying its existing provisions – or, in the case of a disputed power, whether it be between the federal government and one of its coordinates, or between the former and an interposing State, by declaring, authoritatively, what is the Constitution.'

Calhoun's reliance on constitutional conventions and constitutional amendments to resolve conflicts between the federal government and the States has been criticised as unrealistic, unfair, and un-American. As historian Daniel W. Howe concludes in *What Hath God Wrought: The Transformation of America, 1815-1848*, Calhoun's theory of State negatives, State interpositions, and constitutional conventions was 'an impressive argument on behalf of an unworkable proposal.' Calhoun's plan, however, was exactly how Thomas Jefferson had recommended that constitutional disputes be resolved:

> But the Chief Justice [John Marshall] says, 'There must be an ultimate arbiter somewhere.' True, there must; but does that prove that it is either party? The ultimate arbiter is the people of the Union, assembled by their deputies in convention, at the call of Congress or of two-thirds of the States. Let them decide to which they mean to give an authority claimed by two of their organs [i.e. federal or State]. And it has been the peculiar wisdom and felicity of our Constitution, to have provided this peaceable appeal, where that of other nations is at once to force.
>
> But, you may ask, if the two departments [i.e federal and State] should claim the same subject of power, where is the common umpire to decide ultimately between them? In cases of little importance or urgency, the prudence of both parties will keep them aloof from the questionable ground; but if it can neither be avoided nor compromised, a convention of the States must be called to ascribe the doubtful power to that department which they may think best.

If three-fourths of the people of the States amended the Constitution so as to overrule the negative of a State government, continued Calhoun, then the State would be obligated to defer to their amendment, repeal her negative, and obey the act in question. That was not the case, however, if it was an act of State interposition – an act of the people of a State. In a case of sovereignty against sovereignty, the people of the State would have to decide for themselves whether the amendment upheld the liberty and security of society for which governments – including that of the Constitution – were formed in the first place: 'that each and all might enjoy, more perfectly and securely, liberty, peace, tranquility, security from danger, both internal and external, and all other blessings connected with their respective rights and advantages.' If the people of the State decided against the amendment, concluded Calhoun, then they would have no choice but to invoke the same sovereign authority by which they acceded to the Constitution and secede from the Union. 'That a State,' argued Calhoun, 'as a party to the constitutional compact, has the right to secede – acting in the same capacity in which it ratified the Constitution – cannot, with any show of reason, be denied by anyone who regards the Constitution as a compact, if a power be inserted by the amending power, which would radically change the character of the Constitution, or the nature of the system; or if the former should fail to fulfill the ends for which it was established.'

Even James Madison, who during the Tariff Crisis disputed the details of Calhoun's 'Carolina Doctrine,' conceded that 'the right of seceding from intolerable oppression' was but 'another name only for revolution, about which there is no theoretic controversy.'

Calhoun believed that the Constitution did not protect the reserved powers of the States from federal encroachment and that the States must have some power of self-protection: the State negative and State interposition. 'I have shown, that the federal government contains, within itself, or in its organization, no provisions, by which, the powers delegated could be prevented from encroaching on the powers reserved to the several States' declared Calhoun. 'And that, the only means furnished by the system itself, to resist encroachments, are, the mutual negative between the two coordinate governments, where their acts come into conflict as to the extent of their respective powers; and the interposition of a State in its sovereign character, as a party to the constitutional compact, against an unconstitutional act of the federal government.' While these two safeguards were 'sufficient to restrict the action of the federal government to its appropriate sphere,' the amendment power made 'ample and safe provision for their correction' in the event of any 'dangerous derangements or disorders.'

If these safeguards were not maintained, continued Calhoun, then not only would the Constitution be destroyed, but also the entire American federal republic. The 'dominant combination of States' would liberally construe its powers so as to circumvent the Constitution and rule as an absolute majority, oppressing the minority of States for its own 'aggrandisement.' Conservative constructionism, although common sense, would become 'the subject of ridicule and scorn.' While the federal government consolidated power from the States, each federal department would struggle against one another to consolidate power in itself. In the end, the President, the head of the administration of government who benefited from every usurpation of reserved powers, would use his newfound power to become head of the majority party as well, and thus an absolute ruler – a king in all but name. 'Devotion and submission to party and party interest' would replace 'fidelity to the Constitution or to the country,' with Congressmen obeying party lines and serving special interests instead of representing their people. Because of the 'vast extent and diversity of interests' within the American republic, parties would become concentrated in different sections, resulting in the 'dominant section' ruling over the 'subordinate section' as an empire ruled over a colony. 'In this state of things,' predicted Calhoun, 'discontent, alienation, and hostility of feelings would be engendered between the sections; to be followed by discord, disorder, convulsions, and, not improbably a disruption of the system.'

Calhoun was adamant that only the powers of the State negative and State interposition could save the Constitution and the American federal republic from destruction. Other safeguards, such as freedom of speech and the press (supported by suffrage), and the division of power between departments and governments (supported by a written constitution), could delay federal encroachment upon the reserved powers of the States, but without a power of 'counteracting resistance' they would ultimately be 'superseded or rendered obsolete.' In addition to preventing the consolidation of power, however, the State negative and State interposition would actually strengthen the 'moral power' of the federal government. This 'moral power' would encourage States to make compromises with one another and even sacrifice their own interests for the common good. Indeed, there was no reason to suspect that the States, who had 'freely and voluntarily' created the federal government 'for the common good of each and all,' would undermine rather than uphold its rightful delegated powers. 'If its safekeeping cannot be intrusted to its creators,' exclaimed Calhoun, 'it can be safely placed in the custody of no other hands.'

Calhoun concluded that only the full exercise of the delegated and reserved powers could prevent the dissolution or consolidation of the Union and fulfill the hopes of the Founding Fathers for a strong, free, democratic, and federal republic:

> It is by thus bringing all the powers of the system into active operation – and only by this means – that its equilibrium can be preserved, and adjusted to the changes, which the enlargement of the Union, and its increase of population or other causes, may require. Thus only, can the Union be preserved; the government made permanent; the limits of the country be enlarged; the anticipations of the Founders of the system, as to its future prosperity and greatness, be realized; and the revolutions and calamities, necessarily incident to the theory which would make the federal government the sole and exclusive judge of its powers, be averted.

Finished with the section of the *Discourse* which analysed the Constitution and the overall American system of governments, Calhoun turned to history – specifically the question of how and why the American republic had become a national rather than federal government.

As Calhoun saw it, the very first Congress under the Constitution, controulled by the Federalist Party, was where it all went wrong, setting the American republic on a course of consolidation. The worst of all the acts of this Congress was the Judiciary Act, which allowed the federal government, if defeated in the highest court of a State, to appeal to the federal judiciary. 'The effect, so far as these cases extend, is to place the highest tribunal of the States, both of law and equity, in the same relation to the Supreme Court of the United States, which the circuit and inferior courts of the United States bear to it,' explained Calhoun. 'To this extent, they are made equally subordinate and subject to its controul.' In other words, while the Supreme Court was supreme only over other federal courts, the Judiciary Act made it supreme over State courts as well. Thus, the federal judiciary was unconstitutionally granted the right to enforce its judgments as to the extent of federal power against the States. Calhoun conceded that the enforcement was limited to civil cases, but stressed that it set a precedent for further expansions. For instance, Calhoun pointed out, if the Supreme Court determined that a State government did not qualify as republican under the Guaranty Clause (which guaranteed a republican form of government to the States), then the President could, under the Judiciary Act, invade the State and install a new government.

Calhoun was surely recalling President Andrew Jackson's threatened invasion of South Carolina, but he also perfectly anticipated the war rationale of President Abraham Lincoln, who declared that the popular governments of the Confederate States were not republican, but mere 'combinations of criminals' and 'insurgents' – and that the so-called 'Civil War' was not a war at all, but a large-scale law-enforcement operation.

According to Calhoun, the first Congress' consolidations of power were legion. The first Congress deferred to the President's usurpation of its discretionary powers under the Necessary and Proper Clause, allowing him to make appointments and dismissals which he was not authorised to make. The spoils system, by which the President distributed the 'honours and emoluments' of the government among his party, was also introduced during the first Congress. The first Secretary of the Treasury, Alexander Hamilton, ordered his department to accept private banknotes in addition to specie, and convinced the first Congress to establish the First Bank of the United States. During the American Revolution, the United States had been 'inundated' with paper money and suffered severe inflation. To end this 'evil,' the Constitution only allowed the Congress to 'coin' rather than print money, and the first Congress initially required the payment of taxes in specie. The acceptance of bank paper and the creation of a national bank, however, ignored the monetary lessons of the American Revolution and violated the Constitution's provisions to curb paper money and inflation. Acting on the recommendation of Hamilton, the first Congress also laid the foundation for sectional mercantilism, which in time developed into 'the most serious of evils.' In particular, the Congress assumed that it could levy taxes and issue expenditures according to what it deemed the general welfare, without reference to the objects enumerated in the delegated powers. 'On this assumption, thus boldly put forth, in defiance of a fundamental principle of a federal system of government,' objected Calhoun, 'most onerous duties have been laid on imports, and vast amounts of public money appropriated to objects not named among the delegated powers, and not necessary or proper to carry them into execution; to the impoverishment of one portion of the country, and the corresponding aggrandisement of the other.'

Calhoun thought that too much faith was placed in the early actions of the federal government simply because it was composed of many of the framers and thus was supposedly the best expression of their original intentions. Although the 'purity of their motives' was impeccable, Calhoun noted that they lacked experience with the system of governments they had created and thus were unaware of the effects that their acts would have on the balance between the delegated and reserved powers. To prove his point, Calhoun quoted James Madison's admission that experience, not intentions or efforts, was the main flaw in the Constitution: 'Is it unreasonable to conjecture, that the errors which may be contained in the plan of the Convention, are such as have resulted, rather from defect of antecedent experience on this complicated and difficult subject, than from the want of accuracy or care in the investigation of it, and, consequently, that they are such as will not be ascertained, until an actual trial will point them out?'

Resistance to this early consolidation of power rallied around Thomas Jefferson, then serving as the first Secretary of State, and formed the 'Republican Party.' According to Calhoun, 'Its great object was to protect the reserved, against the encroachments of the delegated powers...and hence, they were often called "the State Rights Party."' It was during the presidency of John Adams when the 'State Rights Republicans' (known today as the 'Jeffersonian Republicans' or 'Democratic-Republicans') became an organised party, largely in response to the Alien and Sedition Acts. These detested laws, which permitted the President to deport foreigners arbitrarily and essentially criminalised criticism of the government (which, at that point, meant the Federalist Party), were widely considered unconstitutional violations of civil liberties, the separation of powers between federal branches, and the rights of the States. Virginia and Kentucky spearheaded the opposition, their legislatures adopting resolutions written respectively by James Madison and Thomas Jefferson, declaring that the Constitution was a compact between the States, that the powers delegated to the federal government were limited to those enumerated in the Constitution, and that the States were entitled and obligated to resist any encroachment upon their reserved powers. The resolutions, in effect, were acts of interposition or nullification. When New England's State legislatures rebuked the *Virginia and Kentucky Resolutions*, Madison, on behalf of the Virginia legislature, authored the *Report on the Virginia Resolutions*, 'which triumphantly vindicated and established the positions taken in the resolutions.' According to Calhoun, 'The report of Mr. Madison, and the *Virginia and Kentucky Resolutions*, constituted the political creed of the State Rights Republican Party.' Jefferson won the next presidential election, inaugurating a dynasty of State-Rights Republican Presidents from Virginia as well as the Jeffersonian Republicans' controul of the Congress.

As President, Thomas Jefferson had an 'earnest desire to reform the government' and successfully undid much of the damage done by the Federalist Party. The Alien and Sedition Acts expired and those punished under them were pardoned. Taxes and expenditures were reduced. The national debt was lowered. The power of the national bank was checked and the groundwork laid for its termination. War with Napoleonic France was skillfully averted. Unfortunately, Jefferson treated the symptoms of the disease instead of curing the disease itself, thus limiting the lasting impact of his presidency. State courts remained subjects rather than coordinates with federal courts. The States' rights of interposition/nullification remained a disputed rather than settled subject. The President continued to usurp the discretionary powers of the Congress. The Treasury continued to accept banknotes as payments. The Congress continued to tax and spend without reference to the delegated powers. In short, none of the consolidations of power from the first Congress were reversed. Calhoun believed that the reason Jefferson 'failed to undo, effectually, the consolidating national policy of Hamilton, and to restore the government to its federal character' was because of public complacency and distractions from abroad – the defeat of the Alien and Sedition Acts contented the people and the threat of war with Great Britain and France preoccupied his administration.

The War of 1812, under President James Madison, did not just stop the progress Thomas Jefferson began in office, but reversed many of its gains.

The first national bank had expired without renewal, but a second (the Second Bank of the United States) was chartered to stabilise the currency during the war. Taxes and expenditures had been lowered, but they rose to meet the costs of the war. Due to the wartime embargo, capital was diverted from New England's shipyards to New England's factories, creating a rich and powerful industrial interest which began lobbying for protection from foreign competition and a monopoly over the domestic market. This explosion of power, noted Calhoun, was 'one of the unavoidable consequences of war.' According to Calhoun, 'All these causes combined, could not fail to give a direction to the course of government, adverse to the federal and favourable to the national policy – or, in other words, adverse to the principles and policy which brought Mr. Jefferson and the Republicans into power, and favourable to those for which Mr. Adams and the Federal Party had contended.'

In addition, the War of 1812 destroyed both parties – the Federalists falling into total disgrace for their resistance to the war effort and treasonous collusion with the British and the State-Rights Republicans dividing into the 'National Republicans' (a populist Federalist Party) and the 'Democratic Party' (a populist Jeffersonian Party). James Monroe was the last of the Virginia Presidents – 'the old State-Rights Party, ceased to exist as a party, after having held power for twenty-four years' – succeeded by John Quincy Adams, a National Republican from Massachusetts and the son of the Federalist John Adams. As if to seal their split with the patriarch of their original party, Thomas Jefferson, the National Republicans and Democrats adopted a tariff bill which its opponents branded as the Tariff of Abominations – 'as it truly proved to be,' added Calhoun. What made the Tariff of Abominations worse than all previous tariffs was that it was entirely intended for protection rather than revenue (that is, for politics rather than policy) and came at a time when the federal government was already enjoying an ample surplus and paying down its debts. The Congress, however, only had the constitutional authority to levy taxes for revenue, meaning that taxes for protection were unconstitutional as well as unequal. Furthermore, the Congress desired to distribute the annual surplus among the States, substituting *'individual and local welfare'* (i.e. special interests) for general welfare. To Calhoun, the Tariff of Abominations was a 'gross and palpable perversion of the taxing power,' and the distribution of the surplus 'an extravagant and gross abuse of the money power.' The nail in the coffin, however, came when the Congress almost unanimously obliged Democratic President Andrew Jackson's request for an authorisation of force to collect the Tariff of Abominations. This Force Bill, which Calhoun considered 'grossly unconstitutional and outrageous,' authorised the President to deploy the military for the enforcement of the judgments of the federal government (in effect, the President himself) as to the extent of its power.

Calhoun believed that the Tariff of Abominations and the Force Bill defeated everything that the Jeffersonian Republicans had achieved and practically erased Thomas Jefferson and James Madison from history. 'It was thus, from the identity of doctrine and of policy which distinguished both parties, in reference to the money power, that two of the most prominent articles in the creed of the Republican Party, by force of which Mr. Jefferson, as its leader, came into power, were set aside; and their dangerous opposites, on account of which Mr. Adams, as head of the Federal Party, was expelled, were brought into full and active operation,' claimed Calhoun. 'Namely, the right claimed by the latter for Congress, to pronounce upon what appertains to the general welfare, and which is so forcibly condemned in the *Virginia and Kentucky Resolutions*, and the *Virginia Report* of Mr. Madison; and the right of the federal judiciary to decide, in the last resort, as to the extent of the reserved as well as of the delegated powers.' According to Calhoun, the combined effect of these two laws gave the federal government 'unlimited controul' over the States, 'in utter subversion of the relation of coordinates, and in total disregard of the rights of the several States, as parties to the constitutional compact, to judge, in the last resort, as to the extent of the powers delegated.'

Under the Jacksonian Democrats, party politics and the spoils system also became a vicious cycle: parties politicked to win the spoils of office, then used the spoils of office to solidify the party to win the next election, and so on and so forth. Calhoun gave credit where credit was due, however, and commended the Democrats' stand against the 'money power.' Indeed, the Democrats terminated the Second Bank of the United States, separated the federal government from banking interests through the Independent Treasury System, and lowered taxes and expenditures. Like President Thomas Jefferson, however, the Democrats treated the symptoms rather than cured the disease. 'These are all important measures, and indicate a disposition to take a stand against the perversion of the money power,' admitted Calhoun. 'But, until the measures which led to these mischiefs – and in the adoption of which they bore so prominent a part – are entirely reversed, nothing permanent will be gained.'

Calhoun observed that as the American republic became more centralised, parties became more sectionalised – 'the stronger section with a view to power and aggrandisement' and 'the weaker, for defence and safety.' There were many differences between the sections of the Union, such as 'diversity of interest, of origin, of character, of habits, or of local institutions,' but slavery was an especially sensitive issue – 'at all times, considered by the wise and patriotic, as a delicate point, and to be, with great caution, touched.' Unfortunately, the sectionalisation of the parties was not conducive to statesmanship on this sensitive issue. According to Calhoun, there was a 'happy state of things' until the Missouri Controversy, when the statehood of Missouri was denied due to the fact that her constitution permitted slavery. The debate, though 'long and angry,' settled on a compromise: slave-holding Missouri and non-slaveholding Maine's statehoods were allowed while the existence of slavery in the Territories was divided along the parallel 36°30' north. Southerners uneasily accepted the Missouri Compromise, hoping that the controversy was resolved. Instead, the controversy had 'touched a fanatical as well as a political cord' in the North, leading to the rise of the radical abolitionist movement. When the government was federal, with limited power, opposition to slavery was passive, but as the government became national, asserting the right to enforce its judgments as to the extent of its power against the States, the abolitionists were incited to action. Although the abolitionists were always a loathed minority (even in the North), they gradually grew into a voting bloc capable of determining presidential elections. Since presidential elections had become the 'all-absorbing question' of the United States due to the power and patronage of the presidency, the parties pandered to any and all constituencies to win the election, thus exaggerating the influence of the abolitionists – 'a dangerous system of electioneering.' Calhoun warned that if the North gained controul over the territory conquered in the Mexican War, her representation in corporate character and federal numbers would be increased, she would acquire permanent controul of the federal government, and the South would become a permanent minority. 'The difficulty and danger have been greatly increased, since the Missouri Compromise; and the other sectional measures, in reference to the recently acquired territories, now in contemplation (should they succeed), will centralise the two majorities that constitute the elements of which the government of the United States is composed [i.e. corporate character and representative numbers], permanently in the Northern section,' warned Calhoun. 'And thereby subject the Southern, on this, and on all other questions, in which their feelings or interest may come in conflict, to its controul.'

Given that the American republic had become national and absolute rather than federal and concurrent, Calhoun feared that the Tariff of the Abominations and the Force Bill were the face of the future – that is, a government under the controul of an absolute majority, comprised of the most populous section of the Union, passing whatever laws it pleased (no matter how oppressive and unconstitutional), and using force to execute them against the minority. 'To these fatal measures,' argued Calhoun, 'are to be attributed the violence of party struggles; the total disregard of the provisions of the Constitution in respect to the election of the President; the predominance of the honours and emoluments of the government over every other consideration; the rise and growth of the abolition agitation; the formation of geographical parties; and the alienation and hostile feelings between the two great sections of the Union.' Calhoun was certain that such a system would eventually explode in a civil war between the North and the South.

To prevent the evils of consolidation or dissolution, Calhoun offered two proposals. The first was to make the American republic federal again. 'It is indispensable that the government of the United States should be restored to its federal character,' urged Calhoun. 'Nothing short of a perfect restoration, as it came from the hands of its framers, can avert them.' Only a federal government, in which powers were divided and balanced between all its parts, was capable of lasting in a republic as vast in area and diverse in interest as the United States. Such a restoration, however, involved a host of reforms – what Thomas Jefferson fell short of accomplishing as President and what had been drifting farther out of reach ever since. The States, the sovereign powers who had created the American federal republic in the first place, must be rescued from their 'subordinate and dependent positions' and returned to their 'true position.' According to Calhoun, the repeal of the Judiciary Act and Force Bill would restore the State governments to 'their true relation as coequals and coordinates,' the States to 'the high sovereign power of deciding, in the last resort, on the extent of the delegated powers, or of interposing to prevent their encroachment on the reserved powers,' and the federal government as 'the coequal and coordinate of the separate governments of the several States...restricted to the discharge of the auxiliary functions assigned to it by the Constitution.' In addition, the taxes and appropriations of the Congress must be restricted to the objects enumerated in the delegated powers. Calhoun considered this power 'the most encroaching and comprehensive,' for if the judgment of the Congress determined the general welfare instead of the Constitution, then there would be no limits on its authority and no means to prevent its usurpation of the reserved powers. The power of the President must be restricted, 'divesting [him] of all discretionary powers, and confining him strictly to those expressly conferred on him by the Constitution and the acts of Congress.' The constitutional procedure for the election of the President, which had taken elections out of the hands of the States and into the hands of parties, must be reinstated, and the spoils system, which had turned elections into bonanzas for profit rather than honest debates over policy, abandoned. These reforms would be the first step towards restoring the American republic to a federal system capable of concurrence among its many parts.

The American federal republic, as originally framed, protected the States and the federal government in their rightful spheres and prevented the extremes of consolidation or dissolution. As Calhoun showed, however, the United States had deviated from their federal constitution. Restoring the American republic as a federation would prevent matters from worsening, but could not undo the damage that had already been done – some of which was fundamental and permanent. 'The means which may be sufficient to *prevent* diseases, are not usually sufficient to *remedy* them,' explained Calhoun. 'The very causes which have occasioned its disorders, have, at the same time, led to consequences, not to be removed by the means which would have prevented them.' The consequences that Calhoun had in mind were the disruption of the equilibrium between the North and the South. When the Constitution was ratified, the North and the South were equal in the respects in which the States were represented in the federal government: corporate character and federal numbers. Since then, however, the equality of the sections had been overturned. The cause of this disparity was the constant exclusion of the South from new territory, which had inflated the representation of the North and thus given her 'an overwhelming preponderance in the government' and 'permanently destroyed' the equilibrium between the two sections. Restoring the federal foundations of the American republic was a necessary first step, but it could not change the stark fact that the North, as a permanent majority, could tyrannise the permanent Southern minority. 'So long as it continues, there can be no safety for the weaker section,' averred Calhoun. 'It places in the hands of the stronger and hostile section, the power to crush her and her institutions; and leaves her no alternative, but to resist, or sink down into a colonial condition.'

To restore the sectional equilibrium upon which the Union was founded, concluded Calhoun, the Constitution must be amended to strengthen the minority section's negative power against the majority section. 'Nothing short of this can protect the weaker,' argued Calhoun, 'and restore harmony and tranquility to the Union, by arresting, effectually, the tendency of the dominant and stronger section to oppress the weaker.' Calhoun believed that this was what the framers would have done if they had known that the main danger to the equilibrium of the Union would not be between the States and the federal goverment or the large States and small States, but between sections of States. Therefore, Calhoun's second proposal was to reorganise the single executive into a dual executive, along the lines of Sparta's two kings and Rome's two consuls. The two executives would each represent the two main sections of the American republic, elected among separate, sectional constituencies. The powers of the President would be divided between the two executives (foreign relations to one, domestic affairs to another), but each would have a veto on legislation from Congress. Calhoun was optimistic about this proposed amendment, believing that it would secure the concurrence which the American federal republic was intended to establish. 'It would make the Union a union in truth – a bond of mutual affection and brotherhood,' hoped Calhoun, 'and not a mere connection used by the stronger as the instrument of dominion and aggrandisement, and submitted to by the weaker only from the lingering remains of former attachment, and the fading hope of being able to restore the government to what it was originally intended to be, a blessing to all.'

III

Unlike other small-f federalists and small-r republicans, such as John Randolph of Roanoke, who became voices in the wilderness even in their own time, Calhoun remained extremely influential throughout the United States, and especially the South – a minority section where his argument for consensus rule over majority rule was most resonant. When South Carolina finally convened in Charleston to secede from the Union – a course of action which Calhoun would have found bittersweet – Calhoun presided from beyond the grave. The Secession Convention's President, David F. Jamison, opened the proceedings with a speech on 17 December 1860. 'Gentlemen, we have met here under circumstances more solemn than any of us have ever been placed in before,' began Jamison. 'It is no less than our fixed determination to throw off a government to which we have been accustomed, and to provide new safeguards for our future.' There was no hope of reunion with the North, avowed Jamison. 'What guarantees can they offer us, more strictly guarded or under higher sanctions, than the present written compact between us?' Jamison asked. Indeed, the Constitution had failed to safeguard the liberty and security of South Carolina from the North's 'jealousy and aggressions' in excluding her from the common Territory, 'cupidity' in burdening her with the bulk of the taxes, and 'crusade' of hatred and fear against her citizens and institutions. Without concurrence between all of the parts of society, constitutions were mere 'paper securities,' asserted Jamison. 'Written constitutions are worthless unless they are written at the same time in the hearts, and founded on the interests of a people,' continued Jamison, 'and as there is no common bond of sympathy or interest between the North and the South, all efforts to preserve this Union will not only be fruitless but fatal to the less numerous section.' On political principles (the impotence of written constitutions without a negative, the necessity of a concurrent majority to unite all of the parts of society, and the plight of the minority under an absolute majority) and political issues (territorial expansion, economics, and abolitionism),

Jamison's speech was steeped in the philosophy and history of the *Disquisition* and *Discourse* and was a testament to the enduring power of Calhoun's political philosophy. Indeed, down the street from the convention hall hung a banner of Calhoun holding the broken tablets of 'Truth, Justice, and the Constitution,' with the caption, 'Behold Its Fate.'

To Calhoun, the American federal republic was the embodiment of his theory of the concurrent majority. In a concurrent majority, each part of society had a voice in the formation of the government's acts and the power of self-protection against the execution of oppressive acts. Through the representation of the two capacities of the States (their equality and their population) in the federal government, each of the parts of the American republic had a concurrent voice in the formation of its acts. Through the rights of the States (derived from the coordinate relation of the State governments to the federal government and the sovereignty of the States over the whole), each of the parts of the American republic had the power of self-protection against the execution of oppressive acts. Although the American republic was framed as a concurrent majority, Calhoun despaired that its original foundations had not been preserved. From overreliance on suffrage and written constitutions, rather than the vigilant assertion of the States' reserved powers of the negative and interposition, the American republic had become an absolute majority of the tax-consuming Northern States over the tax-paying Southern States – the former a mortal menace to the security and liberty of the latter. To restore concurrence in the American republic, Calhoun proposed a return to the federal system of governments along with additional reforms to protect the minority section and strengthen the whole. Instead, following Calhoun's death, the centralisation of power and the sectionalisation of politics which he deplored intensified, and the tension between consolidation and dissolution which he dreaded finally erupted, resulting in the bloodiest war in American history – a war which crushed the South, destroyed States' rights, and transformed the concurrent republic into an absolutist nation. 'The nation, not the States, is sovereign,' crowed abolitionist reverend Henry Ward Beecher at a victory ceremony in defeated, destroyed Charleston. 'There may be pardon, but no concession...The only condition of submission is, to submit!' Just as the Redcoats had chopped down and burned Charleston's Liberty Tree (where South Carolinian revolutionaries once gathered to proclaim, 'Don't Tread on Me'), so the Yankees toppled Charleston's statue of Calhoun, aptly signifying the fall of the federal republic for which he stood.

VI. Robert Barnwell Rhett &
Address of South Carolina to the People of the Slveholding States

The one great principle, which produced our secession from the United States – was constitutional liberty – liberty protected by law. For this, we have fought; for this, our people have died. To preserve and cherish this sacred principle, constituting as it did, the very soul of independence itself, was the clear dictate of all honest – all wise statesmanship.
– Robert Barnwell Rhett, 1864

IT IS FASHIONABLE NOWADAYS to regard the constitutional doctrine of States' rights as yet another debunked 'Neo-Confederate' myth, a relic of the slave-holding Old South. More than any other man in his day and age, the South Carolinian Fire-Eater, Robert B. Rhett, stood for the States' rights of 'nullification' and 'secession.' Yet William W. Freehling, a Bancroft-winning historian from the University of Kentucky, takes the incredibly unethical liberty of inserting imaginary thoughts into Rhett's head, having him curse 'St. Thomas' Jefferson, along with 'inalienable rights,' 'rights of revolution,' and 'the principles of 1776,' claiming 'the South had revolted to escape those idiocies.' Never mind the fact that Rhett espoused these very ideals throughout his life, proclaimed that the Confederacy was indeed founded upon them, and personally identified as a 'Jeffersonian Republican.' Elsewhere, Steven Channing, a winner of the Alan Nevins History Prize, writes off the sincerity of States' rights with a few words. 'As for the "dry prattle" about the Constitution, the rights of minorities, and the like, there was never any confusion in the minds of most contemporaries that such arguments were masks for more fundamental emotional issues,' Channing casually asserts. 'State sovereignty was an issue only because the retreat to the inviolability of states' rights had always been a refuge for those fearful of a challenge to their property.' Indeed, it is the current *modus operandi* of historians to discount whatever Southerners said about political, economic, and cultural differences with the North as a false front for the ulterior motive of slavery: Southerners could not possibly have meant what they actually said (except when it was about slavery)!

This essay series aims to set the story straight. The truth is that the great political treatises of the Old South prove that the doctrine of States' rights was never a mere pretence for slavery, but reflected a deep passion for self-government rooted in Southern culture as well as an earnest understanding of the Constitution rooted in Southern history. According to the scholarly, gentlemanly M.E. Bradford, States' rights were part of a Southern political tradition – a 'patrimony' and 'birthright' – dating from the foundation of the Colonies through the independence of the States and to the creation of the Constitution. At the crowning of the Confederate capital in Richmond, President Jefferson Davis honoured this heritage. 'The cause in which we are now engaged is the cause of the advocacy of the rights to which we were born, those for which our fathers of the Revolution bled – the richest inheritance that ever fell to man, and which it is our sacred duty to transmit untarnished to our children,' announced Davis. 'Upon us is devolved the high and holy responsibility of preserving the constitutional liberty of a free government.'

Robert B. Rhett and his *Address of South Carolina to the People of the Slaveholding States*, promulgated in 1860 by South Carolina's Secession Convention, are the subjects of this essay.

I

Robert B. Smith (aka 'Rhett') was born on 21 December 1800, in the old Lowcountry district of Beaufort, South Carolina. With one of the most distinguished lineages in the State (descended from six governors, two landgraves, and the very first settler of South Carolina), Smith aspired to make his ancestors proud and was absolutely committed to protecting his people's identity, interests, and inheritance. Smith's father, James, was a Revolutionary-War veteran who had defended the besieged cities of Savannah and Charleston, and been taken prisoner when the latter fell. Smith attended Beaufort College, where he was impressed with the integrity of the staunch Unionist James L. Petigru. 'It is only the strong man – strong in conscious rectitude, strong in convictions of truth, strong in the never-failing and eternal vindications of time – who can put aside the temptations of present power, and submit to official inferiority,' reflected Smith. 'Superficial observers may not understand the greatness of such a man.' A shy student, Smith was nicknamed 'Madame Modesty.' Due to his father's troubled finances, Smith had to leave Beaufort College and be tutored by his father, who imparted his Jeffersonian politics to his son. 'I was...raised and nurtured a [Democratic-] Republican, in the faith and principles of my father,' recalled Smith.

Smith was born and bred past the glory days of the republic in a time of strife between sections and parties. To Smith, the Union did not stand for peace and prosperity, as it did for his father, but oppression and corruption – a threat to the 'free government' for which his father had fought. Indeed, rumblings of discontent were emerging even in conservative Beaufort (a staunch Federalist stronghold in the Jeffersonian South) over the tariff bills of 1816 and 1824, which enriched Northern industry at the expence of Southern agriculture. These tariffs ('nothing but robbery'), the Missouri Compromise (which 'nullified the sovereignty of the people'), and the corruption of the then-fragmenting Democratic-Republican Party ('little more than a mere association to obtain office and power') convinced Smith to run for office in South Carolina's General Assembly. Elected in 1826, Madame Modesty came out of his shell as a 'brilliant and promising young man,' according to one of his friends.

Amid this tense atmosphere of suspicion between the North and the South, a volcano erupted in Smith's district. At a citizens' meeting in 1827, Smith authored a memorial to the Congress protesting economic protectionism in general (labeled the 'American System' by its supporters) and a proposed tariff on woolens in particular. 'From the moderation of our Northern brethren, who for the last ten years have been beating at our doors for monopolies,' announced Smith, 'we have renounced all hope.' Smith argued that 'free commerce is the true interest of every nation,' but that while the South supplied the bulk of American exports, she also paid the bulk of federal taxes, most of which were redistributed to the North in the form of so-called internal improvements. 'It is immaterial whether that money is received by one man called a king,' exclaimed Smith, 'or by thousands termed manufacturers.' Smith closed with a veiled threat of resistance if the exploitative and unconstitutional tariff were not abandoned. 'Do not add oppression to embarrassment, and alienate our affections from the home our fathers together raised,' warned Smith. 'Do not believe us degenerate from our sires, and that we will either bear or dare less, when the time for suffering or resistance comes.' The Woollens Tariff was defeated – thanks to the tie-breaking vote of Vice President John C. Calhoun – but the next year, in response to the much more comprehensive Tariff of Abominations, Smith authored a second memorial at another citizens' meeting, doubling down on his previous statements and dealing a broadside against the American System. According to Smith, protectionist tariffs were not only 'oppressive' in that they redistributed Southern wealth to the North, making the former 'tributary' to the latter, but also 'unconstitutional' in that they violated the rights of a sovereign State far more flagrantly than anything the British Crown had ever inflicted on the Colonies. From the American Revolution, through the War of 1812, and to the American System, boasted Smith, South

Carolina had sacrificed more in 'blood and treasure' for the Union (and the North) than any other State, yet the 'long, continued, and settled hostility' of the North to the South had pushed her to the realisation that 'our attachment to this Union can only be limited by our superior attachment to our rights.' The summer before, Smith had merely threatened resistance, but now with this latest insult he openly called for it. 'We must either retrograde in dishonour and in shame, and receive the contempt and scorn of our brethren, superadded to our wrongs, and their system of oppression, strengthened by our toleration,' insisted Smith. 'Or we must,' he finished, quoting *Hamlet*, '"by opposing, end them."' According to Smith, resistance to Northern tyranny stemmed 'not from a desire of disunion, or to destroy the Constitution, but...that we may preserve the Union, and bring back the Constitution to its original uncorrupted principles.' Smith's memorials electrified the United States and catapulted him into national prominence. They were his first act of defiance against the federal government and would not be his last.

Smith's memorials made an ultimatum to the Congress: repeal the Tariff of Abominations or South Carolina would secede from the Union. Smith believed that if South Carolina forced the issue by seceding, other Southern States would take her side and the Congress would have no choice but to compromise. When John C. Calhoun, seeking to prevent civil war and preserve South Carolina's rights within the Union, proposed nullification (a renewed application of the Principles of '98 from James Madison and Thomas Jefferson's *Virginia and Kentucky Resolutions*), Smith relented from secession, though he maintained skepticism toward any 'peaceful remedy.' Nevertheless, Smith embraced Calhoun's strategy, leading the call for a State convention and attending States' rights rallies all around South Carolina to galvanise support for nullification. 'Standing, then, upon the very ground which Mr. Jefferson, Mr. Madison, and the whole Republican Party stood in '98,' avowed Smith, 'we think that the time has come when our principles are to be enforced – peaceably – constitutionally enforced – when Carolina, as a sovereign party to the constitutional compact, should interpose "for arresting the progress of evil.'" Revolution? 'What, sir, has the people ever gained, but by revolution?' retorted Smith. 'What, sir, has Carolina ever obtained great or free, but by revolution? Revolution! Sir, it is the dearest and holiest word to the brave and free.' Disunion? 'Washington was a disunionist, Adams, Henry, Jefferson, Rutledge, were all disunionists and traitors, and for maintaining the very constitutional principles for which we now contend. They severed a mighty empire on whose dominion the sun never set [and] cut this empire asunder with the stern energy of the sword,' answered Smith. 'Shall we, standing upon the free soil of Carolina, rendered sacred by the bones of our Revolutionary martyrs and heroes...tremble at epithets?' A serious illness prevented Smith from attending South Carolina's Nullification Convention in 1832, although after the act of nullification was passed he was allowed to add his signature retroactively in recognition of his contribution to the cause.

When no States seconded nullification and President Andrew Jackson prepared for an invasion, South Carolina's position looked grim. In 1833, another State convention reassembled to consider the compromise that John C. Calhoun had helped secure – a gradual reduction of the tariff in exchange for repeal of the act of nullification. Although most South Carolinians came to consider the Compromise of 1833 a success – their small State had singlehandedly won a reduction in federal tariffs! – Smith strenuously objected, arguing that they were betraying their principles for a bribe. 'The enemy is, for the moment, beaten back,' conceded Smith, though he cautioned that 'the disease is still there,' and that 'the true disorder is that pest of our system, consolidation.' Smith was particularly galled that the 'angry tyrant,' Jackson, had resorted to threats of 'coercion' and 'civil war,' and thus admitted that he no longer loved nor was loyal to the United States. 'I cannot love, I will not praise that which, under the abused names of Union and Liberty, attempts to inflict upon us every thing that can curse and enslave the land.' According to Smith, the conflict between the North and the

South was 'a contest which even this compromise can but for a little while avert.'

In 1834, while serving as South Carolina's Attorney General, Smith acquired four plantations and over a hundred slaves in a transaction with an British colonel forced to sell his holdings due to Great Britain's abolition of slavery. Personally attached to his slaves and feeling responsible for their wellbeing, the colonel feared that in selling his slaves, they would be separated and perhaps come under cruel masters. The reason this colonel sold to Smith was because he trusted him to be a benevolent master who would treat his slaves well and keep them together – that what Smith told him about 'my own sense of humanity and Christian duty' was true. Indeed, Smith was a conscientious master who believed that slave ownership carried sacred duties. 'I am responsible to God for their spiritual and temporal welfare, and were I capable of swerving from my engagements express or implied, to man, the accounting, the appalling account over which my heart sometimes almost sinks, which I must render to him who has sanctified us and washed us in his own blood, would terrify me into the path of rectitude,' confessed Rhett. 'God helping me, I am determined that every soul he has committed to my care shall have the considerations of the Gospel brought home to its bearer, and whilst I administer to the necessities of these slaves in this world, the great and one thing needed for eternity shall not be neglected.' This transaction elevated Smith from a lawyer to a planter – from a *bourgeois* profession to the aristocratic ruling class. Despite later financial difficulties, Smith kept his word to the British colonel and never sold the slaves, and employed as many of them as possible after their emancipation.

Smith was elected to the House of Representatives in 1836, where he served until 1848, doggedly defending the rights of the States – and especially those of South Carolina – from usurpation. 'I am a nullifier,' declared Smith, 'and will never consent that more power should be given to this government than strictly belongs to it.' It was at this point that he and his brothers changed their surname to 'Rhett,' to honour a distinguished ancestor – a swashbuckling colonial governor – and restore a historic Carolinian name.

Rhett endorsed President Martin Van Buren's Independent Treasury System (he was one of two South Carolinians who stood with Senator John C. Calhoun on this issue) and opposed the establishment of a third national bank, which he accused of causing the financial panics of 1819 and 1837, robbing Southern planters for the benefit of Northern bankers, and consolidating power in the federal government by giving it controul of the money. Rhett also fought to destroy the American System once and for all, 'that poison still lingering in the veins of the body politic – that unhallowed and corrupt combination by which one section of the Union was plundered for the benefit of another,' and to replace the inequitable tariff system with a more equitable system of direct taxation. Also with Calhoun, Rhett opposed war with Great Britain over the Oregon Territory (denouncing all war as 'an enormous crime, often on both sides, always on one,' in the 'civilised world'), though he broke with Calhoun in wholeheartedly supporting the Mexican War as a just war of self-defence. Slavery became an increasingly important issue during Rhett's career in the House, beginning as a parliamentary dispute over whether the Congress had the right to receive abolition petitions, escalating with the question of admitting slave-holding Texas to the Union, and ending as a debate over the legal status of slavery in the Territories. Underlying all of these issues was a struggle to maintain a balance of power between the North and the South, which had developed into two divergent nations under one government. Rhett resisted these mounting encroachments upon slavery, claiming that the federal government had no authority over the South's peculiar institution and thus could not receive any such petitions, that the South was entitled to the 'common property of the States' (e.g. the Territories) as much as the North, and that any concession from the South would result in her enslavement to the North. 'Here is a subject in which passion, and feeling, and religion, are all involved,' rued Rhett. 'All the inexperienced emotions of the heart are against us; all the abstractions concerning human rights can be perverted against us; all the theories of political dreamers, atheistic utilitarians, self-exalting and self-righteous religionists, who would reform or expunge the Bible – in short, enthusiasts and fanatics of all sorts are against us.'

In 1844, disillusioned with the Democratic Party, angry over the Black Tariff (a tax increase in violation of the Compromise of 1833) and alarmed by Northern opposition to Texas statehood (a sign of Northern determination to limit the growth of the South), Rhett ignited the Bluffton Movement. A revolution among the Lowcountry youth, the Bluffton Movement called for another State convention, where an ultimatum of nullification or secession could be made, causing a crisis which would end with the restoration of the Constitution or the recognition of South Carolina's independence. 'They are raging,' Rhett said of the so-called Bluffton Boys, 'and if the rest of the South was of their temper we would soon bring the government straight both as to Texas and the tariff.' At a banquet in Bluffton, Rhett raised a toast to the proposed convention: 'May it be as useful as the Convention of 1776.' Rhett expected to be branded a 'disunionist, mischief-maker, traitor, etc.,' but he dismissed such epithets as the propaganda of timid and slavish souls against the bold and free. 'My object is not to destroy the Union, but to maintain the Constitution, and the Union too, as the Constitution has made it,' explained Rhett. 'But I do not believe that the government can be reformed by its central action, and that we will probably have to risk the Union itself to save it, in its integrity, and to perpetuate it as a blessing.' Although the Bluffton Movement subsided when Calhoun obtained assurances of tariff reform and Texas statehood from the Democrat presidential candidate, James K. Polk, Rhett had succeeded in radicalising the next generation of South Carolinians. 'The Bluffton Boys have been silenced, not subdued,' claimed Rhett. 'The fire is not extinguished; it smoulders beneath, and will burst forth in another glorious flame that shall overrun the State and place her light again as of old, upon the watchtower of freedom.'

After John C. Calhoun's death in 1850, Rhett was elected to fill his seat in the Senate. Rhett attended a convention of Southern States in Nashville in 1850, as well as South Carolina's Convention of 1852. It was between the two conventions that Rhett renewed his calls for South Carolina to secede separately, although this time the ultimatum was not to the United States to recognise Southern rights, but to the other Southern States to secede and form an independent confederacy. 'Separate State action,' insisted Rhett, would compel the 'cooperation' of the rest of the South. 'Cooperation,' he toasted at a celebration of the American Revolution, 'our fathers obtained it by seizing the stamps, and by firing the guns of Fort Moultrie.' It was around this time when Southern Unionists began referring to Rhett and other secessionists as 'Fire-Eaters,' a derogatory term for brash duelists. After a controversial speech at the Nashville Convention, where he remarked that Southerners 'must rule themselves or perish,' Rhett was branded a 'traitor.' Rhett reveled in the term, however. 'I have been born of traitors, but thank God, they have ever been traitors in the great cause of liberty, fighting against tyranny and oppression,' boasted Rhett. 'Such treason will ever be mine whilst true to my heritage.' Rhett's constituents concurred, hoisting banners which read, 'Oh that we were all such traitors,' and hailing Rhett as Patrick Henry reborn. Indeed, Rhett reveled in the great Southern revolutionary's reputed retort to accusations of treason: 'If this be treason, make the most of it.'

When South Carolina's Convention closed with a resolution upholding the right of secession yet taking no action herself – nothing more than 'solemn and vapid truisms,' according to Rhett – Rhett felt that he was no longer a 'proper representative' of South Carolina and resigned his Senate seat. 'Sensible of the profound respect I owe the State as my sovereign, and deeply grateful for the many favours and honours she has conferred upon me, I bow to her declared will, and make way for those, who, with hearts less sad, and judgments more convinced, can better sustain her in the course she has determined to pursue.' Rhett spent the rest of the 1850s tending to his long-neglected plantations and rebuilding the *Charleston Mercury*, a newspaper which had always served as his mouthpiece and which he and his son had recently acquired.

After the election of the anti-slavery Abraham Lincoln to the presidency, Rhett believed that South Carolina had no choice but to secede from the Union. 'The tea has been thrown overboard,' declared Rhett's *Mercury*. 'The revolution of 1860 has been initiated.' Rhett warned that the Republican Party – a sectional party by, of, and for Northerners – was 'totally irresponsible to the people of the South, without check, restraint, or limitation,' and that its rule would bring 'the total annihilation of all self-government or liberty in the South.' When South Carolina convened to secede, Rhett's hour had finally come. 'Rhett Guards' paraded through the streets of Charleston, carrying banners emblazoned with some of his finest words, and his image was displayed alongside the great John C. Calhoun's. Elected to represent his old district in South Carolina's Secession Convention, Rhett fell to his knees in prayer before signing the act of secession. 'For thirty-two years, have I followed the quarry. Behold! It, at last, in sight!' exclaimed Rhett. 'A few more bounds, and it falls – the Union falls; and with it falls, its faithless oppressions – its insulting agitations – its vulgar tyrannies and fanaticism. The bugle blast of our victory and redemption is on the wind; and the South will be safe and free.'

Rhett's moment of triumph flamed out almost immediately. Rhett was the head of the South Carolina's delegation to the Montgomery Convention, where the Confederate States framed a new constitution, a task which Rhett believed should be 'a matter of restoration' rather than 'innovation,' as the old Constitution was not flawed, but simply perverted by Northern liberal constructionism. Although Rhett obtained prohibitions on the long-detested protectionist tariffs and internal improvements, along with express affirmations of the long-defended principle of State sovereignty, he failed to prevent the admission of non-slaveholding States, which he feared would lead to reconstruction with the North and ultimately recreate all the problems of the old Union – a Northern majority with different ideas, institutions, interests, and identities tyrannising a Southern minority. Furthermore, in forming a provisional government, the conservatives at Montgomery like Jefferson Davis prevailed over the radicals like Rhett – a Thermidor-style counter-revolution which left Rhett embittered and envious. Rhett became a maniacal critic of President Davis, accusing him of assuming the powers of a military despot – worse than Abraham Lincoln, in fact! – and betraying the Confederacy. As Mary Chesnut, the beloved South-Carolinian diarist who once described Rhett as 'mercurial,' observed, Rhett 'had howled nullification, secession, etc. so long, when he found his ideas taken up by all the Confederate world, he felt he had a vested right to the leadership.'

When President Abraham Lincoln summoned troops to crush what he dismissed as a mere rebellion, Rhett's Foreign Affairs Committee was responsible for drafting a declaration of war against the United States. To accompany the declaration of war, Rhett prepared a report presenting the cause and character of the conflict to the world. 'It was plain that it might be no easy task, to make European nations understand the true nature of the contest,' admitted Rhett. 'The rights of the Southern people under the terms of the Constitution, were unfortunately implicated with African slavery; and it might appear to European nations, that not the principle of free government, but the perpetuation of African slavery, was the real issue in the contest.' Rhett, therefore, sought to set the record straight. 'The real issue involved in the relations between the North and the South of the American States, is the great principle of self-government,' explained Rhett. 'Shall a dominant party of the North rule the South, or shall the people of the South rule themselves?' According to Rhett, after 'long forbearance and patience,' stemming from a 'heroic love for the Union' over 'mere interest,' the Southern States were driven to secede from the Union in order to escape the 'ruthless mastery' of the North, which was now threatening 'to subject them by the sword.' Aside from this report, Rhett contributed little to nothing to the Confederate government, seemingly fixated with thwarting President Jefferson Davis at every turn. When elections were held, Rhett did not run for office, but returned home and continued his opposition to 'King Davis' and 'the piddling, prostrate Congress,' from the pages of the *Mercury*.

The hard hand of war fell heavily on Rhett. Two of his sons died in the Confederate army. One of his daughters, unable to cope with her husband's death, drank herself to death. General William T. Sherman's army plundered his plantations, scattering his personal papers and stealing his books. Perhaps Rhett's sole consolation was the loyalty of his slaves, who fled with their refugee-master and worked his land in exchange for a share of the crop even after they were emancipated. Unable to meet his debts after the war, what was left of Rhett's estate eventually went into foreclosure. Rhett closed out his years living with one of his daughters in New Orleans, suffering from skin cancer and toiling on his memoirs, tentatively (and turgidly) titled, *The Last Decade, Seen in the Extinction of Free Government in the United States, and the Downfall of the Southern Confederacy, in Connection with Political Life and Services of the Honourable Robert Barnwell Rhett*. Defiant to the end, Rhett rejected any reconciliation with the North and remained confident that the South would one day rise again. 'Whether sitting around their hearths; or worshipping in the temples of God; or standing over the graves of our Confederate dead,' proclaimed Rhett, 'they will ever remember that they died for them; and spurn from them, as an imputation of the foulest dishonour, the mere suggestion that they can ever abandon their great cause – the cause of free government for which their glorious dead suffered and died.' Upon Rhett's death in 1876, *The Charleston News and Courier* dubbed him 'the father of secession.'

Outside of South Carolina, Rhett was widely detested, and even within South Carolina, Rhett was a controversial figure who could never lead, but only incite and electrify. According to gentleman-amateur historian Walter Brian Cisco, 'Two generations of South Carolinians would come to grin or grimace at the mention of his name.' Indeed, it was Rhett's repulsive public persona, rather than his ideas – visionary in their time and vindicated in the end – which made him so unpopular. One of Rhett's rivals, James H. Hammond, compared him to Cassandra, the mythological Greek priestess blessed with the gift of foresight but cursed for her warnings to go unheeded. 'How unfortunate that Cassandra came to preside over his birth and make him say the wisest things, so out of time and place, that they are accounted by those who rule mere foolishness,' reflected Hammond. 'What a pity that such fine talents should be thrown away on such a perverse temper.' According to Rhett's biographer, Laura A. White, 'It may be said that one can scarcely understand the action of the people of South Carolina in 1860 without including in his ken the remarkable activities of one man, whose eloquent and fiery preaching of the gospel of liberty and self-government, and of revolution to achieve these ends, beat upon their ears in season and out of season for over thirty years.'

II

During South Carolina's Secession Convention there was a dispute over how the State should justify secession. Maxcy Gregg, a friend of Rhett's and fellow Fire-Eater, objected that Christopher Memminger's *Declaration of the Causes Which Induce and Justify the Secession of South Carolina from the Federal Union* focused only on relatively recent grievances related to slavery and thus 'dishonoured the memory of South Carolinians' who had opposed the Tariff of Abominations, the Second Bank of the United States, and internal improvements. Laurence M. Keitt, another Fire-Eater (though no friend of Rhett's), replied that tariffs were now low, the national bank abolished, and internal improvements regularly vetoed, but 'the question of slavery' remained unresolved and thus should take front and centre. As a compromise, South Carolina issued two statements on secession: Memminger's narrow, legalistic *Declaration* (the title of which was amended to read 'immediate causes') and Rhett's *Address of South Carolina to the Slaveholding States*, a fiery manifesto of Southern rights and Northern wrongs. Historian Emory M. Thomas describes the *Address* as 'an extended dissertation which began with the Constitutional Convention of 1787 and rambled through a long catalogue of sectional issues and crises, demonstrating Southern righteousness and Yankee perfidy at every point.' Susan Bradford, a fourteen year-old girl whose father took her to Florida's Secession Convention in Tallahassee, remembered an ambassador from South Carolina reading the *Address* – 'recounting the grievances, which had led her to sever the ties which bound her to the Union' – to the convention. 'You never heard such cheers and shouts as rent the air, and it lasted so long,' she recalled.

From the adoption of the Constitution in 1787 to the secession of South Carolina in 1860, began Rhett, the United States' 'advance in wealth, prosperity, and power, has been with scarcely a parallel in the history of the world.' The 'great object' of forming the Union was 'defence against external aggressions,' which had been amply secured. The United States were safe and free, and Northern ships sailed every sea exporting Southern cash crops to every port. Despite its outward strength, however, the Union was imploding from 'discontent and contention.' In short, summarised Rhett, 'Our internal peace has not grown with our external prosperity.'

Twice in the past three decades – 1832 and 1852 – South Carolina had convened to react to 'the aggressions and unconstitutional wrongs, perpetrated by the people of the North on the people of the South.' Both times, South Carolina had agreed to a compromise, believing that it would resolve the conflict between the sections and restore harmony to the Union. 'But such hope and expectation, have proved to be vain,' claimed Rhett. 'Instead of producing forbearance, our acquiescence has only instigated new forms of aggression and outrage; and South Carolina, having again assembling her people in convention, has this day dissolved her connection with the States, constituting the United States.' The dissolution of the Union, long-feared but long-expected, had finally come to pass.

According to Rhett, 'The one great evil, from which all other evils have flowed, is the overthrow of the Constitution of the United States.' The federal government was no longer 'the government of confederated republics,' as it was founded, but 'a consolidated democracy.' Such a government was 'no longer a free government, but a despotism.' In fact, the federal government had become the same form of government that 'Great Britain attempted to set over our fathers; and which was resisted and defeated by a seven years' struggle for independence.' Throughout the *Address*, Rhett continued to draw parallels between the past revolution of 1776 and the present revolution of 1860, dubbing South Carolinians the true sons of the American Revolution and bestowing upon her the blessing of the Founding Fathers. One of the bitterest ironies and tragedies of the War Between the States was that Northerners and Southerners both believed that they were fighting for the foundational principles of American freedom. 'They fought for the heritage of freedom bequeathed to them by the Founding Fathers,' observes the Princeton historian James M. McPherson, author of *Drawn with the Sword*, *This Mighty Scourge*, and *The War That Forged a Nation*. 'North and South alike wrapped themselves in the mantle of 1776, but the two sides interpreted that heritage in opposite ways.'

'The Revolution of 1776 turned upon one great principle,' claimed Rhett, 'self-government – and self-taxation, the criterion of self-government.' In order to be free, explained Rhett, different people who were united under a common government must have the power to protect their separate and distinct interests, yet the interests of Great Britain and the Colonies had become 'different and antagonistic.' Great Britain's policy towards the Colonies was to exploit them as she did the rest of her empire, 'making them tributary to her wealth and power.' Great Britain had accumulated a high debt from her wars around the world, and intended to recoup the costs of empire from her Colonies. The Colonies, however, opposed British mercantilism and imperialism, desiring freedom from the 'burdens and wars of the mother country.' After all, the Colonies' charters, combined with the English Constitution, granted them the right of self-government, especially regarding the vital issue of taxation. These conflicting interests culminated in the Parliament's infamous assertion of supremacy over the Colonies – 'the power of legislating for the Colonies in all cases whatsoever' – an assertion which the South-Carolinian revolutionary Christopher Gadsden of 'Don't Tread On Me' fame denounced as 'an act that...asserted and maintained the absolute dominion of Great Britain.' This refusal to recognise their chartered rights drove the Colonies to independence. 'Our ancestors resisted the pretension,' declared Rhett. 'They refused to be a part of the consolidated government of Great Britain.'

Rhett stressed that the same causes which justified American secession in 1776 also justified Southern secession in 1860. 'The Southern States,' insisted Rhett, 'now stand exactly in the same position towards the Northern States that the Colonies did towards Great Britain.' Like Great Britain, the Northern States defied the Constitution and claimed 'omnipotence in legislation.' Like Great Britain, the Northern States recognised no constitutional limits upon their power except for the 'the general welfare,' a suitably elastic term of which they were the 'sole judges.' As Great Britain had infamously asserted against the Colonies, the Northern States claimed the power to legislate for the Southern States 'in all cases whatsoever.' The Union no longer resembled the federal republic that the Founding Fathers had created, leaving their sons no choice but to follow in the footsteps of their forefathers and declare their independence. 'Thus,' concluded Rhett, 'the government of the United States has become a consolidated government; and the people of the Southern States are compelled to meet the very despotism their fathers threw off in the Revolution of 1776.' According to Rhett, in declaring independence from tyranny as the Founding Fathers had done, Southerners were the true heirs to the American political tradition.

As the Revolutionary-War veteran Thomas Sumter boasted of South Carolinians during the Tariff Crisis, 'They all know, as their fathers and grandfathers knew, that, in this country, republicanism, in its true sense, was intended to mean, and did mean, that its possessors had both the right and the will to resist effectually unauthorised power, which in every shape means usurpation.' According to Sumter, 'It is a hard matter to enslave a free people, but such a people once enslaved, will hardly regain their liberty.'

As a part of its consolidation of power over the Colonies, the Parliament levied taxes to enrich British interests at the expence of American interests. The Colonies resisted these taxes, however, arguing that they possessed a constitutional and chartered right of self-government and thus self-taxation. The Colonies were represented only in their own legislatures, not in the Parliament, meaning that by the colonial charters and the English Constitution, the Parliament had no authority to tax them. 'Power of regulating trade...is power of ruining us – as bad as acknowledging them a supreme legislative in all cases whatsoever,' Christopher Gadsden grumbled to John Adams at the First Continental Congress. 'A right of regulating trade is a right of legislation, and a right of legislation in one case, is a right in all.' Even when the Colonies were offered representation in the Parliament, they refused to sacrifice their right of local self-government for minority representation in a foreign legislature. 'Between taxation without any representation, and taxation without a representation adequate to protection, there was no difference,' explained Rhett. 'In neither case would the Colonies tax themselves. Hence, they refused to pay the taxes laid by the British Parliament.' The particular issue in 1776 was self-taxation, i.e. 'no taxation without representation,' but the principle was self-government. Rhett would return to this crucial differentiation between the superficial issues and fundamental causes in arguing that secession was about far more than just preserving slavery.

Just as Great Britain attempted to consolidate its power over the Colonies by taxing them without representation – thereby depriving them of their right of self-government – so the North was attempting to use 'the vital matter of taxation' to consolidate her power over the South and rule her as well. Since the Southern States had become a minority in the United States, their representation in the Congress was powerless to prevent 'unjust taxation' in the form of protectionist tariffs. Indeed, for over forty years, 'subserving the interests of the North,' rather than collecting revenue, had been the agenda behind federal taxes. Since the South was an agrarian economy which exported most of her production (cash crops such as cotton, tobacco, and rice) and imported most of her consumption (manufactures such as machinery and textiles), her economic interest was in free trade. The industrial Northern economy, however, had no strong comparative advantages in anything and depended on the federal government for support. Tariffs, by taxing the imports on which the South relied, protected Northern industries from competition but imposed artificially inflated prices upon the South. The South was forced to buy the manufactures she needed in a protected market (choosing between higher prices to parasitic Northern industries or higher taxes to a government which no longer represented them) and sell the cash crops she produced in a competitive market – to buy dearly and sell nearly, so to speak. At the same time, by reducing American demand for foreign imports and foreign currency, tariffs also depressed foreign demand for American exports (in this case, 60% to 90% of which were Southern cash crops) and devalued the pounds and francs which Southern exporters had to redeem for dollars. 'They are taxed by the people of the North *for their benefit*,' Rhett said of Southerners, 'exactly as the people of Great Britain taxed our ancestors in the British Parliament for their benefit.'

The Independent Institute's Jeffrey R. Hummel agrees with Rhett's criticism of the tariff in *Emancipating Slaves, Enslaving Free Men: A History of the American Civil War*. 'At least with respect to the tariff's adverse impact, Southerners were not only absolutely correct but displayed a sophisticated understanding of economics,' argues Hummel. 'The tariff was inefficient; it not only redistributed wealth from farmers and planters to manufacturers and laborers but overall made the country poorer.'

Rhett's protest that tariffs enriched the North at the expence of the South was nothing new in 1860; tariffs had been controversial between the North and the South as early as 1787. At the Constitutional Convention, South-Carolina delegate Charles Pinckney had warned that 'the two great divisions of Northern and Southern interests,' among many other 'minute' economic differences within the United States, 'would be a source of oppressive regulations if no check to a bare majority should be provided.' Since 'the power of regulating commerce was a pure concession on the part of the Southern States,' and the Southern States 'did not need the protection of the Northern States at present,' Pinckney proposed that commercial regulations (not only protectionist tariffs, but also navigation acts) require a two-thirds majority in the Congress. South-Carolina delegate Charles C. Pinckney agreed with his cousin that 'it was the true interest of the Southern States to have no regulation of commerce,' but admitted that the 'liberality' of the Northeastern delegates had overcome his 'prejudices.' South-Carolina delegate Pierce Butler quipped that 'the interest of [the Southern States] and the [North-] Eastern States were as different as the interests of Russia and Turkey,' but was willing to concede to a bare majority on commercial regulation for the purpose of 'conciliating the affection of the [North-] Eastern States.' South-Carolina delegate John Rutledge, who advised his fellow Southern delegates to 'take a permanent view of the subject, and not look at the present moment only,' trusted that Northerners would act honourably and that the Constitution would prevent any abuse of commercial regulation. 'It did not follow, from a grant of the power to regulate trade, that it would be abused,' argued Rutledge. 'At the worst, a navigation act could bear hard only a little while on the Southern States.'

In the end, the South Carolinians came to an accord with the New Englanders, granting the permanent power of commercial regulation and getting a temporary extension of the slave trade – much to the chagrin of the Virginian George Mason and the Marylander Luther Martin. It was a dark bargain which the South Carolinians came to regret, as the slave trade was abolished a generation after the Constitution was ratified while commercial regulation quickly turned from the promotion of the general welfare to the economic exploitation of the Southern minority by the Northern majority. 'Was it consistent with reason, with wisdom, with policy, to suppose in a legislature where a majority of persons sat whose interests were greatly different from ours, that we had the slightest chance of receiving adequate advantages?' asked Rawlins Lowndes as South Carolina's General Assembly considered calling a convention to ratify the Constitution. 'The interest of the Northern States would so predominate as to divest us of any pretensions to the title of a republic.'

'There is another evil, in the condition of the Southern towards the Northern States,' continued Rhett, 'which our ancestors refused to bear towards Great Britain.' Each Colony not only taxed herself, but also spent the taxes she collected on herself. If the Colonies had submitted to taxation without representation, then their taxes would have been spent throughout the British Empire instead of at home. Although this redistribution – 'impoverishing the people from whom taxes are collected, and...enriching those who receive the benefit of the expenditure' – was resisted by the Colonies, the North had, as with oppressive taxation, succeeded against the South where Great Britain had failed. Federal tax revenue, collected primarily from the South, often financed so-called internal improvements in the North, which ranged from legitimate public works to the nineteenth-century equivalent of pork-barrel spending. Either way, Southerners saw their money drained across the Mason-Dixon Line. 'The people of the Southern States,' concluded Rhett, 'are not only taxed for the benefit of the Northern States, but after the taxes are collected, three-fourths of them are expended at the North.'

This exploitative scheme of taxing the South and spending in the North had, argued Rhett, left the South 'provincial' and 'paralyzed' her growth: the North got richer while the South got poorer. One of many indicators of this trend was the decline of South Carolina's maritime trade, an industry that had prospered in the Colony but had been 'annihilated' in the Union due to navigation laws which gave the North a legal monopoly on shipbuilding and shipping. To prove his point, Rhett cited figures contrasting the prosperity of the Colony of South Carolina with the poverty of the State of South Carolina.

As Charles C. Pinckney had predicted at the Constitutional Convention, 'If [the Southern States] are to form so considerable a minority, and the regulation of trade is to be given to the general government, they will be nothing more than overseers for the Northern States,' and as Rawlins Lowndes warned in the General Assembly, 'Behold how our kind friends in the North were determined soon to tie up our hands, and drain us of what we had!'

'No man can, for a moment,' concluded Rhett, 'believe that our ancestors intended to establish over their posterity, exactly the same sort of government they had overthrown.' Indeed, the 'great object' of the Constitution was 'to secure the great end of the Revolution – a limited free government.' Under the Constitution, 'general and common' interests were delegated by the States to the federal government, and 'sectional and local' interests were reserved by the States. This division of power between national and sectional spheres was the only way to unite separate, distinct sections with differing interests such as the North and the South. Unfortunately, Northern treachery and Southern complacency had resulted in the erosion of constitutional limitations on federal power. 'By gradual and steady encroachments on the part of the people of the North, and acquiescence on the part of the South, the limitations in the Constitution have been swept away,' recounted Rhett. 'The government of the United States has become consolidated, with a claim of limitless powers in its operations.'

Rhett viewed Northern 'agitations' against slavery as nothing more than the 'natural results of the consolidation of the government.' Since the North, with her 'interested and perverted' construction of the Constitution, had exceeded national interests and was encroaching upon sectional interests, it was inevitable that she would eventually 'assume to possess power over all the institutions of the country' and 'assail and overthrow the institution of slavery in the South.' Slavery, furthermore, was the only issue against which the North could be united, because it was the biggest difference between the North and the South. 'It would not be united, on any matter common to the whole Union – in other words, on any constitutional subject,' explained Rhett, 'for on such subjects divisions are as likely to exist in the North as in the South.' Because slavery was a 'strictly sectional interest' of the South, however, opposition to it overcame the differences of opinion in the North over other issues, such as economic policy or constitutional interpretation. 'If this could be made the criterion of parties at the North, the North could be united in its power,' continued Rhett, 'and thus carry out its measures of sectional ambition, encroachment, and aggrandisement.' Indeed, Thomas Jefferson and James Madison had observed this ploy at the time of the Missouri Crisis, when the Federalist Party challenged the admission of slave-holding Missouri to the Union in the hopes of restricting Southern political power and reclaiming the North on a new sectional issue. 'To build up their sectional predominance in the Union, the Constitution must first be abolished by construction,' concluded Rhett, 'but that being done, the consolidation of the North, to rule the South by the tariff and slavery issues, was in the obvious course of things.'

In 1820, Charles Pinckney gave a speech in the House of Representatives, warning that the Missouri Crisis presaged a conflict between the North and the South. 'However much I wish to see Missouri admitted, as she ought, on equal terms with the other States, this is a very unimportant object to her compared with keeping the Constitution inviolate,' announced Pinckney. 'On the subject of the Constitution, no compromise ought ever to be made!'

Rhett made a crucial distinction between the overarching cause of the conflict between the North and the South ('the overthrow of the Constitution' and 'the consolidation of the government') and the particular

369

issues which stemmed from that overarching cause (tariffs and slavery). As Rhett put it, the North wanted 'to rule the South by the tariff and slavery issues,' just as Great Britain wanted to rule the Colonies through 'the vital matter of taxation.' In other words, the cause of the conflict was the Northern pretension to rule the South; the issues of tariffs and slavery were merely means to that end. After the war, ex-President Jefferson Davis and ex-Vice President Alexander H. Stephens, along with countless other unreconstructed Confederates, reiterated Rhett's argument in their unapologetic apologias. According to Davis, slavery was 'in no wise the cause of the conflict, but only an incident' – the 'intolerable grievance' being 'the systematic and persistent struggle to deprive the Southern States of equality in the Union.' According to Stephens, slavery was 'unquestionably the occasion of the war...but it was not the real cause, the *causa causans* of it' – the real cause being 'federation, on the one side, and consolidation, on the other.' For differentiating between outer events (slavery, tariffs, etc.) and underlying causes (self-government, States' rights, etc.) as the Father of Secession himself did in a key primary source on the secession of South Carolina, Davis and Stephens have been accused of delusion and deceit. In the neo-conservative *A Patriot's History of the United States*, Davis and Stephens' postbellum crusade to vindicate the Confederate cause is described as 'philosophizing, denials, obfuscation, and constitutional sophistries,' and the term 'rights to own slaves' is suggested as a substitute for the term 'states' rights.'

The Constitution, reflected Rhett, was an 'experiment...in uniting under one government, peoples living in different climates, and having different pursuits and institutions.' In such a constitution, trust between the States was paramount, for the Constitution could not limit itself and would ultimately be interpreted and enforced by the States. 'It matters not how carefully the limitations of such a government be laid down in the Constitution,' admitted Rhett. 'Its success must, at least, depend upon the good faith of the parties to the constitutional compact, in enforcing them.'

As Charles C. Pinckney explained at South Carolina's Ratification Convention, 'On them (I mean the State systems) rests the general fabric: on their foundation is this magnificent structure of freedom erected, each depending upon, supporting, and protecting the other.' It did not matter how strictly the Constitution was written. The South-Carolinian framers John Rutledge and Charles Pinckney had demanded an 'exact enumeration' of powers and the South-Carolinian ratifiers had clearly stipulated 'that no section or paragraph of the said Constitution warrants a construction that the States do not retain every power not expressly reserved by them and vested in the general government of the Union.' Despite these enumerations and reservations, well-meaning errors and self-serving rationalisations had inevitably arisen. 'It is not in the power of human language to exclude false inferences, constructions, and perversions in any Constitution,' noted Rhett. 'And when vast sectional interests are to be subserved, involving the appropriation of countless millions of money, it has not been the usual experience of mankind, that words on parchment can arrest power.' The experiment of the Constitution, argued Rhett, 'rested on the assumption that power would yield to faith – that integrity would be stronger than interest; and that thus, the limitations of the Constitution would be observed.' The experiment, though 'fairly made,' had finally 'failed.'

At South Carolina's Ratification Convention, Charles C. Pinckney called attention to the 'striking difference that there is between the inhabitants of the Northern and Southern States.' According to Pinckney, 'The Southern citizen beholds, with a kind of surprise, the simple manners of the [North-] East, and is too often induced to entertain undeserved opinions of the apparent purity of the Quaker; while they, in turn, seem concerned at what they term the extravagance and dissipation of their Southern friends, and reprobate, as unpardonable moral and political evil, the dominion they hold over a part of the human race.' Pinckney believed that the North and the South's 'marks of distinction in the habits and manners' were 'as strong' as the North and the South's marks of distinction in 'climates and productions.'

From the very beginning, the South had tried to limit the federal government 'within the orbit prescribed by the Constitution.' From when Senator Pierce Butler (a framer in Philadelphia and a ratifier in Charleston) stormed out of the very first Senate in protest of a proposed protectionist tariff and threatened the secession of South Carolina, through when South Carolina nullified the Tariff of Abominations and prepared for war with President Andrew Jackson, and up to when South Carolina actually seceded from the Union over the election of a revolutionary sectional candidate to the presidency, the South had always faithfully honoured the constitutional compact. 'All power being immediately derived from the people, and the State governments being the basis of the general [government], it will easily be in their power to interfere, and to prevent its injuring or invading their rights,' Charles Pinckney assured South Carolina's General Assembly, summarising what would become Southern constitutional orthodoxy. 'The distinction which has been taken between the nature of a federal and State government appeared to be conclusive – that in the former, no powers could be executed, or assumed, but such as were expressly delegated; that in the latter, the indefinite power was given to the government, except on points that were by express compact reserved to the people.' The North, however – from when the Essex Junto plotted to consolidate power by destroying Virginia, through when Senator Daniel Webster reversed his position on tariffs at the behest of industrial interests in Massachusetts, and up to when the Republican Party fanned the flames of the sectional conflict in order to win the presidency – had failed to honour the compact, upsetting the balance of power between the federal government and States at every opportunity.

Indeed, at the Second Continental Congress, South-Carolina delegate Edward Rutledge expressed his disdain for Northern ambition and worried that the North would consolidate power in whatever union the States formed between themselves. 'The idea of destroying all provincial distinctions and making everything of the most minute kind bend to what they call the good of the whole,' worried Rutledge, 'is in other terms to say that these Colonies must be subject to the government of the [North-] Eastern Provinces.' Rutledge held 'the force of their arms' to be 'exceeding cheap,' but confessed that he dreaded 'their overruling influence in council' as well as 'their low cunning, and those leveling principles which men without character and without fortune in general possess.'

As Edward Rutledge feared, Rhett described how in a 'reckless lust for power' the North had 'absorbed' the entire Constitution into the Preamble, claiming that the United States was a nation with a supreme government instead of a federation with a limited government. 'If nothing else, this alone would damn and ought to damn the Constitution,' objected John Rutledge to such a government at the Constitutional Convention. 'Will any State agree to be bound hand and foot in this manner?'

The irony of this sophistic, solipsistic Northern construction, noted Rhett, was that in attempting to strengthen the federal government, it had actually weakened it. The federal government, explained Rhett, was intended to have authority only over 'objects of common interests to all sections.' This, insisted Rhett, was where its 'strength consists.' If the 'scope' of its power were expanded over 'sectional or local interests,' however, it would necessarily face 'opposition and resistance' – the very sort of opposition and resistance which Rhett had led his whole life and which had finally come to a head. Expanding federal power from national interests (the true meaning of the 'general welfare') to sectional interests meant that the minority would not possess the power of self-protection against a potentially tyrannous majority, thus 'necessarily' turning the government into a 'despotism.' 'The majority, constituted from those who do not represent these sectional or local interests, will controul and govern them,' warned Rhett. 'A free people cannot submit to such a government.' As federal power expanded from the national to the sectional, opposition and resistance would weaken the legitimacy of the government. The key to a strong Union, however, was not for the majority section to tyrannise the minority section, but for both sections to cooperate for the common good and respect each other's differences. 'The more it abstains from usurped powers, and the more faithfully it adheres to the limitations of the Constitution, the stronger it is made,' explained Rhett. 'The Northern people have had neither the wisdom nor the faith to perceive, that to observe the limitations of the Constitution was the only way to its perpetuity.' In other words, if the purposes for which the Union was founded, as established in the Constitution, were no longer upheld, then the Union no longer served any purpose and was not worth upholding.

Under a consolidated government of unlimited power – one which made no distinction between national and sectional interests – conflicts would inevitably arise between differing parts of the country, and the North and the South were no exception. 'Under such a government, there must, of course, be many and endless "irrepressible conflicts" between the two great sections of the Union,' explained Rhett, employing the ominous expression of the Republican luminary William H. Seward. Having weakened limited government with liberal constructions of the Constitution, Rhett warned that the Northern majority was now poised to exploit the Southern economy, degrade Southern culture, subvert Southern society, and consolidate all power over the South. Only the goodwill upon which the States created the Union could protect the liberty and security of the South, yet South Carolinians had come to regard Northerners as treacherous and untrustworthy. 'The same faithlessness which has abolished the Constitution of the United States, will not fail to carry out the sectional purposes for which it has been abolished,' held Rhett. Given that 'all confidence in the North is lost by the South,' Rhett claimed that it was 'too late to reform or restore' the Union. 'The faithlessness of the North for half a century,' he concluded, 'has opened a gulf of separation between the North and the South which no promises nor engagements can fill.' Therefore, due to the destruction of the Constitution, the abandonment of the good faith necessary to sustain a compact, and an imbalance of power between the sections of the Union, the South's only hope for 'peace and liberty' was in 'independence of the North.'

Like all Southerners – especially South Carolinians – Rhett was extremely sensitive about the honour of his State, which had acquired a reputation for extremism over the years. The *Address* was a prime opportunity for Rhett to redeem South Carolina and her uncompromising course in the eyes of her Southern sisters. South Carolina had staunchly defended States' rights and resisted Northern consolidation for the past thirty years, yet had been abandoned by the rest of the South and condemned by the North. 'The repeated efforts made by South Carolina, in a wise conservatism, to arrest the progress of the general government in its fatal progress to consolidation, have been unsupported, and she has been denounced as faithless to the obligations of the Constitution, by the very men and States who were destroying it by their usurpations,' stewed Rhett. Given his role in those repeated efforts, Rhett could not have helped feeling some sense of satisfaction.

'It cannot be believed, that our ancestors would have assented to any union whatever with the people of the North, if the feelings and opinions now existing among them, had existed when the Constitution was formed,' argued Rhett. 'There was then no tariff – no fanaticism concerning negroes.' Indeed, Founding Fathers like the Rutledges and the Pinckneys, who had framed the Constitution in Philadelphia and ratified it in Charleston, assured skeptical South Carolinians that the new Constitution did not contain any of the evils which Rhett's generation were now facing. The South-Carolinian framers and ratifiers, trusting that the Northerners would abide by the Constitution and not abuse their powers, had conceded some of their State's own interests in the greater interest of the general welfare. 'The idea that the Southern States would be made to pay that tribute to their Northern confederates which they had refused to pay to Great Britain,' continued Rhett, 'or that the institution of African slavery would be made the grand basis of a sectional organisation of the North to rule the South, never crossed the imaginations of our ancestors.' Rhett pointed out that slavery was one of the building blocks of the Constitution: slavery then existed in the Southern, Middle, and Northern States; the slave trade had been extended for twenty years; three-fifths of all slaves in each State were counted in assessing federal representation and apportioning federal taxes. 'There is nothing in the proceedings of the Constitution, to show that the Southern States would have formed any other Union,' held Rhett, 'and still less, that they would have formed a Union with more powerful non-slaveholding States, having majority in both branches of the legislature of the government.'

Since the adoption of the Constitution, however, the North and the South had separated politically, economically, culturally, and socially/racially; the Union formed by the Founding Fathers was no more. 'That identity of feelings, interests, and institutions which once existed is gone,' explained Rhett. 'They are now divided, between agricultural, manufacturing, and commercial States; between slave-holding and non-slaveholding States.' Given these changes, the North and the South had become 'totally different peoples,' making 'equality between the sections' impossible. 'We but imitate the policy of our fathers,' declared Rhett, 'in dissolving a union with non-slaveholding confederates, and seeking a confederation with slave-holding States.'

Rhett believed that the liberty and security of a society could only be preserved by that society itself. Outside of that society, such power would be perverted and abused. 'No people can ever expect to preserve its rights and liberties, unless these be in its own custody,' claimed Rhett. 'To plunder and oppress, when plunder and oppression can be protected with impunity, seems to be the natural order of things.' At South Carolina's Ratification Convention, James Lincoln stressed this point. 'What have you been contending for these ten years past? Liberty! What is liberty? The power of governing yourselves,' charged Lincoln. 'If you adopt this constitution have you the power? No: you give it into the hands of a set of men who live one thousand miles distant from you.' According to Lincoln, 'let the people but once trust their liberties out of their own hands,' and the result will be 'haughty, imperious aristocracy; and ultimately, a tyrannical monarchy.'

Rhett believed that the controversy over slavery was a prime example of why a society must preserve its own liberty and security – that is, why it must possess the power of self-protection. 'Experience has proved,' argued Rhett, 'that slave-holding States cannot be safe in a subjection to non-slaveholding States.' The British colonies of the West Indies and the French colony of Santo Domingo, where radical abolitionism had been implemented in its purest form, had collapsed into poverty and savagery. 'The fairest portions of the world,' lamented Rhett, 'have been turned into wildernesses, and the most civilised and prosperous communities have been impoverished and ruined by anti-slavery fanaticism.' The fate of Santo Domingo was particularly terrifying to Southerners. When the Jacobins, at the helm of the French Revolution, decreed 'liberty, equality, and fraternity' for the slaves in French colonies, the black population rebelled, wiped out the white and mixed-race population, and repelled efforts to reclaim the island. By nationalising sectional issues such as slavery – in effect, denying the Southern States the power of self-protection – Rhett warned that the North was threatening the South with the same fate as Santo Domingo.

Rhett claimed that the pro-North/anti-South Republican Party had made its intentions against slavery perfectly clear – particularly in the nomination of Abraham Lincoln as a presidential candidate. 'United as a section in the late presidential election,' observed Rhett, 'they have elected as the exponent of their party, one who has openly declared that all the States of the United States must be made *free States or slave States*.' Rhett acknowledged that there were 'various shades of anti-slavery hostility' and a multitude of 'disclaimers and professions' from the Republicans. Indeed, Lincoln himself equivocated on the issue depending upon his audience, telling Northerners that a house divided against itself cannot stand and that the Union could not be half-slave and half-free, but telling Southerners that he had no authority or intention to abolish slavery and just wanted to keep the Territories free for white men. Rhett stressed, however, that the 'inexorable logic' of the Republican Party's premises would eventually end in abolition. 'If it is right to preclude or abolish slavery in a Territory,' asked Rhett, 'why should it be allowed to remain in the States?' Since the Supreme Court's *Dred Scott v. Sanford* decision ruled that the Congress had no constitutional authority to prohibit slavery in the Territories, prohibiting slavery in the Territories was just as unconstitutional as prohibiting slavery in the States. 'When it is considered that the Northern States will soon have the power to make that Court what they please, and that the Constitution never has been any barrier whatever to their exercise of power,' warned Rhett, 'what check can there be, in the unrestrained counsels of the North, to emancipation?'

South Carolina had not signed up for a government controulled by the North with power over slavery, however. As Pierce Butler made plain at the Constitutional Convention, 'The security the Southern States want is that their negroes may not be taken from them, which some gentlemen within or without doors, have a very good mind to do.' When Northern delegates proposed that in the apportionment of representation and taxation slaves should be counted as property rather than people, Butler protested that 'the labour of a slave in South Carolina was as productive and valuable as that of a freeman in Massachusetts, that as wealth was the great means of defence and utility to the nation they were equally valuable to it with freemen; and that consequently an equal representation ought to be allowed for them in a government which was instituted principally for the protection of property, and was itself to be supported by property.' Charles Pinckney agreed that the slave population should be fully counted, adding that 'it will also be politic with regard to the Northern States, as taxation is to keep pace with representation.' When Northern delegates challenged the Transatlantic slave trade, John Rutledge responded that 'religion and humanity had nothing to do with this question' and that 'interest alone is the governing principle with nations.' Reminding the Northern delegates that 'the true question at present is whether the Southern States shall or shall not be parties to the Union,' Rutledge argued that 'if the Northern States consult their interest, they will not oppose the increase of slaves which will increase the commodities of which they will become the carriers.' Rutledge was confident that Carolinians and Georgians 'will never be such fools as to give up so important an interest.' Charles C. Pinckney explained that 'it would be unequal to require South Carolina and Georgia to confederate on such unequal terms' and that a constitution which restricted the slave trade would never obtain 'the assent of their constituents.' In the end, the Constitution counted three-fifths of a State's slave population towards taxation and representation, extended the slave trade by twenty years, and outlawed fugitive slaves.

Today, with slavery 150 years dead, Rhett's staunch support for human property seems repulsive. Slavery was indeed a repulsive institution, physically and psychologically abusive to blacks as well as morally degrading to and disgraceful for whites. 'We have sunk the Africans and their descendants below the standard of humanity,' declared Colonel John Laurens, a young South Carolinian in the Revolutionary War, 'and almost rendered them incapable of that blessing which equal Heaven bestowed upon us all.' In the context of the political, economic, cultural, and social/racial conflict between the North and the South, however, there are four reasons why slave-holders and secessionists like Rhett were justified against the abolitionists and Unionists.

First and foremost is Italian historian Raimondo Luraghi's dictum that the past should be judged *juxta propria principia*, or 'according to its own principles.' By modern standards of egalitarianism and individualism, slavery is seen as an abomination, but by far older standards of Rhett's day and age, slavery was an institution which had existed throughout all of human history (including/especially the esteemed classical civilisations of Greece and Rome) and had been planted in the New World for over three centuries. 'For that some should rule and others be ruled is a thing not only necessary, but expedient,' reasoned Aristotle, the Father of Western Philosophy. 'From the hour of their birth, some are marked out for subjection, others for rule.' In the Bible, slavery was sanctioned by the Law (the Jewish tribes owned slaves) and unchallenged by the Gospel (Jesus never spoke against slavery), leaving slave-holders with clear consciences as Christians. 'Slaves, be obedient to those who are your masters according to the flesh, with fear and trembling, in the sincerity of your heart, as to Christ,' Saint Paul instructed the Ephesian church. 'Masters, grant to your slaves justice and fairness, knowing that you too have a Master in Heaven.' Under the Constitution, slavery was a clearly protected right of the States – no power over slavery having been delegated to the federal government. At the Constitutional Convention, Connecticut delegate Oliver Ellsworth held that 'the morality or wisdom of slavery are considerations belonging to the States themselves,' and at Massachusetts' Ratification Convention, one delegate quipped that Southerners 'would call us pumpkins' if they overheard any talk among the Yankees that the Constitution permitted the national abolition of slavery. On both sides of the Atlantic, the science was settled that there were physical and mental differences between the races, particularly between white (i.e. Caucasian) and black (i.e. sub-Saharan African). Charles Darwin, born to an abolitionist family and one of the fathers of modern science, conceded the existence of 'civilised races' and 'savage races,' which was easily explainable through his theory of evolution: different human groups (subspecies) had adapted to different environments. 'The various races, when carefully compared and measured, differ much from each other,' reported Darwin, not only cataloguing evolutionary differences in skin colour and other physical features, but also in 'the form and capacity of the skull and even the convolutions of the brain,' 'constitution,' 'acclimitisation,' 'liability to certain diseases,' and even 'mental characteristics' such as 'emotions' and 'intellectual faculties.' According to Darwin, 'It would be an endless task to specify the numerous points of difference.'

In Rhett's time and place, slavery was not seen as the abomination that it is today, but as a cornerstone of an established, inherited way of life – a way of life which Southerners felt was worth fighting for. In *The Southern Tradition at Bay: A History of Postbellum Thought*, the paleo-conservative sage Richard M. Weaver argues that 'Southern feudalism,' or plantation society, cultivated 'self-sufficiency,' *'noblesse oblige,'* 'social distinctions' founded in 'respect and loyalty' (as opposed to 'envy and hatred'), and 'kinship with the soil' – the combined effect of which 'gave to the infant republic a wealth of leadership such as might have graced the golden age of another nation...a veritable Plutarchian list of heroes.' Indeed, it was the Southern plantation that fathered many of America's Founders – men such as George Washington (the Father of His Country), Thomas Jefferson (the Father of Democracy), James Madison (the Father of the Constitution), George Mason (the Father of the Bill of Rights), Patrick Henry (the Father of the Revolution), and many more noble men who won American independence and established American self-government. In *The Rise and Fall of the Plantation South*, Raimondo Luraghi traces the history of this 'seigneurial civilization' in the Old South, which he describes as 'a world so far from us, so difficult to understand, endowed with paternalistic institutions, the patriarchal family, the predominance of country over own, [and] the old-fashioned, preindustrial economy.' According to Luraghi, the 'Elizabethan, classically minded, aristocratically individualistic South' was doomed to fight with – and lose to – the 'puritanical, trade-minded, Calvinistic North.'

In glaring contrast to this tradition, Northerners (squeezing every penny of profit out of the federal treasury and Southern pockets, working an industrial proletariat with a lower standard of living than that of the slaves, and bearing no real knowledge of/interest in/or care for the Southern way of life) damned lawful, pious slave-holders as criminals and sinners, denied the scientific consensus on racial inequality for an ideological belief in racial equality, and demanded that slave-holders perform the vastest self-disinheritance in history with nothing but the dire, dismal Santo Domingo and West Indies as precedents. Of course, in the end, the ruling class of the Old South, facing its own extermination, did accept emancipation in order to recruit more soldiers and court European intervention – 'the swan song of the seigneurial class,' according to Raimondo Luraghi. 'Certainly, it is all too easy to scorn the Confederacy because it offered emancipation when it was almost doomed,' comments Luraghi. 'One only has to think that slave-holders were speaking of their own expropriation, and that very rarely in history has an exploiting class ever arrived at such a degree of intellectual independence and self-denial.'

Anti-slavery maximalism was not a reasonable or responsible approach to abolishing slavery (indeed, it was nothing more than political strategy to get elected in the North and never meant to be taken seriously by the South), and thus it was understandable and inevitable that Southerners, who lived in an older world of honour where challenges were answered and insults were avenged, would react with resistance. Indeed, this 'atmosphere of crisis and confrontation' and 'New England-induced hatred of the South' was so counterproductive at actually abolishing slavery that in popular historian Thomas Fleming's myth-busting *A Disease in the Public Mind: A New Understanding of Why We Fought the Civil War*, he titles his chapter on the Northern anti-slavery movement 'How Not To Abolish Slavery.'

In his masterful *Battle Cry of Freedom: The Civil War Era*, the neo-abolitionist historian James M. McPherson argues that in this crisis and confrontation over slavery, the election of Abraham Lincoln (with a one-sided sectional agenda, as opposed to a broad-based national agenda) was indeed a 'revolution,' and that Southern secession was, in fact, a 'counter-revolution.' According to McPherson, Southerners seceded 'to preserve traditional rights and values...to protect their constitutional liberties against the perceived Northern threat to overthrow them,' and to uphold their 'concept of republicanism' (which had resisted nineteenth-century industrialisation and democratisation and retained an eighteenth-century agrarian and aristocratic ethos). 'With complete sincerity,' concludes

McPherson, 'the South fought to preserve its vision of the republic of the Founding Fathers – a government of limited powers that protected the rights of property and whose constituency comprised an independent gentry and yeomanry of the white race undisturbed by large cities, heartless factories, restless free workers, and class conflict.'

The second reason that slave-holders and secessionists like Rhett were justified is that slavery itself was, as John Crowe Ransom observed in the landmark *I'll Take My Stand: The South and the Agrarian Tradition*, 'monstrous enough in theory, but more often than not, humane in practice.' Scholars such as Ulrich B. Phillips, Eugene D. Genovese, Robert W. Fogel, and Stanley L. Engerman have found that slavery was not simply the nightmare from a hell dimension of popular imagination, but rather – as the slave-holders themselves maintained, in fact – a paternalistic institution in which masters and slaves formed one 'family' with mutual rights and duties. 'The Old South, black and white, created a historically unique kind of paternalist society,' explains Genovese, the erudite historian of the Old South, in his sweeping *Roll, Jordan, Roll: The World the Slaves Made*. 'Paternalism's insistence upon mutual obligations – duties, responsibilities, and ultimately even rights – implicitly recognized the slaves' humanity.' Fogel and Engerman, in their controversial *Time on the Cross: The Economics of American Negro Slavery*, actually found that Southern slave labour had a comparable standard of living and level of efficiency with Northern free labour, as well as that the horrors of '*droit du seigneur*' and 'selling down the river' were, for the most part, fables. This is not to romanticise slavery, which Phillips, Genovese, Fogel, and Engerman (and perhaps Rhett himself, who once personally interceded to stop the brutal whipping of a slave) stressed was inherently exploitative and abusive, but simply to reflect on it rationally, in its proper historical context, without the distortion of present-day emotions such as sanctimony or shame. In Phillips' famous phrase from the foundational *Life and Labor in the Old South*, 'All in all, the slave regime was a curious blend of force and concession, of arbitrary disposal by the master and self-direction by the slave, of tyranny and benevolence, of antipathy and affection.'

The third reason that slave-holders and secessionists like Rhett were justified is because his constitutional doctrine and political philosophy (which, in these times of majoritarian democracy and an unchecked, uncontroullable consolidated government, is needed more than ever) can be separated from his outdated social/racial views. As proof of the sincerity of his belief in the constitutional doctrine of States' rights, Rhett first raised those arguments in the midst of the Tariff Crisis (years before slavery became a national issue) and continued to make those arguments long after slavery had been abolished. Furthermore, throughout the 1850s and at the time of secession, slavery was a largely rhetorical issue (for instance, there were only twenty-six slaves in the disputed Territories and no chance of a slave economy taking root there) and was essentially a symbolic struggle between the Hamiltonian-statist North and the Jeffersonian-liberal South for political power. States' rights and slavery, though intertwined issues, were also independent of one another, yet if it were true that the right of secession were, as the Declaration of Independence proclaimed, 'unalienable,' that government derives its authority from the 'consent of the governed,' and that the people may 'alter or abolish' or 'throw off' any government to which they no longer consent, then Rhett's reasons for secession (even if they were simply to preserve slavery) were ultimately irrelevant. Jeffrey R. Hummel, in his groundbreaking libertarian-revisionist history, *Emancipating Slaves, Enslaving Free Men: A History of the American Civil War*, grasps this basic, yet elusive, truth. 'The Confederate revolution of 1861, despite deep commitment to the peculiar institution, clearly carried on the radical tradition of '76 in its drive toward self-determination, decentralization, and *laissez-faire*,' concludes Hummel. 'As a legal recourse, the legitimacy of secession was admittedly debatable...but as a revolutionary right, the legitimacy of secession is universal and unconditional.' Indeed, to drive this point home, Hummel quotes the anti-war abolitionist George W.

Bassett: 'The same principle that has always made me an uncompromising abolitionist, now makes me an uncompromising secessionist. It is the great natural and sacred right of self-government.'

The fourth reason that slave-holders and secessionists like Rhett were justified is that even if the sole cause of secession were the preservation of slavery (which, of course, would have been understandable and justifiable under the circumstances), the cause of the war which followed was certainly not the abolition of slavery. At the top level of the Northern war effort, the ruling Republican Party denied that its invasion was about abolishing slavery and insisted that it was about establishing the authority of the federal government. In his First Inaugural Address, President Abraham Lincoln repeated his longstanding position that he had 'no lawful right' nor even an 'inclination' to 'interfere with the institution of slavery in the States where it exists.' After Lincoln's unilateral, unconstitutional proclamation of war, the Congress passed the 'War Aims Resolution,' clarifying that the war was not for 'overthrowing or interfering with the rights and established institutions of those States,' but to 'defend and maintain the supremacy of the Constitution and to preserve the Union.' To Horace Greeley (the famous abolitionist editor of *The New York Tribune*, a Republican newspaper), Lincoln laid out his priorities in painstaking detail. 'My paramount object in this struggle is to save the Union, and is not either to save or to destroy slavery,' explained Lincoln. 'What I do about slavery, and the colored race, I do because I believe it helps to save the Union; and what I forebear, I forebear because I do not believe it would help to save the Union.'

In the middle level of the war effort, Northern commanders agreed with the Republican politicians that they were fighting to enforce the government's authority, not to free the slaves. 'Help me dodge the nigger,' General George B. McClellan confided to a friend. 'I am fighting to preserve the integrity of the Union ... To gain that end we cannot afford to raise up the negro question.' In public, McClellan declared, 'The people of the South should understand that we are not making war upon the institution of slavery.' Even the radical generals who eventually replaced the conservative McClellan agreed. General William T. Sherman, who believed that 'the question of the national integrity and slavery should be kept distinct,' frankly admitted, 'I would not, if I could, abolish or modify slavery.' General Ulysses S. Grant explained that he was fighting solely 'to put down the rebellion,' with 'no hobby of my own with regard to the negro, either to effect his freedom or continue his bondage.'

At the ground level of the war effort, Northern soldiers agreed with their commanders and the politicians. A New-York officer argued that the war was 'for the preservation of the Union, the putting down of armed rebellion,' and added that if the President 'gives way to these "Black Republicans," and makes it an abolition war...I for one shall be sorry that I ever lent a hand to it.' According to an Illinois private, 'I am the boy that can fight for my country, but not for the negroes.' When the prospect of emancipating and enlisting the slaves was raised, the troops revolted and desertions spiked. 'We don't want to fight side by side with the nigger,' insisted a New-York private. 'We think we are too superior a race for that.' A New-York officer explained that his troops were 'much dissatisfied' with the idea of a 'nigger war,' and that 'all are anxious to return to their homes for it was to preserve the Union that they volunteered.' An Illinois soldier grumbled about 'the cost of freeing the black devils' and added that 'I consider the life and happiness of my family or more value than any nigger.' An Illinois officer aptly described why both sides were fighting. 'We are fighting for the Union...a high and noble sentiment, but after all a sentiment,' he explained 'They are fighting for independence and are animated by passion and hatred against invaders.'

After studying 25,000 letters and 250 diaries from Federal and Confederate soldiers, Princeton historian James M. McPherson, author of *What They Fought For* and *For Cause and Comrades*, concludes that both sides were, in a sense, fighting over opposing interpretations of the American Revolution. Specifically, explains McPherson, while the Confederates 'fought for liberty and independence from what they regarded as a tyrannical government,' as well as 'the defense of home and hearth against an invading enemy,' the Federals fought for 'the conviction that preservation of the *United* States...was indeed the last, best hope for the survival of republican liberties in the Western world' and 'were willing to risk their lives for the Union, but not black freedom.'

In sum, slave-holders and secessionists like Rhett should be viewed not from our present looking backward, but from his present looking forward. This is the only way to understand the past – anything else is, at best, the error of oversimplification, or at worst, the sin of politicisation.

Slavery was certainly not the sole cause of conflict between the North and the South, continued Rhett in his *Address*. In addition to economic issues like the tariff and internal improvements, the North and the South clashed over opposing political philosophies. As Rawlins Lowndes had reminded his fellow South Carolinians, Northerners were 'governed by prejudices and ideas extremely different from ours.' 'Not only their fanaticism,' claimed Rhett, 'but their erroneous ideas of the principles of free governments, render it doubtful whether, if separated from the South, they can maintain a free government amongst themselves.' According to Rhett, the North had abandoned small-r republicanism and small-f federalism, and had instead embraced a 'free society' of egalitarianism and individualism. 'Numbers, with them, is the great element of free government,' explained Rhett. 'A majority is infallible and omnipotent.' The whole purpose of constitutions, however, was to limit the power of the majority and protect the liberty and security of the minority. 'The very object of all constitutions, in free popular government,' argued Rhett, 'is to restrain the majority.' To the egalitarian, individualist North, however, constitutions were not blessings to be upheld, but 'unrighteous inventions' which limited the 'will of the majority.' In a single, small society with 'identity of interests and pursuits,' such as an ancient Greek city-state, the absence of a constitution was 'harmless,' as there was unanimity among the polity. In a larger society, however, such as an American State, and especially in a 'vast confederacy' such as the United States, 'various and conflicting interests and pursuits' necessitated a constitution; otherwise, the government would become a 'remorseless despotism' of the majority over the minority.

'Notwithstanding self-serving rhetoric, the slave-holders did believe themselves to be defending the ramparts of Christianity, constitutional republicanism, and social order against Northern and European apostasy, secularism, and social and political radicalism,' admits Eugene D. Genovese, author of *The Mind of the Master Class: History and Faith in the Southern Slaveholders' Worldview*. 'Viewing the free states, they saw vicious Negrophobia and racial discrimination and a cruelly exploited white working class.' According to Genovese, 'The Transatlantic revolutionary movement of 1789-1848 proposed a new understanding of freedom as the freedom of the individual, but slave-holders, slaves, and non-slaveholding whites all descended from cultures that viewed family, clan, and community as more important than the individual.'

Rhett declared that it was such a majoritarian despotism from which South Carolina was seceding. 'We are vindicating the great cause of free government, more important, perhaps, to the world, than the existence of all the United States.' Secession, insisted Rhett, was but a peaceful dissolution of bonds between sovereignties – a declaration of independence, not a declaration of war. 'In separating from them, we invade no rights – no interest of theirs,' stressed Rhett. 'We violate no obligation or duty to them.' Indeed, in seceding from the Union, South Carolina was doing nothing more than repealing the act of ratification for a constitution which she had helped frame and by which she originally acceded to the Union. 'As separate, independent States in convention, we made the Constitution of the United States with them; and as separate, independent States, each State acting for itself, we adopted it,' explained Rhett. 'South Carolina, acting in her sovereign capacity, now thinks proper to secede from the Union.' Rhett denied that the States sacrificed their sovereignty to the Union. 'She did not part with her sovereignty in adopting the Constitution.' Indeed, since sovereignty was a State's 'life,' it was 'the last thing a State can be pressured to surrender.' Even then, such a serious sacrifice could not be signified by mere 'inference,' as the North interpreted the Preamble, but by nothing less than a 'clear and express grant.'

As that inimitable, irrepressible old Virginian, John Randolph of Roanoke, quipped, 'Asking one of the States to surrender part of her sovereignty is like asking a lady to surrender part of her chastity.'

Rhett scoffed at this Northern attempt to construe away something as fundamental as the sovereignty of the States and sighed at the Northerners' predictability. 'It is not at all surprising that those who have construed away all the limitations of the Constitution, should also by construction, claim the annihilation of the sovereignty of the States,' remarked Rhett. 'Having abolished all barriers to their omnipotence, by their faithless constructions in the operations of the general government, it is most natural that they should endeavor to do the same towards us in the States.'

All told, concluded Rhett, the North had violated the Constitution so pervasively that it was no longer a 'compact' at all, and certainly no longer 'morally obligatory' upon the States. According to Rhett, the North, by breaking the trust of the compact, was the true disunionist section. 'South Carolina,' declared Rhett, 'deeming the compact not only violated in particular features, but entirely abolished by her Northern confederates, withdraws herself as a party from its obligations.' Yet the North, noted Rhett, seeing an opportunity to consummate her longstanding lust for dominion over the Union, was refusing South Carolina this basic right – the freedom to leave. 'They desire to establish a sectional despotism, not only omnipotent in Congress, but omnipotent over the States,' raged Rhett, 'and as if to manifest the imperious necessity of our secession, they threaten us with the sword, to coerce submission to their rule.'

At South Carolina's Ratification Convention, Patrick Dollard warned that 'my constituents are highly alarmed at the large and rapid strides which this new government has taken towards despotism' – a government 'big with political mischiefs, and pregnant with a greater variety of impending woes to the good people of the Southern States, especially South Carolina, than all the plagues supposed to issue from the poisonous box of Pandora.' According to Dollard, 'They will resist against it...they will not accept of it unless compelled by force of arms, which this new Constitution surely plainly threatens...your standing army, like Turkish janissaries [the elite guard of the Ottoman sultan] enforcing despotic laws, must ram it down their throats with the points of bayonets.' Ultimately, South Carolina peaceably consented to the Constitution, yet Dollard had peered into the future: several generations later, when South Carolina peaceably withdrew her consent, 'the Constitution' would indeed be rammed down her throat with bayonet points.

Aware of South Carolina's reputation even among other Southern States as a radical, Rhett defended her conduct and called for Southern unity. South Carolina did not wish to be the first State to secede, assured Rhett, but felt that the decision had been forced upon her – what choice did she have, in the face of Northern consolidation? 'Circumstances beyond our controul,' pled Rhett, 'have placed us in the van of the great controversy between the Northern and Southern States.' South Carolina had no ambition to rule a new Southern Confederacy, either. 'Independent ourselves, we disclaim any design or desire to lead the counsels of other Southern States.' The Southern States, the seals of which were emblazoned upon a banner hanging in the hall where South Carolina had just convened, belonged together. 'Providence has cast our lot together, by extending over us an identity of pursuits, interests, and institutions,' urged Rhett. 'South Carolina desires no destiny separated from yours.'

Hoping to stir South Carolina's sisters to her cause, Rhett ended his *Address* with a Southern call to arms. It was Southern statesmanship and

Southern valour which had always strengthened and secured the Union. 'In the field, as in the cabinet, *you* have led the way to renown and grandeur.' The South had always honoured the Union, doing her duty even when it came with costs. 'You have loved the Union, in whose service your great statesmen have laboured, and your great soldiers have fought and conquered – not for the material benefits it conferred, but with the faith of a generous and devoted chivalry.' In spite of Northern treachery, the South had always remained loyal to the Union. 'You have long lingered in hope over the shattered remains of a broken Constitution,' seethed Rhett. 'Compromise after compromise, formed by your concessions, has been trampled underfoot by your Northern confederates.' With the triumph of a sectional Northern party within the Union, determined to consolidate its power and rule the South, Southern patience and benevolence was exhausted. 'All fraternity of feeling between the North and the South is lost, or has been converted into hate,' announced Rhett. 'We, of the South, are at last driven together by the stern destiny which controuls the existence of nations.' If there were a silver lining to the South's 'bitter experience of the faithlessness and rapacity' of the North, it was that the conflict had forced the South 'to evolve those great principles of free government, on which the world depend,' and prepared her 'for the grand mission of vindicating and reestablishing them.'

Rhett denied that Southerners had any reason to apologise for their agrarian, slave-holding, *Gemeinschaft*, which he argued was superior to the Northern industrial, capitalist, *Gesellschaft*. 'We rejoice that other nations are satisfied with their institutions,' offered Rhett. 'We are satisfied with ours.' According to Rhett, the North was infected with class warfare stemming from the exorbitance of industrial capitalism. 'If they prefer a system of industry, in which capital and labour are in perpetual conflict – and chronic starvation keeps down the natural increase of population – and a man is worked out in eight years – and the law ordains that children shall be worked only *ten hours a day* – and the sabre and bayonet are the instruments of order

– be it so,' shrugged Rhett. 'It is their affair, not ours.' Yet in contrast to the North, the South was peaceful and prosperous. 'We prefer, however, our system of industry, by which labour and capital are identified in interest, and capital, therefore, protects labour – by which our population doubles every twenty years – by which starvation is unknown, and abundance crowns the land – by which order is preserved by an unpaid police, and many fertile regions of the world, where the white man cannot labour, are brought into usefulness by the labour of the African, and the whole world is blessed by our productions,' boasted Rhett. 'All we demand of other people is to be left alone, to work out our own high destinies.' Southerners like Rhett sincerely believed that the paternalistic institution of slavery, by which capital cared for labour and whites controulled blacks, was the alternative to the revolutionary 'levelling' which had consumed Europe and was sweeping the United States.

'When this new Constitution should be adopted,' prophesied Rawlins Lowndes in 1788, 'the sun of the Southern States would set, never to rise again.' Other South Carolinians made sport of Lowndes' phrase. On the contrary, retorted Edward Rutledge, if the Constitution were not ratified, then 'the sun of American independence would indeed soon set – never to rise again.' John Rutledge agreed with his younger brother. 'So far from thinking that the sun of this country was obscured by the new Constitution, [I do] not doubt but that when it was adopted, the sun of this State, united with twelve other suns, would exhibit a meridian radiance astonishing to the world.' The Rutledges carried the day, but history would vindicate Lowdnes. By 1860, the sun of the Southern States was indeed setting, but Rhett finished his *Address* with the hope that it would soon rise again in a new, independent confederacy:

> United together...we must be the most independent, as we are among the most important, of the nations of the world. United together...we require no other instrument to conquer peace, than

our beneficent productions. United together...we must be a great, free, and prosperous people, whose renown must spread throughout the civilised world, and pass down, we trust, to the remotest ages.

III

In 1882, six years after Rhett's death, the First South Carolina Volunteers, the former command of fellow Fire-Eater Maxcy Gregg, held a reunion in Barnwell County. Colonel Edward McCrady, Jr., a respected historian and lawyer from Charleston, addressed what remained of the regiment. As Confederate veterans faded away, urged McCrady, those few left behind should unite and commemorate the sacrifices they made 'for the cause which we maintain to have been righteous – even though lost.' At the same time, however, Confederate veterans should also transmit the truth to posterity – 'tell to those who are growing up around us what were the great causes which impelled the young and the old of that time, the rich and the poor, the learned and the ignorant, to take up arms and risk their lives in battle.' As Rhett had always insisted, McCrady denied that slavery was the cause of the conflict between the North and the South, but merely an issue of a much deeper conflict. 'We did not fight for slavery,' insisted McCrady, who explained that slavery 'was not the *cause* of the war, but the incident upon which the differences between the North and the South, and from which differences the war was inevitable from the foundation of our government, did but turn.' Again in accordance with Rhett, McCrady maintained that States' rights were the root cause of the conflict. 'We fought for States' rights and States' sovereignty as a political principle,' declared McCrady. 'We fought for the State of South Carolina, with a loyal love that no personal sovereign has ever aroused.' If slavery had never existed in America, continued McCrady, the North and the South would still have gone to war, for the 'seeds' of the conflict were planted in the Constitution itself, growing from the opposing interpretations of Thomas Jefferson's 'Federal

Party' and Alexander Hamilton's 'National Party.' As McCrady put it, 'The Convention which framed the Constitution was itself divided into the two parties which, after seventy years of discussion in the Senate chamber, adjourned the debate to the battlefields of our late war.' Like Rhett, McCrady believed that the battle lines of the war were drawn when the President and the Congress threatened South Carolina with invasion for nullifying the Tariff of Abominations. In 1832 and 1860, explained McCrady, the 'incident' differed – the tariff and slavery, respectively – but the underlying 'question' of 'the sovereignty of the State' remained the same. 'Would that we might have fought and shed our blood upon the dry question of the tariff and taxation,' bemoaned McCrady, 'instead of one upon which the world had gone mad.'

McCrady believed that South Carolina's Secession Convention was mistaken to have centered its *Declaration* solely on grievances related to slavery, as did Rhett. 'It is a matter of satisfaction to us, my comrades,' remarked McCrady, 'that our first and beloved commander, General Maxcy Gregg, as a member of the Convention, opposed the adoption of the declaration on this very ground.' McCrady claimed that Rhett's *Address* – 'in which was so ably and well shown that the issue was the same as that in the Revolution of 1776, and like that turned upon the one great principle, self-government, and self-taxation, the criterion of self-government' – was a vastly superior 'justification of the secession of the State.' According to McCrady, Rhett's *Address* demonstrated that the South faced the same threats from the North that all Americans had once faced from the British – a majority with 'omnipotence in legislation' judging the extent of the limitations on its own power – and thus that 'the government of the United States had become a consolidated government, and the people of the Southern States were compelled to meet the very despotism their fathers threw off in 1776.'

McCrady's speech at the Confederate reunion was a testament to the power of Rhett's ideas, specifically how they had shaped the course of States' rights. From 1828, when he took the United States by storm, to 1860, when he and South Carolina dissolved the Union, Rhett saw clearly that the North and the South were separate peoples, with starkly differing political beliefs, economic interests, cultural values, and social/racial identities. At first, Rhett saw States' rights as the only safeguard of the South's liberty and security *in* the Union, but as the conflict between the North and the South deepened, he saw States' rights as the South's only way *out* of the Union.

Rhett stood at the culmination of the sectional conflict and in the shadow of a distinguished Southern political tradition: the Founding Fathers James Madison and Thomas Jefferson, who first enunciated States' rights in the *Virginia and Kentucky Resolutions*; the jurists St. George Tucker and Abel P. Upshur, who systematised States' rights in their scholarly works; the philosopher John Taylor of Caroline, who defended States' rights in his elaborate treatises; and the statesman John C. Calhoun, who honed States' rights in many political battles and sought to unify the Southern minority in the Union. Rhett turned States' rights from a constitutional doctrine into a battle cry, putting into action what his predecessors had put down into words. Thus, when Confederates like McCrady took up arms, they were not fighting for slavery, but for States' rights – the same cause of independence and self-government which had fired the hearts and minds of their Revolutionary forefathers. McCrady closed his speech with a poem which beautifully captured their defeated, but not dishonoured, cause:

> *Believing*
> *That they fought, for Principle against Power,*
> *For Religion against Fanaticism,*
> *For Man's Right against Man's Might,*
> *These Men were Martyrs of their Creed;*
> *And their Justification*
> *Is in the holy keeping of the God of History.*
>
> *But, for as much*
> *As alike in the heat of Battle,*

JAMES RUTLEDGE ROESCH

In the weariness of the Hospital,
And in the gloom of hostile Prisons,
They were faithful unto death,
Theirs is the Crown
Of a loving, a glorious, and an immortal Tradition,
In the Hearts, and in the Holiest Memories
Of the Daughters of their People;
Of the Sons of their State;
Of the Heirs Unborn of their Example;
And all of for whom
They dared to die.

Conclusion

Every brave people who considered their rights attacked and their constitutional liberties invaded, would have done as we did. Our conduct was not caused by any insurrectional spirit, nor can it be termed a rebellion; for our construction of the Constitution under which we lived and acted was the same from its adoption, and for eighty years we had been taught and educated by the Founders of the Republic, and their written declarations, which controulled our consciences and actions. The epithets that have been heaped upon us of "rebels" and "traitors" have no just meaning, nor are they believed in by those who understand the subject, even at the North.
– Robert Edward Lee, 1869

THE AIM OF THIS ESSAY SERIES has been to bring to light suppressed Southern political treatises and restore the honour of the constitutional doctrine of States' rights. 'There has been for many years a historical canard afoot that says that the States' Rights philosophers of the Old South were pettifoggers, lost in tedious abstract arguments that had no relevance to real life and were merely rationalizations for an indefensible society of limited intellect and imagination,' explains Clyde N. Wilson, the M.E. Bradford Distinguished Chair of the Abbeville Institute, who adds that 'nothing could be further from the truth.' According to Wilson, 'The Southern view of the Constitution was always philosophical and historical...it was the Northerners who were pettifogging legalists, resorting to semantics and often outright deception to prove a bad case.' Indeed, from the Founding Fathers to the Fire Eaters, States' rights were the cornerstone of a rich

Southern political tradition which defended American small-f federalism and small-r republicanism against overwhelming numbers – first at ballot-boxes and finally on battlefields. 'A better case can be made for the persistence of Revolutionary republicanism in the South than can be made for its persistence in the North,' argues the Independent Institute's Joseph R. Stromberg. 'Southern republicanism was the inheritance the South received from its Revolutionary forefathers, and right or wrong, the South had remained truer to the original understanding of it than had the North.' As Eugene D. Genovese, who began his career as a Communist in New York City and ended it as a 'Southern Agrarian' in Georgia, put it in a lecture series on 'the Southern tradition' at Harvard University, 'The principal features of the Southern worldview – for example, its republicanism – had roots in the history of Western civilization, most notably in the history of Britain, and cannot be regarded as an ideological projection of slavery ... The Old South was a continuation of the mainstream of the development of Christendom and...the North was a heretical deviation.'

Far from solely synonymous with slavery, States' rights were also synonymous with liberty – that is, the foundational principle of American freedom, the right of self-government. Slavery was ultimately incidental to States' rights, as all conceivable constitutional questions – whether slavery, territories, tariffs, internal improvements, banking, civil liberties, or any other of the myriad antebellum issues – were ultimately reducible to a question of power between the States and Washington, D.C. As John Randolph of Roanoke – that old-fashioned Virginian who was more Jeffersonian than Thomas Jefferson himself – summed up, 'The question for every honest man to ask himself is, to which of these two divisions of government does the power in contest belong?' Slavery was *a* question, but not *the* question; self-government was *the* question. That this right of self-government became inextricably intertwined with the institution of slavery is one of the great tragedies of American history.

Whatever the history of slavery and States' rights, the *Kulturkampf* has transformed slavery from a long-dead national tragedy into a 'volcano god' to which superstitious whites must ritually sacrifice increasing shares of their heritage and identity. The Old South will be the first to go, of course, but by the logic of this particular superstition and the demographic trends of the country, it will not be long before all of American history is sacrificed as well. Today's vitriolic, violent attack of Confederate history, waged by fifth columnists on the Left and supported by useful idiots on the Right, is not the end, but merely the beginning – a beachhead for a massive invasion of all American history. The cowardly, foolhardy 'conservatives' who are complicit in this attack are opening the castle gates to their enemies, hoping that only the 'racists' and 'rebels' will be massacred, but will soon find that to these barbarians and fanatics, nothing is sacred and nothing will be spared. The politicisation of history, which has subverted and degraded our national self-consciousness (our sense of heritage and identity) as well as our national self-confidence (our love of and loyalty to our country), must be stopped. History is a story, not an ideology – the story of who we are, where we came from, what we believe, and why it matters today – and should unite us around the answers to those questions. Slavery is long since dead, but rather than buried, its rotting corpse has been left out to 'guilt' whites into surrendering their birthright – not just dry constitutional doctrines like States' rights, but Western Civilisation's whole way of life and standard of living. 'Unless whites – Southerners as well as non-Southerners – learn to have the courage to demand that the symbols of their heritage and their identity be respected and honored in the places where they have always been respected and honored, what we can expect to see, as whites cease to be a majority in the country, is the continuing destruction of those symbols and with them of the heritage and identity they symbolize,' warns the paleo-conservative renegade Samuel T. Francis. 'And what that means eventually is that whites will cease to have any identity, any collective sense of themselves as a people or a culture, and when that occurs, they will simply become an underclass to be exploited and oppressed by whatever race or people has seized cultural dominance.'

On 20 April 1861, shortly after President Abraham Lincoln's proclamation of war against the newly free and independent Lower South and the resultant secession of the Upper South, the *Charleston Mercury*, a prominent Southern newspaper helmed by the Fire-Eater Robert B. Rhett, asked and answered 'For What Are We Contending?'

> For more than thirty years the people of South Carolina have been contending against the consolidation of the government of the United States. Created a confederation of republics whose central power, authority, and jurisdiction, were carefully limited by the compact of the Constitution, and made conformable to, and within its proper limits, coordinate with the original and reserved powers, authority and jurisdiction of the several States which it was composed, the United States government has steadily usurped powers not granted – progressively trenched upon States' rights. Not a bald, irresponsible, unchecked, vulgar democracy of mere numbers, was organised by the instrument of the federation between the States; but a well-adjusted, duplicate system harmonious and complimentary – the central common government performing its allotted functions within its prescribed sphere, and each State government performing all other functions of government not expressly yielded to the other. If that government became practically omnipotent, it was clear that it must be a most fearful despotism – a despotism of one section of the Union over the other – a despotism of manufacturing over agricultural States – of free States over slave-holding States. Earnestly and faithfully have our public men at Washington contended against this fatal consummation. It was not for free trade only in 1833 – it was not against antislavery fanaticism only in 1852, it is not now against our preclusion from our Territories or the vulgar crew who fill the high places at Washington, that we have set up for ourselves a separate destiny.

These are all effects of one great cause – the consolidation of the federal government. As facts, we have been obliged to meet them – but the facts themselves were comparatively insignificant. They were like the ship money [a tax levied by King Charles I to finance the navy] which Hampden [an English statesman who defended the Parliament against the Crown] refused to pay [because only the Parliament had the power of the purse] – like the three pence a pound on tea, which our fathers resisted. They proved to us that we were the slaves of a consolidated despotism – that self-government, and the security which self-government alone can impart – and liberty, and the priceless self-esteem and proud repose, which liberty can only inspire – were no longer our inheritance or possession. South Carolina, by her secession, forced the test of the nature of the government under which we lived. It has proved itself. As one scale of hypocrisy after another fell off of its poisonous surface, it stood forth a pure, fierce monster of despotism...in the grand effort to establish, by the sword, what has long existed as a policy – the despotism of a consolidated government under the Constitution of the United States. The matter is now plain. State after State in the South sees the deadly development, and are moving to take their part in the grand effort to redeem their liberties. It is not a contest for righteous taxation. It is not a contest for the security of slave property. It is a contest for freedom and free government, in which everything dear to man is involved. Shall we submit to the sectional and remorseless despotism of a majority of the Northern States, with no restraints on their lawless will, no checks on their omnivorous rapacity? That is the question. Every man, every boy in the South answers NO! And they will fight the foul usurpers and tyrants, if they dare the issue of war, as long as the streams run and the sun shines on our valleys.

On the eve of war, Confederate President Jefferson Davis reminded his fellow Southerners that 'the only way of preserving our slave property, or what we prize more than life, our LIBERTY, is by a UNION WITH EACH

OTHER.' To Southerners, therefore, 'slave property' and 'liberty' were not just separate questions, but unequal ones as well – the former certainly a social cornerstone and an economic interest, but the latter a principle more precious than life itself. 'We are not fighting for slavery,' Davis later declared. 'We are fighting for INDEPENDENCE – and that, or extermination, we will have.' To those 'who speak of reconstruction with slavery maintained' and 'would thus measure rights by property,' Davis gagged, 'God forbid.' The right of a State to govern herself, as Southerners like Thomas Jefferson, James Madison, St. George Tucker, John Taylor of Caroline, Abel P. Upshur, John C. Calhoun, Robert B. Rhett, and many more had defended all along, was the strongest safeguard of this precious liberty. That States' rights stood for liberty, not slavery, was why Lord Acton, the great English classical liberal, consoled the defeated Robert E. Lee after the war. 'I saw in State rights the only availing check on the absolutism of the sovereign will, and secession filled me with hope, not as the destruction, but as the redemption of democracy,' Acton told Lee. According to Acton, 'You were fighting the battles of our liberty, our progress, and our civilisation.' That States' rights stood for liberty rather than slavery was also why Lee replied to Acton that 'the maintenance of the rights and authority reserved to the States and to the people' were 'the chief source of stability to our political system' and that 'the consolidation of the States into one vast republic, sure to be aggressive abroad and despotic at home, will be the certain precursor of that ruin which has overwhelmed all those that have preceded it.' Sadly, however, Lee admitted that 'the judgment of reason has been displaced by the arbitrament of war.'

Jefferson Davis, who never lost his heart for the Confederate cause even as the Old South collapsed around him, was confident that 'the principle for which we contend is bound to reassert itself, though it may be at another time and in another form.' Although the rights of the States seem to have been crushed along with the Old South, force can only settle questions of might, not of right. Threats and coercion are not moral substitutes for reason and consent. No matter how many Southern cities were put to the torch or Southern people put to the sword, the Southern political tradition still stands proudly as an alternative to today's Yankee leviathan – a government winning hatred around the world for its provocations, passing whatever laws it pleases in defiance of democracy, electing a new electorate through mass-immigration, crushing dwindling tax-payers beneath the burden of ballooning tax-consumers, and collapsing beneath its own weight in general. In a time of such atrocious tyranny, the constitutional doctrine of States' rights, however unjustly downtrodden, could, should, and shall rise again.

Source Material

Books & Articles

Alden, John Richard. *The First South*. Baton Rouge, LA: Louisiana State University Press, 1961.

Banner, James M. *To the Hartford Convention: The Federalists and the Origins of Party Politics in Massachusetts, 1789-1815*. New York, NY: Alfred A. Knopf, 1970.

Barry, Richard. *Mr. Rutledge of South Carolina*. New York, NY: J.J. Little & Ives Company, 1942.

Bassani, Luigi Marco. *Liberty, State, & Union: The Political Theory of Thomas Jefferson*. Macon, GA: Mercer University Press, 2010.

Belz, Herman, ed. *The Webster-Hayne Debate on the Nature of the Union: Selected Documents*. Indianapolis, IN: Liberty Fund, 2010.

Birzer, Bradley J. *American Cicero: The Life of Charles Carroll*. Wilmington, DE: ISI Books, 2010.

Bledsoe, Albert Taylor. *Is Davis a Traitor? Or Was Secession a Constitutional Right Previous to the War of 1861?* Baltimore, MD: Innes & Company, 1866.

Reprint. Brion McClanahan and Mike Church, eds., Mandeville, LA: Black Hat Publishing, 2013.

Bradford, M.E. *Remembering Who We Are: Observations of a Southern Conservative*. Athens, GA: University of Georgia Press, 1985.

——. *The Reactionary Imperative: Essays Literary & Political*. Peru, IL: Sherwood Sugden & Company, 1990.

——. *Against the Barbarians, and Other Reflections on Familiar Themes*. Columbia, MO: University of Missouri Press, 1992.

——. *Original Intentions: On the Making and Ratification of the United States Constitution*. Athens, GA: University of Georgia Press, 1993.

——. *A Better Guide Than Reason: Federalists and Anti-Federalists*. New Brunswick, NJ: Transaction Publishers, 1994.

——. *Founding Fathers: Brief Lives of the Framers of the United States Constitution*. Lawrence, KS: University of Kansas Press, 1994.

Burstein, Andrew, and Nancy Isenberg. *Madison and Jefferson*. New York, NY: Random House Trade Paperbacks, 2013.

Calhoun, John Caldwell. *A Disquisition on Government and A Discourse on the Constitution and Government of the United States*. Columbia, SC: A.S. Johnston, 1851.

Carpenter, Jesse Thomas. *The South as a Conscious Minority, 1789-1861: A Study in Political Thought*. New York, NY: New York University Press, 1930.

Cheek Jr., H. Lee. *Calhoun and Popular Rule: The Political Theory of the Disquisition and Discourse*. Columbia, MO: University of Missouri Press, 2001.

Cheek Jr., H. Lee, ed. *John C. Calhoun: Selected Writings and Speeches.* Washington, D.C.: Regnery Publishing, 2003.

Chernow, Ron. *Alexander Hamilton.* New York, NY: The Penguin Press, 2004.

——. *Washington: A Life.* New York, NY: The Penguin Press, 2010.

Chitwood, Oliver Perry. *John Tyler: Champion of the Old South.* Newton, MA: American Political Biography Press, 1939.

Cisco, Walter Brian. *Taking a Stand: Portraits from the Southern Secession Movement.* Shippensburg, PA: White Mane Books, 1998.

Coit, Margaret L. *John C. Calhoun: American Portrait.* Columbia, SC: University of South Carolina Press, 1991.

Coleman, Mary Haldane. *St. George Tucker: Citizen of No Mean City.* Richmond, VA: The Dietz Press, 1938.

Cooper, William J. *Liberty and Slavery: Southern Politics to 1860.* New York, NY: Alfred A. Knopf, 1983.

——. *Jefferson Davis, American.* New York, NY: Alfred A. Knopf, 2000.

Davidson, Donald, John Gould Fletcher, H.B. Kline, Lyle H. Lanier, Stark Young, Allen Tate, Andrew Nelson Lytle, H.C. Nixon, F.L. Owsley, John Crowe Ransom, John Donald Wade, and Robert Penn Warren. *I'll Take My Stand: The South and the Agrarian Tradition, by 12 Southerners.* New York, NY: Harper & Brothers, 1930.

Davis, William C. *Jefferson Davis: The Man and His Hour.* New York, NY: HarperCollins Publishers, 1991.

——. *A Fire-Eater Remembers: The Confederate Memoir of Robert Barnwell Rhett.* Columbia, SC: University of South Carolina Press, 2000.

——. *Rhett: The Turbulent Life and Times of a Fire-Eater.* Columbia, SC: University of South Carolina Press, 2001.

Davis, Jefferson. *The Rise and Fall of the Confederate Government.* 2 vols. New York, NY: D. Appleton and Company, 1881. Reprint. James M. McPherson, ed. New York, NY: Da Capo Press, 1990.

DeRosa, Marshall L. *The Confederate Constitution of 1861: An Inquiry into American Constitutionalism.* Columbia, MO: University of Missouri Press, 1991.

DiLorenzo, Thomas J. *The Real Lincoln: A New Look at Abraham Lincoln, His Agenda, and an Unnecessary War.* New York, NY: Three Rivers Press, 2003.

——. *Lincoln Unmasked: What You're Not Supposed to Know About Dishonest Abe.* New York, NY: Three Rivers Press, 2006.

——. *Hamilton's Curse: How Jefferson's Archenemy Betrayed the American Revolution – and What It Means for Americans Today.* New York, NY: Three Rivers Press, 2008.

Elliott, Jonathan, ed. *The Debates in the Several State Conventions on the Adoption of the Federal Constitution, as recommended by the General Convention of Philadelphia in 1787. Together with the Journal of the Federal Convention, Luther Martin's Letter, Yates' Minutes, Congressional Opinions, Virginia and Kentucky Resolutions of 98-99, and other illustrations of the Constitution.* 5 vols. Philadelphia, PA: J.B. Lippincott Company, 1836.

Fleming , Thomas: *A Disease in the Public Mind: A New Understanding of Why We Fought the Civil War.* New York, NY: Da Capo Press, 2013.

Fogel, Robert William, and Stanley L. Engerman. *Time on the Cross: The Economics of American Negro Slavery.* New York, NY: Weber, Norton & Company, 1974.

Francis, Samuel T. *Beautiful Losers: Essays on the Failure of American Conservatism.* Columbia, MO: University of Missouri Press, 1993.

——. "After the Republic." *Chronicles.* Aug. 1991.

——. "Why Race Matters: The assault on our race and culture must be met in explicitly racial terms." *American Renaissance.* Sep. 1994.

——. "Race and the American Identity: To claim that we are a 'universal nation' is to deny the past." *American Renaissance.* Dec. 1998.

——. "The War on White Heritage: The attack on the battle flag is only a preliminary skirmish." *American Renaissance.* Jul. 2000.

——. "Historical Basis for the Second Amendment." Address to the Sixth Annual Conference on the Great Revival in the Southern Armies, Jul. 12, 2000.

——. "In Defense of Symbols: Southern and Otherwise." Address to the Sixth Annual Conference on the Great Revival in the Southern Armies, Jul. 13, 2000.

——. "Abolishing America: What Gilmore's Latest Grovel Means about the 'European-American' Place in the Multicultural New Order." *VDare.com.* May 21, 2001.

——. "Abolishing America: Guess What Flag's Not Coming to Dinner." *VDare.com.* Jul. 2, 2001.

——. "Abolishing America: The Logic of the Attack on Southern Symbols." *VDare.com*. Jul. 10, 2003.

——. "The Return of the Repressed." Introduction to *Race and the American Prospect*. Mt. Airy, MD: The Occidental Press, 2006.

Freehling, William Wilhartz. *Prelude to Civil War: The Nullification Controversy in South Carolina, 1816-1836*. Oxford, UK: Oxford University Press, 1965.

——. *The Road to Disunion, Volume I: Secessionists at Bay, 1776-1854*. Oxford, UK: Oxford University Press, 1990.

——. *The Road to Disunion, Volume II: Secessionists Triumphant, 1854-1861*. Oxford, UK: Oxford University Press, 2007.

Genovese, Eugene D. *Roll, Jordan, Roll: The World the Slaves Made*. New York, NY: Pantheon Books, 1974.

——. *The Southern Tradition: The Achievement and Limitation of an American Conservatism*. Cambridge, UK: Harvard University Press, 1994.

——. *The Southern Front: History and Politics in the Cultural War*. Columbia, MO: University of Missouri Press, 1995.

Genovese, Eugene D., and Elizabeth Fox-Genovese. *The Mind of the Master Class: History and Faith in the Southern Slaveholders' Worldview*. Cambridge, UK: Cambridge University Press, 2005.

——. *Slavery in White and Black: Class and Race in the Southern Slaveholders' New World Order*. Cambridge, UK: Cambridge University Press, 2008.

——. *Fatal Self-Deception: Slaveholding Paternalism in the Old South*. Cambridge, UK: Cambridge University Press, 2011.

Gobold Jr., E. Stanley, and Robert H. Woody. *Christopher Gadsden and the American Revolution*. Knoxville, TN: University of Tennessee Press, 1982.

Graham, John Remington. *Principles of Confederacy: The Visions, the Dreams, and the Fall of the South*. Salt Lake City, UT: Northwest Publishing, 1990.

Gutzman, Kevin R.C. *Virginia's American Revolution: From Dominion to Republic, 1776-1840*. Lanham, MD: Lexington Books, 2007.

——. *James Madison and the Making of America*. New York, NY: St. Martin's Press, 2012.

——. *Thomas Jefferson, Revolutionary: A Radical's Struggle to Remake America*. New York, NY: St. Martin's Press, 2017.

Hall, Claude Hampton. *Abel Parker Upshur: Conservative Virginian, 1790-1844*. Madison, WI: State Historical Society of Wisconsin, 1964.

Carey, George W., and James McClellan, eds. *The Federalist*. Indianapolis, IN: Liberty Fund, 2001.

Hamilton, Phillip. *The Making and Unmaking of a Revolutionary Family: The Tuckers of Virginia, 1752-1830*. Charlottesville, VA: University of Virginia Press, 2003.

Haw, James. *John Rutledge & Edward Rutledge of South Carolina*. Athens, GA: University of Georgia Press, 1997.

Haws, Robert J., ed. *The South's Role in the Creation of the Bill of Rights*. Jackson, MS: University Press of Mississippi, 1991.

Hill, Jr., Charles William. *The Political Theory of John Taylor of Caroline*. Cranbury, NJ: Associated University Presses, 1977.

Howe, Daniel Walker. *What Hath God Wrought: The Transformation of America, 1815-1848.* Oxford History of the United States. Oxford, UK: Oxford University Press, 2007.

Hummel, Jeffrey Rogers. *Emancipating Slaves, Enslaving Free Men: A History of the American Civil War.* Chicago, IL: Open Court, 1996.

James, Marquis. *The Life of Andrew Jackson.* Indianapolis, IN: The Bobbs-Merrill Company, 1938.

Johnson, David E. *John Randolph of Roanoke.* Baton Rouge, LA: Louisiana State University Press, 2012.

Kauffman, Bill. *Forgotten Founder, Drunken Prophet: The Life of Luther Martin.* Wilmington, DE: ISI Books, 2008.

Kidd, Thomas S. *Patrick Henry: First Among Patriots.* New York, NY: Basic Books, 2011.

Kirk, Russell. *John Randolph of Roanoke: A Study in American Politics.* Chicago, IL: University of Chicago Press, 1951.

——. *The Conservative Mind: From Burke to Eliot.* Chicago, IL: University of Chicago Press, 1953.

——. *The Roots of American Order.* La Salle, IL: Open Court, 1974.

Lind, William. "Cultural Marxism: The Poison and the Antidote." *Chronicles.* Aug. 2017.

Livingston, Donald, ed. *Rethinking the American Union for the Twenty-First Century.* Gretna, LA: Pelican Publishing Company, 2012.

Luraghi, Raimondo. *The Rise and Fall of the Plantation South*. New York, NY: New Viewpoints, 1978.

Lytle, Andrew Nelson. *From Eden to Babylon: The Social and Political Essays of Andrew Nelson Lytle*. Washington, D.C.: Regnery Gateway, 1990.

Malone, Dumas. *Jefferson and His Time*. 6 vols. Boston, MA: Little, Brown & Co., 1948-1981.

——. *Jefferson the Virginian*. vol. 1. Boston, MA: Little, Brown & Co., 1948.

——. *Jefferson and the Rights of Man*. vol. 2. Boston, MA: Little, Brown & Co., 1951.

——. *Jefferson and the Ordeal of Liberty*. vol. 3. Boston, MA: Little, Brown & Co., 1962.

——. *Jefferson the President: First Term, 1801-1805*. vol. 4. Boston, MA: Little, Brown & Co., 1970.

——. *Jefferson the President: Second Term, 1805-1809*. vol. 5. Boston, MA: Little, Brown & Co., 1974.

——. *The Sage of Monticello*. vol. 6. Boston, MA: Little, Brown & Co., 1981.

Masters, Edgar Lee. *Lincoln: The Man*. New York, NY: Dodd, Mead & Co, 1931.

May, John Amasa, and Joan Reynolds Faunt, eds. *South Carolina Secedes, with Biographical Sketches of Members of South Carolina's Secession Convention*. Columbia, SC: University of South Carolina Press, 1960.

McClanahan, Brion. *The Founding Fathers' Guide to the Constitution*. Washington, D.C.: Regnery History, 2012.

McClanahan, Brion, and Clyde N. Wilson. *Forgotten Conservatives in American History*. Gretna, LA: Pelican Publishing Company, 2012.

McCoy, Drew R. *The Last of the Fathers: James Madison & the Republican Legacy*. Cambridge, UK: Cambridge University Press, 1989.

McDonald, Forrest. *We the People: The Economic Origins of the Constitution*. Chicago, IL: University of Chicago Press, 1958.

———. *Novus Ordo Seclorum: The Intellectual Origins of the Constitution*. Lawrence, KS: University of Kansas Press, 1985.

———. *States' Rights and the Union: Imperium in Imperio, 1776 to 1876*. Lawrence, KS: University of Kansas Press, 2000.

McDonald, Forrest, ed. *Empire and Nation: Letters from John Dickinson and Letters from Richard Henry Lee*. Englewood Cliffs, NJ: Prentice-Hall, 1962.

McPherson, James M. *Battle Cry of Freedom: The Civil War Era, 1848-1865*. Oxford History of the United States. Oxford, UK: Oxford University Press, 1988.

———. *What They Fought For, 1861-1865*. Baton Rouge, LA: Louisiana State University Press, 1994.

———. *Drawn with the Sword: Reflections on the American Civil War*. Oxford, UK: Oxford University Press, 1996.

———. *For Cause and Comrades: Why Men Fought in the Civil War*. Oxford, UK: Oxford University Press, 1997.

———. *This Mighty Scourge: Perspectives on the Civil War*. Oxford, UK: Oxford University Press, 2007.

Merchant, Holt. *South Carolina Fire-Eater: The Life of Laurence Massillon Keitt, 1824-1864.* Columbia, SC: University of South Carolina Press, 2014.

Middlekauf, Robert L. *The Glorious Cause: The American Revolution, 1763-1789.* Oxford History of the United States. Oxford, UK: Oxford University Press, 1982.

Moore, Glover. *The Missouri Controversy, 1810-1821.* Lexington, KY: University of Kentucky Press, 1953.

Murchison, William. *The Cost of Liberty: The Life of John Dickinson.* Wilmington, DE: ISI Books, 2013.

Peterson, Merrill D. *The Jefferson Image in the American Mind.* Oxford, UK: Oxford University Press, 1960.

——. *Thomas Jefferson and the New Nation: A Biography.* Oxford, UK: Oxford University Press, 1970.

——. *The Great Triumvirate: Webster, Clay, and Calhoun.* Oxford, UK: Oxford University Press, 1987.

Peterson, Merrill D., ed. *Jefferson: Writings.* New York, NY: Library of America, 1984.

Phillips, Ulrich Bonnell. *Life and Labor in the Old South.* Boston, MA: Little, Brown & Co. 1929.

——. *The Course of the South to Secession.* New York, NY: Hill and Wang, 1939.

Pollard, Edward A. *The Lost Cause: A New Southern History of the War of the Confederates.* New York, NY: E.B. Treat & Co. Publishers, 1867.

Price Jr., William S. *Nathaniel Macon of North Carolina: Three Views of His Character and Creed.* Raleigh, NC: North Carolina Offices of Archives and History, 2008.

Rakove, Jack N., ed. *Madison: Writings.* New York, NY: Library of America, 1999.

Reese, George H., ed. *Proceedings of the Virginia State Convention of 1861.* 4 vols. Richmond, VA: Virginia State Library, 1965.

Rhett Jr., Robert Barnwell. "The Confederate Government at Montgomery." In *Battles and Leaders of the Civil War.* vol. 1. New York, NY: The Century Company, 1887.

Risjord, Norman K. *The Old Republicans: Southern Conservatism in the Age of Jefferson.* New York, NY: Columbia University Press, 1965.
Rothbard, Murray N. *Conceived in Liberty.* Auburn, AL: Ludwig von Mises Institute, 1999.

Royster, Charles. *Light-Horse Harry Lee and the Legacy of the American Revolution.* Baton Rouge, LA: Louisiana State University Press, 1981.

Shalhope, Robert E. *John Taylor of Caroline: Pastoral Republican.* Columbia, SC: University of South Carolina Press, 1980.

Sheldon, Garrett Ward, and C. William Hill, Jr. *The Liberal Republicanism of John Taylor of Caroline.* Cranbury, NJ: Rosemont Publishing and Printing.

Simms, Henry H. *Life of John Taylor: The Story of a Brilliant Leader in the Early Virginia State Rights School.* Richmond, VA: The William Byrd, 1932.

Smith, Oran P., ed. *So Good a Cause: A Decade of Southern Partisan.* Columbia, SC: Foundation for American Education, 1993.

Stephens, Alexander Hamilton. *A Constitutional View of the Late War Between the States: Its Causes, Character, Conduct, and Results*. Philadelphia, PA: National Publishing Company, 1868.

Storing, Herbert J., ed. *The Anti-Federalist: Writings by the Opponents of the Constitution*. Chicago, IL: University of Chicago Press, 1981.

Storing, Herbert J. *What the Anti-Federalists Were For: The Political Thought of the Opponents of the Constitution*. Chicago, IL: University of Chicago Press, 1981.

Tate, Adam L. *Conservatism and Southern Intellectuals, 1789-1861: Liberty, Tradition, and the Good Society*. Columbia, MO: University of Missouri Press, 2005.

Taylor, John. *An Inquiry into the Principles and Policy of the Government of the United States*. Fredericksburg, VA: Green & Cady, 1814.

——. *Arator: Being a Series of Agricultural Essays Practical and Political*. Petersburg, VA: Whitworth & Yancey, 1818. Reprint. M.E. Bradford, ed. Indianapolis, IN: Liberty Fund, 1977.

——. *Construction Construed and Constitutions Vindicated*. Richmond, VA: Shepherd & Pollard, 1820.

——. *Tyranny Unmasked*. Washington, D.C.: Davis & Force, 1822. Reprint. F. Thornton Miller, ed. Indianapolis, IN: Liberty Fund, 1992.

——. *New Views of the Constitution of the United States*. Washington, D.C.: Way & Gideon, 1823. Reprint. James McClellan, ed. Washington, D.C.: Regnery Publishing, 2000.

Taylor, Richard. *Destruction & Reconstruction: Personal Experiences of the Late War*. New York, NY: D. Appleton & Company, 1879. Reprint. Clyde N. Wilson, ed. Nashville, TN: J.S. Sanders & Company.

Tucker, St. George. *View of the Constitution of the United States.* Philadelphia, PA: William Young Birch and Abraham Small, 1803. Reprint. Clyde N Wilson, ed. Indianapolis, IN: Liberty Fund, 1999.

Upshur, Abel Parker. *A Brief Enquiry into the True Nature and Character of Our Federal Government: Being a Review of Judge Story's Commentaries on the Constitution of the United States.* Petersburg, VA: Edmund and Julian C. Ruffin, 1840.

Walther, Eric H. *The Fire-Eaters.* Baton Rouge, LA: Louisiana State University Press, 1992.
Weaver, Richard M. *The Southern Tradition at Bay: A History of Postbellum Thought.* New Rochelle, NY: Arlington House, 1968.

——. *The Southern Essays of Richard M. Weaver.* Indianapolis, IN: Liberty Fund, 1987.

——. *In Defense of Tradition: Collected Short Writings of Richard M. Weaver, 1929-1963.* Indianapolis, IN: Liberty Fund, 2000.

White, Laura A. *Robert Barnwell Rhett: Father of Secession.* New York, NY: Appleton-Century-Crofts, 1931.

Wilson, Clyde N., ed. *The Essential Calhoun: Selections from Writings, Speeches, and Letters.* New Brunswick, NJ: Transaction Publishers, 1992.

——. *A Defender of Southern Conservatism: M.E. Bradford and His Achievements.* Columbia, MO: University of Missouri Press, 1999.

——. *Chronicles of the South: Garden of the Beaux Arts.* Rockford, IL: Chronicles Press, 2011.

——. *Chronicles of the South: In Justice to so Fine a Country.* Rockford, IL: Chronicles Press, 2011.

Wilson, Clyde N. "'Free Trade: No Debt: Separation from Banks': The Economic Platform of John C. Calhoun." In *Slavery, Secession, and Southern History*. Robert Louis Paquette and Louis A. Ferleger, eds. Charlottesville, VA: University Press of Virginia, 2000.

——. *From Union to Empire: Essays in the Jeffersonian Tradition*. Columbia, SC: Foundation for American Education, 2003.

——. *Defending Dixie: Essays in Southern History and Culture*. Columbia, SC: Foundation for American Education, 2006.

Wood, Gordon S. *Empire of Liberty: A History of the Early Republic, 1789-1815*. Oxford History of the United States. Oxford, UK: Oxford University Press, 2009.

Woods Jr., Thomas E. *Nullification: How to Resist Federal Tyranny in the 21ˢᵗ Century*. Washington, D.C.: Regnery Publishing, 2010.

Lectures

Bassani, Marco Luigi. "Is There a Federal Common Law? Jefferson, John Taylor, and Spencer Roane." 2004 Abbeville Institute Summer School: The Southern Critique of Centralization and Nationalism, 1798-1861.

——. "The Anti-Federalists and the Ratification Debates." 2003 Abbeville Institute Summer School: The American Decentralist Tradition.

——. "The Nullification Crisis." 2003 Abbeville Institute Summer School: The American Decentralist Tradition.

——. "The Principles of '98 and the Hartford Convention." 2003 Abbeville Institute Summer School: The American Decentralist Tradition.

——. "Thomas Jefferson's States' Rights Agrarianism." 2006 Abbeville Institute Summer School: The Southern Agrarian Tradition.

Brown, Kent Masterson. "An Indissoluble Union: The Ultimate Nonsequitur." 2010 Abbeville Institute Scholars Conference: State Nullification, Secession, and the Human Scale of Political Order.

Cheek Jr., H. Lee. "The Southern Constitutional Tradition: Keeping and Restraining the Republic." 2013 Abbeville Institute Summer School: Understanding the South and the Southern Tradition.

DeRosa, Marshall L. "The Confederate Constitution." Abbeville Institute Summer School: The American Decentralist Tradition, 2003.

——. "The Confederate Rule of Law." Abbeville Institute Summer School: The American Decentralist Tradition, 2003.

——. "States' Rights versus National Wrongs: The Tenth Amendment Awakening, the Supreme Court be Damned." Abbeville Institute Scholars Conference: State Nullification, Secession, and the Human Scale of Political Order, 2010.

Devanny, John. "The Origins of the Jeffersonian Economic Program." 2004 Abbeville Institute Summer School: The Southern Critique of Centralization and Nationalism, 1798-1861.

——. "The Federalist Crucible and the Renascence of the Jeffersonian Program." 2004 Abbeville Institute Summer School: The Southern Critique of Centralization and Nationalism, 1798-1861.

——. "Post-60s Neo-Abolitionist Historiography." 2008 Abbeville Institute Summer School: Northern Anti-Slavery Rhetoric.

——. "The Aims of Anti-Slavery in the Missouri Compromise." 2008 Abbeville Institute Summer School: Northern Anti-Slavery Rhetoric.

——. "John Taylor: Agrarian Prophet." 2011 Abbeville Institute Summer School: The Greatness of Southern Literature II.

——. "John Randolph versus the War Hawks." 2011 Abbeville Institute Scholars Conference: The South and America's Wars.

Graham, John Remington. "The Glorious Revolution of 1688 and the Origins of Southern Constitutionalism." 2004 Abbeville Institute Summer School: The Southern Critique of Centralization and Nationalism, 1798-1861.

Kickler, Troy. "Nathaniel Macon's Resistance to the War of 1812." 2011 Abbeville Institute Scholars Conference: The South and America's Wars.

Landess, Thomas. "Southern Scholarship vs. Neo-Conservatism: M.E. Bradford and the National Endowment for the Humanities." 2010 Abbeville Institute Summer School: The Greatness of Southern Literature I.

Lence, Ross. "The Federalists at the Philadelphia Convention." 2003 Abbeville Institute Summer School: The American Decentralist Tradition.

——. "Seminar on Calhoun." 2003 Abbeville Institute Summer School: The American Decentralist Tradition.

Livingston, Donald. "What Secession Is." 2003 Abbeville Institute Summer School: The American Decentralist Tradition.

——. "The Secession of an American State." 2003 Abbeville Institute Summer School: The American Decentralist Tradition.

——. "Centralization and Modern Barbarism." 2004 Abbeville Institute Summer School: The Southern Critique of Centralization and Nationalism, 1798-1861.

——. "Abel Upshur's Critique of Joseph Story's Commentaries on the Constitution of the United States." 2004 Abbeville Institute Summer School: The Southern Critique of Centralization and Nationalism, 1798-1861.

——. "The Origin of New England Sectional Nationalism." 2007 Abbeville Institute Summer School: The Origin of Southern Identity and the Culture of the Old South.

——. "New England Cultural Imperialism." 2007 Abbeville Institute Summer School: The Origin of Southern Identity and the Culture of the Old South.

——. "Secession: The Founding Principle of American Republicanism." 2010 Abbeville Institute Scholars Conference: State Nullification, Secession, and the Human Scale of Political Order.

——. "Calhoun as Political Philosopher." 2011 Abbeville Institute Summer School: The Greatness of Southern Literature II.

——. "The North and the Moral Challenge of Slavery." 2013 Abbeville Institute Summer School: Understanding the South and the Southern Tradition.

——. "The South and the Moral Challenge of Slavery." 2013 Abbeville Institute Summer School: Understanding the South and the Southern Tradition.

——. "What They Were Fighting For: the Confederate Constitution." 2014 Abbeville Institute Summer School: The War for Southern Independence.

——. "The Moral Challenge of Slavery and Confederate Emancipation." 2015 Abbeville Institute Summer School: The Southern Tradition.

Roberts, Carey. "Were the Articles of Confederation a Failure?" 2003 Abbeville Institute Summer School: The American Decentralist Tradition.

——. "Why Were the Articles Dissolved?" 2003 Abbeville Institute Summer School: The American Decentralist Tradition.

——. "Slavery and the Philadelphia Convention." 2008 Abbeville Institute Summer School: Northern Anti-Slavery Rhetoric.

——. "'Negro Presidents and Negro Congresses': Abolitionism and the First Congress." 2008 Abbeville Institute Summer School: Northern Anti-Slavery Rhetoric.

——. "The Southern Political Tradition." 2009 Abbeville Institute Summer School: The Meaning and Legacy of Reconstruction.

Sale, Kirkpatrick. "To the Size of States there is a Limit: The Human Scale of Secession." 2010 Abbeville Institute Scholars Conference: State Nullification, Secession, and the Human Scale of Political Order.

Stromberg, Joseph R. "John Taylor's Critique of Political and Economic Centralization." 2006 Abbeville Institute Summer School: The Southern Agrarian Tradition.

White, Jonathan. "Virginia's Reluctant Secessionists, Dutiful Sons, Fierce Warriors." 2011 Abbeville Institute Scholars Conference: The South and America's Wars.

Wilson, Clyde N. "St. George Tucker's A View of the Constitution." 2004 Abbeville Institute Summer School: The Southern Critique of Centralization and Nationalism.

——. "The Lincoln Fable." 2005 Abbeville Institute Summer School: Rethinking Lincoln: The Man, The Myth, The Symbol, The Legacy.

——. "The Republican Party: America's Peculiar Institution." 2005 Abbeville Institute Summer School: Rethinking Lincoln: The Man, The Myth, The Symbol, The Legacy.

——. "The Work of the Late M.E. Bradford." 2006 Abbeville Institute Summer School: The Southern Agrarian Tradition.

——. "Society Before Government." 2007 Abbeville Institute Summer School: The Origin of Southern Identity and the Culture of the Old South.

——. "'Tiger's Meat': Abolitionism in Antebellum America." 2008 Abbeville Institute Summer School: Northern Anti-Slavery Rhetoric.

——. "Steady Habits vs. Chivalry: Sectional Antagonism Before Abolition." 2008 Abbeville Institute Summer School: Northern Anti-Slavery Rhetoric.

——. "Thomas Jefferson, Southern Man of Letters." 2011 Abbeville Institute Summer School: The Greatness of Southern Literature II.

——. "John C. Calhoun: Anti-Imperialist." 2011 Abbeville Institute Scholars Conference: The South and America's Wars.

——. "Lost Causes Regained: The Wisdom of M.E. Bradford." 2011 Abbeville Institute Summer School: The Greatness of Southern Literature II.

——. "A Jeffersonian Political Economy." 2015 Abbeville Institute Summer School: The Southern Tradition.

About the Author

JAMES RUTLEDGE ROESCH received his Bachelor of Arts in Classics from Bucknell University and his Master of Business Administration from Claremont Graduate University. He is married to a beautiful and brilliant Armenian woman whom he met in California. He lives in Florida, where he is an active member in the Sons of the American Revolution and Sons of Confederate Veterans. Despite his respect for Lee's character, he shares Longstreet's love of whiskey and tobacco.

Available from Shotwell

A Legion of Devils: Sherman in South Carolina by Karen Stokes

Annals of the Stupid Party: Republicans Before Trump by Clyde N. Wilson (The Wilson Files 2)

Carolina Love Letters by Karen Stokes

Confederaphobia: An American Epidemic by Paul C. Graham

The Devil's Town: Hot Spring During the Gangster Era by Philip Leigh

Dismantling the Republic by Jerry C. Brewer

Dixie Rising: Rules for Rebels by James R. Kennedy

Emancipation Hell: The Tragedy Wrought By Lincoln's Emancipation Proclamation by Kirkpatrick Sale

Lies My Teacher Told Me: The True History of the War for Southern Independence by Clyde N. Wilson

Maryland, My Maryland: The Cultural Cleansing of a Small Southern State by Joyce Bennett.

My Own Darling Wife: Letters From a Confederate Volunteer by John Francis Calhoun. Edited with Introduction by Andrew P. Calhoun, Jr.

427

Nullification: Reclaiming Consent of the Governed by Clyde N. Wilson (The Wilson Files 2)

The Old South: 50 Essential Books by Clyde N. Wilson (Southern Reader's Guide, vol. I)

Punished with Poverty: The Suffering South by James R. & Walter D. Kennedy

Segregation: Federal Policy or Racism? by John Chodes
Southern Independence. Why War? by Dr. Charles T. Pace

Southerner, Take Your Stand! by John Vinson

Washington's KKK: The Union League During Southern Reconstruction by John Chodes.

When the Yankees Come: Former South Carolina Slaves Remember Sherman's Invasion. Edited with Introduction by Paul C. Graham

The Yankee Problem: An American Dilemma by Clyde N. Wilson (The Wilson Files 1)

———————

Green Altar Books (Literary Imprint)
A New England Romance & Other SOUTHERN Stories by Randall Ivey

Belles: A Carolina Romance by Karen Stokes

Honor in the Dust by Karen Stokes

The Immortals by Karen Stokes

The Soldier's Ghost: A Tale of Charleston by Karen Stokes

Tiller by James Everett Kibler

GOLD-BUG (Mystery & Suspense Imprint)
Billie Jo by Michael Andrew Grissom

To Jekyll and Hide by Martin L. Wilson

Splintered: A New Orleans Tale by Brandi Perry

Publisher's Note

IF YOU ENJOYED THIS BOOK or found it useful, interesting, or informative, we'd be very grateful if you would post a brief review of it on the retailer's website or your social media feed.

In the current political and cultural climate, it is important that we get accurate, Southern-friendly material into the hands of our friends and neighbours. *Your support can really make a difference* in helping us unapologetically celebrate and defend our Southern heritage, culture, history, and home!

Free Book Offer

SIGN-UP FOR NEW RELEASE NOTIFICATIONS and receive a FREE DOWNLOADABLE EDITION of *Lies My Teacher Told Me: The True History of the War for Southern Independence* by Dr. Clyde N. Wilson by visiting FreeLiesBook.com or by texting the word "Dixie" to 345345. You can always unsubscribe and keep the book, so you've got nothing to lose!

Southern without Apology

54441516R00252

Made in the USA
Columbia, SC
31 March 2019